| | | |
|---|---|---|
| | | |
| | PR 6005. | O6A6 |
| | | 2012 |
| Mage ? or | WDR | |
| | | |
| | | |
| | | |
| | | |
| | | |

**Renew items by telephone or online,**
**24 hours a day, 7 days a week:**

Tel: 028 9036 8530
http://library.ulster.ac.uk/renew

45200U/416/9/2012

DANIEL CORKERY'S CULTURAL CRITICISM
*Selected Writings*

Daniel Corkery with a bronze bust he commissioned from Joseph Higgins.
Courtesy of the Boole Library, University College Cork.

# Daniel Corkery's Cultural Criticism

## SELECTED WRITINGS

EDITED AND WITH AN INTRODUCTION

*by*

Heather Laird

First published in 2012 by
Cork University Press
Youngline Industrial Estate
Pouladuff Road, Togher
Cork, Ireland

**British Library Cataloguing in Publication Data**
A CIP catalogue record for this book is available from the British Library

ISBN 978–1–85918–455–4

This book was grant-aided by the National University of Ireland; the
College of Arts, Celtic Studies and Social Sciences, University College
Cork; and the School of English, University College Cork.

Typeset by Carrigboy Typesetting Services
Printed in Spain by Grafo
www.corkuniversitypress.com

In memory of Andrew Dolan
(1991–2012)

# Contents

# Preface

Daniel Corkery was one of the foremost Irish cultural critics of the early Free State. His contemporary prominence as a cultural commentator is evidenced by the flurry of interest that his criticism generated. Aodh de Blácam, writing in 1934, stated that Corkery's *The Hidden Ireland* (1924) had 'kept Irish literary and historical criticism in a ferment' since its publication a decade previously.[1] Corkery's second major critical study, *Synge and Anglo-Irish Literature* (1931), also generated considerable debate and, like *The Hidden Ireland*, was reviewed and discussed in almost every notable Irish and British newspaper and journal publication of his day.[2] Following the publication of *Synge and Anglo-Irish Literature*, Daniel Corkery's name became increasingly synonymous with a narrow-gauge nationalism that, in the eyes of many, sought to stifle an emerging 'modern' Ireland. The initial interest that had greeted his writings was, consequently, largely replaced by disdain or indifference. In the aftermath of Corkery's death in 1964, Seán Ó Tuama, an Irish-language scholar and former student of Corkery's, contacted Radio Éireann to enquire about a memorial programme and, to his proclaimed astonishment, ended up in conversation with a staff member who had never heard of Daniel Corkery.[3] In a later publication, Ó Tuama was to refer to Corkery as 'an undeserving casualty of ideological warfare' whose writings have not received the scholarly attention they deserve.[4] The present publication is designed to facilitate the critical analysis that Ó Tuama called for, and to reveal that the commonplace depiction of an insular, racist and parochial Corkery, while not entirely groundless, is based on a reading of his cultural criticism that is both selective and reductive.

*Daniel Corkery's Cultural Criticism* is testimony to the sheer productivity of Corkery's eighty and more years. This collection – the bulk of which comes from the Corkery Archive in University College Cork – both provides a representative sample of Corkery's cultural criticism and traces significant moments in this branch of his writing career. Key writings from Corkery's published corpus, including oft-cited chapters from *The Hidden Ireland* and *Synge and Anglo-Irish Literature*, are included in this book. Throughout his life, Corkery was an active participant in public debates on cultural issues. This publication contains a selection from the vast number of newspaper articles written by Corkery. The topics discussed in these articles range from the applicability of Russian literary forms to Irish-language prose fiction ('Russian Models for Irish Litterateurs'), to the definition of the nation provided by the Indian poet, Rabindranath Tagore ('What is a Nation?').

Corkery's writing career began in D.P. Moran's polemical nationalist weekly, *The Leader*. Three of Corkery's *Leader* articles are included in this collection: 'Mr. Yeats in Cork', 'Russian Models for Irish Litterateurs', and 'The Modernisation of Irish Poetry'. The earliest of these articles, 'Mr. Yeats in Cork', is signed 'Lee', one of Corkery's many pen-names.[5] Early examples of his cultural commentary can also be found in the journal *New Ireland*. *Daniel Corkery's Cultural Criticism* contains 'The Peasant in Literature', a *New Ireland* article that Frank O'Connor drew on when formulating his notion of the short story as the voice of a 'submerged population group'.[6]

Following the ratification of the Treaty that established the Irish Free State, Corkery, who was to take the anti-Treaty side during the subsequent Civil War, published articles in the new republican weekly, *Poblacht na h-Éireann*. 'Their First Fault', published just three weeks after the ratification, is included here. This book also contains Corkery's previously unpublished essay 'The Literature of Collapse' and his review of Liam O'Flaherty's *The Tent and Other Stories*. In both of these pieces, Corkery denounces the trend in Free State literature to devalue the romantic nationalism that propelled the independence movement. In 'The Literature of Collapse', he goes on to argue for a counter-discourse that would challenge the aesthetics that reflected pro-Treaty values and norms.

Corkery was a regular contributor to *The Irish Tribune*, a short-lived newspaper that was established in March 1926 as a nationalist alternative to *The Irish Statesman*. In June, July and August of the same year, Corkery engaged in a bitter exchange in the columns of this newspaper with his former protégés, Frank O'Connor and Seán O'Faoláin. Corkery's article 'A Landscape in the West', and O'Connor's and O'Faoláin's initial responses to this article ('The Heart has Reasons'; 'The Spirit of the Nation') are in this collection. At the time that this exchange was taking place, O'Faoláin was in the process of writing a series of articles for *The Irish Tribune* on the future of the Irish language. 'Irish – An Empty Barrel?', which contains a scathing attack on Corkery's *The Hidden Ireland*, is included here. In a letter to *The Irish Tribune* written in defence of this series of articles, O'Connor is equally damning of *The Hidden Ireland*. This letter ('Have We a Literature?') can also be found in this book. In 1937, this public 'spat' was resumed in a series of articles published in *The Irish Press*, a newspaper that Corkery regularly wrote for in later life, on the future of literature in Ireland. Corkery's contribution to this series, 'The Colonial Branch of Anglo-Irish Literature', is in this publication, as are the articles written by Frank O'Connor and Seán O'Faoláin for the series ('Ireland Reads – Trash!'; 'Let Ireland Pride – In What She Has').

Corkery contributed numerous reviews of contemporary Irish-language and English-language literary works to newspapers and journals, and a sample of these reviews are contained here, including his Irish-language reviews of Máirtín Ó Cadhain's *Cré na Cille* and Máire Mhac an tSaoi's 'Inquisitio 1584'. This latter review is one of the few times that Corkery directly engaged, in his cultural criticism, with a woman writer.[7] A water-colourist of some distinction, Corkery took a keen interest in the visual arts and his review of a Jack B. Yeats exhibition is included in this book. The collection also contains extracts from a 1946 radio broadcast, 'The Book I am Writing Now', in which he discusses an unfinished work that he provisionally titled 'The Romance of Nation Building'. *Daniel Corkery's Cultural Criticism* concludes with a range of contemporary responses to Corkery's critical writings, including the aforementioned pieces by O'Connor and O'Faoláin. This section of the publication clearly indicates the strong reactions, both positive and negative, that his work originally elicited.

The overall structure of this book, thematic as opposed to chronological, is designed to reveal the central and recurring concerns of Corkery's cultural criticism. Within each section, however, the writings have been arranged chronologically so that the sequential pattern of Corkery's thoughts on particular issues can be traced. English-language translations of the Irish-language reviews contained in Part One have not been provided as including same, without including Irish-language translations of Corkery's English-language reviews, would bestow a normative status on his English-language writings. Corkery, I like to think, would have approved of this gesture. Names of people, texts and organisations are annotated on their first appearance in this collection. I have used the endnote numerical system to annotate Corkery's writings. The footnote asterisk system is used for Corkery's own annotations. Corkery's original use of spelling, grammar and punctuation has, for the most part, been preserved, though some necessary standardisation has taken place and what are clearly typographical errors have been corrected. Occasional omissions are indicated by ellipses in square brackets: [. . .]. Corkery's own omissions are indicated, as is the case in the originals, by ellipses with no brackets.

*Daniel Corkery as Cultural Critic* would not have been realised without the support of my family, friends and colleagues. In particular, I want to thank Eibhear Walshe for his help and encouragement in the preparation of the collection, and Hilary Lennon for generously sharing books and insights with me. As I have 'school Irish' and, consequently, only a limited knowledge of Irish-language literature, the assistance of Irish-language scholars and speakers was invaluable in making possible the completion of this book in its present form. Farrell McElgunn was kind enough to provide me with translations of the Irish-language reviews included in this publication and to contextualise these reviews. Pat Coughlan took time out from her very busy schedule to elucidate and discuss Irish-language articles on *The Hidden Ireland*. Louis de Paor gave me an English-language translation of Seán Ó Ríordáin's 'Do Dhomhnall Ó Corcora'. Kevin Murray provided information about some of the more elusive Irish-language poets and poems. The contribution of others is also very much appreciated. Joe Cleary offered sound advice on the content of this collection. Informative conversations with Patrick Maume and Colbert Kearney helped fill some of the many gaps in my knowledge. Mark Quigley promptly responded to a request for a journal article. Barry Monahan was very patient when I phoned him at unsociable hours with grammar-related queries. Clíona Ó Gallchoir and Mary Breen read and commented on the chronology. Lee Jenkins and Alex Davis lent me books. David Bickerdike gave guidance when my computer misbehaved.

Throughout the project, I have received invaluable assistance from the Special Collections staff in the Boole Library, University College Cork. In particular, I want to thank the archivists, Carol Quinn and Emer Twomey, for their friendly efficiency. Heartfelt gratitude is also owed to the courteous staff of the National Library of Ireland. The Boole Library and the National Library kindly gave permission to reproduce materials from their collections. I am grateful to the vivacious storyteller Kate Corkery for her interest in this publication and for granting me permission to publish her granduncle's writings. Harriet O'Donovan Sheehy generously allowed me to include some pieces by Frank O'Connor in this collection. Julia O'Faolain kindly gave permission for writings by Seán O'Faoláin to be published here. Every effort has been made to establish contact with other copyright holders; where this has not been possible I hope this general acknowledgement will be taken as sufficient. I am very grateful to everyone at Cork University Press, and in particular Maria O'Donovan, for their invaluable work in preparing this book for publication.

I would like to thank the following for their companionship and scholarship: Dermot Dix, Tadhg Foley, Sinéad Kennedy, Chandana Mathur, Conor McCarthy, Caoilfhionn Ní Bheacháin, Emer Nolan, Maureen O'Connor and Lionel Pilkington. My hard-working colleagues and friends in the School of English at University College Cork are a constant source of inspiration and support. Evenings spent eating, drinking, chatting and, occasionally, arguing around Eddie Lahiff and Mairead O'Neill's kitchen table have provided just the right combination of intellectual stimulus and frivolous fun. The friendships of Helen Finney and Rosaleen Laird have sustained me throughout my academic career and are never taken for granted. Special thanks go to Adrian Kane, my comrade and companion, whose tireless campaign for a more just world is always inspirational. Last (but certainly not least), I would like to thank my children, Shane and Róisín. Their patience with a mother who spends long periods of time in her office engrossed in seemingly very dull topics has made so many things possible.

HEATHER LAIRD
Cork

# Chronology of Corkery's Life

# Chronology of his Times

| Year | Age | Life | Irish Cultural Context | Irish Historical Events |
|---|---|---|---|---|
| 1876 | | | Society for the Preservation of the Irish Language founded | |
| 1878 | | Born in Cork city; son of William, a carpenter, and Mary (Barron) Corkery; educated initially at Presentation Brothers Elementary School, where he taught for some years as a monitor | Standish O'Grady, *History of Ireland: The Heroic Period* | |
| 1879 | | | Irish language sanctioned as an 'extra' school subject | National Land League founded |
| 1880 | | | Gaelic Union founded | Ladies' Land League founded |
| 1882 | | | *Irisleabhar na Gaedhilge/The Gaelic Journal* established | |
| 1884 | | | Gaelic Athletic Association founded | Fenian dynamite campaign |
| 1886 | | | Douglas Hyde, 'A Plea for the Irish Language' | First Home Rule Bill |
| 1893 | | | W.B. Yeats, *The Celtic Twilight*; Douglas Hyde, *Abhráin Grádh Chúige Connacht, or Love Songs of Connacht*; Gaelic League founded | Second Home Rule Bill |
| 1899 | | | Commission on Intermediate Education; heated debate as to whether the Irish language should be on the school curriculum | |

| Year | Age | Life | Irish Cultural Context | Irish Historical Events |
|------|-----|------|------------------------|-------------------------|
| 1900 | | | *An Claidheamh Soluis* is established as newspaper of the Gaelic League<br>Catholic Truth Society of Ireland founded | |
| | | | D.P. Moran founds *The Leader*<br>Stopford A. Brooke and T. W. Rolleston, *A Treasury Of Irish Poetry in the English Tongue* | Cumann na nGaedheal founded<br>First meeting of Inghinidhe na hÉireann<br>Queen Victoria visits Ireland |
| 1901 | 23 | Joins the Gaelic League<br>Writes his first article for *The Leader* (under the pen-name 'Lee') | Douglas Hyde's *Casadh an tSúgáin* performed at the Irish Literary Theatre; first play in the Irish language to be professionally produced<br>Patrick Dinneen, *Cormac Ua Conaill*, the first historical novel in the Irish language | |
| 1902 | | | W.B. Yeats, *Cathleen ni Houlihan*<br>Lady Gregory, *Cuchulain of Muirthemne*<br>Dun Emer Press founded (renamed Cuala Press in 1908) | |
| 1903 | 25 | Short stories by Corkery are published in *The Irish Rosary* and *The Leader*<br>Attends a performance of Douglas Hyde's *An Pósadh* in which Hyde plays Raifteirí | J.M. Synge, *In the Shadow of the Glen*<br>George Moore, *The Untilled Field*<br>Irish National Theatre Society founded | Wyndham's Land Act |
| 1904 | | | G.B. Shaw, *John Bull's Other Island*<br>J.M. Synge, *Riders to the Sea*<br>Michael Davitt, *The Fall of Feudalism in Ireland*<br>Peadar Ó Laoghaire, *Séadna*<br>Opening of the Abbey Theatre | |

| Year | Age | Life | Irish Cultural Context | Irish Historical Events |
|---|---|---|---|---|
| 1905 | 27 | Appointed assistant teacher in St Francis's National School, Cork<br><br>Attends lecture given by W.B. Yeats in Cork | J.M. Synge, *The Shadow of the Glen*<br>J.M. Synge, *The Well of the Saints*<br>G.B. Shaw, *Man and Superman*<br>Padraic Colum, *The Land*<br>Jack B. Yeats, *The Man from Aranmore*<br>D.P. Moran, *The Philosophy of Irish Ireland*<br>Gaelic League opens teacher-training college at Ballingeary, Co. Cork | Sinn Féin founded by Arthur Griffith |
| 1906 | 28 | Undertakes teacher training at St Patrick's College, Drumcondra, Dublin | | |
| 1907 | 29 | Resumes teaching at St Francis's National School, Cork<br><br>Visits Abbey Theatre for the first time<br><br>Attends Abbey production of J.M. Synge's *Riders to the Sea* in Cork | J.M. Synge, *The Playboy of the Western World*; riots at Abbey Theatre production<br>J.M. Synge, *The Aran Islands*<br>Patrick Pearse, *Íosagán agus Sgéalta Eile* | |
| 1908 | 30 | Co-founds the Cork Dramatic Society<br><br>Commissions a bronze bust of himself from the Cork-based sculptor Joseph Higgins | | Irish Women's Franchise League founded |
| 1909 | 31 | Corkery's first play, *The Embers*, is staged by the Cork Dramatic Society<br><br>*The Hermit and the King* is staged by the Cork Dramatic Society<br><br>Attends a summer course at the Gaelic League's teacher-training college at Ballingeary, west Cork; while there forms a friendship with Terence MacSwiney | | Irish Transport and General Workers' Union founded |

| Year | Age | Life | Irish Cultural Context | Irish Historical Events |
|---|---|---|---|---|
| 1910 | 32 | *The Onus of Ownership* is staged by the Cork Dramatic Society<br>Defends *The Playboy of the Western World* in a lecture to the Cork Literary and Scientific Society | Cork premier of *The Playboy*<br>James Connolly, *Labour in Irish History*<br>Pádraic Ó Conaire, *Deoraidheacht* | Irish Countrywomen's Association founded |
| 1911 | 33 | *The Epilogue* is staged by the Cork Dramatic Society | | Irish Women Workers' Union established, with James Larkin as president and his sister, Delia, as secretary |
| 1912 | 34 | *Israel's Incense* (later revised as *Fohnam the Sculptor*) is staged by Cork Dramatic Society | James Stephens, *The Charwoman's Daughter*<br>G.B. Shaw, *Pygmalion*<br>Paul Henry, *The Potato Diggers* | Third Home Rule Bill<br>Ulster Rebellion<br>Irish Labour Party founded by James Connolly, James Larkin and William O'Brien |
| 1913 | 35 | Transfers to St Patrick's National School, Cork; amongst the students he teaches at this school are Michael O'Donovan (Frank O'Connor), the author, and Seamus Murphy, the sculptor | Irish language becomes a compulsory matriculation subject for entry into the National University of Ireland | The Great Dublin Lockout<br>Ulster Volunteer Force founded<br>Irish Volunteers founded<br>Irish Citizen Army formed |
| 1914 | | | James Joyce, *Dubliners*<br>Pádraic Ó Conaire, *An Chéad Chloch* | First World War commences<br>Cumann na mBan founded |
| 1915 | 37 | Delivers a lecture titled 'The Hidden Ireland' to the Cork Literary and Scientific Society<br>Co-founds the Twenty Club | Peadar Ó Laoghaire, *Mo Scéal Féin*<br>Sean Keating, *Men of the West* | |
| 1916 | 38 | *A Munster Twilight* (short stories)<br>Delivers a lecture titled 'A Plea for the European' to the Cork Catholic Young Man's Society | James Joyce, *A Portrait of the Artist as a Young Man*<br>Patrick Pearse, *An Mháthair agus Sgéalta Eile*<br>Thomas MacDonagh, *Literature in Ireland* | Easter Rebellion and executions |

| Year | Age | Life | Irish Cultural Context | Irish Historical Events |
|---|---|---|---|---|
| 1917 | 39 | *The Threshold of Quiet* (novel)<br>*The Yellow Bittern* is staged by the Munster Players | | |
| 1918 | 40 | Resigns his post at St Patrick's National School having been refused the headmastership and is employed as a teacher of art, woodwork and Irish by the County Cork Technical Instruction Committee<br>Declines the offer of a nomination by the local Sinn Féin organisation for Cork City in the forthcoming General Election<br>Commissions a portrait of himself from the Cork-born artist William Sheehan | Brinsley McNamara, *The Valley of the Squinting Windows*<br>James Joyce, *Exiles* | Sinn Féin electoral triumph<br>Countess Markievicz elected to Dáil Eireann<br>Granting of vote to women over thirty |
| 1919 | 41 | *An Clochair* (play co-written with Séamus Ó hAodha)<br>*The Labour Leader* is staged by the Abbey Theatre | | Establishment of First Dáil |
| 1919–21 | | | | War of Independence |
| 1920–4 | | | | Dáil Courts |
| 1920 | 42 | *Three Plays: King and Hermit, Clan Falvey, The Yellow Bittern*<br>*The Hounds of Banba* (short stories)<br>*The Labour Leader* (play)<br>*The Yellow Bittern* is staged by the Abbey Theatre<br>*Clan Falvey* is staged in Cork; Seán O'Faoláin plays one of the lead roles | W.B. Yeats, *Michael Robartes and the Dancer*<br>Lady Gregory, *Visions and Beliefs of the West of Ireland* | Deaths of Tomás MacCurtain and Terence MacSwiney<br>'Bloody Sunday' |
| 1921 | 43 | *I Bhreasail* (poems and lyrics) | Seumas MacManus, *The Story of the Irish Race*<br>Sean Keating, *Men of the South* | Anglo-Irish Treaty |

| Year | Age | Life | Irish Cultural Context | Irish Historical Events |
|------|-----|------|------------------------|-------------------------|
| 1922 | 44 | *Rebel Songs* published under pen-name 'An Réilthín Siúbhalach'; dedicated to Erskine Childers. Adopts an anti-Treaty position; criticises the Irish Free State in the republican weekly, *Poblacht na b-Éireann* | James Joyce, *Ulysses* | Anglo-Irish Treaty ratified by Dáil; Establishment of Irish Free State. W.B. Yeats becomes a senator of the Irish Free State. Death of Erskine Childers |
| 1922–3 | | | | Irish Civil War |
| 1923 | 45 | Appointed clerical assistant to the County Cork Inspector of Irish. Lectures at the first summer school held at University College Cork to train secondary teachers to meet the new Irish-language requirements | Sean O'Casey, *The Shadow of a Gunman*. Liam O'Flaherty, *Thy Neighbour's Wife*. Jack B. Yeats, *The Liffey Swim*. W.B. Yeats receives Nobel Prize. Censorship of Films Act | Irish Free State joins League of Nations. Cumann na nGaedheal founded. Cork Lock-Out |
| 1924 | 46 | *The Hidden Ireland* (cultural history) | Sean O'Casey, *Juno and the Paycock* | |
| 1925 | | | Liam O'Flaherty, *The Informer*. E. Somerville and M. Ross, *The Big House at Inver*. G.B. Shaw receives the Nobel Prize | Partition confirmed |
| 1926 | 48 | Extended exchange in print between Corkery, O'Connor and O'Faoláin in *The Irish Tribune* | Sean O'Casey, *The Plough and the Stars*; protests at Abbey Theatre production. Lennox Robinson, *The Big House*. Establishment of Irish-language publishing house, An Gúm. Establishment of national radio service | Fianna Fáil founded by Eamon de Valera |
| 1927 | 49 | 'The Literature of Collapse' (literary criticism). Addresses mass meeting called to demand a ban on immoral publications | An Cumann le Béaloideas Éireann founded. *An Taibhdhearc* Irish-language theatre founded | |

| Year | Age | Life | Irish Cultural Context | Irish Historical Events |
|---|---|---|---|---|
| 1928 | 50 | Appointed 'Irish Organiser', County Cork Vocational School Educational Committee | Peadar O'Donnell, *Islanders* <br> Sean O'Casey, *The Silver Tassie* <br> Irish Manuscripts Commission founded | |
| 1929 | 51 | *The Stormy Hills* (short stories) <br> Awarded Honours MA for independent research on Synge | Elizabeth Bowen, *The Last September* <br> Tomás Ó Criomhthainn, *An tOileánach* <br> Peadar O'Donnell, *Adrigoole* <br> Austin Clarke, *Pilgrimage and Other Poems* <br> Harry Clarke, *The Geneva Window* <br> Censorship of Publications Act | Official opening of Ardnacrusha hydro-electric power station |
| 1930–1 | 52/3 | Engages in a debate with the Irish-language scholar and translator Pádraig de Brún in the journal *Humanitas* about the translation of the classics into the Irish language | | |
| 1931 | 53 | *Synge and Anglo-Irish Literature* (literary criticism) <br> Appointed Professor of English at University College Cork | Frank O'Connor, *Guests of the Nation* <br> Teresa Deevey, *A Disciple* <br> Kate O'Brien, *Without my Cloak* | Public Safety Bill <br> First number of *The Irish Press* issued |
| 1932 | 54 | Declines a founding membership of the Irish Academy of Letters on the basis that such an academy, so named, and meaning literature in the English language, was a contradiction in terms | Seán O'Faoláin, *Midsummer Night Madness* <br> Peadar O'Donnell, *The Gates Flew Open* | Fianna Fáil forms government; re-elected with overall majority <br> International Eucharistic Congress in Phoenix Park <br> Northern Ireland parliament buildings at Stormont formally open |
| 1933–8 | | | | Anglo–Irish Trade War |
| 1933 | | | Muiris Ó Súilleabháin, *Fiche Bliain ag Fás* | Introduction of Marriage Bar for women national teachers |

| Year | Age | Life | Irish Cultural Context | Irish Historical Events |
|---|---|---|---|---|
| 1934 | 56 | Publicly denounces Blueshirt protests against the effects of the Economic War | Kate O'Brien, *The Ante-Room* Samuel Beckett, *More Pricks than Kicks* Robert Flaherty, *Man of Aran* | |
| 1935 | | | Irish Folklore Commission founded Teresa Deevy, *The King of Spain's Daughter* The Dance Halls Act | Marriage Bar extended to all civil service posts The Irish Nationality and Citizenship Act |
| 1936 | | | Peig Sayers, *Peig* Kate O'Brien, *Mary Lavelle* Elizabeth Connor (Una Troy), *Mount Prospect* | IRA declared illegal in Irish Free State Aer Lingus founded |
| 1937 | 59 | Corkery, O'Connor and O'Faoláin contribute to a series of articles published in *The Irish Press* on the future of literature in Ireland | Conrad Arensberg, *The Irish Countryman* Frank O'Connor, *The Big Fellow* | New Constitution approved by Dáil |
| 1938 | | | Samuel Beckett, *Murphy* Seán O'Faoláin, *King of the Beggars* W.B. Yeats, *Purgatory* | Douglas Hyde elected President of Ireland |
| 1939–45 | | | | Second World War; Irish neutrality |
| 1939 | 61 | *Earth out of Earth* (short stories) *Fohnam the Sculptor* is staged by the Abbey Theatre | James Joyce, *Finnegans Wake* Flann O'Brien, *At Swim–Two–Birds* | |
| 1940 | | | Seosamh MacGrianna, *Mo Bhealach Féin* C.M. Arensberg and S.T. Kimball, *Family and Community in Ireland* Seán O'Faoláin founds *The Bell*; O'Faoláin is editor from 1940 to 1948 | |

| Year | Age | Life | Irish Cultural Context | Irish Historical Events |
|---|---|---|---|---|
| 1941 | | | Flann O'Brien, *An Béal Bocht*<br>Kate O'Brien, *The Land of Spies* | |
| 1942 | 64 | *Resurrection* (play)<br>*What's This About the Gaelic League?* (pamphlet)<br>In response to an editorial by O'Faoláin, writes a letter to *The Bell* which the journal refuses to print | Patrick Kavanagh, *The Great Hunger*<br>Mary Lavin, *Tales from Bective Bridge*<br>Elizabeth Bowen, *Bowen's Court*<br>Eric Cross, *The Tailor and Ansty* | |
| 1943 | 65 | *The Philosophy of the Gaelic League* (pamphlet) | | Eamon de Valera's St Patrick's Day broadcast |
| 1944 | | | Frank O'Connor, *Crab Apple Jelly* | |
| 1945 | | | Frank O'Connor's translation of *The Midnight Court*<br>Establishment of Irish-language publishing house, Sáirséal agus Dill | Congress of Irish Trade Unions formed |
| 1946 | | | Jack B. Yeats, *Men of Destiny*<br>Second Censorship of Publications Act | |
| 1947 | 69 | Retires from Professorship at University College Cork | Seán O'Faoláin, *The Irish* | |
| 1948 | 70 | Awarded Honorary D.Litt by the National University of Ireland | Patrick Kavanagh, *Tarry Flynn*<br>Seán O'Faoláin, *The Short Story* | Declaration of Irish Republic |
| 1949 | | | Máirtín Ó Cadhain, *Cré na Cille*<br>Francis Stuart, *Redemption*<br>Thomas Bodkin, *Report on the Arts in Ireland*<br>Cultural Relations Committee founded | Éire formally becomes a Republic |

| Year | Age | Life | Irish Cultural Context | Irish Historical Events |
|---|---|---|---|---|
| 1950 | 72 | *The Wager* (selected short stories from previous collections) | | |
| 1951 | 73 | Nominated to Seanad by Fianna Fáil | Arts Council founded in Irish Republic | |
| 1952 | 74 | Appointed to first Arts Council | Seán Ó Ríordáin, *Eireaball Spideoige*; Evie Hone completes *The Crucifixion and the Last Supper* | |
| 1953 | 75 | *An Doras Dúnta* (play) | Liam O'Flaherty, *Dúil*; Samuel Beckett, *En attendant Godot*; Gael-Linn founded | |
| 1954 | 76 | *The Fortunes of the Irish Language* (cultural history); One-man exhibition of paintings in Dublin | | |
| 1955 | | | J.P. Donleavy, *The Ginger Man*; Brian Moore, *The Lonely Passion of Judith Hearne*; Elizabeth Bowen, *A World of Love*; Irish premiere of Samuel Beckett, *Waiting for Godot* | Irish Republic admitted to the United Nations |
| 1956–62 | | | | 'Border Campaign' |
| 1956 | | | Seán O'Faoláin, *The Vanishing Hero*; Brendan Behan, *The Quare Fellow* | Ireland adopts UN Convention on Human Rights |
| 1957 | | | Samuel Beckett, *Endgame* | Boycott at Fethard-on-Sea commences |
| 1958 | 80 | Biography of Tomás MacCurtain published with an Introduction by Corkery | Brendan Behan, *Borstal Boy*; Samuel Beckett, *Krapp's Last Tape*; Thomas Kinsella, *Another September* | Sean Lemass and T.K. Whittaker launch the First Programme for Economic Expansion; Ireland first contributes to the United Nations Peacekeeping Mission |

| Year | Age | Life | Irish Cultural Context | Irish Historical Events |
| --- | --- | --- | --- | --- |
| 1959 | | | Seán Ó Riada, *Mise Eire* | Eamon de Valera elected President of Irish Republic |
| 1960–4 | | | Edna O'Brien's *The Country Girls* trilogy | |
| 1961 | | | Frank O'Connor, *An Only Child*; National television service commences | |
| 1962 | 84 | Biography of Terence MacSwiney published with an Introduction by Corkery | Frank O'Connor, *The Lonely Voice*; Samuel Beckett, *Happy Days* | |
| 1963 | | | John McGahern, *The Barracks* | State visit of John F. Kennedy |
| 1964 | 86 | Dies in Cork; as previously requested by Corkery, his headstone is carved by the Cork-based sculptor and stonecarver Seamus Murphy | Flann O'Brien, *The Dalkey Archive*; Brian Friel, *Philadelphia, Here I Come!*; Ulster Folk Museum opens | |
| 1965 | | | Seán O'Faoláin, *Vive Moi!*; John McGahern, *The Dark* | |
| 1967 | | | Frank O'Connor, *The Backward Look* | |
| 1969 | | | L.M. Cullen, 'The Hidden Ireland: Re-assessment of a Concept' | |

# Introduction: Daniel Corkery as Postcolonial Critic

Daniel Corkery – writer, language activist, teacher and painter – was born in Cork in 1878 and died in the same city in 1964. He was educated at the Presentation Brothers, Cork, and at St Patrick's College of Education, Dublin. He worked as a primary school teacher in Cork, taught art for the local technical education committee and was Professor of English at University College Cork from 1931 to 1947. Corkery was a mentor to younger writers and artists; Frank O'Connor, Seán O'Faoláin and Seamus Murphy were amongst his most celebrated protégés.[1] He was an active member of the Gaelic League[2] and a prominent proponent of the Irish Ireland movement.[3] He was also involved in a number of local organisations, most notably the Cork Dramatic Society. In his later years, he served in the Seanad and on the Arts Council. He was a republican in politics and a close friend of Tomás MacCurtain and Terence MacSwiney, successive Lord Mayors of Cork who died in tragic circumstances during the War of Independence.[4] He was one of the foremost Irish cultural critics of the 1920s and 30s.

Corkery began his writing career at the turn of the twentieth century in the columns of D.P. Moran's polemical nationalist weekly, *The Leader*. An Irish-language enthusiast who was not a native speaker, he wrote primarily, though not exclusively, in the English language. His literary writings are comprised of four collections of short stories; a number of plays, including the Irish-language play, *An Doras Dúnta*; a novel and some poetry. His non-fiction writings, which are the focus of this publication, include two major critical studies, *The Hidden Ireland* (1924) and *Synge and Anglo-Irish Literature* (1931); writings on the Irish language and on the Irish-language movement; newspaper articles on a wide range of cultural issues; and reviews of Irish-language and English-language literary works.

While the contemporary response to his critical writings was mixed, by the late 1990s Corkery had been firmly established in Irish scholarship, particularly amongst those who worked on English-language material, as, in Declan Kiberd's words, a 'whipping boy for all right-on pluralists'.[5] A 1969 article by the historian L.M. Cullen, now considered a foundational text in Irish revisionism, was fundamental in assigning that role to Corkery. In this article, 'The Hidden Ireland: Re-assessment of a Concept', Cullen argued that Corkery's *The Hidden Ireland* 'simplifies Irish history' and 'seems to impoverish Irish nationality and sense of identity, seeing it in the context of settlement and oppression and not in the rich, complex and varied stream of identity and racial consciousness heightened in the course of centuries of Anglo-Irish relations'.[6] In this and subsequent critiques of Corkery's critical writings, Corkery is depicted as the chief spokesman for a narrow, repressive and backward-looking Gaelic nationalism from which 'modern' Ireland is struggling to escape. In Volume III of *The Field Day Anthology of Irish Writing*, for example, Corkery is described by Terence Brown as an 'able polemicist' for an Irish Ireland movement which 'insisted that the only authentic Irish identity was the rural Gaelic/Catholic one'. Corkery's influential critical writings, Brown states, 'gave intellectual sanction to an attitude that in its less refined form often expressed itself as a strident xenophobia or a bigoted social triumphalism'.[7] More sympathetic accounts of Daniel Corkery, such as Patrick Maume's critical biography of 1993 and Colbert Kearney's writings on Corkery's short stories, have, in the main, accepted this interpretation of Corkery's cultural criticism, arguing, however, that this was only one facet of a Daniel Corkery whose early writings and/or literary works reveal a more complex and contradictory figure than such an interpretation suggests.[8]

Irish-language scholarship has been more divided in its response to Corkery's cultural criticism. Breandán Ó Buachalla's 'Ó Corcora agus an Hidden Ireland' and Seán Ó Tuama's 'Dónall Ó Corcora', both published in a 1979 special edition of *Scríobh* in honour of Daniel Corkery, largely represent the opposing viewpoints held by Irish-language scholars on his writings and legacy. Corkery's *The Hidden Ireland* is referred to in both of these essays as a 'leabhar ann féin' [unique book],[9] but the scholars' understanding of the nature and significance of the book differs substantially. For Ó Tuama, *The Hidden Ireland*, written at a time when the Irish-language poems of Aodhagán Ó Rathaille and Brian Merriman were as strange to the Irish people as Chinese poetry, captured Corkery's elation at the discovery of an Irish-language poetry tradition and provided, for the first time, an appraisal of the poets and poetry that belonged to that tradition.[10] Ó Tuama concedes that the limited historical knowledge of the eighteenth century that Corkery had at his disposal distorted his understanding of the mindset of that period, but insists that *The Hidden Ireland* should not be dismissed on the basis of its historical inaccuracies as the book was never intended as a work of social or economic history.[11]

In Ó Buachalla's analysis, *The Hidden Ireland* fails to provide an objective and consistent analysis of the poetry it features and ignores generic differences.[12] Furthermore, the mode of production of the poetry is omitted and the poems treated as social documents.[13] Based on these 'documents', the history that Corkery provided in *The Hidden Ireland* is both inaccurate and incomplete. Ó Buachalla, who chides Corkery for failing to acknowledge the impact of the patronage system on the content of eighteenth-century Irish-language poetry,[14] draws attention, in the opening pages of his essay, to the uneven power relations, reminiscent of such a system, which existed between Corkery and his protégés. According to Ó Buachalla, it was these uneven power relations that the Irish-language poet Seán Ó Ríordáin was referring to when he mockingly described Corkery and those who gathered around him as 'an Máistir agus a dheisceabail' [the master and his disciples].[15]

Ó Ríordáin's view of Corkery was less resolute than is suggested by Ó Buachalla in 'Ó Corcora agus an Hidden Ireland'. In a 1977 RTÉ broadcast, Ó Ríordáin makes reference to Corkery's devotees, emphatically stating that he himself never belonged to their ranks. To be one of Corkery's disciples, Ó Ríordáin states, you would have to close your mind as his opinion was the only one that mattered. Corkery's role as 'an Máistir', Ó Ríordáin makes clear, however, was not solely dependent upon his forceful personality. People listened to Corkery, according to Ó Ríordáin, because Corkery had significant things to say. Indeed for Ó Ríordáin '[ní] raibh ionad ar domhan níb fhearr chun radharc cothrom d'fháil ar an saol ná an seomra ina raibh Dónal Ó Corcora suite i ndeireadh a shaoil' [there was no better place on earth to get a balanced view of life than the room in which Daniel Corkery was seated at the end of his life].[16] Ó Ríordáin's conflicted stance on Corkery, which overlaps with elements of both Ó Buachalla's and Ó Tuama's appraisals, is perhaps best captured in his poem 'Do Dhomhnall Ó Corcora' [To Daniel Corkery]. The poem opens with an eloquent celebration of Corkery's role as chronicler of Irish-language poetry.

> Éirigh is can ár mbuíochas croí dhó,
> Do mhúin sé an tslí,
> Do dhúisigh eilit ár bhfilíochta
> I gcoillte blian.[17]

> [Rise and sing our heart-thanks to him,
> He showed the way,
> He woke the doe of our poetry
> In the woods of the years.]

In the penultimate verse of the poem, however, Corkery's weighty influence is a shackle that stifles and curbs the individual poet's creativity:

> Braithim é gan sos ag éisteacht
> Mar athchoinsias;
> Tá smacht a chluaise ar lúth mo véarsa,
> Trom an chuing.[18]

> [I feel him listening constantly,
> A second conscience;
> The pace of my verse is controlled by his ear.
> A heavy chain.]

In recent years, a number of reappraisals of Corkery's critical writings have appeared, the most notable of which draw on postcolonial theories and frameworks. In 'Becoming Minor', Conor Carville discusses *The Hidden Ireland* and *Synge and Anglo-Irish Literature* in relation to Homi Bhabha's thesis that underlying even the most authoritarian nationalist sentiment is an awareness of the nation as a performative assemblage of multiple identities and disparate referents. In 'Becoming National', which is a re-working of elements of Carville's argument, Paul Delaney suggests that Corkery's criticism is best interpreted in the context of a 'decolonising politics which deterritorialise[s] in order to reterritorialise'.[19] Corkery's work, Delaney goes on to argue, is symptomatic of the processes 'whereby the minor becomes major', with the 'inventive potential' of that work ultimately becoming 'swamped by the rhetoric of official nationalism'.[20] In addition to being viewed through a postcolonial lens, Corkery's writings have of late been cited as examples of early Irish postcolonial criticism. In *Inventing Ireland*, for example, Declan Kiberd refers to Corkery as 'the nearest thing Ireland produced to a post-colonial critic' in the first half of the twentieth century.[21] Indeed, notwithstanding his aforementioned comments in *The Field Day Anthology*, Terence Brown, in *Ireland: A Social History, 1922–1985*, paved the way for just such an approach by including Corkery in a list of figures whose advocacy of Gaelic Ireland stemmed not from 'racial chauvinism' but from 'a concerned awareness of the psychological distress suffered by countless individual Irishmen and women because of colonial oppression'.[22]

As indicated by Kiberd and Brown, Corkery, in his critical writings, offered valuable insights into the cultural and psychological effects of colonialism. It could be argued, in fact, that the central, and interrelated, concerns of his criticism – language displacement, cultural dislocation, a disconnect between dominant literary forms and local reality, 'fractured' identity, education as a colonial tool, the gaps and silences of official historiography, the relationship between settler and native – have, until recently, been the central concerns of postcolonial criticism. *The Hidden Ireland*, which is a study of the eighteenth-century remnants of an earlier thriving Irish-language literary culture, touches on a number of these concerns. The dominant narrative of Ireland's cultural past, Corkery reminds us in his Introduction to *The Hidden Ireland*, is essentially the story of the cultural achievements of the Anglo-Irish community. The Irish language was considered by this community to be little more than 'a *patois* used by the hillmen among themselves' and certainly not the basis for a literary culture. In the course of time, Corkery tells us, Irish people from a non-Ascendancy background internalised the notion of their cultural inferiority, developing what he refers to as a 'slave-mind'.[23]

In *The Hidden Ireland*, Corkery reveals the gaps and silences of official historiography by imaginatively reconstructing a world outside of its parameters. In one section of the book, the famous Irish travel journals of Arthur Young are employed by Corkery to demonstrate the invisibility of this world to those who did not know to look for it.[24] The passage of the journal that he cites contains Young's description of an 'enlightening' conversation he had with a woman called Mrs Quinn in Adair about the history of the locality. It is the information that Young received from this woman that is included in his journal; information which, according to Corkery, was only partial. Mrs Quinn failed to tell Young about the death the previous year of the eighteenth-century Irish-language poet Seán Ó Tuama, and Young lacked the knowledge required to seek out this information. Moreover, even if asked about Ó Tuama, Mrs Quinn, Corkery tells us, would in all likelihood have referred to him not as a poet but as the servant who looked after her hens.

Corkery's eighteenth-century Ireland is a place of parallel universes, whose inhabitants are often forced to lead a dual existence. In the 'hidden Ireland' that Corkery is seeking to document, Seán Ó Tuama is the poet who took on a leadership role amongst the poets of the district when Seán Clárach MacDomhnaill died. In the world of Mrs Quinn, John O'Twomey (Seán Ó Tuama) was a disgruntled and possibly not very effective hen-keeper. Similarly, in the 'darkened land' that Corkery writes about, Eoghan Ruadh Ó Súilleabháin was 'one of our greatest lyric poets', while in the Ireland that the renowned historian W.E.H. Lecky documented in his *History of Ireland in the Eighteenth Century,* Ó Súilleabháin would have been referred to as 'a farm labourer, a *spailpín*'.[25] Parallel universes can also be found in a number of Corkery's short stories, most notably in 'Solace' which is included in the 1916 collection *A Munster Twilight.* The protagonist of this story is both Eoghan Mor of the Aislings who calls all the poets of the locality to a Bardic session so that he can recite a new song, 'a riot of words, golden and flashing with fire and sound and colour', and an impoverished tenant-farmer who, in the eyes of a passing English traveller modelled perhaps on Arthur Young, is merely 'a huge gaunt man [. . .] reciting what was apparently a very violent poem' in 'a miserable hut' which was 'crowded to the door with wild and picturesque figures'.[26]

L.M. Cullen's previously mentioned critique of *The Hidden Ireland* was one of a number of texts that emerged from the history departments of Irish universities in the 1950s and 60s that drew attention to the flawed methodology of the nationalist historiography of the first part of the century. This critique consists for the most part of a bombardment of facts designed to reveal the paucity of Corkery's sources and, consequently, the largely fictional nature of his historical narrative. As Seán Ó Tuama, the twentieth-century Irish-language scholar, and, more recently, Patrick Walsh have suggested, however, such a critique misconstrues what Corkery was setting out to achieve in *The Hidden Ireland* and, more significantly, disregards the actual practice of the book.[27] Factual accounts of Irish history, Corkery points out elsewhere, are for the most part based on state papers. Consequently, 'our histories' are 'the story of the struggle of the English state to maintain its position in our midst'.[28] *The Hidden Ireland* demonstrates the limitations of historical accounts of Ireland based on the information supplied in these state papers by imaginatively constructing, largely from Irish-language cultural sources, a world and worldview that they omitted. In a later publication, *The Fortunes of the Irish Language*, Corkery states that 'in our case [where] native state-papers of the usual type do not exist', cultural artefacts can function to 'mitigate, if not contradict, the alien state-papers'.[29] The significance of such artefacts in this context, he goes on to argue, lies less in the 'points of information' they contain than in the extent to which they allow us 'to feel our way into the deeper past'.[30] In Corkery's *The Hidden Ireland*, voices from the past that had gone unheard in mainstream historiography speak to us.[31] Corkery's treatment of these voices is very different from the historian's treatment of archival evidence. His interest in them lies less in the factual information they provide than in the extent to which they allow us, 'in our very different world', to take an imaginative leap and speculate on how it might have felt to be part of the hidden, and rapidly transforming, world of the eighteenth-century Irish-language poet.[32] *The Hidden Ireland*, Corkery acknowledges in the book's Introduction, probably contains errors of fact, but these errors, he goes on to state, will not prevent the book from achieving its primary goal: the 'lighting up' of that which previous accounts of eighteenth-century Ireland had kept in the 'dark'.[33]

In Corkery's second major critical work, *Synge and Anglo-Irish Literature*, it is the literary culture of the 'visible' Ireland recorded by W.E.H. Lecky and others that is the focus of attention. *The Hidden Ireland* challenges the dominant narrative of Ireland's cultural past by constructing an alternative narrative of a cultural past that it omits; *Synge and Anglo-Irish Literature* challenges the dominant narrative of Ireland's cultural past by calling into question the nature and value of the cultural past that it documents. J.M. Synge, referred to by Corkery as 'a true child of the Ascendancy', belonged to that cultural past and his plays are praised, in Corkery's study of them, in direct proportion to their distance from the 'norms' of Ascendancy culture.[34] It is the opening chapter of *Synge and Anglo-Irish Literature* that has received the most critical attention, much of it hostile. In this chapter, 'On Anglo-Irish Literature', Corkery outlined, with reference to form, content, and perspective, the chief characteristics of a literature that he believed should be categorised as colonial as opposed to Anglo-Irish. The main points of comparison between this literature and other colonial literatures, such as Rudyard Kipling's Indian books, according to Corkery, were that its intended audience was an external one and its treatment of its Irish subject-matter broadly-speaking anthropological: 'This Colonial literature was written to explain the quaintness of the humankind of this land, especially the native humankind, to another humankind that was not quaint, that was standard, normal.'[35] Its depiction of 'quaint' Irish people led this external audience to 'picture us as given over either to a wild whirl of fox-hunting and rioting, or as spell-bound by fairies that troop nightly from our prehistoric ruins'.[36] Moreover, its particular brand of Irish subject-matter marked it, in Corkery's eyes, as colonial literature; the story that Ascendancy literature from Edgeworth's *Castle Rackrent* to Somerville and Ross's *Big House of Inver* told, over and over again, was the story of 'the decline and fall of an Ascendancy "Big House"'.[37] Literature about Ireland written by the Ascendancy was also colonial in form, characterised, Corkery argued, by a disconnect between literary 'moulds' that had originated elsewhere and, consequently, 'do not willingly receive the facts of Irish life', and local reality.[38]

For Corkery, since the literature written by the Ascendancy had established the norms of English-language literary culture in Ireland, the characteristics of Ascendancy literature were the dominant characteristics of that literary culture. Consequently, the bulk of English-language literature in Ireland, even the works of non-Ascendancy writers, was colonial in form, content, and perspective. Gerald Griffin, whose novel *The Collegians* features 'an Englishman to whom the quaintness of the folk is exhibited with the accompanying stream of comment, exactly in the Colonial manner', is cited by Corkery as an example of a 'non-Ascendancy writer who under the stress of the literary moulds of his time wrote Colonial literature'.[39]

In 'On Anglo-Irish Literature', Corkery divides the literary works associated with Ireland into three distinct categories. He names the first of these categories Irish literature, stating emphatically that this term should only be used to refer to literature written in the Irish language. The second of these categories, colonial literature, includes the bulk of the literature written in the English language by Ascendancy and non-Ascendancy writers. While this second category is dealt with in some depth in Corkery's opening chapter to *Synge and Anglo-Irish Literature*, I would suggest that it is, in fact, the third category that is the main focus of the chapter. The name that he gave this category, Anglo-Irish literature, in Corkery's view, had been wrongly applied to literature written by the Ascendancy and instead should be used to refer to a literature that did not, as yet, exist in its proper state and may, in fact, never fully come into being. With the introduction of this third category of literature, we see a shift in approach from an analysis of that which is, to the establishment of a framework for that which might be. 'Genuine' Anglo-Irish literature, for Corkery, is Ireland-centred literature written in the English language by writers born in Ireland that is not colonial literature. In the logic of Corkery's argument, it is a literature that 'canalise[s] some share of Irish consciousness so that that consciousness would the better know itself' as opposed to a literature that 'canalises' Irish consciousness so that 'the strange workings of that consciousness might entertainingly be exhibited to alien eyes'.[40] Synge is the focus of the subsequent chapters of the book because his plays, Corkery tentatively suggests, do not fit neatly into the category of colonial literature and might possibly be a 'portent', signalling the arrival of non-colonial or 'genuine' Anglo-Irish literature.[41]

For Corkery, however, the development of a 'genuine' Anglo-Irish literature would not be a straightforward process. This development could only take place if the dominant 'mould' of English-language literature in Ireland, the colonial 'mould', was displaced by native 'moulds', and native 'moulds', he argues, would require a stronger base than 'fractured' Irish identity:

> The difficulty is not alone a want of native moulds; it is rather the want of a foundation upon which to establish them. Everywhere in the mentality of the Irish people are flux and uncertainty. Our national consciousness may be described, in a native phrase, as a quaking sod. It gives no footing. It is not English, nor Irish, nor Anglo-Irish.[42]

Corkery located the origins of this 'fractured' identity in a cultural dislocation that permeated all aspects of Irish life, including the education system that he, having worked for many years as a primary school teacher, was so familiar with:

> [The Irish child] cannot find in [his] surroundings what his reading has taught him is the matter worth coming upon. His surroundings begin to seem unvital. His education, instead of buttressing and refining his emotional nature, teaches him the rather to despise it, inasmuch as it teaches him not to see the surroundings out of which he is sprung, as they are in themselves, but as compared with alien surroundings: his education provides him with an alien medium through which he is henceforth to look at his native land![43]

Corkery's analysis of colonial cultural alienation in 'On Anglo-Irish Literature' offers insights into the relationship between education and colonialism and pre-empts such influential writings as Frantz Fanon's *Black Skin, White Masks* (1952) and Ngũgĩ wa Thiong'o's *Decolonising the Mind* (1986), but his attempt to counteract the effects of this cultural alienation by establishing a framework for native literary 'moulds' gives rise to what is often interpreted as a crude essentialism. There are 'three great forces', Corkery tells us, which have ensured that the 'Irish national being' is different from the 'English national being'.[44] Consequently, these three forces – religion, nationalism and land – should provide the basis for the native 'moulds' of literature required for a 'genuine' Anglo-Irish literature.

*Synge and Anglo-Irish Literature* was written in 1929. As is clear from the tentative tone of sections of its introductory chapter, Corkery was already sceptical at this point in time about the possibility of establishing an English-language literature in Ireland that was not colonial literature: '[T]he difficulties in creating genuine Anglo-Irish literature are so immense. It seems indeed an almost impossible task.'[45] By the time the book was published two years later, Corkery had abandoned the notion of a 'genuine' Anglo-Irish literature.[46] From that point on, he was to proclaim that Irish-language literature was the only literature in Ireland that could provide native 'moulds' of literary representation. Consequently, in *The Philosophy of the Gaelic League*, published in 1943, no distinction is formed between colonial literature and a 'genuine' Anglo-Irish literature. Anglo-Irish literature, even Anglo-Irish literature that is about Irish 'matter', is, we are told, merely a branch of English literature.[47] The 'Irish tradition', Corkery proclaimed in this publication, cannot 'go on living in English with either usefulness or dignity'.[48] It demands 'its own way, its own technique, its own media'.[49]

In the one-paragraph dismissals of Corkery that are to be found in so many post-1960s studies of Irish history, literature and culture, Corkery's analysis and the questions that he posed tend to be disregarded in favour of the solutions that he offered. This has facilitated the commonplace one-dimensional portrayal of a bigoted, fanatical Corkery. Corkery's solutions, while at times clearly questionable, emerged out of his often insightful analysis and, consequently, are best viewed, and critiqued, in conjunction with this analysis. Corkery's wholesale renunciation, in his later writings, of English-language literature in Ireland is undeniably open to challenge, particularly when taking into account the profound decentring of English-language literature that has taken place in the last forty and more years: 'What seems [. . .] to be happening is that those peoples who were once colonised by the [English] language are now rapidly remaking it – assisted by the English language's enormous flexibility and size, they are carving out large territories for themselves within its frontiers.'[50] Indeed, in *Finnegans Wake*, published just four years before *The Philosophy of the Gaelic League*, James Joyce's 'remaking' of the English language was so extreme that, in the words of Terry Eagleton, he 'estrange[d] [it] in the eyes of its proprietors'.[51] This renunciation, however, was based on Corkery's awareness of the significance and ramifications of language displacement in the colonial context; an awareness shared by such influential scholars of colonialism as Frantz Fanon.

Fanon opened *Black Skin, White Masks*, his 1952 study of the 'arsenal of complexes' that results from colonialism, with an analysis of how language contributes to and is affected by the feelings of inadequacy and dependence experienced by colonised peoples.[52] 'A man who has a language,' Fanon tells us, 'possesses the world expressed and implied by that language.'

Consequently, 'mastery of language affords remarkable power.'[53] In the colonial context, the colonised, who have internalised the notion of their own inferiority and, hence, the inferiority of 'native' languages, covet the agency or subjectivity ensured by the ability to speak the language of the coloniser. In the words of Fanon, '[t]he Negro of the Antilles will be proportionately whiter – that is, he will come closer to being a real human being – in direct ratio to his mastery of the French language.'[54] For Fanon, the assimilation and valorisation of the coloniser's language undermines the workings of the anti-colonial revolution on a number of fronts. By adopting the language of the coloniser, the colonised reinforces the notion of the superiority of the coloniser's language and culture over the so-called 'jabber' of native languages. Furthermore, 'to speak', according to Fanon, means not only 'to use a certain syntax, to grasp the morphology of this or that language, [. . .] it means above all to assume a culture, to support the weight of a civilisation'.[55] For Fanon, as for Corkery, language was more than a mere means of communication. Both held that in the colonial context to adopt the coloniser's language was not only to speak in a different way but to think in a different way; it was to adopt the perspectives, points of view and cultural assumptions that were encapsulated in that language.

Furthermore, Corkery's preoccupation in 'On Anglo-Irish Literature' with native literary 'moulds' and his accompanying attempt to differentiate the 'Irish national being' from the 'English national being' emanated from his awareness of the possible consequences of a cleavage between literature and local reality. In 'On Anglo-Irish Literature', the outcome of the splitting of the sign and the referent in the colonial classroom is a devaluing of the child's world: '[The Irish child] cannot find in [his] surroundings what his reading has taught him is the matter worth coming upon. His surroundings begin to seem unvital.'[56] Elsewhere, in a description of his own schooling, Corkery outlined the self-negation that results from this disconnect between the world of the classroom curriculum and the child's actual physical and material conditions; a disconnect that is sometimes referred to in post-colonial studies as 'the daffodil gap':[57]

> We were taught implicitly, and indeed almost explicitly, not to seek a reflection of our own thoughts and feelings in literature [. . .] We were supposed to read English literature with English eyes [. . .] [S]uch English texts as I studied for examination had nearly all been edited for nice little Protestant English boys by nice old English Protestant rectors or head-masters of English Public Schools [. . .] Knowledge that I had not – of English customs, religion, home-life, etc. – was taken for granted. Feelings that I had not, prejudices that I had not, were taken for granted. The knowledge, the feelings, the prejudices I had were never mentioned at all; I was, therefore, all the time being

implicitly instructed that all these were somehow wrong, that they had no right to be there at all, in me or in anyone else – and that I was somehow out of it, not normal, a kind of freak.[58]

As Corkery clearly surmised, one of the most pervasive and debilitating features of colonialism is the establishment, within colonial discourse, of a normative imperial culture and worldview, against which all other cultures and worldviews are deemed to be abnormal deviations. Indeed, Corkery's incessant use of the terms 'abnormal' and 'freakish' in his cultural criticism, and his accompanying determination to establish a literature, a people and a nation that was 'normal', 'typical', 'natural' and, therefore, not 'freakish', indicates that not only was he conscious of, and attempting to counteract, the damaging psychological effects of this aspect of colonialism, but that he himself was a product of it.[59] Corkery, having internalised the normal/abnormal binary opposition of colonial discourse, sought to reposition Ireland within this binary. To achieve 'normal' status, Ireland would have to assert its political and cultural independence: 'In a country that for long has been afflicted with an ascendancy, an alien ascendancy at that, national movements are a necessity: they are an effort to attain to the normal.'[60] For Corkery, the national in Ireland was the 'normal' in that it sought to undo the colonial. 'Normal' literature in Ireland, Corkery argued, would have the same relationship to Irish life as English literature had to English life and French literature had to French life.[61] A 'normal' literature, in the logic of his argument, was a non-colonial literature, a national literature, whose 'moulds' matched local reality.

Corkery, in *The Hidden Ireland*, had commended eighteenth-century Irish-language poets for 'gradually changing the old moulds into new shapes, and [...] filling them with a content that was all of the passing day and their own fields'.[62] In 'On Anglo-Irish Literature', he suggests that English-language literature in Ireland, in the form of a 'genuine' or 'true' Anglo-Irish literature, could establish a similarly close relationship between form and local reality. When in the process of writing *Synge and Anglo-Irish Literature*, Corkery clearly believed, therefore, that twentieth-century English-language literature in Ireland could be 'normal' in the way that eighteenth-century Irish-language poetry had been 'normal' and contemporary English and French literature was 'normal'.

Reconnecting literary 'moulds' to Irish life, however, involved determining what exactly was meant by Irish life and, for Corkery, this entailed forming a distinction between the 'Irish national being' and the 'English national being'.[63] He based this distinction, as any reader of the aforementioned one-paragraph dismissals of Corkery will be aware, on the three elements that he considered of key importance to Irish life: religion, nationalism and land.[64] Corkery, in pinpointing these elements, was, however, less concerned with uncovering intrinsic or essential Irish characteristics than with devising an ABC of 'genuine' Anglo-Irish literature. Indeed, religion, nationalism and land, in Corkery's analysis, are external forces that, due to specific cultural, historical and economic circumstances, have shaped the Irish national being. The religious consciousness referred to in 'On Anglo-Irish Literature' appears to be a relatively recent phenomenon in that it had displaced an alternative belief-system that 'still float[s] in the minds of a tiny percentage of the people'.[65] 'Hundreds of battlefields, slaughterings, famines, exoduses' are listed amongst the factors that have established the centrality of nationalism to Ireland.[66] It is at least partially due to the comparatively large percentage of people 'actually working in the fields' in Ireland that the land 'is a huge force in Irish life'.[67] Moreover, 'centuries of onslaught', according to Corkery, meant that all three forces acquired an 'intensity' that they lacked in countries with a less violent history.[68] Having '*work[ed]* for long in the Irish national being', these three forces, he argued, had ensured that the Irish national being differs from the English national being [my emphasis].[69]

The principle problem with this contentious section of 'On Anglo-Irish Literature' is not, therefore, that it attempts to uncover the essential Irish mind but that, in laying down coordinates for a non-colonial literature, it establishes rigid and exclusive artistic and national parameters. Having clearly outlined the often devastating effects of colonial cultural alienation on the individual and on society, Corkery sought to offset these effects by devising a set of criteria for a literature in which the Irish reading public could find its reflection. His coordinates were, however, notably narrow. Moreover, the individual writer, as Terence Brown has pointed out, is unlikely to obey any such prescriptive imperatives, even if less restrictive.[70] The result was an increasingly embittered relationship between Corkery and a younger generation of writers, including some of his former protégés, who were understandably reluctant to play their designated role in his cultural programme and, consequently, found themselves rejected from his literary canon. 'It is an odd type of criticism,' Seán O'Faoláin was to state, 'which would dictate to an artist as if he were a building contractor.'[71] Indeed O'Faoláin, a former protégé turned vehement critic, was to indict Corkery for 'lay[ing] down for Ireland' the 'same excluding law' that Goebbels and Hitler were 'laying down' for Germany. According to O'Faoláin, the only response that any self-respecting writer could have to the person 'who takes up a Hitlerian attitude' and demands that '*you* write what *we* want or you can get out' is 'we will write what we honestly feel to be the truth, and we will not get out' [O'Faoláin's emphasis].[72]

Kiberd's description of Daniel Corkery as 'the *nearest* thing Ireland produced to a post-colonial critic' in the first half of the twentieth century is as significant for its equivocality as it is for its choice of appellation [my emphasis].[73] This description suggests that notwithstanding the considerable overlap between his work and the writings of a number of seminal post-colonial critics, attempting to categorise Corkery as a postcolonial scholar can give rise to tensions and anxieties. Given the present-day dominance of a poststructuralist strand of postcolonial studies that is characterised by an undifferentiated disavowal of all forms of nationalism and a corresponding exaltation of the liminality, hybridity, ambivalence and multiculturality that results from colonialism, it is perhaps not surprising that doubt might arise about Corkery's suitability to this scholarly field. Homi Bhabha has proposed that postcolonial studies be more attentive to 'the complex cultural and political boundaries that exist on the cusp' of the political spheres of the coloniser and the colonised.[74] Corkery recognised, as do recent critics of Bhabha, that colonialism was 'a historical project of invasion, expropriation and exploitation' and, consequently, not 'a symbiotic encounter'.[75] For Corkery, colonialism was first and foremost disabling. Consequently, his writings do not fit easily into a body of work which, by deploying categories that lace colonised into colonising cultures, 'effectively [becomes] a recon-ciliatory rather than a critical, anticolonialist category'.[76]

Corkery's cultural criticism belongs, therefore, I would suggest, to what we might refer to as the anti-colonial branch of postcolonial studies in that, as L.M. Cullen recognised, he was more concerned with the antagonistic relationship between the opposing spheres of the coloniser and colonised than with the cultural and political interconnections that exist on the cusp of these spheres. His anti-colonialism was, however, limited in that what he sought for Ireland was the 'normal' or non-colonial as defined by colonial discourse. Contrary to claims otherwise, Corkery was not a nativist. The solution to the cultural and psychological effects of colonialism for Corkery was not to go back to a pre-colonial past, but to create a contemporary Irish society that functioned as other contemporary non-colonised societies functioned. As has been recognised in postcolonial societies across the globe, however, it is simply not possible to 'undo' colonialism in this way. The only conceivable outcome of a cultural programme designed for such a purpose is a restrictive and exclusive cultural atmosphere of the sort that stifled Seán Ó Ríordáin and enraged Seán O'Faoláin.

Corkery was a perceptive colonial commentator whose insights were echoed in later postcolonial writings now considered seminal. He was also, however, a product of the colonialism he so fiercely opposed. Corkery recognised and drew attention to connections between Ireland and other colonised locations, but the Ireland he sought to bring into being was a 'modern' nation-state on a par with the non-colonised nation-states of Europe; an Ireland that had surmounted the uneven power relations of colonialism and, consequently, could partake in a cultural exchange with its neighbours on an equal footing. Ironically, much of the post-1960s discussion of his work has been shaped by a modernisation discourse that has its origins in the colonial project and seeks to rid Ireland of the recalcitrant elements that prevent it from becoming just such a 'modern' nation-state. One of Corkery's principal strengths as an anti-colonial commentator was his understanding that colonialism is a pervasive force that shapes how we view ourselves and the world around us. The widespread portrayal of Corkery's cultural criticism within Irish scholarship as retrograde writings that sought to hinder Ireland's journey on the path to Progress gives credence to Corkery's claims for the ubiquitous nature of the colonial mindframe.

# Further Reading

Carville, Conor. 'Becoming Minor: Daniel Corkery and the Expatriated Nation', *Irish Studies Review*, 6.2 (August 1998), 139–47.

Condon, Janette. '"A Quaking Sod": Ireland, Empire and Children's Literary Culture', in P.J. Matthews (ed.), *New Voices in Irish Criticism* (Dublin: Four Courts Press, 2000), 189–96.

Cullen, Louis M. 'The Hidden Ireland: Reassessment of a Concept', *Studia Hibernica*, 9 (1969), 7–47.

— 'Postscript', *The Hidden Ireland: Reassessment of a Concept* (Mullingar: Lilliput Press, 1988), 47–53.

Delaney, Paul. 'Becoming National: Daniel Corkery and the Reterritorialised Subject', in Kelly, Aaron and Gillis, Alan A. (eds), *Critical Ireland: New Essays in Literature and Culture* (Dublin: Four Courts Press, 2001), 41–8.

— '"Fierce Passions for Middle-Aged Men": Frank O'Connor and Daniel Corkery', in Hilary Lennon (ed.), *Frank O'Connor: Critical Essays* (Dublin: Four Courts Press, 2007), 53–66.

— 'A Lack of Invention': Corkery, Criticism and Minor Fatigue', *The Irish Review*, 33 (Spring 2005), 96–109.

Kearney, Colbert. 'Daniel Corkery: A Priest and his People', in Jacqueline Genet (ed.), *Rural Ireland, Real Ireland?* (Gerrards Cross: Colin Smythe, 1996), 201–12.

— 'Dónall Ó Corcora agus an Litríocht Angla-Éireannach', *Scríobh*, 4 (1978), 138–51.

Kiberd, Declan. 'Dónall Ó Corcora agus Litríocht Bhéarla na hÉireann', *Scríobh*, 4 (1978), 84–93.

Larkin, Emmet. 'A Reconsideration: Daniel Corkery and his Ideas on Cultural Nationalism', *Éire-Ireland*, 8 (Spring 1973), 42–51.

McCaffrey, Lawrence. 'Daniel Corkery and Irish Cultural Nationalism', *Éire-Ireland*, 8 (Spring 1973), 35–41.

Maume, Patrick. *'Life that is Exile': Daniel Corkery and the Search for Irish Ireland* (Belfast: Institute of Irish Studies, 1993).

— *The Rise and Fall of Irish Ireland: D.P. Moran and Daniel Corkery* (Coleraine: University of Ulster, in association with Colin Smythe Ltd., 1996).

Murphy, Seamus. 'Mr Daniel Corkery: An Appreciation', *The Irish Times* (2 Jan 1965), 12.

Ní Bheacháin, Caoilfhionn. 'Beyond the State: Narrative and Agency in the Irish Free State', unpublished Ph.D. Thesis, NUI Galway, 2005, 57–115.

Ó Buachalla, Brendán. 'Ó Corcora agus an Hidden Ireland', *Scríobh*, 4 (1979), 109–37.

O'Connor, Frank. *An Only Child* (London: Macmillan & Co. Ltd., 1961).

O'Faoláin, Seán. *Vive Moi!: An Autobiography* (London: Rupert Hart-Davis, 1965).

Ó Tuama, Seán. 'Daniel Corkery, Cultural Philosopher, Literary Critic: A Memoir', in *Repossessions: Selected Essays on the Irish Literary Heritage* (Cork: Cork University Press, 1995), 234–47.

— 'Dónall Ó Corcora', *Scríobh*, 4 (1979), 94–108.

— 'Dónall Ó Corcora agus Filíocht na Gaeilge', *Studia Hibernica*, 5 (1965), 29–41.

Saul, G.B. *Daniel Corkery* (Lewisburg PA: Bucknell University Press, 1973).

Sewell, Frank. 'Seán Ó Ríordáin: Joycery-Corkery-Sorcery', *The Irish Review*, 23 (Winter, 1998), 42–61.

Walsh, Patrick. 'Daniel Corkery's *The Hidden Ireland* and Revisionism', *New Hibernia Review*, 5.2 (2001), 27–44.

— 'Daniel Corkery: Tradition and an Individual Talent', unpublished M.A. Thesis, University of Ulster, 1993.

— *Strangers: Reflections on a Correspondence between Daniel Corkery and John Hewitt* (Coleraine: The University of Ulster, in association with Colin Smythe Ltd., 1996).

PART ONE

# The Irish Language and Gaelic Culture

# Russian Models for Irish Litterateurs[1]

When a modern literature began to be created in Irish there were practically only two sources to which the writers went for models. These were English literature and the old Irish literature. English literature was on all counts a disastrous model. It was disastrous when the writers went to the English of the Elizabethans, as some did when they set about writing drama. It was no less disastrous when they went to Sir Walter Scott,[2] as others did when they set out to write historical novels. Few went to the English moderns – perhaps some instinct saved them. There are perhaps no two countries in Europe which present two such different schemes of life to the artist as do Ireland and England. The problems of sex are the stock-in-trade of modern English novelists. If the artist is to grow in his own soil and to flower as the nation flowers, it is evident these problems are not for the Irish writer. They are not the sources of passionate endeavour in Ireland. So much for English models. As for the Irish models, it is I think to be accepted that even yet as much has not been done with them as might. The unfortunate thing is, however, that we have little or no prose models from the more recent centuries in Irish. The prose models go too far back to be of immediate service. Verse models there are in plenty – and it is of these I am thinking when I say that they have not at all been used to the extent they might.

A few writers went to the French dramatists; surely not wisely: to the courtly life of France in the seventeenth century is surely a far cry from modern Ireland.

Russian literature on the other hand uses for its own end a scheme of life which has much in common with Irish life; and at the same time it is a modern literature. It practically did not exist before the nineteenth century. These earlier Russian litterateurs – Pushkin,[3] Lermontov,[4] Gogol[5] – when they looked from their own eyes out on Russia found in the first place the cultures of other peoples and languages seated in the high places. Looking more intimately at life they found a horde of officials, a bureaucracy; and behind all this a peasant nation. And the one great central fact in that peasant nation was its religion; religion coloured every strand of the web of its life. They also found revolutionaries.

I need not point out the closeness of the parallel, it is so obvious. But it is to be insisted on that these writers did not look out on this life as from alien eyes: they were above all things Russians. Religion in the Russian peasant often intensifies into fanaticism; and we find the same thing happening in these writers, both in their books and their lives. Politics in the Russian revolutionary often seems to die away into a sullen despair; and so too with Russian writers. Need it be said also that one finds examples among the minor writers of people developing the smugness of the official both in their lives and writings – a thing not undreamt of in Ireland.

I mention this identity of the Russian writer with his people as a sort of hint of my fear that the same thing is not being done in Ireland. Is there not a touch too much of the schoolmaster in our Irish writers? Not in all, but in too many. Is there not a certain want of frankness, a fear of being real? Is there not a touch too much of the idyllic?

Because of this desire of ours to turn out a side of things which is perfectly blameless (as if the trick cannot be seen through at a glance!) we are not getting up the power or putting forth any of these studies of life which would do more in the end to forward everything Irish than political movements. What would one not give for a passionately real study of Irish life before the famine! Or for a study – not idyllic – of life in the Land League days? Or for a story which – again predicating passionate reality – would have, say, Egan O'Rahilly[6] or Eoghan Ruadh[7] or Pierce Fitzgerald[8] or Cathal Buidhe[9] for its central figure, grouping up the life of their extraordinary days about them!

These are yet to come. If I point out Russian literature as a storehouse of models – (and this much good we may credit to the war – that translations of Russian writers are now easily to be had)[10] – I do so remembering a vast gallery of figures met with in Russian pages that may have walked the roads of Ireland itself. And indeed I am not forgetting, too, the fact that one of the most successful pieces of work in modern Irish is obviously coloured with the tints of Russia – I mean Pádraic Ó Conaire's *Deoraidheacht*.[11]

\* \* \*

# The Modernisation of Irish Poetry[1]

When I see finicky schemes for the betterment of Irish education I find myself smiling, wanly smiling; for who that knows anything of Irish educational systems does not know the uselessness of tinkering with them at all until about at least four times the present total grant of money is available to put things aright? In somewhat the same way, I suspect, in the problem of modernising Irish verse, there must be some great simple factor, overlooked by outsiders, constantly riding like a nightmare the thoughts of the initiated, sealing their lips in the silence of despair. In this matter I suppose I am like the simple folk who would settle Irish education by clipping programmes here and strengthening them elsewhere – I know enough to appear impressive to those who know nothing. Well, be it so. If discussion discover to us that grand single factor which I must, through ignorance, overlook just now, so much will have been gained.

I will begin by telling how I stand with regard to the subject, enlightening, perhaps, just a little, the professors, whose way it is to get apart from the tents of the tribes. I can read modern Irish verse. I can tolerably well read the verse of the 18th century. Perhaps I could, with some study, make out 17th century verse. With the aid of notes I have done some of the poetry of the 16th century. But beyond that is chaos. And, tantalisingly, the farther back one goes the better the verse appears to become. Of the very early Irish verse my knowledge is confined to translations, mostly to Kuno Meyer's translations. I have never met with anyone who ever even saw the originals of the poems in his *Ancient Irish Poetry*.[2]

What I wish to inquire is, is there no one to do for Irish verse what Canon Peter O'Leary has done for Irish prose?[3] Or is the thing impossible? (By the way, the only specimen of ancient Irish poetry I have ever seen done into modern Irish came from the same daring pen.)

I will give my own simple views on the matter, quietly, timidly, as befits one who does not grasp the whole difficulty.

The difficulty, of course, is form. The overweening concision implied in the very verse-structure of old Irish verse is antagonistic to the verse forms in modern Irish, perhaps even antagonistic to the, comparatively speaking, broken-down grammatical structure of modern Irish (it may be well to explain to the English-minded reader that the 'broken-down' grammar system of modern Irish is granite itself compared with the grammar-system of English). At the same time it must be obvious that if the English had never invaded Ireland, ancient Irish literature would have, by some means or other, modernised itself, just as English literature modernises itself – almost unconsciously, so to speak. The problem, therefore, does not seem impossible. Every circumstance of our history has, of course, complicated it and added to the difficulty; still, intrinsically, there does not seem to be any factor that makes the thing impossible.

We must be prepared to sacrifice something – maybe a great deal. The modern Englishman does not read Shakespeare as it was written. Perhaps not even one of his vowel-sounds is the same as the corresponding vowel-sound in Shakespeare's own mouth, not to speak of consonantal and stress changes. Perhaps the great dramatist, if he re-visited the glimpses of the moon, could not understand one of his own plays, at least at a first hearing? He would feel very savage at the loss of the full-vowelled beauty he loved so well. Irish verse in modernisation would suffer a greater time-change, but then we have to deal with verse written eleven centuries ago instead of three centuries ago. Let us be prepared for this loss; and Time is not without his compensations as well as his revenges. Stray gleams of beauty will arise where formerly, perhaps, there was none – a patina on the bronze. But the thing is to be prepared to lose something.

If verse translates, then, surely, it ought to modernise. And old Irish verse translates not alone well, to judge by Kuno Meyer's examples, but excellently well. The concision of old Irish verse that must hinder, in a way, modernisation, at the same time proves that modernisation is possible.

So far as I know, old Irish verse did not depend on its metre for its beauty; neither did it depend on verbal graces nor on assonance; these graces were in it, contributing their quota towards the final result; but there was in it, as there is in Browning,[4] to choose a modern parallel, a beauty that would still remain, and remain almost in its entirety, if all these were blotted away – the beauty of vision. And vision knows only one tongue – the concrete. Vision appeals always in concrete terms – fortunately, since it gives all peoples a chance of translating into their own parochial languages the greatest literature in all other languages. If the great outstanding excellence of ancient Irish verse consist in its keenness of vision, then I can see no reason why it should not be modernised, even if new verse forms, more modern verse-forms, had to be used for the purpose.

Every living literature modernises itself from day to day: is it not time to begin to do this with more modern Irish poems? No one, of course, would ask that it be done in the case of poems now published for the first time, like those in Thomas F. O'Rahilly's *Dánta Grádha*,[5] but why not make an effort to do so in the case of Keating?[6]

Perhaps I speak as a fool. Perhaps also it is a question on which the professors, being professors, are admirably qualified to give a perfectly wrong decision: do we not see them hankering after quaint spellings in the case of even Milton,[7] after the capital letters found in early Goldsmiths?[8]

\* \* \*

# The Hidden Ireland[1]

## I

In the latter half of the eighteenth century, whether Catholics should be free to enlist in the British Army was warmly debated by the ruling caste in Ireland. It was, of course, the Penal Laws that stood in the way: according to these, no Catholic could do so, for it was not thought wise that Catholics should learn the use of firearms. However, Townshend became Viceroy,[2] and took a new view of the matter.

He argued that 'as the trade and manufactures of Ireland are almost totally carried on by Protestants, the number of whom is very small in proportion to the number of Papists,' it was of the utmost importance that Protestants should not be taken away for foreign service, and he proposed that Papists, and Papists alone, should be enlisted. 'A considerable number of able men might be raised from amongst them in a short space of time in the provinces of Leinster, Munster, and Connacht.' Rochford[3] answered that the arguments of Townshend had convinced the King of the impropriety of drawing off a number of Protestants from those parts of the country where the chief manufactures were carried on; that he could not without a special Act of Parliament order the recruiting agents to restrict themselves to Roman Catholics, but that in the present very pressing exigency he authorised them to make Leinster, Munster, and Connacht their recruiting grounds.*

In this manner, adds Lecky, the Catholics were silently admitted into the British Army (1771).

A few years later, among the Catholics who took advantage of this hoodwinking at the Law was a poor Munster peasant, a labourer, a wild rake of a man, named Eoghan Ó Súilleabháin. He had misbehaved himself whilst in the service of the Nagle family,[4] whose place was not far from Fermoy, and enlisting in the Army was his way of escaping the consequences. From Fermoy he was sent to Cork, transferred to the Navy, and straightway flung into England's battle-line, thousands of miles away.

If one dwells on the incident, a great deal of Irish history, Irish history in any century, may be realised. Townshend, the Viceroy, the representative of Law, rough-rides over it when it suits him. The penalised Catholic, living from day to day, is callous whether his act is thought lawful or unlawful, if only it helps him here and now. In between English Viceroy and Gaelic peasant, strongly contrasted types as they are, we have the Nagle family, not greatly surprised, it is likely, at all this, they having seen what they had seen.

If one could, with imaginative assurance, enter first the life of the Townshend circle, and explore it; enter then the life of the Nagle family – a house where Irish was spoken to their Kerry labourers and English to their visitors from Dublin – and absorb it; and from this circle pass on and make one's own of the world of the labourer – that hidden, teeming and ragged world that threw him up, a genius! – then one should be qualified to tell the story of Ireland in the eighteenth century. As yet, unfortunately, no historian of it has been so qualified.

The story of the Townshend circle has been shredded out patiently enough by the historians, to be again woven into something like coherency

* *History of Ireland in the Eighteenth Century* – Lecky.[5]

and shapeliness. Novelists have dealt with such houses as that of the Nagles, chiefly Maria Edgeworth;[6] and writers of history have discovered interesting matter in the memoirs such families have, in rare instances, left behind them. But neither novelist nor historian has dealt with that underworld which threw up the silver-voiced labourer, Eoghan an Bheóil Bhínn – Owen of the Sweet Mouth – as his own people named him then, as they name him still, affection warming the soft Gaelic syllables – for with that hidden land neither historian nor novelist has ever thought it worth his while to deal.

Lecky imagined he had dealt with it! Not without pity for them, he wrote of the people of that darkened land as an almost countless mob – plague-stricken, poverty-stricken, shiftless, thriftless, desperate. He numbered them, as best he might, and traced their sufferings to the causes – and what else remained to be told? Of a mob, what else is there to tell?

This book, too, must touch on their sufferings, their degradation; but afterwards will move on to hint, at least, that all the time much else remained to be told. If only one could do it with as much patience, with as much learning, as Lecky did his share of the work! But even to dream of that, much less to attempt it, is not the task for the day. The immediate task is to show that Lecky presents us, for all his industry and learning, with only a body that is dead and ripe for burial; to show that this is far from being the truth; that all the time there is a soul under the ribs of this death; that the music which was the life of that soul had strength and beauty in it; and that to remain a clod to that music is for us not only to misunderstand the period, but unnaturally to forego our happiness and our privilege.

To that Hidden Ireland of the Gaels, then, we turn our faces.

II

To reach it one must, leaving the cities and towns behind, venture among the bogs and hills, far into the mountains even, where the native Irish, as the pamphleteers and politicians loved to call them, still lurked. 'The savage old Irish,' Swift named them;[7] and Berkeley wrote of them as growing up 'in a cynical content in dirt and beggary to a degree beyond any other people in Christendom.'[8] So far down in the depths were they that to the law of the land, though three times more numerous than all the others, they had no existence at all! In times of peace even, they were referred to as 'Domestic enemies.' 'The phrase "common enemy" was, in the early part of the eighteenth century, the habitual term by which the Irish Parliament described the great majority of the Irish people.'* And elsewhere Swift wrote (1720): 'Whoever travels through this country and observes the face

* *History of Ireland in the Eighteenth Century* – Lecky.[9]

of nature, or the faces and habits and dwellings of the natives, would hardly think himself in a land where either law, religion, or common humanity was professed.'\* 'Torpid and degraded pariahs,' is the epithet of the balanced Lecky, speaking for himself;[10] and Chesterfield, a mind still more balanced, said: 'The poor people in Ireland are used worse than negroes by their lords and masters, and their deputies of deputies of deputies,'[11] while Madden spoke of all Ireland as 'a paralytic body where one half of it is dead or just dragged about by the other,'[12] which, perhaps, is the unforgettable phrase.

The Hidden Ireland, then, the land that lies before us, is the dead half of that stricken body; it is the terrain of the common enemy, ruled by deputies of deputies of deputies, and sunk so deep in filth and beggary that its people have been thrust, as torpid and degraded pariahs should, beyond the household of the law.

This Hidden Ireland we will first look at and see as the travellers who dared to open it up beheld it; that is, we shall see its face rather than its heart; its body, but not its soul. It will be only a glance; for the historians, Lecky especially, have made their own of this aspect of it, and their books are there for the reading. But that glance given, we shall make on for thresholds that they never crossed over, in hope that what we shall further discover will not only complete the picture they have given, but frankly alter it, as a dead thing is altered when the spirit breathes upon it and it speaks.

### III

The Hidden Ireland was in a sense coterminous with Ireland itself, bounded only by the same four seas. Even the children of the Cromwellians who themselves, hardly fifty years before, had come to live in it, could not now speak English.† Into the very heart of the Pale, into Dublin itself, this Gaelic-speaking Ireland flowed in many streams. The nobility, coming from their big houses in the provinces, spoke Irish to their servants. Those society people were not Gaels either in blood or feeling, and many of their descendants have become bitterly anti-Irish, yet it is certain that the Colthursts of Blarney and the Lord Kenmare family in Kerry, were at this time speakers of Irish; it was necessary for them to be so, for otherwise they could not direct their workmen, who often knew no English; and those two families may be taken as typical of the county class. Among such people the new-born child was put out to nurse with a neighbouring peasant woman, and the intimacy thus established was frequently maintained in after years. It may also be taken as certain that the hangers-on about these large houses

\* *A Proposal for the Universal Use of Irish Manufacture.*[13]
† *Irish Nationality* – Mrs. J.R. Green.[14]

– the land stewards, agents, bailiffs, were frequently ignorant of English. We hear of a 'well-bred boy' in the County Down as speaking no language but Irish in 1744;* while in the lives of the Gaelic poets we may note that many of them went into the cities and settled down in them, still singing their songs. Donnchadh Ruadh Mac Conmara (MacNamara)[15] completed his education in the city of Limerick; there in Mungret Street Seán Ó Tuama (O'Twomey)[16] lived for a good many years; while Brian Merriman[17] died there, in Old Clare Street, in 1805. Donnchadh Caoch Ó Mathghamhna (Denis O'Mahony the Blind, died 1720),[18] lived in Cork city, as also did Father William English,[19] a witty poet, whose songs are still favourites among Gaelic speakers. And Father English had scarcely died there, in 1778, when another Gaelic poet, Micheál Ó Longáin,[20] settled in it for some time. These poets, unlike the Colthursts and the Brownes (the Kenmare family), were of the Hidden Ireland; but we do not need such evidence to show that its Gaelic waters reached everywhere, either in occasional streams or concealed floodings. Into all these cities, as into all the towns, there was a never-ceasing flowing of the country people, an intercourse that was then far more human and intimate than it is to-day. The roads were always alive with traffic, for country produce was brought in on horse-back or, though not so frequently, in wagons and carts; and arriving at all hours of day and night, and stopping at a hundred different warehouses and inns, the trafficking kept up a chatter and bustle and give and take of mind and wit that similar commerce in our own day knows but little of. Even in Dublin those traffickers were Irish speakers, if necessary; while in places like Cork and Limerick and Waterford their business was very often carried on in that language, as it is in Galway to this very day.

Young, who made his tour in 1776–78,[21] says he found the English language spoken without any mixture of the Irish language only in two places, in Dublin and in the baronies of Bargie and Forth in County Wexford† – a statement easily credible when one thinks of the children of the Cromwellians themselves having had to make it their mother tongue.

For all this widespread use of their language, however, the Gaels never made their own of the cities and towns: many of them trafficked in them, lived in them, yet were nevertheless little else than exiles among the citizens. Gaelic Ireland, self-contained and vital, lay not only beyond the walls of the larger cities, if we except Galway, but beyond the walls of the towns, if we except Dingle, Youghal, and a few others in Connacht and Donegal. For Irish Ireland had, by the eighteenth century, become purely a peasant nation.

---

* *Two Centuries of Life in Down, 1600–1800* – John Stevenson.[22]
† 'The inhabitants of the Barony of Forth, near Wexford, are descendents of the first followers of Strongbow. They have never mixed with the Irish, and still speak a singular language, which is more akin to Flemish than to modern English.' – *A Frenchman's Walk through Ireland* (1796–7).[23]

Indeed not only did it lie beyond the walls of cities and towns, but the strongholds lay far away beyond all the fat lands, beyond the mountain ranges that hemmed them in. History had seen to that: the rich lands had been grabbed from the Gaels centuries before by successive swarms of land pirates who, in a phrase written by one of themselves (an Elizabethan Browne of Killarney) 'measured law by lust and conscience by commodity.'[24] In the softer valleys those land pirates had built their houses, and Irish Ireland had withered away in the alien spirit that breathed from them. Even to-day we come on the remains of this Gaelic Ireland only in places where there have been no such alien houses for some hundreds of years.

Irish Ireland, then, while in a sense coterminous with Ireland itself, had its strongholds in sterile tracts that were not worth tilling. The hard mountain lands of West Cork and Kerry, the barren Comeraghs in Waterford, hidden glens in the Galtee and other mountains, the wild seaboard of the South and West, the wind-swept uplands of Clare, the back places in Connemara, much of Donegal – in such places only was the Gael at liberty to live in his own way. In them he was not put upon. Big houses were few or none. Travellers were rare; officials stopped short at the very aspect of the landscape; coaches found no fares, the natives being home-keeping to a fault: 'They seem not only tied to the country, but almost to the parish in which their ancestors lived,' Arthur Young wrote of the Catholics, who had not yet learned to emigrate.[25] Among themselves they had a proverb: 'Is maith an t-ancoire an t-iarta' ('The hearth is a good anchor').

The eighteenth century was everywhere a time of violence and hard-drinking for the rich, and for the poor a time of starvation and brutality. If that period was hard on the poor who tilled the plains of France, the rich lands of England, the golden soils of central Ireland, we may conceive how it must have been with the Gaels, whose only portion was rock and bog and wind-swept seashore!

It is only weakness to sentimentalise away the filth, the degradation, the recklessness that go with hardship, starvation and tyranny, when these are continued from generation to generation. If we would realise both the staunchness of the martyr and the blossom-white beauty of his faith, we must understand the rigour of the trial that tested him. In that dreadful century our forefathers were tested as never previously; and one cannot but think that Dr. Sigerson is justified in writing: 'For a time, Anti-Christ ruled in Ireland. Cromwellian cruelty looks mild, and the pagan persecution of the early Christians almost human when compared with the Penal Code.'* The test that they underwent we will realise, as we learn of the ways of their daily lives, only if we keep in mind that the insult that went, and will always go, with poverty was the bitterest thong in the manifold lash. Illiterate peasants

* *The Last Independent Parliament of Ireland.*[26]

still keep in mind, as if they thought the lines worth remembering, a certain quatrain, which they attribute to that Eoghan of the Sweet Mouth, that wild rake of a man we have already come upon:

> Ní h-í an bhoichtineacht is measa liom,
> Ná bheith síos go deó,
> Ach an tarcuisne a leanann í,
> Ná leighisfeadh na leóin.

> 'Tis not the poverty I most detest,
> Nor being down for ever,
> But the insult that follows it,
> Which no leeches can cure.

## IV

All that has been written about rural Ireland in that century, whether by contemporaries like Young, Miss Edgeworth and Barrington,[27] or later writers like Carleton,[28] O'Neill Daunt[29] or Lecky, leave us with the impression of a land of extraordinary slatternliness – slatternliness and recklessness: while sorrowing, one could not help laughing. There were brighter spots, but these were due to chance or to individual effort. A landlord happened to be a philanthropist, or some tract or other fell out of the memories of the officials and began to fruit of itself. That these very infrequent cases were due to personal efforts speaks plainly enough for the slatternliness of the rest of the country. And it was a striking slatternliness, as common to the rich as to the poor: the typical Big House was as ill-cared for as the cabin – as untidy in its half-cut woods, its trampled avenues, its moss-grown parks, its fallen piers, its shattered chimney stacks, as the cabin with its dung-pit steaming at the door, its few sorry beasts gathered within doors for the night, its swarm of scarce-clad children running wild on the earthen floor. The slatternliness of the Big House was barbaric: there was wealth without refinement and power without responsibility. The slatternliness of the cabin was unredeemed, unless one looks into the soul of things. And between high and low there was, all authorities agree, no middle class; and consequently a dearth of the virtues for which that class stands. Domesticity must have seemed disparate to the very genius of the time. Anti-Christ governed the Catholic poor, not without difficulty; but the Lord of Misrule governed everything; and did so with merely a reckless and daring gesture: at his behest it was that everyone lived well beyond his means.

It is with the state of things after the Union that Miss Edgeworth's book, *The Absentee*, deals: the appearance of the countryside, however, changed but little in all the years of misery between 1690 and 1881 – indeed much later than 1881 one could discover whole landscapes – in the Congested Districts of Connacht and Kerry, for instance, where little or nothing had changed: in Miss Edgeworth's book, then, when we find this description of what was called a town, 'Nugentstown,' we may take it as equally true of the Nugentstown of the eighteenth century:

> This *town* consisted of one row of miserable huts, sunk beneath the side of the road, the mud walls crooked in every direction; some of them opening in wide cracks or zig-zag fissures, from top to bottom, as if there had just been an earthquake – all the roofs sunk in various places – thatch off, or overgrown with grass – no chimneys, the smoke making its way through a hole in the roof, or rising in clouds from the top of the open door – dung-hills before the doors, and green standing puddles . . . .[30]

This I take for a quite true description of the small towns and villages of that period. Considering everything, they could not have been otherwise. Who was there to keep order, to set a model? If one reap and reap and never restore to the ground what it loses in each harvest, one should be as careful and as wise as were the rulers of the soil of Ireland in those days.

The larger towns were tidier, for their Protestant inhabitants enjoyed those rights of property that were denied to the Catholics of places like Nugentstown.

But of Irish Ireland it is, perhaps, better to realise the cabin as a thing in itself, than any hamlet, however small; for being then a peasant nation, the cabins, as might have been expected, were the custodians of its mind.

When Michael Doheny was an outlaw in 1848 on the mountains near Glengariff a rainstorm forced him to shelter in a hut which he thus describes in his book, *The Felon's Track*:

> The cabin was ten feet square, with no window and no chimney. The floor, except where the bed was propped in a corner, was composed of a sloping mountain rock, somewhat polished by human feet and the constant tread of sheep, which were always shut up with the inmates at night. The fire, which could be said to burn and smoke, but not to light, consisted of heath sods, dug fresh from the mountain. A splinter of bog-wood, lurid through the smoke, supplied us with light for our nightly meal. The tea was drawn in a broken pot, and drunk from wooden vessels, while the sheep chewed the cud in calm and happy indifference. They were about twelve in number, and occupied the whole space of the cabin between the bed and the fireplace.[31]

Elsewhere in the same book he describes a 'cabin in the hills' near Kenmare:

> In the house where I slept – as indeed in every house of the same character in the county – the whole stock of the family, consisting chiefly of cows and sheep, were locked in at night. Such was the extreme poverty of the people that they would not be otherwise safe . . . . There was a slight partition between the room where my bed was and the kitchen, where there were three cows, a man, his wife and four children. It is impossible to convey any idea of the sensations which crowd upon one in such a scene. I fell asleep at last, lulled by the heavy breathing and monotonous ruminating of the cows. Never was deeper sleep.[32]

Catholic Munster certainly was no poorer, if indeed not richer, in 1848 than in 1748, and from these passages we learn how things then were. Doheny himself was sprung from the poorest class of Irish farmers, and followed the plough in his youth, yet it is clear that these cottage interiors surprised him: they would certainly not have surprised the son of any Catholic farmer in 1748, a hundred years before, for, as we know from Young's pages, such cabins might have been met with right up to the gates of Dublin. In 1915, near Ventry, in West Kerry, I found a windowless, one-roomed cabin which could be described in lines taken from Brian Merriman's poem, *Cúirt an Mheadhon Oidhche* (*The Midnight Court*), written in 1780:

> Bothán gan áit chun suidhe ann,
> Ach súgh sileáin is fáscadh aníos ann,
> Fiadhaile ag teacht go fras gan choímse
> Is rian na gcearc air treasna scríobtha,
> Lag ina dhrom 's na gabhla ag lúbadh
> Is clagarnach dhonn go trom ag túirlint.[33]

> A cabin with no place to sit down,
> But dripping soot from above and oozings from below,
> No end of weeds growing riotously,
> And the scrapings of hens across it,
> Its roof-tree sagging, its couples bending,
> And brown rain falling heavily.

*Brown* rain, because it had come through the soot-impregnated thatch.

These cabins were thrown up anyhow and almost in any place. In the time of the Land League, when evictions were frequent, exactly the same kinds of huts were often thrown up in a few hours in the shelter of a ditch, to house the suddenly dispossessed family: though not meant for permanent abodes, some of them were still being lived in forty years after – which should teach us how slowly a landscape wins back to comeliness after a period of disturbance, and enable us further to realise something of the slatternliness of that period in which there had been not even the beginning of recovery.

The cabins of the eighteenth century were sometimes built of stone, mortared or unmortared, but far more frequently of sods and mud. They were thatched with bracken, furze, fern or heath; and must have been often indistinguishable from the bogland, perhaps with advantage. Usually there was but one room, sometimes divided by a rough partition; and often a sort of unlighted loft lay beneath the roof. Chimney there was none, but a hole in the roof allowed portion of the smoke to emerge when the interior had become filled with it. The smoke was often seen to rise up like a cloud from almost every inch of the roof, percolating through as the thatch grew old and thin. The soot that in time came to encrust the walls and thatch within was occasionally scraped off and used as manure.

Between the absence of windows and the ever-present clouds of smoke, the people dwelt in darkness: it did not make for health, nor for quick convalescence when sickness broke out; quite commonly it led to blindness; though one must not forget to add the many prevalent fevers and plagues if one would understand why in any list of the poets of these days one comes so frequently on the word 'Dall' (blind) – Tadhg Dall Ua h-Uigín,[34] Liam Dall Ua h-Ifearnáin,[35] Seumas Dall Ua Cuarta,[36] Donnchadh Dall Ua Laoghaire;[37] Carolan[38] might also have been called 'Dall,' while Donnchadh Ruadh Mac Conmara (MacNamara) became blind in his old age. Blind poets, blind fiddlers, blind beggars of all kinds were to be seen tapping their way on every road in the country, from fair to fair, from house to house.

Without as within, the hut had a haphazard appearance. Seldom was there a lease, either of house or land; and to improve either led to an increase of rent, perhaps to eviction. No attempt was, therefore, made at tidiness. A hundred years later, in 1838, Lady Chatterton, a lady with a taste for sketching, wrote in charming simplicity of mind: 'The only thing I miss in Ireland is my favourite rural scenery; I mean by rural, the neat honey-suckled cottages with their trim little gardens and bee-hives.'[39] She would have missed them still more had she come sooner. Every hut had its dung-pit in front of the door, with a causeway of boulders giving passage through it; not far away stood a rick of turf; and practically nothing else: no barns, no sheltering plantations, no market garden, no orchard – and yet it might be a farmer's house.

In appearance the inmates were one with their cabin. Both man and woman usually went barefoot, were scantily clad, and what they had of clothing was some other person's cast-off, patched and re-patched.

The life about the hearth was one with the cabin and its people: it could not be further simplified. House and dress were so miserable that food was almost the only expense; and it was computed that £10 was more than sufficient for the whole annual expense of the family: yet even one bad year brought starvation.

The food consisted almost entirely of buttermilk and potatoes. Morning, noon and night, their dish was the self-same:

> Prátai istoidhche,
> Prátai um ló,
> Agus dá n-eireóchainn i meadhon oidhche,
> Prátai gheóbhainn![40]

> Potatoes by night,
> Potatoes by day,
> And should I rise at midnight
> Potatoes still I'd get.

Towards the end of summer their stock of potatoes ran out; and then they went hungry. Conditions improved again in the autumn, and if at this time a person showed any signs of giddy vigour in him, the others said mockingly: 'There's flour in the potatoes' – it was breaking out in him as in the tubers. In the winter when the milk was scarce they ate the potatoes with a kitchen made of salt and water, or with a herring, or even a pinch of a herring: 'From time to time each one of the family nipped with finger and thumb a little bit of the herring; to give a flavour to his potato.'* An old peasant, living beyond Dingle, told me that the fishermen, unlike the landsmen, were not so badly off in 1847 – the time of the Great Famine – they had the periwinkles! Scraps of food, like periwinkles, all through the eighteenth century were reckoned essential foodstuffs along the coasts.

In some places, Donegal and Kerry, to name two, when everything else had failed, they had the habit of bleeding the cattle, 'which they had not the courage to steal,' says a contemporary account:[41] mixing sorrel through it, they boiled the blood into a broth, and 'Kerry cows know Sunday' became a proverb, for it was to provide the Sunday dinner that they had to suffer.

In the winter months, when the work of the farm could be done in a few hours, the whole family, by rising late and going to bed early, managed to survive on two, and sometimes on one meal in the day.

Some corn, some vegetable, a little poultry, were also raised on the farms, which were always small, but these were sold to pay the rent, as also were the live stock, if any, the family knowing the taste of meat only at Christmas and Easter, if even then.

Archbishop King tells us that 'one half of the people of Ireland eat neither bread nor flesh for one half of the year, nor wear shoes or stockings.'†

---

\* *Seventy Years of Irish Life* – Le Fanu.[42]
† King, to the Lord Bishop of Carlisle, Feb. 3rd, 1717.[43]

When life struggled along thus, on its hands and knees, so to speak, there could have been no reserves of goods, foodstuffs or gold. Nor were there any, for whenever, after a prolonged season of rain, famine swooped on them out of a black mist, the poor souls went down like flies. The world rang with the havoc of 1847, but no one hearkened to the periodic famine cries in the eighteenth century. In the famine of 1740 – that famine which set Berkeley ruminating on the virtues of tar-water – 400,000 are said to have perished. One writer says that the dogs were seen to eat the dead bodies that remained unburied in the fields. Another contemporary wrote:

> Want and misery in every face; the rich unable almost, as they were willing, to relieve the poor; the roads spread with dead and dying bodies; mankind the colour of the docks and nettles which they feed on, two or three, sometimes more, on a car going to the grave for want of bearers to carry them, and many buried only in the fields and ditches where they perished.*

'I have seen,' wrote still another contemporary,

> the labourer endeavouring to work at his spade, but fainting for want of food, and forced to quit it. I have seen the aged father eating grass like a beast, and in the anguish of his soul wishing for dissolution. I have seen the helpless orphan exposed on the dung-hill, and none to take him in for fear of infection; and I have seen the hungry infant sucking at the breast of the already expired parent.†

And if we move either backward or forward from this midmost period of 1740, things are found to be no better. In 1720 Archbishop King writes: 'The cry of the whole people is loud for bread; God knows what will be the consequence; many are starved, and I am afraid many more will.'[44]

Bishop Nicholson, an Englishman, tells how one of his carriage horses, having been accidentally killed, was at once surrounded by fifty or sixty famished cottagers struggling desperately to obtain a morsel of flesh for themselves and their children. In Swift's terrible pages – his *Modest Proposal* was published in 1729 – the temper of the time looks out at us: we shudder at Swift's self, we imagine, but the only thing then wrong with Swift was that he had a large heart and a seeing mind .... And if instead of backwards we go forward twenty years from 1740 we are entering the period of

---

\* *The Groans of Ireland* – a pamphlet published 1741.[45]
† Letter from a Country Gentleman in the Province of Munster to His Grace the Lord Primate. Dublin, 1741. (For these quotations, and much other evidence, see Lecky, Vol I.)[46]

Whiteboyism – evidence enough that the sufferings had come to a head and broken out.

A new harvest might delay the distress of hunger, but the consequences remained in fevers, fluxes, blindness, insanity, demoralisation. Even in a love lyric one comes on lines like these:

> 'S gurab í do phóigín thabharfadh sólás
> Dá mbeinn i lár an fhiabhrais.[47]

> And 'tis your little kiss would comfort me
> Were I in the midst of fever.

while the crowds were thinned at Art O'Leary's[48] funeral (1773) by the small-pox, the black death, the spotted fever:

> Mura mbéadh an bolgach
> Agus an bás dorcha
> 'S an fiabhras spotuighthe
> Bhéadh an marc-shluagh borb san
> 'S a srianta d'á gcrothadh acu,
> Ag déanamh fothraim,
> Ag teacht dod shochraid,
> A Airt an bhrollaigh ghil.[49]

> Only for the small-pox,
> And the black death,
> And the spotted fever,
> That mounted spirited troop,
> With their bridles clattering
> And making a noise,
> Would be coming to your funeral,
> O Art of the white breast.

And to the Gall, Seán Clárach MacDomhnaill (MacDonnell) wished

> Peannaid is fiabhras dian i dteas na dteinteadh.[50]

> Torment and gripping fever in the heat of hellfire.

But indeed from any one of the poets of that time a collection of such phrases as these – phrases that touch the life of the folk so intimately – might easily be gathered.

As hinted, the conditions of life were such as worsened every plague striking a countryside: the very huts themselves seemed to grip the wandering disease, to hug it, to keep it, until indeed its venom had entirely outworn itself. They were crowded with life, yet, as a rule, contained only two beds, the father and mother sleeping in one, the children in the other, lying heads and points, the boys at one end, the girls at the other. There were no candles nor lamps: at night the family sat and talked around the turf fire, and if anything had to be searched for they lit a rush-light (the pith of rushes, dried and drawn though melted grease or oil), or else a splinter of bog-fir.

Such, then, was the life that went on in and around each of these cabins, if anything so poverty-stricken, so fever-plagued, so uncomely, could be called life.

V

Let us now give a swift glance at the country – the fields, the roads, the woods, the landscape in general. Agriculture was in a poor state, as might be expected when the cottiers were mostly tenants at will. Ploughs were scarce – often only a half-dozen of them in a parish; and these were hired out, as is done to-day in the case of a huge threshing engine. A *meitheal*, a gathering of the neighbours, assisted in the ploughing; and two, three, or even four horses, all abreast, were attached to the plough: the process had not become the lonesome task it is to-day. In the early part of the century, the plough was sometimes hitched to the horses' tails – a custom not peculiar to Ireland alone. But the bulk of the crops were raised by spade labour, and not by ploughing. These labourers earned from twopence to fivepence a day; Eoghan Ruadh Ó Súilleabháin, one of them, threatens in one of his poems to go down to Galway, a fat land where the daily wage was sixpence; and there were always complaints and bickerings over the accounts as between middlemen and tenants; the tenant by all sorts of dodges being defrauded of the cash, if not indeed of his earnings: the chronic shortage of small coin, by leading to elaborate systems of barter, conduced towards this everlasting pilfering.

> 'A great number of the peasantry in Ireland,' we read, 'know perfectly well that for the same work they would receive in England two shillings, and in Ireland only sixpence. And further, they would be much more sure of getting their two shillings in the one country than their sixpence in the other.'*

All the farm gear was as primitive as the plough. Carts or any sort of wagons were rarely owned or used by the landsmen; and any rough contrivances employed as such had solid wheels beneath them.

* *A Frenchman's Walk through Ireland* (1796–7).[51]

The roads were better than might have been expected, and the bye-roads often superior to the highways, for there was a system of local contract labour which gave the Big House care of the bye-roads about it, and a chance of making money into the bargain.

The roads were, of course, the only highways; and vast crowds of beggars, many of them blind, swarmed upon them. In 1742, it is calculated, 30,000 of them were moving from place to place; they were for ever coming between the wind and the nobility – that nobility that Young spoke of as 'vermin.' Berkeley thought out a scheme by which these vagrants might be set to work, loaded with chains; between them, however, and the cottiers – who never knew when they themselves would also be out on the roads – a great spirit of camaraderie existed, and the footweary found it easier to obtain a lodging for the night than he would to-day along the same roadsides. But there were others as well as beggars upon the highways – pedlars, packmen, horses laden with goods, wagons, carriages, coaches – and occasionally highwaymen.

Everywhere the giant woods were being cut down – the woods that like a magic cloak had sheltered the Gael in every century. The undertakers, the land pirates, not ever quite sure of their standing in so strange a country, were selling the timber on the estates at sixpence a tree – they were rifling the ship they had boarded. 'Trees to the value of £20,000 were cut down, soon after the Revolution, upon the single estate of Sir Valentine Browne in Kerry.'*

An English lawyer named Asgill, who had married the daughter of Sir Nicholas Browne, and bought the estates of the attainted family, was responsible for this. Aodhagán Ó Rathaille, who was born not far from Killarney, sorrowed with the Brownes – 'Is díth chreach bhur gcoillte ar feóchadh' ('Woe, your woods withering away'). But indeed all the poets lamented the vanishing woods: the downfall of the Gaelic or even the Gall-Gaelic nobility, the downfall of the woods – these two went together in their verses. One of our most beautiful lyrics, mourning over the ruin that had come upon the Butlers of Kilcash, begins:

> Cad a dhéanfaimíd feasta gan adhmad,
> Tá deire na gcoillte ar lár.[52]

> What shall we henceforth do without timber,
> The last of the woods is fallen.

And in a lyric of about the same time we have:

---

* Lecky, Vol. I.[53]

Anois tá 'n choill dá gearradh,
Triallfaimíd thar caladh.[54]

Now the wood is being cut,
We will journey over the sea.

This destruction was taking place all over Ireland: it was as if the undertakers had suddenly recollected Spenser's words: 'goodly woods fit for building of houses and ships, so commodiously as that if some princes in the world had them, they would soon hope to be lords of all the seas, and ere long of all the world.'[55] It was just then that the English were indeed becoming lords of all the seas, for the industrial revolution had begun, and markets needed to be established all over the world. The English adventurers in Ireland, the Bishop of Derry, the Bishop of Kilmore, to name only two, were, as always, in want of ready money; and so between one thing and another the Isle of the Yellow Woods was stripped of its beauty.

These half-felled woods were to be seen everywhere, even in the farthest places; there was, for instance, a great clearance made at Coolmountain in West Cork, a place where even to-day a stranger's face is hardly ever seen. Some evil genius, it might seem, was labouring to harmonise all things into an equal slatternliness. The country, moreover, was speckled with ruins – broken abbeys, roofless churches, battered castles, burnt houses, deserted villages, from which the inhabitants were being cleared to make room for beasts; and these ruins were, for the most part, still raw, gaping, sun-bleached, not yet shrouded in ivy nor weathered to quiet tones.

• • •

Such, then, was in general the face of Ireland, such, more particularly, the face of Irish Ireland – that hidden land whose story has never been told. Poverty was its only wear – poverty in the town, the cabin, the person, the gear, the landscape. Civic life was not only broken, but wiped away. Institutions, and the public edifices, ceremonies, arts into which the institutional blossoms in home-centred countries, had ceased to exist. Life did no more than just crawl along, without enough to eat, unclothed, fever-stricken, slow: how could it have a thought for anything beyond mere existence from day to day!

## VI

The facts here gathered are the commonplaces of the social history of eighteenth century Ireland; and the political history of the period explains the causes of the whole frightful disorder: for the better understanding, however, of the remaining chapters of this book, as well as for the completion of this, it may be as well to touch upon the immediate causes here.

The rack-rents, that had so much to do with the poverty and the instability of the time, were, of course, themselves the result of the Middleman system, or, as Chesterfield stigmatised it, the deputy of deputy of deputy system of land-tenure.[56] That system worked like a screw-press: the increase in the rent of any farm at the close of any half-year might be small, but the screw still went on revolving, the pressure increasing until, at last, human nature could no longer endure it: agrarian outrages burst out; and on these the man-hunt followed, the noble lords blooding their young dogs. That system one may simplify thus: The landed proprietor – the undertaker or the undertaker's descendant – would let his estate or portion of it, ten thousand acres perhaps, to a middleman: having done this, the noble lord went away to the delights of London or Bath. The middleman, renting a large house in Dublin, then became one of the crowd of place-hunters who, in the phrase of the day, spent their time in Ploughing the Half Acre – that is, the Castle yard – keeping their eyes open, pushing their children forward, and periodically petitioning the King, through the subservient Parliament in Dublin, not to grant relief to the Catholics. The middleman usually acted as agent to a number of noble lords: impossible to oversee his far-flung and scattered acres, he in turn had recourse to men living in various districts. These local agents, these under-agents, squireens, or stewards, usually kept an office in or near the local town. They in turn again employed bailiffs to collect the rents. These bailiffs were, in many cases, renegade Gaels and renegade Catholics; they were, indeed, the actual torturers, the actual headsmen under the horrible system. It was with them, and with the next nearest circle above them, the squireens, that the peasant came in contact; and the poets, who were, of course, peasants themselves, make us bitterly aware of what that contact meant for the harried people. But these poems will be glanced at later; here it may be better to see these squireens as Young saw them:

> This is the class of little country gentlemen; tenants, who drink their claret by means of profit rents; jobbers in farms; bucks; your fellows with round hats edged with gold, who hunt in the day, get drunk in the evening, and fight the next morning – these are the men among whom drinking, wrangling, quarrelling, fighting, ravishing, etc. etc., are found as in their native soil, once to a degree that made them the pest of society.[57]

There was no trick of squeezing money or value out of their tenants at will that these creatures did not know and make use of – from the canting of farms, without a day's warning, to the cadging of poultry from the farmyards, or the juggling with figures at the end of the half-year.

The peasant had to wring from the soil the gold that supported this huge and artificial superstructure – the bailiff in the village, the steward in the town, the agent in Dublin, the lord in England. Living from hand to mouth, with no reserves, the cottier was at the mercy not only of winds and rains, but of every change, and even threat of change, in the body politic, the body economic. It happened that just as the Industrial Revolution had begun to open up new avenues of wealth to the big landowners in England, to woo them into the ways of commerce, disease on a large scale broke out among the herds of cattle in England; and the remedy shows the new direction that men's thoughts had taken: Ireland began to be envisaged as England's feeding ground of the future. A beginning was made by the raising of the embargo on Irish cattle, whereupon vast herds of Irish bullocks were set upon the roads towards the Irish ports. Then followed huge clearances: the landlords became suddenly aware that continuous cropping impoverishes the soil; moreover, no tithes needed to be paid on pasture: in what way they justified their grabbing of the commons is not very clear: the result of all was that herds of dispossessed human beings, as well as the herds of beasts, began to darken the roads. To know with any sufficiency what it meant one must take up some such book as MacKenzie's *Highland Clearances*.[58] Needless to say, 'crime' followed, the Whiteboys swooping headlong across the countryside in the dark nights.

Such economic-political storms were, it would seem, as frequent as the famines, which indeed were so often their aftermath. Every such storm stretched the peasant out longer on his rack of torture; and yet the whole tale is not yet told, for one cannot omit mention of the Penal Laws. Only for certain of them the Gael might, by becoming an owner of land, win beyond the rack-renting, and only for those others that forbade him the professions, he might occasionally win away from the land altogether; but no, there was to be no way out: those Penal Laws that denied him ownership, that forbade him education, that closed the professions to him – those laws were as so many nails that held him fast in the bondage where half a century of warfare had left him – a hewer of wood and a drawer of water – 'to his conquerer,' as Swift significantly added.[59] And this, of course, was the purpose of those laws; and this the Gael knew and felt; so that in picturing to ourselves his condition in that wretched time – his town, his hut, his poor farm-gear, the dismal landscape – all one in misery – let us not forget to realise also that darkness which a mind in which hope is extinguished throws not only on the surrounding fields, but on the very heavens themselves – to picture the Gael's way of life in those days is to feel that one has gone away from the human lands and wanders in a dream which must presently break. And as yet no word has been said about the laws against his religion, the one retreat where his heart might have eased itself of its stifling emotions. The Gael's sufferings had not begun with the eighteenth century, nor was it then for the first time that his religion had been attacked; his cathedrals, his abbeys, his churches, had long since been stolen from him or destroyed. But there was a great difference between the old and the new assaults on his ancient faith. The old assault was open, and had indeed something of manliness in its hot-tempered violence. The new assault, on the other hand, was all lawyer-like with cunning – temptations, rewards and penalties. The children were to be bribed to barter faith for wealth and authority – over their own parents. They were to be wheedled into the luxurious service of God. 'All this will I give thee if . . . .' There were no longer any cathedrals to be battered down or monasteries to be dispersed; what remained to be done was the crushing of private devotions, of even the smallest gatherings for religious practices. Not a relic, not a ceremony, not a memorial of the faith was to be allowed. The bells were silenced. The holy wells deserted. The priests banished, a certain number of them bought by gold. The dead must not be laid with their fathers in the abbey grounds. Mass could be said only in secret rock-clefts, with sentries posted on the hilltops; if said in some hidden garret in the town, then a curtain had better be hung between priest and people, so that the flock might afterwards truthfully swear, if put to it, that they knew not who the celebrant was. And this flock had better bring no prayer-books with them, and if they need a beads, let its appearance be disguised and its pendant any shape but a cross!

· · ·

We have now glanced at the state of Catholic Ireland in the eighteenth century, viewing first the appearance of the land and then, very briefly, inquiring into the economy of life which led to this dire aspect. 'But this much,' one hears whispered, 'we knew before; and why do you speak of the *Hidden* Ireland?' So much, and indeed much else, is known before, to all, it would seem: and were nothing further to be revealed of that unique people, one could not make the complaint that their story had never been told. Implicitly, if not explicitly, Lecky says that nothing else was to be revealed; and the novelists of that period bear him out. And yet this is not so, for a whole world, the world of mind and spirit, remains still to be unveiled. Yes, one might take the facts we have gathered and add life to them, vividly showing those peasants as grubbing their bit of rock-strewn land, 'breaking the hill,' as the Irish phrase has it, the mists and sea-winds about them, or as cloud-swarms of beggars wandering from fair to fair, or, maddened at last, as converging to a churl's fields of a night-time and reaping and carrying off his harvest before the dawn, or as being dragged before the land-bailiff for daring to gather brosna in the woods, or as dying of starvation in their cabins, their mouths green with the munge of nettles; – and over against all this, one might, vividly again, evoke the wine-flushed revelry of the alien gentry, the hunting, the dancing, the drinking, the gambling, the duelling, with the Big House itself in the background, its half-felled woods hanging like dishevelled garments about it – one might do all this, as to the life, and still leave the secret of that land and people unrevealed. The truth is, the Gaelic people of that century were not a mob, as every picture given of them, whether by historian or novelist, would lead one to think. They were mob-like in externals; and one forgives the historians if those externals threw them out, but how forgive the novelists? If not a mob, what then were they? They were the residuary legatees of a civilisation that was more than a thousand years old. And this they knew; it was indeed the very pivot of all they did know, and the insult that followed on their poverty wounded them not only as human beings but as 'Children of kings, sons of Milesius!' ('Clanna righthe, maca Mileadh').[60] With that civilisation they were still in living contact, acquainted with its history; and such of its forms as had not become quite impossible in their way of life, they still piously practised, gradually changing the old moulds into new shapes, and, whether new or old, filling them with a content that was all of the passing day and their own fields. What of art they did create in their cabins is poor and meagre if compared with what their fathers had created in the duns of kings and grianans of queens; yet the hem matches the garment and the clasp the book.

Here hinted, then, what the historians scanted; and scanting the soul and the spirit of a people, what of that people have they profitably to speak? But history has belied the historians, for that people, if they were but a mob, had died, and their nationality died with them: instead of which that nationality is vigorous today, not only at home, but in many lands abroad – 'translated, passed from the grave.'

* * *

# Eoghan Ruadh Ó Súilleabháin[1]

Aodhagán Ó Rathaille, that spirit so quick with all the proud and lonely sorrows of the Ireland of his time, had been buried only a little more than twenty years when, almost in the same spot of outland – one mile away, to be exact – another poet was born who also may be said to have been quick with Ireland's sorrows, no longer proud and lonely sorrows, however, but reckless and wild. Ó Rathaille is a tragic figure, mournful, proud; Eoghan

Ruadh's life was even more tragic, but then he was a wastrel with a loud laugh.

That piece of outland, in which both were born, was truly Irish in its fortunes, and its story is full of meaning. It stretches eastward from Killarney to Rathmore, the Abhainn Ui Chriadh (the Quagmire River) running through it southwards to join the Flesk. On the north-east lies the mountain mass known as Sliabh Luachra; and the school of poets, of which Eoghan Ruadh is the greatest, is known as the Sliabh Luachra school. When the Geraldines were crushed, the piece of outland was swept and harried and left desolate – houseless and unpeopled. In time, some few of the O'Sullivans came northwards from Kenmare and set up new homesteads in it, undoing with patient labouring the work of the despoiler; and from these O'Sullivans sprang the boy Eoghan Ruadh.

In another way, too, the piece of land helps us to realise history. Let us look at it: All to the west of the little river belonging then to the MacCarthy Mór;[2] all to the east was part of the Kenmare estate.[3] That estate was in the grip of the middlemen, those 'deputies of deputies of deputies';[4] but the MacCarthys' tenants do not seem to have been rack-rented at all: it was probably one of those half-forgotten spots where many immemorial customs supplied the place of law; and, as compared with the rack-rented eastern riverbank, was a land flowing with milk and honey. Milk and honey may, indeed, have been actually the most plentiful of foods in it; and if it were so it was only fitting, for nowhere else in Ireland were so many sweet singers gathered together: the south-west corner of Munster was the Attica of Irish Ireland and Sliabh Luachra its Hymettus.[5]

We are told there was a 'classical school' in it – but what we are to understand by the phrase is that the Irish tradition had somehow never been quite extinguished there; that one or more bardic schools[6] had flourished in the district of old; that a broken-down bardic school or Court of Poetry[7] still assembled there; that the study of Irish poetry was the chief business of that school; that among the students would be found certain 'poor scholars' who had travelled thither on foot, some of them hundreds of miles, from those places where such schools had ceased to exist; that of those students some would later enter Continental universities and become priests, while others would obtain Commissions in the armies of France, Austria or Spain.

> On Sunday evenings throughout the summer season a 'patron,' or dancing festival, was held at Faha, and in the plain beneath, a vigorous hurling match was carried on . . . . The whole district on both sides of the river was permeated with the spirit of learning and the spirit of song. The O'Rahillys, the O'Scannells, the O'Sullivans and other families included men of conspicuous ability and no mean poetical talents. Between the people on either side of the river a rivalry,

reminding one of the supposed derivations of that word, sprang up in hurling and in poetry. The people grew critical; each new poem or song was subjected to a severe examination, and if approved was inserted in a book specially kept for the purpose, called 'Bolg an tSoláthair.'* In the winter evenings the neighbours assembled to see what new piece was added to the *bolg*, and thus a constant stimulus to poetic effort was maintained. Native music, too, was fostered with native song, and an Irish piper was an institution at Faha which the surrounding rent-crushed villages could not afford.

The academy at Faha prepared students for the more advanced seminary at Killarney, where candidates were educated for Holy Orders, and was not a mere grinding establishment, but fostered poetry and music and supplied a strong stimulus to the efforts of genius. The course comprised, besides Irish, English, Latin and Greek. In Greek, Homer seems to have been a favourite, and in Latin, Virgil and Cæsar and Ovid.†

'The more advanced seminary at Killarney' – yes, for the penal laws against religion were being relaxed; and the Church was just beginning to re-organise itself as an institution with a body as well as a spirit. From day to day, the passing of priests to and from the Continent was quickening; and parishes were beginning to set up regular services in buildings set apart for the purpose. But though the penal laws were becoming less rigorous, the condition of the people was worsening rather than improving; they were growing poorer and poorer. The peasants, almost all Catholics, were increasing rapidly, while the whole political and social economy of the country was still working towards their extinction, a tug-of-war that led to widespread brutality and wretchedness. The Church had begun to grow active, and only in time, for the long period of social disorganisation had undoubtedly sapped some of the moral stamina of the people: in ever-growing numbers the richer Catholics were openly turning Protestant to save their estates; and the example both of these and the hard-drinking and boisterous squirearchy was influencing the mind of the labourers: Jack would have his fling as well as his master. The Church had not yet, however, had time to chasten, except in the least degree, the almost melodramatic spirit of violence that was abroad, common to both high and low, so that the peasants still took to the cudgel as readily as the squires to the pistol. All this we note as we turn the pages of Arthur Young, who went through the country just when Eoghan Ruadh was in the prime of life; and all this we should keep in mind if we would understand the tragic wayfaring of this child of song.

* 'Bolg an tSoláthair' ('The Wallet of the Provider').
† *Amhráin Eoghain Ruaidh Uí Shúilleabháin*, leis an Athair Pádraig Ua Duinnín.[8]

I

Meentogues, where he was born, was a place of poor land, of small holdings, of struggling people. Across the river was Faha, where the school was. Over the threshold of this school, a sooty cabin, it is likely, no boy of the place ever stepped who more quickly won the attention of the poet-teacher, for Eoghan came of a household where poetry was still, in the Gaelic mode, accounted as riches and as a stay against misfortune. He quickly learned to read in tattered and dirty manuscripts those great Gaelic stories and poems, the outlines of which he had already become acquainted with at home. So, too, in Latin and Greek he made his own of the world-famous stories that he would have heard already spoken of among his people and their visitors: ever afterwards the bright figures of those stories were to haunt his imagination. In English he must have learned to read with ease, to judge by the occasional poems he wrote in it.

The 'poor scholars' caused him but little surprise, for these were now an old institution in the place. To such a school they were accustomed to come without books, without money, without a way of supporting themselves; and Eoghan's people, not the poorest in the countryside, would very likely have had, in the traditional way, one or more of them as guests upon their hearthstone. But he might have wondered at the differences between their language and his own; certain poets, that he would have little or no difficulty in understanding, must have, in many cases, needed much study from them; and beginning with this fact, he might have learned that his native parish was not typical of all Ireland. It took him a longer time, probably, to realise that he himself was not typical of even the boys of Sliabh Luachra.

One morning, we are told, he was late for school, and that he made his excuse in verse:

Ar dhrúcht na maidne is mé ag taisteal go ró-mhoch.[9]

In the dew of the morning while journeying early.

And the story is credible, since no day would pass over those fields about his house without impromptu verses having been made, the labourers flinging them out almost as readily as the schoolmasters. But it is not right to think of him as a studious boy. If it is true that he was intended for the priesthood, it is only fitting to imagine him as restrained and docile; but remembering what he became while still in his young manhood, and the name he left behind him, to do so is impossible. One pictures him as good-looking, with hair as golden as red – not, indeed far different from the colour of his sun-tanned brow and cheeks – as narrow-headed, high-crowned, lithe, tall, sinewy; as carrying himself well, daring, and not easily put down; as full of life, witty, and given to laughing; yet one must also recollect that he could be very still over a book and very patient in copying a manuscript.

When he was eighteen he opened a school on his own account at Gneeveguilla, a place two miles to the north of Meentogues. A contemporary of his, out of bitter experience, had called schoolmastering an empty trade, yet all his life through, whenever his fortunes were hopeless, on this empty trade Eoghan was to fall back. This first school of his did not last long – 'an incident occurred, nothing to his credit, which led to the break-up of his establishment.'* Such incidents, it may be as well to say it, were afterwards to occur frequently; and because of them, and the want of self-control they denote, we may be certain that from this time, when he had to fly Gneeveguilla, with a threatening priest behind him, he scarcely ever afterwards knew what peace was, however much he laughed or sung. He returned to his home.

The boy-schoolmaster then became a *spailpín*, a wandering farm labourer. It may not have been necessary for him to start off on such unprofitable wayfaring, but the life of itself had much in it to appeal to one of his gifts and years. It was when the turf had been brought in from the bogs and had been built into stacks, that the *spailpíní* of Kerry tied up a few oaten cakes in their handcloths, shouldered their spades, and set off for the rich lands of Limerick, of North-East and East Cork. Their wives would then lock up their cabins, and, with their children swarming about them, set off to beg along the roads until their men returned at Christmas-time. Year after year this break-up and re-union of the family took place; and one imagines those *spailpíní* as railing at their lot, and yet finding it not easy finally to give it up, as is the way with sailors and wanderers of every description; the charms of the change of skies, the change of companions, the freedom, renewing themselves in the memory the moment the home-life sinks again into dullness. But, of course, it was only rarely that the *spailpín* had any choice in the matter, no other way of living being left him: when the rich Catholic was hemmed in on every side, the poverty-stricken peasant must have had about as much freedom as a slave in choosing how he should live.

One can imagine, too, how eagerly a band of these labourers, and it was in squads that they traversed the countryside, would entice a young man of Eoghan's character to accompany them; for since the beginning of the world wit and song have not failed to shorten a lengthy road. Whatever the reason was, before he was twenty years old he shouldered his spade and set off to mow the meadows and to dig the potatoes in the County Limerick. One thinks of him as setting out with high heart and quick nostril: the roads were crowded with life; and taverns were frequent, the coaches swinging up to

* *Amhráin Eoghain Ruaidh Uí Shúilleabháin*, leis an Athair Pádraig Ua Duinnín.[10]

them in noise and dust and bustle; and in every tavern there would be new stories of highwaymen, of duelling, of kidnappings, of elopements and forced marriages, for it was the heyday of that melodramatic tragi-comedy that meant life for the Anglo-Irishman. For Eoghan, moreover, there would be a Court of Poetry here and there, hidden away in quiet villages, to be discovered; and in any countryside a poet, or a group of them, with their manuscripts and their traditions, might be come upon. Yes, at least on his first round, for he was never to cease making them, what between his youth, the novelty of the roads, and the freedom, his heart must have been high and his eyes alert at this setting out for the unknown.

There remain three poems of his, with which we will afterwards deal, that keep still fresh for us, in spite of the century and a half that has since gone by, those autumn wanderings on the roads of Munster of the young Kerryman in his knee-breeches and peaked cap. They make us certain of everything: of his wit, his daring, his way with the lasses: certain, too, that the memory of him that even to-day still lingers on these roads is not far astray when it recalls him as a playboy, a Mercutio,[11] albeit a rustic one, with the same turn for fanciful and even dainty wit joined to the same fatal recklessness of spirit.


II


A little before Christmas he returned to his homeland by the little river; and it so happened that the stage was set, as if for his coming. The unmarried and the married men of the place had met in the hurling-field, and the ancients had won the bout. To perpetuate the triumph, songs had been written; and these songs had not gone unanswered; so that presently the hurling contest was thought of as but the cause of the greater effort in song that, before Eoghan's arrival, had, like a fever, overtaken every poet from Knocknagree to Ballyvourney. As is usual, the younger generation were being scoffed at for their having dared to knock at the door. In their extremity, it had become necessary for them to induce an aged poet, Tadhg Críonna Ó Scannail (Old Theig O'Scannell), by dosing him with whiskey, to take their side, and write them verses satirising the feebleness and the ineptness of old men (the poor poet needed but to behold himself!). These verses, however, Matthew Hegarty of Glenflesk had roundly replied to, calling the writer of them a senseless renegade to deny his friends for the sake of drink; so that the married men still maintained their pride of place. The battle stood thus when Eoghan Ruadh returned from his first round on the roads of Munster.

In a poem he had previously written on his having to mind his own illegitimate child while its mother was out, he promised it, to quiet it, with a hundred other dainty and impossible gifts, the staff of Pan:[12] to read now the poem he contributed to the contest, its assurance, its hearty gesture, its boastfulness, is to see him entering the fray armed, indeed, with that selfsame staff, wherever he, not yet twenty years of age, had come by it. He took the part of youth, and without misgivings he might well have done so, for he was never to reach middle age, not to mention old age; and his song sung, there was an end to the struggle. Indeed, there are nooks in Munster to this very day where, if an old man, forgetting his impotence, raises his voice against the young, he will find himself answered in one or another couplet from that headlong poem that the young labourer then flung disdainfully from his lips, as if to show what youth could do when it had gone afield and mixed with many men.

III

For the next ten years he wandered annually, either as *spailpín* or schoolmaster, over the roads of the South. Sometimes, it is likely that instead of returning to Sliabh Luachra when the crops were all gathered in and no further work was required in the farms, he would remain where he was, open a school, and carry it on until the coming of the summer again. We know for certain that at one time he did keep school at Donoghmore, which is not more than ten miles from Cork – a countryside that was then and for long afterwards well known for Irish scholarship and poetry. In other places, of which we have now no record, he must have done the same; but again he made his way back to Meentogues, never, however, to settle down or make himself a home. His wanderings have not yet been traced on any map; perhaps they never will; and our only way of filling up this period of ten years is to think of him as travelling the autumn roads with his spade on his shoulder, or as seated in a hut or by a farmer's hearth, a group of young men about him, all of them deep in the story of Ulysses,[13] another wanderer, while the red glow of the turves lights the pages for them and the winter's winds sweep past outside.

So went the years; but how passed the slowly trailing days of them? – those days with their tally of pain, insult, longing, sickness, fierceness, weakness; with their fits of wild love-making, drunkenness; with their dull slavery of teaching, of turf-cutting, of potato-digging, of grass-mowing; with their discovery of kindred spirits, of young poets, of Courts of Poetry; with their patient labouring upon almost indecipherable manuscripts; with their ecstasies of new songs dreamed or fashioned or sung in a triumphant voice – how those slow-trailing days passed for him, dark or bright or wild or slow or fast, we shall never be able to imagine, except dimly and, therefore, wistfully.

Tidings of him are to be found in every county of Munster. There is no town nor stronghold nor fort from the Siuir to Beara that he did not walk there; and in them there remained the memory of him so long as even a remnant of the Irish language remained in the mouths of the people. Here he was a teacher; there a labourer. In this town he drank and took his pleasure. At fair and market he was often seen with a crowd about him, for whom he made sport or poured out verses, or retaliated on someone who had tried to put him down. Usually he was among the poets, making sport for them, answering and counter-answering them, satirising or making a laughing-stock of someone who appeared too officious. Often, again, he went on foot from house to house, spending a night here, another there, letting on to be a poor, simple man that had had no rearing or schooling, putting foolish questions to the woman of the house, and failing to understand her replies, speaking out clearly at last his own opinion, and praising or dispraising the family in good verses. Sometimes, again, he made bold on some priest, in the form of a poor tramp who did not know the Commandments; only to break out, when the priest had done his best to teach him them, in impromptu verses, satirising the priesthood. He was fine company for the labourer. Neither conversation nor song nor story failed him from morning till night.*

Except in some such general terms, we cannot speak of the ten years from 1770 to 1780 – that is, from his twenty-second to his thirty-second year. It is probable that it was during these years he made the greater number of his poems, verses of pure poetry, of poet's poetry; but it is certain that it was during them he established the tradition of himself that the winds of a century and a half have not quite swept from the roads of Munster. In point of character, he was sinking lower and lower; and at last it became necessary for him to take refuge in the army, although every better impulse of his nature must have rebelled against the act. He was at the time schoolmaster to the children of the Nagle family, whose place was near Fermoy, and how, from being one of their farm-labourers, he had come to be in this position lingers still as a legend in the Irish-speaking parts of Munster. I have had it told to myself that one day in their farmyard he heard a woman, another farm-hand, complain that she had need to write a letter to the master of the house, and had failed to find anyone able to do so. 'I can do that for you,' Eoghan said, and, though misdoubting, she consented that he should. Pen and paper were brought him, and he sat down and wrote the letter in four languages – in Greek, in Latin, in English, in Irish. 'Who wrote this letter?'

---

* I translate from *Beatha Eoghain Ruaidh Uí Shúilleabháin*, leis an Athair Pádraig Ua Duinnín.[14]

the master asked the woman, in astonishment; and the red-headed young labourer was brought before him; questioned, and thereupon set to teach the children of the house. Other accounts vary slightly from this, but it may be taken as illustrating the legends of him that even yet survive in corners of Munster. Owing to his bad behaviour he had to fly the house, the master pursuing him with a gun. Fermoy was an important military station, and he soon put the walls of the barracks there between himself and his pursuer. From Fermoy he was sent to Cork, and from Cork he sailed almost immediately in a transport for the West Indies – and a new chapter had opened for him.*

IV

To say nothing of the alien rabble of the lower decks, the scourings of the English prisons, among whom he now found himself, to be thus caged in was a dismal change for one who had had whole counties for his adventurous feet. What manner of men swarmed in a man-of-war at that period, as well as what manner of men ruled over them with ruthless authority, we know from the realistic pages of *Roderick Random*;† and Mr. John Masefield has in our own days written for his countrymen these terrible words:

> Our naval glory was built up by the blood and agony of thousands of barbarously maltreated men. It cannot be too strongly insisted on that sea life, in the late eighteenth century, in our navy, was brutalising, cruel, and horrible; a kind of life now happily gone for ever; a kind of life which no man today would think good enough for a criminal. There was barbarous discipline, bad pay, bad food, bad hours of work, bad company, bad prospects.‡

And stressing the phrase 'bad company,' he quotes from the contemporary Edward Thompson:

> In a man-of-war you have collected filths of jails: condemned criminals have the alternative of hanging or entering on board . . . . There's not a vice committed on shore that is not practised here; the scenes of horror and infamy on board a man-of-war are so many and so great that I think they must rather disgust a good mind than allure it.[15]

---

* But see the later edition of these poems, where the editor throws doubt on the whole story. It may be yet proved that the poet was pressed for the Navy, as he himself states in one of his poems.[16]
† Published 1748.[17]
‡ *Sea Life in Nelson's Time*, by John Masefield (p. 123).[18]

Between these lower decks, then, Eoghan Ruadh, the landsman, the wandering minstrel, was now imprisoned, one of those thousands of barbarously maltreated seamen. His own talent was no longer of use: if in his few hours of sleeping, *aisling* poems still brightened in his brain,[19] it was only bitterness to recall them once they had scattered in the hurry-scurry of the seaman's uprousing. In those silent night watches of his across the unfamiliar waters, he no doubt comforted himself with the quiet singing of the songs of Munster, his own and others; and also, doubtless, he would often astonish his illiterate English shipmates with his strange stories of Greece and Rome, with his amazing gift of tongues; he was not, therefore, utterly forlorn both of moments of forgetfulness and moments of triumph. Must we not also recollect, however, that as surely as it was in his nature to give way to wild fits of loud-voiced recklessness, it was also in him to sit tongue-tied, revolving his fate, and finding but little comfort in looking either backwards or forwards. In such moments he saw himself with clear eyes: in one such, the Spirit of Ireland came before him, as radiant as ever, with reproach in her eyes:

> 'Do not insult me, Bright Shape of the Fair Tresses,' the tortured poet cried to her; 'by the Book in my hand I swear I am not of them; but by the very hair of the head I was snatched away and sent over the floods, helping him (the English Monarch) that I do not wish to help, in the ships of the bullets on the foaming sea, I that come of the stock of the Gaels of Cashel of the Provincial Kings!'

> Ná tarcuisnigh mé, a gheal-scéimh na gcúil-fhionn,
> Dar an leabhar so im ghéag, níl braon dá gcrú ionnam,
> Ach taistealach théid tar chaise le fraoch,
> Do stracadh i gcéin ar úrla,
> Ag cabhair don té nár bh-fonn liom,
> I mbarcaibh na bpiléar ar chubhar-mhuir,
> Is gur scagadh mo thréad as caise d'fhuil Ghaedheal
> I gCaiseal na réacsa cúigidh![20]

To the longing that is so heavy a weight in every exile's heart was added in his case the pain of helping those whom he, the descendant of Provincial Kings, despised. Though it is quite certain that in the rough-and-tumble of the seaman's life, he could, as well as the next, take care of himself – the Munster of his day being no bad training ground in such arts, there was still an implacable round of circumstances leagued against him: he was one of a despised race; he was a peasant; his strange accents were an offence; his messmates, we have seen what they were; and he was a poet. Taking everything into account, among the thousands of maltreated men between the decks of Rodney's ships,[21] perhaps there was not one more miserable than this baffled son of music and dreams.

It was his lot to assist in one of England's most famous sea-fights.

The ship in which he sailed joined the English fleet under Rodney, then vice-admiral of Great Britain, somewhere before the West Indies were reached. On the morning of the twelfth of April in that year, 1782, Rodney, who had lately been blundering, was awakened by Sir Charles Douglas[22] with the intelligence that God had given him the French enemy on the lee bow 'not far from old Fort Royal.' De Grasse,[23] the French admiral, in vain tried to get to the windward. The engagement began at seven o'clock, and at close quarters. As the French line got southward under the lee of Dominica, it was gapped by varying winds. Through one of the gaps Rodney's own vessel, the 'Formidable' passed, the 'Bedford' followed, another leading vessel found also a passage. The ships astern followed. The French fleet were routed, and De Grasse's flagship, the 'Ville de Paris,' surrendered to the 'Barfleur.' Rodney, whose recent manœuvres had ended in failure, was in ecstasies of delight. He had won a victory, perhaps hitherto unsurpassed in the annals of British naval warfare, and was fully conscious of the importance of his triumphs. In an account of the fight, written by himself, we read: 'The battle began at seven in the morning and continued till sunset, nearly eleven hours, and by persons appointed to observe, there never were seven minutes' repose during the engagement, which, I believe, was the severest ever fought at sea, and the most glorious for England. We have taken five and sunk another.'\*

On that fight Eoghan Ruadh, almost before the heat of battle had left him, wrote this curious song in English:

> 'Rodney's Glory'
> Give ear, ye British hearts of gold,
> That e'er disdain to be controlled,
> Good news to you I will unfold,
> 'Tis of brave Rodney's glory,
> Who always bore a noble heart,
> And from his colours ne'er would start,
> But always took his country's part
> Against each foe who dared t' oppose

---

\* *Amhráin Eoghain Ruaidh Uí Shúilleabháin*, leis an Athair Pádriag Ua Duinnín.[24]

Or blast the bloom of England's Rose,
So now observe my story.

'Twas in the year of Eighty Two,
The Frenchmen know full well 'tis true,
Brave Rodney did their fleet subdue,
Not far from old Fort Royal.
Full early by the morning's light,
The proud De Grasse appeared in sight,
And thought brave Rodney to affright,
With colours spread at each mast-head,
Long pendants, too, both white and red,
A signal for engagement.

Our Admiral then he gave command,
That each should at his station stand,
'Now, for the sake of Old England,
We'll show them British valour.'
Then we the British Flag displayed,
No tortures could our hearts invade,
Both sides began to cannonade,
Their mighty shot we valued not,
We plied our 'Irish pills' so hot,
Which put them in confusion.

This made the Frenchmen to combine,
And draw their shipping in a line,
To sink our fleet was their design,
But they were far mistaken;
Broadside for broadside we let fly,
Till they in hundreds bleeding lie,
The seas were all in crimson dye,
Full deep we stood in human blood,
Surrounded by a scarlet flood,
But still we fought courageous.

So loud our cannons that the roar
Re-echoed round the Indian shore,
Both ships and rigging suffered sore,
We kept such constant firing;
Our guns did roar and smoke did rise,
And clouds of sulphur veiled the skies,

Which filled De Grasse with wild surprise;
Both Rodney's guns and Paddy's sons
Make echo shake where'er they come,
They fear no French or Spaniards.

From morning's dawn to fall of night,
We did maintain this bloody fight,
Being still regardless of their might,
We fought like Irish heroes.
Though on the deck did bleeding lie
Many of our men in agony,
We resolved to conquer or die,
To gain the glorious victory,
And would rather suffer to sink or die
Than offer to surrender.

So well our quarters we maintained,
Five captured ships we have obtained,
And thousands of their men were slain,
During this hot engagement;
Our British metal flew like hail,
Until at length the French turned tail,
Drew in their colours and made sail
In deep distress, as you may guess,
And when they got in readiness
They sailed down to Fort Royal.

Now may prosperity attend
Brave Rodney and his Irishmen,
And may he never want a friend
While he shall reign commander;
Success to our Irish officers,
Seamen bold and jolly tars,
Who like darling sons of Mars
Take delight in the fight
And vindicate bold England's right
And die for Erin's glory.

The ode was sent to the Admiral in the flush of triumph. He was delighted with the composition, and asked the author to be brought to him. An officer named MacCarthy, a Kerryman, accompanied the poet in his visit to the Admiral. Rodney was gracious, and offered promotion, but Eoghan only wanted to be set free from service. Ere the Admiral could reply to his request, MacCarthy interposed and said: 'Anything but that; we would not part with you for love or money.' Eoghan turned away, saying: 'Imireochaimíd beart éigin eile oraibh' ('I will play some other trick on you'). MacCarthy, who understood his remark, replied: 'I'll take good care, Sullivan, you will not.*

The group makes a curious cabin interior: The proud Admiral, new-flushed with victory; the officer, MacCarthy, representing, it is likely, one of those Gaelic families that had changed their religion for the sake of retaining their lands and, generally, winning to worldly honours; and then the drab seaman, the heart-sick exile, the darling of the peasantry of Munster, the self-conscious descendant of the Provincial Kings of Cashel. The song, which, doubtless, the heady seamen in the revel of victory had sent roaring across the waves, lies there on the table beneath the Admiral's eyes. We know it for a song written in a language which never crossed the poet's lips whenever he spoke what was in his own heart or in the heart of his race; yet Rodney, though it was his privilege to have the living poet there before his eyes, could not have known this: to him the song is complete in itself, a good song, worthy of being paid for somehow or other. One thinks of him as looking from manuscript to poet and from poet to manuscript, not without some sense of wonder; and one further reflects: How much greater wonder if in this rough seaman, awkward as one in a strange place, he could have seen the author of 'Do rinneadh aisling bheag aereach' or 'I gcaol-doire chraobh-chluthmhar néamh-dhuilleach bhíos,' two perfect lyrics, with the refined artistry of the intuitional poet in every line of them! What would his wonder have been could it have been revealed to him that only more than a century later this peasant-sailorman would begin to come into his due; or that one hundred and forty years later a certain warm feeling of envy would arise in at least one narrator of the episode to think that he can never, except in fallacious vision, behold what he, Rodney, then looked upon with his mortal eyes!

V

We do not know how it came about that the poet was transferred from the navy to the army: as a soldier, however, stationed in England, we find him no less unhappy than he had been at sea. Beyond the poems that he wrote at this time, no other information either of his whereabouts or his condition, seems to have been discovered; and in these poems what we are chiefly aware of is his disgust at being mistaken for a rake from London, his

---

* *Amhráin Eoghain Ruaidh Uí Shúilleabháin*, leis an Athair Pádraig Ua Duinnín.[25]

bitterness at having had to undergo some term of imprisonment, and in 'Ceo draoidheachta i gcoim oidhche' (A fog of wizardry in the depths of night) – as good a poem as he ever wrote – we find him again visited by the Spirit of Ireland, with whom he makes equal sorrow, finishing, however, on the universal hope: 'Should our Stuart come to us from beyond the sea with a fleet from Louis and from Spain, in the sheer dint of joy I'd be mounted on a swift, stout, vigorous, nimble steed, driving out the "ospreys" at the sword's edge' – and then, with this couplet, he entirely and triumphantly shakes the trouble from his mind:

> Is ní chlaoidhfinn-se m'intinn 'na dheághaidh sin
> Chum luighe ar sheasamh gárda lem rae.[26]

'And after that, as long as I lived, never more would I dull my mind with mounting guard' – an unforced expression that opens up for us the many-sided miseries of a soldier who is aware that he has any mind to dull.

Aching still to be at home, he blistered his shins with spearwort when all other stratagems to get free had failed him. His companions, it is said, refused to mess with him, so terrible had the sores become; and doctor after doctor having tired in vain to cure him, he was at last free to go home.

He seems to have made straight for Kerry. Arrived there, he sent a letter to Fr. Ned Fitzgerald, asking him to publish from the alter that he was about to open a school at Knocknagree – a bleak, wind-swept hamlet, only a few miles from his birthplace. The letter, which was in verse, was written both in Irish and English, and it is strange that only the English portion has come down to us in its entirety:

> Reverent Sir –
> Please to publish from the alter of your holy Mass
> That I will open school at Knocknagree Cross,
> Where the tender babes will be well off,
> For it's there I'll teach them their Criss Cross;
> Reverend Sir, you will by experience find
> All my endeavours to please mankind,
> For it's there I will teach them how to read and write;
> The Catechism I will explain
> To each young nymph and noble swain,
> With all young ladies I'll engage
> To forward them with speed and care,
> With book-keeping and mensuration,
> Euclid's Elements and Navigation,
> With Trigonometry and sound gauging,
> And English Grammar with rhyme and reason.

With the grown-up youths I'll first agree
To instruct them well in the Rule of Three;
Such of them as are well able,
The cube root of me will learn,
Such as are of a tractable genius,
With compass and rule I will teach them,
Bills, bonds and informations,
Summons, warrants, supersedes,
Judgement tickets good,
Leases, receipts in full,
And releases, short accounts,
With rhyme and reason,
And sweet love letters for the ladies.[27]

The school did not last long; it may be that it broke up naturally at the approach of summer, or that the ex-soldier, though not yet thirty-six years of age, had lost the power of working on steadily day after day. In either case, in the early summer of 1784, he paid a visit to Colonel Daniel Cronin, of Park, near Killarney: it was only lately that Cronin had become colonel of a body of yeomanry, and before his honours had had time to dull, the poet thought to present him with a complimentary poem in English. The Colonel either neglected or refused to acknowledge the song in the only way that could now recompense the poet. When we learn that he thereupon blazed up and put all his wits into composing a fierce satire on the Colonel, we somehow indulge the thought that the unfortunate poet had not even yet quite come to the dregs of his self-respect; for the faculty of resentment finally ceases altogether in those whose only plan is to live on the bounty of others. Soon afterwards some of Cronin's servants and himself chanced to meet in an ale-house in Killarney and a quarrel arose between them; blows followed, and the Colonel's coachman is said to have struck the poet a sharp blow on the head with a pair of tongs – the weapon first to hand in the place. The one blow was sufficient: with his head bound, and hot with fever, he made his way back to Knocknagree.

On that wind-swept hilltop, 'at the eastern side of the fair field on the northern side of the road opposite the gate of the pound,' was a hut for fever patients. It was about two hundred yards distant from the houses – far enough away to prevent contagion, far enough also to be as lonely and desolate to the dying man as the middle of the sea. In this hut he was laid, and some woman of the place went in and out, attending on him. He was putting the fever off him, he was convalescent, when 'an act of self-indulgence, it is said, brought on a relapse from which he never rallied.'*

---

* *Amhráin Eoghain Ruaidh Uí Shúilleabháin*, leis an Athair Pádraig Ua Duinnín.[28]

When his end was not far off, he sat up in bed, asked for pen and paper, and set himself to write his last verses, his poem of repentance, as the Irish fashion was; but he was weaker in limb than brain – the pen slipped from his fingers, to his own sudden enlightenment, it seems, for

> Sin é an file go fann
> 'Nuair thuiteann an peann as a láimh,[29]

> Weak indeed is the poet
> When the pen falls from his hand,

he whispered, lay back, and in silence died. Eoghan an Bheóil Bhínn – Eoghan of the Sweet Mouth!

'Pen,' 'poet' – a poet, in his own thought, to the very end, no matter to what misguided uses the rough racket of the world had put him while he lived.

The winds still played with him: though it was mid-summer (1784), a thunderstorm broke upon the uplands as he lay in the midst of the keeners, and had not ceased when the time for burial was come. To reach Muckross Abbey, the Blackwater had to be crossed, but there being no bridge, the floods made this impossible. A temporary grave was, therefore, quickly dug, and the mourners dispersed for the night. On the following day the coffin was shouldered again, and he was carried over the river and laid with his people in the Abbey. This, though it is now generally accepted as the truth, has been always disputed, and even to-day some of the people of that countryside assert that the poet lies at Nohavile, where the first grave was dug.


VI


He was dead for almost a century and a half when his poems were collected from various sources by Father Dinneen and, for the first time, published in book-form. Perhaps from time to time some few others may be added to this collection; but there is scarcely a doubt that we have in it practically the entire harvest that remains to us of that vagrant and feverish life. It is certain that many of his songs are lost, and among them some, perhaps, that we should especially value, for the bye-poems of that period, with their intimacy and human interest, were not the sort of poetry that the rather academic, though peasant, scribes thought best worth copying and preserving; yet, taking one thing with another, this book of 121 pages is as large as one could fairly expect. With a passing thought that the poet himself never had the wistful, gentle pleasure of turning its pages, let us first roughly reckon up what it contains, afterwards trying to feel the qualities that made these poems the dear inheritance of a province.

In the book there are nineteen *aisling* (vision) poems. The specimen we have examined in the chapter on the *Aisling* is one of these nineteen, and some authorities would not agree that it is the best of them.[30] The high level of this whole set of *aisling* poems is surprising; and to determine for ourselves that this or that is the best of all is straightway to have the opening lines of some other one begin to sing in our ears. The *Aisling* beginning:

> Cois na Siúire maidean drúchta
> is mé támhach lag faon,[31]
>
> Beside the Suir one dewy morn
> and I weak, cast down and faint,

is a perfect lyric; as indeed also is:

> Do rinneadh aisling bheag aerach
> gan bhréig trím néal dam[32]
>
> In sleep there came a vision
> light, fleeting and true

– a poem full of the most beautiful lyric qualities; and who definitively would place

> Trím aisling araoir do smuaineassa[33]
>
> In my vision last night I fancied

second to any of these mentioned without lingering regret for the tripping and dainty music that hovers above its firm resolve? And so one goes from one to another, the charm in each varying as the mood. What distinguishes one from another is the temper of its mood, that dictating the music, the colour, everything. Yet there are some readers – and even writers! – who find these *aisling* poems 'all the same'; and no kind friend whispers them that it may not be unwise for them to keep their colour-blindness, their tone-deafness, to themselves.

Following these nineteen *aisling* poems we have two songs classed as Songs Against the Pirates (that is, the Planters). The first of the two is interesting as being one of those poems, so frequent in the Munster manuscripts, which glance at political disturbances on the Continent, their writers still clinging to the hope that France or Spain, or both together, would yet come to help the Gaels.[34] The second is interesting as a versification of the names of the Cromwellian settlers in the poet's district: here are the concluding stanzas of it:

('is' = 'agus' = 'and')
Gibson, Brown, Townsend, Gill, Tonson, is Gore,
Dickson, Nowls, Boulton is Buttons is Bowen,
Kickson, Southwell, Moulton, Miller is Dore
Glas is gobhann is lom ar a maireann dá bpór.

Southwell, Steelman, Stephens, Stanner is Swain,
Parnell, Fleetwood, Reeves, is Shutman is Lane,
Gach crochaire coimhightheach, ciar-dhubh, ceannan, dá bpréimh,
Treascartha claoidhte sínte i gcaismirt na bpiléar.

Lysight, Leader, Clayton, Compton is Coote,
Ivers, Deamer, Bateman, Bagwell is Brooks,
Ryder, Taylor, Manor, Marrock is Moore,
Is go bhfaiceam-na traochta ag tréin-shliocht Chaisil na búir.

Upton, Evans, Bevins, Basset is Blair,
Burton, Beecher, Wheeler, Farren is Fair,
Turner, Fielding, Reeves, is Wallis is Dean,
Cromwell 's a bhuidhean sain scaoileadh is scaipeadh ar a dtéid.[35]

The list of names in every verse is followed by an imprecation, thus the last line in the third stanza quoted may be translated:

May we see the boors routed by the mighty descendants of Cashel.

The interest in the poem is many-sided: the preserving of the vowel-music of Irish verse in the mere listing of alien names is of itself testimony to his lyrical ear; then, if for Eoghan Ruadh's own day it had the immediate interest of the topical, for our time it has the aloofness of a passionate face on which the coldness of death has fallen: it is one of those invaluable poems which confront the historian with a challenge that cannot be put aside, testing his message or, on the other hand, adding to it the poignancy of flesh and blood. The opening of the poem may be translated: 'O keen and correct poet who reads the old authors and quickly solves each hard difficulty, do you relate to us completely and with learning, are the Gaels to be long under the sharp yoke of the pirates (the Cromwellians)?' And the close is:

> A Íosa, a Dhia aoibhinn, is a Athair an Uain,
> Do chídheann sinn i gcuibhreacht's i gceangal go cruaidh –
> A Rígh néimhe díonta, freagair mo dhuan,
> Scaoil agus díbir an ghraithin seo uainn.[36]

> O Jesus, O dear God, and O Father of the Lamb,
> Who beholds us hard bound in fetters and bonds –
> O mighty King of Heaven, answer my poem,
> Scatter and banish from us this contemptible breed.

And between opening and close we have the actual names of the local Cromwellians who in those days ruled with such strong and surly power the poet's countryside, and who in our days are vanished from the place; vanished, moreover, with no song sung nor any other work of the spirit left in their wake to save their name from oblivion; they live now lonely in the passionate verse of the *spailpín* who in a 'sconnsa fhliuch' a wet trench, dug out their potatoes for them or, heavy with weariness, ploughed their wide lands for them 'ag treabhadh go tréith do dhaoscur Cailbhinists,' crying out:

> An réidhfidh Críost ar gcás go deo?

> Will Christ ever ease our lot for us?

The wheel has come full circle. These *spailpíns'* estimation of their masters we must accept, since, as has been said, the Cromwellians have left no perdurable monument that would contradict it.

Reading such verses, one often wonders if those hard-drinking, duelling, gambling buckeens that Arthur Young in those very days questioned so closely ever realised how passionately the peasants who swarmed about their lands felt towards them? or ever dreamt that in a century and a half practically all their houses and lands would have reverted to the Gaels? Again, to the reader who is not ignorant of his literary history, the list of names will remind him of other such lists, for the homeliness, the plebeianism, rather, of the Cromwellian surnames caused great humour among the highly-descended Irish people; they made many rhymes of these names both in English and Irish, as the one in English that begins:

> The Fairs, the Blacks, the Blonds, the Brights,
> The Greens, the Browns, the Greys, the Whites,
> The Parrotts, Eagles, Cocks and Hens,
> The Snipes, Swallows, Pies, Robins, Wrens, etc.*

---

* See 'Cromwell in Ireland,' by Rev. Denis Murphy, S.J.[37]

While Dáibhidh Ó Bruadair was making one in Irish: –

> Gúidí Húc is múdar Hammer
> Róibín Súl is fádur Salm
> Geamar Rú is goodman Cabbage
> Mistress Cápon Cáit is Anna
> Ruiséal Rác is Maighistir Geadhar, etc.[38]

almost at the very time that Milton was writing of those Gaelic names that would, to his mind, have made Quintilian stare and gasp[39] – and so we have glanced at both sides of the picture.

Following on these there come a very interesting group of poems dealing with his own life. The first, that addressed to a love-child of his, is full of daintiness and bright music. Then we have three poems which renew for us his life as a *spailpín*. Each is addressed to some smith or other of his acquaintance: a spade is to be made, or a handle fitted in one, or thanks returned for work done. These songs are not alone interesting as bearing directly on his own life, but each is self-centred, sterling poetry, as good to-day as when written; and it is certain that the second of them would be known to the world if Villon[40] had made it. In it are found the lines, already quoted, where he tells his friend James Fitzgerald, smith, that should the steward begin to chide him as not of great account at spadework, he, the poet, will gently begin to relate the adventurous wanderings of Death, or the tale of the Grecian battles at Troy, where the princes fell. The poem grows swifter then, and finishes with a wild gesture: He will not spend a sixpence of his wages, stored away and tied with hemp in the bosom of his shirt, until, returned home, he finds himself in the smith's company. 'Then since like myself you are a man that Old Thirst has often tortured – to the tavern at the stage with us, and let the tables be struck until the wines and ales are spread, and no stop to the carousing while even a halfpenny remains!' In the original the lines rush ahead to the perfect climax.

The next poem in this group is a request to a priest to announce that he intends to open a school in the neighbourhood – sixteen lines that remind us how the *spailpín* would pass the winter months when the land was idle. Then we have a 'Confession' of a rather conventional type, though some of the verses are striking, now for their quaintness, and then for their frankness. In the Mass, he confesses, he took but little interest, failing in reverence even at the most sacred moments, moments when the fish in the stream stood still, owning to the miracle (of the Consecration). We then find a curious poem beginning: 'Here's what I think of a rake's life' ('Sin agaibh mo theastas ar beathaidh gach réice') – and, indeed, it is little else than a frank account of what he thought of himself when the heat of excitement had passed and thought began to say its bitter word:

An uair tigeann an laige, agus druideann an t-aos liom,
'S mé ar uireasbaidh éadaigh, is caillim mo threoir,
Bíonn pairthis creathach gach maidean im ghéagaibh,
Ní blasta mo bhréithre is níl tathach im ghlór;
Is searbh an aiste liom labhairt ar chéithlinn,
Tigh an tabhairne séanaim mar chaitheas mo stór,
Dearbhaim, admhuighim feasta, 'gus géillim
Gur damanta an chéird í, is go mb'fheárr léigeann dóibh.[41]

When weakness comes and old age draws up to me,
I lack for clothing, I lose my strength,
My limbs in the morning shake and shiver,
My words are savourless, and weak my voice;
Bitter it is to me to speak of a woman,
I shun the tavern where I spent my all,
I swear, I admit henceforth, I yield
That it is a damned business and they are better let alone.

He finishes by counselling the free and manly youth to settle down and marry, to avoid drinking and quarrelling at the fairs. The two remaining songs in the section are also concerned with drinking.

Then we pass to the satires. Of the most famous of them, 'An t-Arrachtach Sean' (The Aged Monster), we have already given some account. Perhaps the next most famous is a poem satirising the priests of his time. He addresses one of them, evidently a poet, praising him at the expense of his brethren; and the burden of his song is twofold: once there was a Church that was friendly to the poets, the priests generous in their houses, feast-giving, humane, charitable; but now there is left to us only the chaff after the sieving – a rabble of dunces: the other burden is that while a rich man may do as he likes, let a poor man but look at a girl and there's 'running routing' for him and the curse of clergy and bell. In his next satire he relieves his mind on Kate O'Leary, who had 'sequestered' his pair of stockings because he owed her fourpence – a right good poem, flung out, hot and heady and as reckless as it could be. 'May I see you with an ugly child in your lap, and neither father nor tidings of father to be had for ever':

Go bhfeicead-sa gárlach gránna id chlúid agat
Is gan a athair le faghbháil go bráth ná cunntas ann[42]

– one of the many curses in it – may be taken as a sample of the whole. All over it we find those touches of time and place that make all his poems, except, possibly, the decorative *aisling* poems, so real and alert. He wishes that she may die without the priest and be waked without keeners – a hard wish in the Munster of that time:

> Gan ola chum báis ná gáir ós cionn do chuirr.[43]

It is not very intellectual, perhaps, but as one reads it one fancies that Villon or Rabelais[44] would have howled it out with vast delight, so full of verve is it, so lacking in all restraint: it is, moreover, an example of that headlong run of overpowering invective, so common in Irish poets, that influenced John M. Synge both in his dramas and poems.*

We have only one elegy in the book. It was written on the death of Father Con Horgan, 20th January, 1773; and in every line of it one feels the influence of Ó Rathaille. This verse might be taken from almost any of his famous keens:

> Uaill is gáir is crádh-ghol éagnach,
> Is gruaim is glámh is lán-tocht éighmhe,
> Greadad bas is stracadh céibhe,
> Brón is caoi go cíocrach céasta.[45]

What is said in the lines is not of the same importance as the solemn music in which the message is wrapped up, the dark vowels resounding, one to another – the very note of Ó Rathaille's keens. Here are two other lines which nobody would believe were written by any other poet except him:

> An bocht's an nocht go docht 'san mhéala
> Tré theascadh an bhile ceann urraidh na cléire.[46]

But here we have two lines with Eoghan's tenderness in them:

> Níl agam ach guidhe le h-intinn éagnaigh
> Chum aingil is naoimh bheith síor dá aodhaireacht.[47]

> What can I do but pray with wistful mind
> That angels and saints may shepherd him for ever.

The very thought, however, which these two lines round to a close tells us that the poet was all the time aware of the difference between himself and Ó Rathaille as keeners. Where is the genealogy? The priest that he was lamenting was, the poet tells us, learned in song, practised in the difficult lore of the poets, trained in the genealogy of the race:

---

* See his curse on the sister of an enemy – not wholly serious, one believes.

> Do chuireadh le slacht 'na gceart gach Gaedheal-treabh
> I nBanba ghluais anuas ó Éibhear.[48]

Literally:

> Who used to put neatly right every Gaelic tribe
> In Banba that descended from Éibhear.

The poet himself felt very unlearned in all this; his head is empty of *ogham*,[49] he tells us. All he can do is to pray the angels and saints to take the dead priest into their shepherding – a prayer possible to the most ignorant of men. But in many another of his poems he is also conscious of this want of the old learning: and the solacing thought that he may have been better without it never broke even once upon his mind.

The next five poems are grouped under the heading 'Amhráin Molta Ban', 'Poems in Praise of Women', but, though in each of them there are very beautiful and tender lines, they are only the conventional love-poetry that was then in fashion.

Then we have a few 'Warrants' – humorous verses which are all readable, but of little importance. The first is called 'A Warrant against Some Person Who Stole his Hat,' and while conventional in the scheme, the handling is as neat as it could well be: who could think of bettering these lines in point of style?

> Cá tairbhe damh-sa a mhaitheas do chómhaireamh,
> D'éis a ghuidighthe?
> Is gur bh'álainn gleoidhte sásda an t-seod é
> Ag soar-fhlaith chumasach:
> Níl ainnir ná bé do dhearcadh an té
> Ar a shuidhfeadh seal
> Ná tabharfadh searc rún is gean
> A cléibh 's a cumainn dó.[50]

And another verse is curious:

> As I am informed that pilfering roving
> Rakes gan dearmaid,
> Juris quoque contemptores,
> Fé mar mheasaim-se,
> Nightly strollers haunt these borders,
> Déanaidh faire ceart
> To apprehend aon chladhaire faolchon
> Claon-sprot cealgach.[51]

VII

In reading Ó Rathaille we cannot help thinking of him as an 'Oisin in the Fenians' Wake': a new world had come upon the Gael, but to its strangeness he would most willingly shut his eyes. His world was the few scattered big Irish houses still remaining in his countryside rather than the thousands of dismal huts where the swarming peasants gathered themselves at nightfall. Of the Big Houses, of their sorrows, it was that he sung; to and fro amongst them he made his way; when they failed him he died, stepping into the grave, as one may recollect, with the name of the most memorable of them all on his lips – the MacCarthys.

Far otherwise it is with Eoghan Ruadh. He was a stranger to the Big House; he trudged the roads with his spade on his shoulder, truly one with the other labourers in whose gang he was numbered. Yet, while it was for them he sung, he was not a folk-poet, as the term is now understood: he was a literary man singing for a literary audience, though it was in a tavern or in a farmer's kitchen that that audience assembled. Every day, however, both the language and the speakers of it were becoming less literary and more folk, if one may so speak; and of this the poet was very conscious – we have seen how he frequently refers to himself as an unlearned poet, unlearned, that is, in the craft of song, which then, of course, included both history and genealogy.

Though only a little more than twenty years had passed between the death of Ó Rathaille and the birth of Eoghan Ruadh, there is, due to the decaying of all things Gaelic, a world of difference between the feeling in the verses of the one and the other; the difference, therefore, is not so much the measure of the disparity between two poets as between two periods.

Knowing Eoghan Ruadh, then, as the wandering labourer who sung his own songs in the wayside tavern, we feel ourselves, while we read them, warm as with the very breath of the peasants who crowded about him while he did so. For them he wrote; and always, it is evident, in hot haste, fitting the song to the day that was passing over. Those peasants, then, what manner of learning they set store on, how they felt towards their masters, their sense of race, of religion – all this we cannot help apprehending while we read him, their poet. But of himself we are also poignantly made aware; of himself at his almost every new fling at fortune. His opening of the school, while still a boy, at Gneeveguilla and what happened there; his travelling the roads; his taking the part of youth in the famous contest; his venturing over the sea; his home-sickness in exile; his return; his love of the great stories of Greece; his love of learning – all this is, even to-day, fresh and vivid in his songs. In them also his revelry, as well as the repentance that followed it; no phase of his stormy life remains unsung, while his last moment of consciousness is enshrined for us in a memorable couplet. Indeed, so marked is the personal note in the greater part of his work that one can understand how those who will not, or cannot, content themselves with sheer artistry, find the decorative *aisling* poems uninteresting and pale.

Yet, close-linked as are his songs with the real things of his days, there never was a mind more essentially poetic; that is, a mind on which no vision shone that was not fledged with music.

There is always music, and most frequently it is the very heart of the poem, not a running accompaniment. 'Is that Eoghan an Mhéirin?' we are told a priest once cried from the altar, only to be answered: 'No, it is Eoghan an Bhéil Bhínn' – Eoghan of the Sweet Mouth; and when the people put this name upon him they did so with the sure instinct that had come of a thousand years of literary traditions. In one of his *aisling* poems the Spirit of Ireland recalls the great past when her lot was chieftainship and feasting 'le seascaireacht ceoil'[52] ('with the comfort of music') – the comfort of music! – the one phrase to denote the excelling charm in his own verse, the exact phrase to describe what it was he gave his down-trodden and hungry people, endearing himself to them in spite of his recklessness and his wilfulness.

The critics of our own day who have tried to reverse the judgement of his contemporaries forget all this, or, rather, while they begin by paying tribute to his gift of music, do not seem to have anything pregnant to remark of his work until they have first put that music aside – as if, that put aside, anything of great importance remained to be said! Surely the critic's task is to give a fuller sense of the masterpiece he deals with (just as a poet's task is to deepen our sense of life); and the fuller sense of this man's poetry is the proper realisation of the music that is in it – the realisation of it, not only as the hidden vital force from which the song took being, but as the bloom, the charm of perfection, in one word, the achievement which, when he had sung his song, left the poet himself full of ease and sighing for content, as a woman who has been delivered.

There might be some sense in this impatience with the orchestration of these poems if the rich medley, whether by its self-willed frenzy or loudness or unmanageability, had made foolish or niggard or weakling the musician who attempted it. But this did not ever happen: in not even one song, one verse, does he go astray in the whirlwind he has raised about him, or forget his destination. No other lines were ever more spontaneous, free-running, unburdened, triumphant, carrying their message up to the very gate intended, laying it there on the threshold of our consciousness, clean and beautiful: if we do not glow to receive it, it is because we have given our hearts away, if ever we had any.

Thinking of him, so gifted, 'born with thy face and throat, Lyric Apollo!';[53] thinking of the *Aisling*, a form created as if in expectation of such a singer, one wonders how much of him is due to the *aisling* songs his young fancy dwelt upon as in his boyhood he roamed the slopes of Sliabh Luachra. It was these *aisling* songs made him what he was; in turn he left other *aisling* poems to those who should come after him – not for their good: the form had reached perfection in him; and there is a weariness and a hint of coldness in all of them that were to be made after his time. But in his own, what brilliancy! What perfect understanding of what lyric poetry should be – the music arising from the perfect blending of the word, as a word, heavy with its own especial treasures – music, colour, associations – the blending of this word with the thing it represents, that also heavy with its own enrichments, haphazard or integral:

> Mar a raibh cantain na n-éan ar ghéagaibh crainn ghlais,
> Lachain is éisc ag scéitheadh ón dtaoide,
> An eala go glé ag téacht ar tuinn ann,
> 'S an péarla i n-íochtar trath as cómhair.[54]

These four lines I recall to justify the common peasants' appreciation of Eoghan Ruadh as their best singer. Are they not perfect as lyric verse – spontaneous, swift-running, light, unburdened, a shower of sweet sounds – the perfect blending of the word and the thing? The choiring birds on the green tree-branches, the sea-birds and fish swarming from the tide, the swan brightly taking the wave's crest, and – perfect artist! – he reserves to the close the touch that will add radiance to all the others – the pearl in the water's depth, *sometimes visible* – this is how they translate into English prose, the lightness, the music, the swiftness, the brilliancy destroyed.

He brought something of that fresh radiance to all that his young eyes rested on. The old names in those Greek stories he loved, it is seldom that he invokes them without some life-giving word in his mouth. Hebe is 'an réilteann óg' ('the young star').[55] Helen is 'ríobh chailce an choimheascair thug ár na Trae' ('the lime-white lady of the conflict who brought destruction to Troy').[56] Elsewhere she is 'an bhríghdeach Hélen' ('the bride Helen'). Not since the days of the Pléiade,[57] if even then, did the bright-robed Grecians play their various parts so entirely unburdened of text-book scholarship. The Irish poets of that time read those classic tales as good, bright stories: they seem, happy folk, to have had the blessed privilege of reading them as the far-off creators of them intended – greedily rather than critically; with the glory that was Greece they made free, finding entrance to it through their own sagas, where there are grotesque figures as well as lovers and queens; of the warriors and, indeed, deities of Greece they expected the same homeliness, none welcoming their gracious presence as did Eoghan Ruadh.

They crowd pell-mell upon his vision; and the living word that thereupon leaps quickly from his mouth lets us know the heart-ease he has always found in their coming. So, too, when that more frequent visitant of his sad hours – the Spirit of Ireland – brings speech to his lips, there is sure to be some unexpected word that, piercing our imagination, makes us at once, and whether or not we will it, initiate of what is towards. Only a truly poetic mind is so seized upon by its own visions as to be unaware of what the next word will be until it falls upon the air; and it is strange that the more entirely the mind is in the grip of the vision, the more precise and hard-edged will be those sudden and unpremeditated words that describe what is happening in the happy trance. Saluting, once, that great Spirit of Ireland, Eoghan Ruadh, without ado, tells us he bowed to the grass 'with his (three) cornered hat in his hand':

Is tapa d'umhluigheas lem hata cúinneach im lámh go féar.[58]

This swift daring is to be seen almost in all his songs: is it the 'invention' that Keats thought of as the quality most necessary of all to a poet?[59] It, anyway, achieves; for whenever that assured timbre rings in a poet's accents, one accepts his statement as the living truth, no matter what the dimensions, the colours, the topsy-turvy or the impossibility may be.

To his climax he sweeps on; and it is always effective. Take any one of the *aisling* poems: imagine it recited or sung in a voice equal in earnestness to the artistry in the song, and one cannot help hearing the applause at the end, more especially when the close of the poem is loud and triumphant:

'S dá bhfeichinn-se, mar shamhluighim,
na samharlaidhe treascartha,
Do bhéadh lampaí ar lasadh agam le éigean spóirt.[60]

And were I to see, as I dream,
the churls overwhelmed
Lamps would I set blazing in the dint of joy.

But when the song dies gently, or even sadly, it is no less the firm closing of the tale: the song has been sung cleanly to its end. How praise sufficiently the last line of the song in which he requests a smith to make him a new spade? He describes in rapid and dainty verse of great dexterity exactly the sort of spade he wants, and then:

Is mar bharra ar gach nídh bíodh sí i mbinneas an chluig![61]

And, crowning all, let it have in it the sweetness of a bell!

Every inch a poet! That is what one exclaims of him; and it includes all.

A mind enamoured of music, bestowing radiance, is rightly described as lyrical; yet this sense of form that was his, this sweeping along to his climax and then ceasing, bespeaks a strength that was capable of something on a higher, if not a lovelier, plane than the lyric. This mastery of form is seen in almost every poem that remains to us; but in 'An t-Arrachtach Sean' (The Aged Monster) there is in addition a sense of reality, a grip on the lie of the human land, a certain hardness of vision that surprises one who thinks of it either as written by one who had just reached his twenty-first year or as written by the singer of the decorative *aisling* poems at any age. It is boastful, vigorous, mature, assured – the work, one would take it, of a man who had not sufficient tenderness in him ever to write lyric poems of any worth either as regards lightness or music. Critics have wondered at Brian Merriman's view of life in his *Midnight Court* (Cúirt an Mheadhon Oidhche); they have praised him for his grip, his substance, and his disregard for the merely lyrical; but even in these qualities is he so far ahead of the young lad who wrote these lines? –

> 'Nuair d'amharcann ainnir do snaidhmeadh le h-ársach,
> Faraire bláthmhar álainn ar each,
> Go meanmach acfuinneach abaidh glan ceáfrach,
> Lannmhar láidir lan-chumais mear,
> Biodhgann a croidhe-sin is líonann le taithneamh dhó,
> Tigheann dortadh díleis is caoi-ghol 'na haigneadh,
> Adeir, galar gan chasadh go leagaidh mo cháirde
> Cheangail go bráth mé le harrachtach sean![62]

Here, surely, we find the 'modern' note; though not quite so strongly, perhaps, as in 'Cailleach Bhéara,' which was written in the tenth century![63]

And how Molièresque[64] is this:

> Ar shéadaibh na hÉireann ní thréighfeadh an seanduine
> Aodhaireacht a chéile tré éad leis na fearachoin.[65]

> For the jewels of Ireland the Ancient would not cease
> Shepherding his wife through jealousy of heroic youths.

That 'shepherding' is a good word.

This core of hardness is scarcely ever lacking to the Gaelic poet; track him right down the centuries, and one never finds it missing. It is intellectual in its nature: hard-headed and clear-sighted, witty at its best, prosaic when not eager; and to its universality in the truly Gaelic world is due the fact that one can turn over the pages of the Gaelic book of poetry, century after century, without coming on any set of verses that one could speak of as sentimental:

Tennyson's 'Queen of the May'[66] would have thrown Eoghan Ruadh or indeed, any of his companions, whether poets or not, into wild fits of laughter. Brian Merriman had so much of that hardness in him that one could not expect delicacy or sensibility to go with it; of his one gift he certainly made the best use; yet, when we keep this whole poem of Eoghan Ruadh's, 'An t-Arrachtach Sean', in mind, we find it hard to account for the rhapsodies that Merriman's *Cúirt an Mheadhon Oidhche* has excited. Great it is, but those who have spoken of it as a thing unique in Gaelic literature must have forgotten, not only this whole poem of Eoghan Ruadh's, but the whole vast volume of Irish proverbial lore, not to say those numerous floating quatrains that Professor Thomas F. O'Rahilly has gathered into his book, *Dánfhocail*.[67]

No, *Cúirt an Mheadhon Oidhche* (The Midnight Court) is not a unique thing in Irish literature; it is, however, a big thing successfully wrought. But we must not attempt to group Eoghan Ruadh and Brian Merriman together either as opposed, one to the other, or as kindred spirits: they were contemporaries (though Brian Merriman lived on for twenty years after Eoghan Ruadh); otherwise they had only very little in common. Brian Merriman's vision was prosaic: the distance between his verse and good idiomatic prose is, or seems to be, measurable; but the distance between even the best prose and almost the weakest of Eoghan Ruadh's work is immeasurable; for it is always in that higher plane where the thirst of music is necessary to full understanding. Brian Merriman may be said to derive from Dáibhidh Ó Bruadair, with a loss of sensibility, of flexibility; and Eoghan Ruadh from Aodhagán Ó Rathaille, with a loss of intensity and high-mindedness.

Eoghan Ruadh's gifts, then, were manifold: there was that intellectuality that so effectually staved off the sentimental; there was that intuitional sense of form which accounts for the perfect articulation of his most winged lyrics; there was that freshness of vision which accounts for his daring epithets; there was, above all, his thirst of music, his lyric throat. Of these great gifts he did not make the most; but how could he have done so, even were his passions less violent and his will-power greater, in the Irish Munster of his day? What was all that land but a death-stricken country, an outland, one might say, far from the stir of life? In such a land, he could have done nothing were it not for those thousands of other Gaelic poets who for a thousand years had been using the Gaelic language and enriching the Gaelic mind.

## VIII

'What Pindar is to Greece, what Burns is to Scotland, what Béranger is to France, what nobody in particular, unless it be Mr. Kipling, is to England, that and much more is Eoghan Ruadh to Ireland.'*

Alas! it is by no means so; but were Fr. Dinneen to write: 'that and much more was Eoghan Ruadh to Gaelic Munster,' he would have understated rather than overstated the matter. When I first learned Eoghan's language I went, summer after summer, now to one, now to another, Irish-speaking district in Munster; and, city-born and city-bred, I for some time found it difficult to find matter to chat about with the peasant ancients of those hidden vales: later on, however, I found there were two subjects which never failed to arouse the dying fires, to bring light into the fading eyes, and a flood of speech to the toothless gums: the Great Famine of '47 was one, and Eoghan Ruadh, the wastrel poet, whose voice had been stilled for more than a hundred years, whose poems they had never seen printed, whose life they had never seen written, was the other. One who has been trying to raise an interest in Irish literature among the teachers of Munster tells me: 'When I speak of the other poets they pay no heed, but when I mention Eoghan Ruadh, the old men raise their heads.' 'Among labourers,' writes one[†] who, living not far from Eoghan's homeland, has always taken a deep interest in all that concerns the poet –

> Among labourers, 'A Ghaibhne Chláir Fódla' was very popular. The cultivated Irish speakers favoured 'Seó Hó, a Thoil', and I've heard a good old singer giving 'Mo Léan le Luadh'. 'An t-Arrachtach Sean' and 'Eascaine ar Cháit ní Laoghaire' were well known to the last generation. My father used to sing 'Mo Chás mo Chaoi mo Cheasna'. 'Ag Taisteal na Blárnan' and 'Cois na Siúire' were very popular.

In the back lanes of the city of Cork I have met old women who at the mention of his name forgot all the hardship they had come through since their young days in the country; and once I remember meeting in a lodging-house with two very old men who were full both of his life and his poetry and wit; one helping out the other: when they had gone I was told that they had just come from Chicago, in the toil of which they had spent a full half-century of years.

> Though quite a distance from there now, in my mind's eye I can see the spot where, as I was shown, Eoghan's house stood, that is the house in which he died, about two hundred yards from the village of

---

* *Amhráin Eoghain Ruaidh Uí Shúilleabháin*, leis an Athair Pádraig Ua Duinnín.[68]
† Mr. John Kiely, of Cullen, Co. Cork.

Knocknagree, in the County Cork; the place is called Park. I was born myself about half a mile from there, and I well remember the old people years ago tell about Eoghan a hundred stories illustrative of his peculiar life. Such discussions relative to Eoghan usually wound up with a reference to his last days, the penniless and impoverished condition to which he was reduced, dying of fever in that little hovel.*

• • •

Such, then, is an account, altogether inadequate, of the life, the works, the genius and the legend of Eoghan an Bheoil Bhínn – Eoghan of the Sweet Mouth.

\* \* \*

# The Philosophy of the Gaelic League[1]

The philosophy of such an association as the Gaelic League means no more than the body of thought by which it lives, the reasons it goes upon. One who is anything but a philosopher may attempt at least a sketch of these. In general the philosophy of the Gaelic League is nothing else than that of Irish Ireland, of the National Ideal, of Ireland a Nation, of Irish Nationality. Irish mind restored, living, in action, is the vital principle of each. Of the existence of a national mind the Gaelic League is assured, assured even of its having continuously existed for something like two thousand years. Irish history of itself is firm enough basis for that belief. Irish literature of itself is confirmative of the history, at least for half-way back. To dwell upon either, or both, is to be aware of a homogeneous community dwelling in its own island-country for a vast number of years, a community sensitively aware of itself as a historic entity, and endowed with character enough either to absorb invading forces or finally to eject them, if their will is, not to be absorbed. Only nationality can be the cohering principle where history can be summarised in such terms.

---

\*  See *Beatha Eoghain Ruaidh Uí Shúilleabháin*, leis an Athair Pádraig Ua Duinnín. The words quoted are from a letter received by Fr. Dinneen from a gentleman in America who wished to erect a monument to the poet.[69]

### THE NATIONAL MIND

Yes, but the world, even before that two thousand years began, had come to know of frustrated nationhoods. Nations had been led away in captivity, set to make bricks without straw. Others had been made captive within their own confines. Only when an imperial system consists entirely of colonies flung abroad by itself, can it be anything else than a single (overweening ?) nationality and a conglomerate of frustrated nationhoods (that is, if it has dared to enslave civilised peoples).

A frustrated nationhood is not however an obliterated nationality. The national mind is no longer a free agent, is thwarted indeed at every hand's turn, but it has not ceased to be. It may still be making a constricted use of its own modes and forms. As, under the stress of circumstance, it gives these up one after another it is drawing nearer and nearer to extinction. Finally there will remain to that people only memorials of those modes and forms. If however these memorials have still for them more than aesthetic meaning, that is, if they can stir them *as a people*, it cannot be said that the national mind is quite obliterated. On the other hand, if such memorials are possessed of no more appeal for them than for any other people, a nationality has vanished, and can never be brought back.

Those modes and forms are of course the media through which a national mind expresses itself, so coming to know itself in the first instance for a national mind. Indeed until the 'national mind' comes to know itself as such, it is straining language to use this term at all. For when it comes to know itself as such, it cannot be what it was before. There is henceforth what we may call a *tensioned* use of those modes and forms (for the Greeks there was consciously a Greek way, for the Irish an Irish way). Each mode and form is henceforth a national piety. Among them we may enumerate the language (and all its own proper modes – literature, history, law, etc.), all the arts (if the nation practises them all), social customs, games (if the nation is fortunate enough to have them of its own), etc., etc. These modes and forms constitute a sort of spiritual organism, the members of which are unequal in rank and great in variety. Any pair of them may at first view seem to be of disparate genera: actually they harmonise one with another, each with all, all with each – for the reason that the one mind has made each of them what it actually is. They are organically co-ordinated.

Of those national pieties, the language is unique. It is the mother-form. It is the one form that every single individual in the community practises, day in day out, and for his whole life long. It feeds and sustains all the other forms. It justifies them, and clarifies them. The musician can think and imagine in musical forms; but wherefrom in innumerable cases come the thoughts, the feelings, the desires, which his compositions formulate for us? The history of his craft is written in words; in words its criticism. What is said of music is true of the other arts as well – indeed of all the other modes, since ordinarily it is in language we think. Our intellectual operations depend on language.

## THE GAELIC LEAGUE'S TASK

When the Gaelic League was founded over fifty years since, Ireland had abandoned almost all its own significant modes and forms; such of them as survived were death-stricken; its national mind was not alone frustrated, it was approaching extinction. It was no longer creative. Even in the religion of the nation – and a religion that offers such a field for creation in – there was no Irish way of any significance.

The significant thing about the Gaelic League is that from the start it has worked in the spirit of nationhood. *Tír gan teangain tír gan anam* – a country without a language is a country without a soul – soon became its favourite slogan. The League's task specifically has always been to restore to Irish nationhood its supreme mode – its language. It has never been merely to preserve an ancient language, as well as its literature, for cultural or antiquarian purposes. One cannot recall that it has ever hindered other societies whose aim was such, nor societies of any kind whose propaganda and activities encouraged the use of Irish, even when the members of such societies confessed themselves cold to its own dream of a full nationhood, that is, a nationhood with a full canon of national modes and forms. In its own affiliated membership, however, it could not naturally include partial adherents: such would, or might, induce 'doubt, hesitation, and pain.' A constitution has at least to be logical in its articles; the imperfect practice of them is a less grievous failing.

## ITS AUXILIARS

The Gaelic League has never been unaware of the immensity of its task. It has perhaps greater auxiliars than it first knew of. And others were to come along: they have not ceased to come. Of these auxiliars a word or two:

Our tradition is easily the greatest of them. Merely to speak of it as a national tradition is to say nothing of it, national traditions can vary so much. The quality, the temper, of ours is not to be come upon as yet in our histories: they for the most part speak of other matters. Fifty years ago that tradition was rife in the minds of the people rather than in their infrequent books; was at their hearths rather than in their schools. One may liken it to a vast music with vital strains in it, legendary, historical, religious, secular. There was not one of those vital strains which some ruin, or place-name, or well, or other local memorial could not awaken into life, so vouching in a way for the tradition as a whole as well as for that portion of it intimately apprehended. Part and parcel of that whole tradition, indeed the summing up of it, was, that defeat had never been accepted, nay, further, that it never was to be accepted. Was this an ordinary normal national tradition? Finland would easily apprehend its temper, or Poland, or the Jewish people in ancient days.

The founders of the Gaelic League were Irish scholars; yet even they could hardly have made any adequate image of how that tradition was, almost of itself, to take to the Gaelic League, to spread it from parish to parish throughout the land. But then, was it really the farmers and their helpers in the towns who had just won out in the Land League struggle? Was it not rather that same tradition? (Those who aspersed that struggle as mere agrarianism were woefully astray). And was it not that self-same tradition which was carrying the G.A.A. from triumph to triumph? The success of those two movements, the result of that success on the people's mind, everywhere assisted the League to find its feet. To point all this out is not to take either from the wisdom or the energy of the founders of the Gaelic League. Still they could not have foreseen it. Nor could they have foreseen the triumph of 1916, which indeed was a triumph of the Gaelic League's own. Our tradition remains therefore, and strengthened rather than weakened, the greatest of our auxiliars.

The fact that countries like Finland and Czechoslovakia and Hungary had succeeded in bringing down-trodden languages back to full strength was, and is, another great auxiliar. That small countries, and others, consciously and of set purpose, succeeded in doing this, may yet be counted for perhaps the greatest of the few original contributions of the nineteenth century to the enrichment of the equipment of culture. What previous century had brought back whole languages? Those small countries have since given more than their due to the cultural output of the world. And not without reason. For a language struggle in its essence is a spiritual impulse. What is it anywhere except a rising against an illegitimate overlord, against the stranglehold of the culture he has established in the wrong place? It is usually an effort to right an ancient wrong, to free forces that have been wrongfully impeded.

Of the newer auxiliars that are come into the field we may mention, and there is space only to mention, the almost world-wide recognition of the foolishness of modern peoples everywhere in trying to rid themselves of the sense of tradition; and, secondly, the growing appreciation of the fact that only in deep-rooted, slowly-ripening nationhoods has man's personality shown itself at its best, certainly at its finest.

## THE STRUGGLE MUST BE MAINTAINED

Other auxiliars newly become of force, because newly prominently before the world's mind, which might be commented on are: the greater appreciation of the intrinsic virtues that lie potentially in a language as an implement of culture; the recognition of the inability of one language adequately to take the place of another; the appreciation of the fact that Wireless has in a sense made every nation in the world language-proud, that is, every nation that has a language to be proud of.

Philosophy interprets facts. What we have been speaking of as auxiliars are admitted facts. Irish tradition is a reality, a reality demanding its own way, its own technique, its own media – that is if it is to create, to express itself, even to live at harmony with itself. The manifestations of that tradition in the political sphere during our own times show it to be resilient, resurgent, triumphant. The Gaelic League's interpretation of such facts is that this tradition of ours cannot go on living in English with either usefulness or dignity. Doing so it is going counter to what must be the most innate desire of such a tradition, namely, to be itself not only in spirit but in form. It cannot be satisfied to give it to say to Finland, Poland, Bohemia, Denmark, that unlike themselves, it will continue to make do with the language that the conqueror superimposed upon it. If to others than Gaelic Leaguers this country appears content to do so, these others may be basing their opinion on a page here and there of modern Irish history; they cannot certainly be basing them on the trend and pressure of Irish history since the founding of the Land League.

The Gaelic League, because of its intimate knowledge of, and feeling for, what the last seventy or eighty years have engendered in the Irish tradition, cannot for a moment doubt that this language fight is to go on, and finally to win. Anyway, in the light of what that same period has given it of new inspiration based on solid facts – the sense of language movements as spiritual impulses (Did not the *Divine Comedy* arise in one of them?), the sense of nationality as a refiner and inspirer of personality (All the art and life of old Greece), the certainty that Wireless reinforces the sense of language as a people's most national asset (Only listen!) – in the light of these the League's thought is that for Ireland to refrain from going back to its native speech is for Ireland to choose to play the dullard.

## OURS MUST NOT BE THE ENGLISH WAY

We are therefore asking the doubter to try better to estimate that new temper come to this nation; the Anglo-Irish intellectual we ask to take stock of what is being thought everywhere abroad. Since the propaganda of the latter is still loud in the land, it may be necessary to look at how his cult of this speech superimposed on us must continue to hinder us, if he have his way, from ever being able to march side by side with such small countries as we have named, our head as high as theirs.

Every national tradition is a unique thing, standing apart. It does not follow that each is possessed of the same valuable foison for the human spirit. The opposite is the truth. There have been great trading nations in the world, rich, with far-flung connections, with argosies coming and going between them: what however they had to say of value in the way of literature or art is almost unknown to us. It is held that their trafficking 'in the monarch Thought's dominion' bore no proportion to their far questings on land and sea.[2] Perhaps in their time they had not suffered enough to understand what spirit is. If our tradition can give no better account of itself in literature than it has been doing for the last century and a half in English – and where is the evidence that it can? – it is not for want of significant matter to go on. *That* it cannot lack, for its experiences have been of the spirit stripped of the institutional and embodied sheerly in flesh and blood, and not at all of what either spirit or flesh and blood may wrap themselves around with or dandle to pass the time away. Our tradition has been experiencing reality bone to bone, and from age to age. It cannot but have much to say. And its way of saying it ought to be of moment, too. But to be of moment, and to be consonant with, and agreeable to the matter, this must be its own way. It must not be the English way; for the English way is, it must be remembered, integral in the English language, even as the Latin in the Latin language, and the Greek in the Greek. If Ireland succeed in expressing in English, so as fully to satisfy itself, what the ages have engendered in it, then the English language will have within it two national literatures, or more simply and as equally truly, two literatures. How can that be? It can never be. When we have said this, we have said all. Considered deeply enough, it proves the whole case of the Gaelic League.

## ANGLO-IRISH LITERATURE A BRANCH OF ENGLISH LITERATURE

We may be reminded: 'We do not envisage an Irish literature in English; but what of an Anglo-Irish literature?' If by an Anglo-Irish literature is meant a literature with a genius of its own, then again we are to have two disparate literatures in the one tongue. There certainly can be literature in English about Irish *matter*. There is a fair amount of such literature already in existence, much of it quite interesting. But no one thinks of it as having a genius, a way, of its own. It has no way which would be discernible if the matter treated of were not Irish. It is of course a branch, and nothing but a branch, of English literature. It is recognised as such. If all our writers in English were to set up a Kiltartan League, and by dint of propaganda to get this 'dialect' adopted by the nation at large, and then, rejecting English literary forms and contemning English syntax, were to write and publish all their books in this Kiltartanese,[3] these works of theirs should have a fair claim to be called Anglo-Irish literature, even Irish literature, for it would have developed a way of its own, and so become capable of dealing with universal literary material. One does not think, however, that our writers in English will even make the attempt. It would not succeed. It would meet with too hilarious a reception everywhere. And yet a phenomenon not quite dissimilar is, one thinks, succeeding in America. Indeed one cannot see how there it can eventually fail. But Ireland is not America. It has not a population of one hundred and thirty millions; nor is it thousands of miles away from England's manner of using her own language. There is therefore no means by which Ireland can come at a literature in English, which shall have a way of its own. Why this cannot come to pass is clear enough. The English language (any language) of itself is prepossessive. The corpus of English literature, as self-contained a thing as the language itself, is equally prepossessive. Both know, as if beforehand, what they want, and they get it. Is there any considerable piece of English from the pen of an Irishman which does not exhibit this prepossessive power of both language and literature? It is certain that many writers of such literature wished their work to be Irish, probably even thought that it was so. But in such a case neither wishing nor thinking counts. Their work is in the English way because it is in the English language. And whether it be called Anglo-Irish or Irish does not alter that fact. Nor does it matter whether it has been written solely for the people of Ireland, or for those of England or America, or for all three. The naming of it, the classification of it does not matter. If thought worth while from the English point of view, it is all, to use Tennyson's phrase, 'swallow'd in the conqueror's chronicle,'[4] and deservedly so.

The fact, however, that such literature as Irishmen write in English falls of itself into two classes has much significance for those who would understand it. The matter in both cases is Irish. It is, however, looked at from different angles. The result is that the literature written for Ireland alone is frequently immodest with too much modesty, while that written for foreign markets is frequently immodest with a cold and calculated recklessness. The overweening tone of either is to be understood only by considering the overweening tone of the other. There is falseness in each. There is unreality. And as long as English is our medium for literary expression, only in these intrinsically unreliable mirrors is our immemorial tradition, our own mind, to be contemplated! That tradition which in itself is so real, so sheer, so factual, so unexuberant, so hard, so homely, so human. Coming out of Gaeldom, only in the Irish language has it found such expression as is consonant with itself. The integrity of that real literature of ours, the way in which it has kept its own notes, should teach us how thoroughly Gaelicism, that is, Irish mind, assimilated whatever it took from Dane or Norman, or Elizabethan or Cromwellian, or from Continental sources. Because it was a real thing, self-subsisting, it had the capability of doing this, that is, of assimilating foreign matter and yet remaining its own self. But what we have done in English wears ever in its face the reflex of whatever expression is to be found in the contemporaneous writing of Englishmen. In Irish literature one has to look twice, and more than twice, to come upon its borrowings; in what we have done in English what one feels like looking twice for is its own self! It lacks character; has never developed from within. It is thereby unfitted to represent that reality that is Irish mind.

## THE GAELIC LEAGUE'S SENSE OF REALITY

Have we been saying something too much of literature? The making of literature is not all, nor half, the task that lies upon a language. In the end, however, it is its power to deal with the soul's way (as in literature) as well as with the mind's way (as in science) that decides whether or not a language is capable of bearing the burden of a national tradition. Ireland can of course continue to live its life in English – only, however, a constricted sort of life, ever in part prepossessed, as we have shown, by the English way. It is curious to reflect that if our minds were under the full control of the Irish language and its literature, it would not be, as it now is, impossible for us to come into loving and intimate contact with both the language and literature of our neighbour (a thing well worth doing) without at the same time ceasing in some degree to be our own selves.

To be our own selves – that is, to be real; and, to turn from literary considerations, it is the Gaelic League's sense of reality which leaves it quite unimpressed by the business man's sweeping gesture as he cries out: Changing one language for another is not a commercial proposition. For it knows that the Finns, the Czechs, the Danes have found that it was! These countries date their entry not only into the cultural life, but also into the commercial life, of Europe from the making of such a change. We have not heard that any one of them, or any one of those other countries that did the same, regret its having the pluck to do so. The answer is complete, although the Gaelic League itself would have the temerity to continue its propaganda if it had been proved even up to the hilt that changing our language would mean our having less of the world's goods in our larders. It is, again, its sense of reality that would prompt it to do so.

## THE DEBUNKERS

In recent years the League has been having to meet the questionings of those who are being instructed, first, by the debunkers of our nationality, and, secondly, by innumerable pamphlets and books from across the sea. Our debunkers prepare them to receive the doctrines propounded in the incoming print. The Irish tradition they are told is essentially aristocratic: to go back to it is like going back to feudalism, from which of course the world has wrenched itself free. As if anyone wants them or others to go 'back' to anything! Bringing a national tradition alive is not going 'back,' unless we think that in recovering from an illness one is going back. To become so much ourselves as to begin to create in a way natural to ourselves can hardly be the same thing as going back; it surely seems more like going forward. So much for that. As for our 'aristocratic' past. Aristocratic and feudal are words which carry their own atmosphere. That atmosphere is all over the English language as it is found in English literature; and not without reason. If our debunkers do not like the atmosphere those two terms create, one would think that they would turn their guns on English literature rather than on ours, in which no such atmosphere abounds at all. It would be very extraordinary if it did. To apply aristocratic or feudal to the political and social economy of the old Irish Ireland, or to the literature nurtured in it, is as wrong, one thinks, as to apply them to the life that we have pictured for us in the Old Testament. Patriarchal would of course fit much closer than either. Into that old patriarchal economy whatever the Normans brought with them of feudalism was absorbed, so ceasing to be feudalism in any real sense of the word. Whatever of it remained still unabsorbed in certain parts of the country was soon narrowed into the Pale, and kept there while, even in England itself, feudalism under the pressure of rising municipalities was losing its force and colour. The Elizabethans who came here after the Normans were not feudal nobles, nor aristocrats for that matter. Still less so were the Cromwellians. Each as known to us was an alien ascendancy, freed unfortunately from even what was left of the tradition of feudalism in England. It is from the domination now of one, then of another ascendancy, and not from feudalism or the aristocratic spirit, that Ireland suffered in the past. Furthermore, with the flight of the Earls at the beginning of the seventeenth century, with the Cromwellian harrying and dispossessions in the middle of it, and the going of the Wild Geese at the end, whatever of feudalism in any shape or form had become indued in Irish life was brought to an end. Not so the patriarchal spirit – a fact which is clear from such accounts as we have of many of the big houses of the eighteenth century. Patriarchalism, like feudalism, is not well dead; so for what reason our debunkers should try to excite animosity against Irish literature for any such reason is not very obvious; nor is it obvious why such misreadings of history as theirs should carry weight any longer. As to the incoming print. That would pull down nationality in general, whereas what we have been speaking of would debunk only Irish nationality. In England, as also in most European countries, nationalism is, one might say, peculiarly the consciousness of the rich. In Ireland for the last two and a half centuries, it has been the appanage – not of the rich, very unfortunately for themselves. It has, on the other hand, been the one and only means by which our own ordinary people have won up from slavery. Without knowledge of this simple fact, the history of modern Ireland is not credible. Communism abroad has much to go on when it would deflate nationalism. Those who preach it in Ireland must obviously find some other scapegoat. The Gaelic League, noting that Labour circles in our midst are beginning to understand that this fundamental difference is to be found between English and Irish nationalism, feels that another auxiliar is coming to its aid, for in coming on an understanding of this difference our Labour circles will no longer be tempted to follow English or other alien headlines.

ONLY THROUGH A NATIVE LANGUAGE

To finish: The Gaelic League builds on the Irish tradition. That tradition it would reinforce by restoring to it its mother-form – the language. Modern thought on the nature of nationality confirms its own thought that only through a native language can this country become possessed of a feeling for culture, for the things of the mind. To continue to use English, means clinging on to what is an unreality in our intellectual operations. The final result of the action of this unreality in our life will be that our nationality must become nothing more than a romantic memory, as in the case of Scotland and Wales. The example of other small countries makes us aware that a change of language is likely rather to improve than to injure our economic standing. Unity can be brought into Irish life only by the use of a language that is not the mouthpiece of any other nation.

\* \* \*

# Review: *Cré na Cille*
# Le Máirtín Ó Cadhain[1]

Na tuairimí atáthar a chur in iúl le níos mó ná bliain ní gá iad d'athrá. Glactar leis gur leabhar tábhactach *Cré na Cille*, gur scríbhneoir ó thalamh a údar.[2]

Is mian liom féachaint ar an leabhar ó dhearcadh fé leith. Is é an modh ina bhfuil an scéal curtha le chéile atá ag cur ceisteanna chugam go dteipeann orm iad a réiteach. A leithéid seo: Bhfuil dlúth-bhaint ag Réim an leabhair le tát an scéil? Sidé a réim do réir an údair féin: An Chré Dhubh. An Chré dhá Sreathnú. An Chré dhá Slámadh. An Chré dhá Meilt. An Chré dhá Cnáimhleasú – agus mar sin dóibh go dtí an chaibidil dheireannach – An Chré Gheal. Teidil iad san a dheineann ana-luí isteach ar an samhlaíocht. An bhfreagraíonn an scéal don luí-isteach san? Bhfuil sé leathan a dhóthain? doimhin a dhóthain? cumasach a dhóthain? Ba dheacair dó a bheith, mar is leor aon cheann amháin de na teidil sin d'úrscéal mór gan trácht ar chaibidil, ná ar eadarlúid, d'úrscéal. Agus tá deich gcinn do na teidil sin luaite ag an údar. Fágaimis an cheist sin gan réiteach. Má thógaimid na teidil sin le chéile chífear dúinn gur nod cheart dúinn iad ar an saghas aigne atá ag an scríbhneoir seo: tá sé i ngrá le focail díreach mar a bhíonn péintéir i ngrá le dathanna. Maith an comhartha san ar phéintéir, ar scríbhneoir. Ach aibiúlacht éigin do dhul ar an bpéintéir ní fada go dtagann an smaoineamh so dó agus é ag féachaint ar phictiúir ó láimh mháistir: 'Nach spárálach ar na dathanna atá sé!' Ní fada go mbíonn á rá aige leis féin: 'Cumasach! agus gan ach cúig cinn de dhathanna ann!'

Is cuma nó bean seoil an scríbhneoir a bhfuil leabhar á scríobhadh aige – is é Newman a dúirt. Muran mar sin atá ag Máirtín Ó Cadhain fós is mar sin a bheidh aige an túisce a dhéanfaidh sé iarracht ar last trom do thabhairt leis in árthach bheag. Ar ádhmharaí an tsaoil pé smacht agus pé scagadh a imreoidh sé ar fhriotal a phinn beidh an oiread san fágtha aige agus a dhéanfaidh cúis go cruinn agus go breá dhó. Is ar thréithe eile seachas brí agus dath gach abairte agus gach focail dá scríobhann sé ba cheart dó a aire a dhíriú feasta.

Ó leathanach a 81 go deireadh an leabhair tá dhá shaghas ceapadóireachta ar siúl aige. Caint na ndaoine ceann acu agus prós liteartha an ceann eile. Sé an tarna ceann atá i gceist agam. I dtosach na n-eadarlúd atá sé le fáil – leathanach nó leath-leathanach de. Ar shlí is iad na píosaí próis sin amháin a thagann chugainn glan ón údar féin. 'Sé féin a chum; níorbh iad an pobal. Ach b'é a leas é, im thuairimse, dá nglacadh sé cúnamh ón bpobal agus go fiú an phíosa is liteartha acusan á scríobhadh aige.

Féach an píosa so: (1. 142). 'Is seol dó an bruscar crannaí ar ar dhréim aislingeachaí an té údan a chuingrigh a charbad don réalt is gleoraí i mbuaic Nimhe, nó a bhain crobhaing den toradh is teiriúla sa duibheagán is doimhne.'[3]

Ní mór do dhuine é sin a léamh cúpla uair ar a laghad sar a bhfaigheann sé greim ar a rithim. Tá a lán píosaí den tsaghas san le fáil sa phrós litearta atá aige. Iontu san bíonn fuaimeanna ag treasnaíl a chéile, uaireanta chomh minic céanna leis na béimeanna. Agus nuair a bhíonn an rithim réitithe ag an léitheoir chomh maith agus is féidir dó é cad deireann sé i dtaobh a bhfuil aige as ucht an píosa a léamh? I gcéad do Hamlet, sé a deireann sé na 'Focail, focail, focail.'[4]

Samhlaítear dom ná fuil á dhéanamh ag an údar. sna píosaí sin ach iarracht ar chúlráid rómánsach Ghallda do cheapadh d'fhonn an saothar go léir do mhóradh agus do dhéanamh doimhin. Rómánsaíocht mar thaca le caint na Gaeltachta agus í againn ó láimh mháistir!

Ar an dtaobh eile dhe is deimhin nach gan dua a scríobh an t-údar na píosaí liteartha san, agus go bhfuil rud foghlamtha aige dá mbarr. Níl slí eile chun teacht isteach ar chúrsaí rithime ach amháin an abairt chéanna do mhúnlú arís agus arís eile go dtí go ritheann sí leí uaithi féin.

Ach i dtaobh an phíosa san a bheith gan substaint is é atá le rá ná gur greannmhar ar fad é an saghas friotail rómánsaigh sin a bheith ag imeacht as litríocht an Bhéarla agus ag teacht isteach i litríocht na Gaeilge – litríocht ina bhfuil a cineál féin rómánsaíochta, fé mar atá i ngach sean-litríocht eile.

Tá cúpla gné eile sna píosaí sin nach mór tagairt dóibh freisin. Ar leathanach a 82 tá timpeall le ceithre cinn déag d'abairtí i ndiaidh a chéile gur tosnú do gach abairt acu an focal Tá. Tá . . . Tá . . . Tá. Is fíor gur minic i scéalaíocht simplí a thagaimid ar shreath d'abairtí as a chéile gur tús dóibh an focal Bhí. Ach ní scéalaíocht atá ar siúl sna píosaí sin a deirim. Uaireanta ní hé an focal Tá a úsaideann sé mar sin ach Níl . . . Níl . . . b'fhéidir. Nó Is . . . Is . . . Nó Ná . . . Ná . . . Dá bhrí sin ní fhéadfadh an léitheoir gan an cleas do thabhairt fé ndeara. Nós a chleachtaíodh Macaulay uaireanta is ea é – agus do dheineadh na Francaigh gáire fé.[5] Sé atá de laige ar an nós san ná é a bheith meicniúil – agus ní holl-táirgeadh (mass production) is aidhm do scríbhneoir muran nuachtánaí é.

Ní leis an leabhar ar fad a bhaineann an méid sin ach le cuid bheag de – cuid nach ceart a bheith ann in aon chor, im thuairimse. Caint na ndaoine ar fad is meán ceapadóireachta aige lasmuigh de na píosaí sin – caint na ndaoine – ach ní gan chabhair ón scríbhneoir atá an chaint sin sa leabhar mar atá, agus ar an dtaobh eile dhe, ní gan chabhair ó na daoine, agus a lán di, a d'éirigh leis an údar an tuile sin d'agallamh iontach do choimeád ar siúl go ceann trí céad leathanach gan leamhas do theacht uirthi. An t-údar, an pobal – eatarthu araon a scaoileadar chugainn í – Dia dá bheannacha, Dia dá mbeannacha. Agus Máirtín Ó Cadhain á scaoileadh uaidh bhí traidisiún ní hamháin na Gaeltachta ach na teangan féin beo ina chroí, ina intinn agus sa pheann a dhein an pár a bheacadh dhó.

Féach anois, ní sa tuile cainte sin a thánamar ar shamplaí den droch-rithim, ná ar an easpa substainte sin, ná ar an slí mheicniúil sin. Tá caint an scéil saor ar fad óna leithéid sin de lagracha. Ó chuir an tAthair Peadar nua-phrós na Gaeilge ar shlí a leasa, á bhunú aige ar an dteangain labhartha,[6] bhíodar ann a dhein a ndícheall d'fhonn caint na ndaoine do thabhairt na beo leo. Sa Mumhain, i gConnachtaibh, i gCúige Uladh bhíodar ag gabháil dó. Ní déarfadh éinne ná gur éirigh leo. Ach mar sin féin is minic a ghéilleadh an bheocht don dílseacht agus an dílseacht don bheocht. Ní dímholadh ar éinne de na scríbhneoirí sin mé a rá go bhfuilid sáraithe ag an údar so.

Idir prós liteartha agus fíorchaint samhlaíotar dúinn gur fé anál úrscéalaíochta na Meiriceánach a scríobhadh an leabhar so. Na tréithe dhe atá lochtaithe againn, agus cinn nach iad, táid le fáil go tiubh sa litríocht thall. Údair acu, bíonn siad fé dhraíocht ag an liricíocht ar leathanach amháin agus fé dhraíocht ag clabaireacht na sráide ar an gcéad leathanach eile – Dos Passos cuir i gcás agus Thomas Wolfe. Táid tugtha d'eadarlúidí idir na caibidle, freisin, agus go minic don nuachtánachas. Sidé Dos Passos agus é ag cleachtadh nuachtánachais:–

> U.S.A. is the slice of a continent. U.S.A. is a group of holding companies, some aggregations of trade unions . . . . U.S.A. is the world's greatest rivervalley fringed with mountains and hills, U.S.A. is a set of big-mouthed officials . . . . U.S.A. is a lot of men buried in their uniforms in Arlington cemetery. U.S.A. is the letters . . . . But mostly U.S.A. is the speech of the people.[7]

Agus sidé é agus eadarlúid liriceach ar siúl aige: tugtar fé ndeara an saghas maoineachais is dual don rómánsaíocht Ghallda (murab ionann do rómánsaíocht na teangan céanna sna meán-aoiseanna): 'westbound to Havana Puerto-Mexico Galveston out of Santander (the glassy estuary the feeling of hills hemming the moist night an occasional star drips chilly out of the rainy sky a row of lights spills off the muffled shore) the twinscrews rumble . . . .'[8] (Gan dabht dob é James Joyce a mhúin dóibh a éifeachtúla a bhí sé gan na poncanna do chur isteach.) Ní mór dúinne, ámh, an abairt seo do thabhairt fé ndeara. 'But mostly U.S.A. is the speech of the people', mar is nod í chun an nua-litríocht do thuiscint. Tosaíonn litríocht Mheirice sa bhliain 1918. Ansan is ea do thuig na scríbhneoirí thall nárbh í *vernacular* Shasana a *vernacular* féin le fada an lá; thuigeadar gur mó na U.S.A. ná New York. Thuigeadar diaidh ar ndiaidh nárbh fhéidir litríocht Mheirice do chumadh i *vernacular* Shasana. Theastaigh uathu scarúint ghlan do bheith ann idir an nua-litríocht agus litríocht Shasana. Gabhadar chucu caint na ndaoine. Bhí acu go dtí go raibh gá acu le saghas eile próis seachas caint –

prós liteartha, prós fileata. Is léir dúinn cad a tharla. An túisce a chuireann siad an chaint i leataoibh titeann said isteach i bhfriotal na rómánsaíochta Gallda – 'the feeling of hills hemming the moist night.'

Sé an difríocht atá idir a gcássan agus ár gcásna féin ná traidisiún liteartha a bheith againn agus gan a bheith acusan ach traidisiún na teangan go raibh a *vernacular* féin tar éis scarúint léi.

D'fhéadfaí úsáid a dhéanamh de cháilíochta áirithe atá sa lítríocht nua thall – an méid di go mbeadh saol na coitiantachta mar bhun leis, abair. Ach más prós d'aon tsaghas atá a lorg againn ní í Meirice ná sa Bhéarla atá san le fáil. Déarfainn féin gur i gcaint na ndaoine atá sé le fáil againn – an chaint sin agus í saothraithe smachtaithe ag fílíocht gach aoise againn.

Focal anois uaim ar an scéal féin. An béaloideas a bhunús. Ach níl de bhunús leis an mbéaloideas féin ach amháin an tsamhlaíocht. Ní mór bunús eile seachas béaloideas chun cruinn-litríocht do chumadh.[9] Níl i mbéaloideas i gcomórtas leis an mianach eile ach góil (giost) do chíste. Ar an ngóil a bhíonn ár mbraith chun na hábhair eile a thabhairt chun beochta. Is fíor go raibh mianach eile, nó mianaigh eile, ag an údar so – a leithéid seo cuir i gcás: go dtéann éirí-in-airde i dtreise sa duine fé mar a bheireann an tseanaois greim ar cholainn air. I ndomhan an bhéaloideasa is cuma ciacu a bhíonn éirí-in-airde ar dhuine nó ná bíonn, nó aon locht eile. Ní thagann aithreachas air – beo nó marbh. Níl rian de le feiscint ar Chaitríona an scéil seo. Ní taise don chuid eile acu atá ann. Tuigtear dúinn ná fuil aon athrú tar éis teacht orthu, sé sin go raibh anam gach duine acu 'untroubled by a spark' riamh. Sé sin is é an béaloideas féin atá ag an údar so mar an t-aon bhunús amháin – níl sa chíste aige ach góil. Do chuir sé teora leis féin nuair a thaoibh sé roilig mar shuíomh dá scéal. Dá bhféadaimis – rud ná féadaimid – ár n-eolas féin ar mhuintir na Gaeltachta do chur ar ceal, d'fhéadfaimis suim do chur i muintir an scéil seo mar dhaoine a bhí ar aon dul leo san atá ann fós. Ach ní raibh na daoine seo beo riamh. Ní chreidimid go ndúradar riamh aon fhocal eile ach amháin iad san a tugadh dóibh le rá. Ar ádhmharaí an tsaoil tá píosa de theangain na Gaeltachta againn ná déanfar é a shárú go ceann i bhfad.

\* \* \*

# Review: 'Inquisitio 1584'
# Le Máire Mhac an tSaoi[1]

'Inquisitio 1584'

Sa mbliain sin d'aois ár dTiarna
Cúig céad déag ceithre fichid,
Nó blianta beaga ina dhiaidh sin,
Seán mac Éamoinn mhic Uiliuig,
Lámh le Sionainn do crochadh.

Tréas an choir, is a thailte
Do tugadh ar láimh strainséara,
Is anois fé bhun Chruach Mhárthan
Níl cuimhne féin ar a ainm,
Fiú cérbha díobh ní feasach ann.

Lámh le Sionainn na scuainte
I Luimnigh, cathair na staire,
Seán mac Éamoinn mhic Uiliuig,
Aniar ó pharóiste Mhárthan,
Ba thaoiseach ar Bhaile an Fhianaigh.

Nára corrach do shuan,
A Sheáin mac Éamoinn mhic Uiliuig
Ar bhruach na Sionainne móire,
Nuair shéideann gaoth ón bhfarraige
Aniar ód cheantar dhúchais.[2]

Is ar éigean atá dán dá bhfuil de dhánta i *Nuabhéarsaíocht** is minicí a thagann os comhair m'aigne ná 'Inquisitio 1584' ó pheann Mháire Mhac an tSaoi, agus níl uair dá dtagann ná go dtugaim taitneamh dó. Tá dánta eile sa leabhar luachmhar san a bhfuil níos mó sonnrachais ag roinnt leo, ach má tá féin ní thagaid thar n-ais chun na cuimhne chomh minic leis, chun mo chuimhne-se ach go háirithe, agus ní hí an fháilte chéanna a gheibhid ar a dteacht.

Cad fé ndear an síor-fhilleadh agus an taitneamh?

Na tréithe is cúis leis an síorfhilleadh agus an taitneamh, táid chomh soiléir sin sa dán gurb ar éigean is gá aon iniúchadh cruinn a dhéanamh orthu ach amháin iad a dheighilt óna chéile agus focal nó dhó a rá orthu ina dtréith agus ina dtréith.

Os cionn píosa ceoil is minic ná feicimid mar theideal ach 'Op. No. 2' nó a leithéid, agus os cionn lirice 'Soinéad' nó 'Amhrán'. Teipeann ar an gcumadóir, ar an bhfile, teacht ar theideal a chuirfeadh le brí a iarrachta, nó tuigtear dó nach gá teideal ar bith. Ní mar sin don dán so. Gan 'Inquisitio 1584' a bheith os a chionn ní thuigfimis é. Cuid cheart den dán isea é, agus cuid tábhachtach. Oibríonn sé ar shamhlaíocht an té a thuigeann é go díreach fé mar a dhéanfadh *prelude* do phíosa ceoil – dornán de chórdaí, abair. Cuireann a leithéid ár n-aigne in oiriúint chun glacadh le brí an ceoil; agus is minic a dhéanann *prelude* níos mó ná san. Is minic is ionann agus dúshlán é, isé sin is ionann agus caighdeán é: tugann sé slat tomhais don

* *Nuabhéarsaíocht*. Sáirséal agus Dill, Foilsitheoirí Gaeilge, Baile Atha Cliath. 7s. 6d.[3]

lucht éisteachta. Is mar sin don teideal 'Inquisitio 1584'. B'fhearr liom i nGaeilge é ná sa Laidin, ach ní fheicim go bhféadfaí teacht ar fhocal Gaeilge fé láthair a mbeadh baint aige le cúrsaí dlí agus cúrsaí staire agus le ré áirithe aimsire chomh maith. Ní hé sin amháin é, ach tá blas na croinice, blas na stáidiúlachta ar an bhfocal inquisitio féin. Idir seo agus siúd tá an teideal rícheart.

Tá dhá chuid sa dán – trí bhéarsaí agus ceangal. Tá na trí bhéarsaí ar dhul fé leith. Tá an ceangal ar an ndul gcéanna i bpáirt méadair agus ceoil agus urlabhra dhe; ach maidir le spiorad tá sé ar dhul is airde, is treise, is paisiúnta. Chífimid ar ball fé mar a théann an ceangal do na bhéarsaí sin. Agus ní trí sheans atá an difríocht idir an dá chuid ann; agus difríocht suaithinseach isea í. Chífimid é sin freisin.

Uaireanta déanann péintéir stánadh agus síor-stánadh ar an bpictiúir a bhíonn idir lámhaibh aige. Níl ag éirí leis; agus ní ró-chruinn a thuigeann sé cad í an léic atá ann. Ansan cuireann sé, abraimis, iarracht eile de dhath ar bhall airithe den bpictiúir – é eaglach go loitfidh sé é. Ach ní i gcónaí a loiteann. Uaireanta chíonn sé láithreach go bhfuil aige. 'Tá agam', adeireann sé go buachach. Ach cad é a bhíonn aige? Aon rud amháin, dar lena aigne, seachas cnuasach de rudaí arb ábhar pictiúra gach ceann acu, dar lena aigne.

Agus isé an t-aon iarracht amháin de dhath ar leith a oibríonn an mhíorúilt sin dó. Don bhfile a scríobh 'Inquisitio 1584' isé an ceangal a dhein an mhíorúilt. Do bhí aici! Isé sin do bhí aon rud amháin aici – agus é beo!

Is ionann aon rud amháin agus aontacht. Agus ní beocht go haontacht. Ach ní dhéanfaidh aontacht de shaghas ar bith cúis i gcónaí. Cuir i gcás an aontacht a shásódh an aigne ach ná sásódh an tsamhlaíocht.

Tá an dá shaghas san aontachta le fáil in 'Inquisitio 1584'. Tá saghas amháin acu sa gceangal – (ní miste an ainm sin a thabhairt ar an bhéarsa deireannach) – agus an saghas eile sa gcuid eile den dán.

Is beag ná go bhfuil dán cruinn againn sa 'gcuid eile' sin. Tá iomlán an scéil ann. Scéal bróin isea é, scéal uafáis. Ach d'imeodh an scéal san láithreach, uafás agus eile, ó aigne an té a léifeadh é. Léimid scéalta chomh lán donais leis ar na nuachtáin gach lá: ní fhágaid rian ar bith ar ár n-aigne. Ba chuma le léithneoir na dtrí bhéarsaí sin ciacu ar mhair Seán mac Éamoinn mhic Uiliuig riamh nó nár mhair; ba chuma leis muintir Bhaile an Fhianaigh do dhéanamh dearmaid de.

Ach féachaimis ar na trí bhéarsaí sin: Níl iontu ach léiriú an ábhair – cnámha an scéil; agus ní miste 'cnamha' a thabhairt ar a bhfaigimid iontu, táid chomh tirim chomh lom chomh cruaidh sin. Agus is gairid grod an tslí ina dtugtar dúinn iad:

> Tréas an choir, is a thailte
> Do tugadh ar láimh strainséara –

go grod, go gonta. Agus is beag ná go bhfuil insint féin an scéil gan trua gan taise. Tabhair fé ndeara go bhfuil dul an phróis ar na bhéarsaí sin. Má dhéanaimid 'do crochadh' a aistriú go tosach na ceathrú líne, píosa glan-phróis isea an chéad bhéarsa. Ach go deimhin féin ní miste píosa próis a tabhairt air sa chuma ina bhfuil sé. Ná ar an dá bhéarsa eile a leanann é. Agus cá bhfuil le fáil sna bhéarsaí sin na haidiachta bláthmhara dathmhara a gabhann le filíocht de ghnáth? Agus cad chuige go bhfuil samhailteacha suaithinseacha ar iarraidh ar fad? – an gléasadh san atá chomh beo leis an mbeocht féin nach mór. Ní hann dóibh. Ach ná tuigtear ná fuil cur amach ag an bhfile orthusan go léir. Gheibhimid i ndán eile léi sa leabhar céanna:

> Le coinnle na n-aingeal tá an spéir amuigh breactha,
> Tá fiacail an tseaca sa ghaoith ón gnoc –[4]

Agus b'fhéidir gur leor an dá líne sin chun a chur í dtuiscint dúinn nach gan fáth atá 'Inquisitio 1584' folamh óna leithéid. Ach féach freisin ná fuil fiú agus aon fhocal liteartha amháin sna trí bhéarsaí sin. Agus is ar éigean a airimid an ceol agus an méadar atá iontu ar a shimplí atáid araon.

Ach dá loime, dá fhuaire, dá phléineálta atá na trí bhéarsaí, idir mhianach agus stíl, gabhann a dtréithe go rí-dhlúth le chéile. Táid na tréithe sin, ar shlí, ar nós tréithe teachtaireachta, ar nós tréithe cáipéise, ar nós tréithe croinice. Tá blas na staire orthu go léir. Luíod ar phlána na staire – plána ná baineann spiorad leis. Agus de bhrí gur ar phlána airithe dhóibh tá saghas áirithe aontachta iontu. Ach ní hé an saghas é a dhúisíonn samhlaíocht an duine.

Is beag ná go bhfuil teideal an dáin curtha ar ceal ag na bhéarsaí sin mar, fé mar aduart, dúisíonn an teideal iarracht de chuimhne ina bhfuil meascadh d'uafás agus d'fheirg. Agus dá mba ná beadh sa dán ach na trí bhéarsaí sin do bheadh díomá dian orainn tar éis a léite. Ní shásódh an plána san na staire gona cháipéisí agus croinicí agus eile sinn. Ní ar a leithéid a chuir an teideal sinn ag lorg, bíodh go bhfeicimid gur nadúrtha cáipéisí agus croinicí a theacht i gceist le teideal dá short. I gan fhios dúinn tá plána eile á lorg againn.

Agus isteach linn ar an bplána san agus gan ach cúpla focal eile ráite ag an bhfile. Ní léir, ámh, an iad na focail féin a dhéanann an tsóinseáil nó teocht an ghutha atá á rá. Ní ar chúrsaí staire atá an guth ag labhairt ach le *duine*.

> Nára corrach do shuan,
> A Sheáin mac Éamoinn mhic Uiliuig –

agus na línte a leanann iad san, is beag má tá fiú agus líne orthu ach gur léamar cheana é sna bhéarsaí eile – ach cad é mar athrú atá tar éis teacht orthu! Déanann *rudaí* de *fhocail*, déanann *áiteanna* de *logainmneacha* – Márthan, Baile an Fhianaigh, Bruach na Sionainne. Agus as ucht na sóinseála san déanaid go léir dian-luí isteach ar an samhlaíocht. Is beag ná go dtugann an guth daonna san an teocht féin thar n-ais i mballa beatha an duine a crochadh i Luimnigh na céadta bliain ó shoin. Airimid, tá a *fhios* againn, go bhfulaingeodh sé pianta níba dhéine ná iad san a ghabh é le linn a chrochta dá ndúisíodh sé agus an ghaoth aniar a bheith ag séideadh!

Tá sé ag rith chugainn um an dtaca so nárbh ann in aon chor don chumhacht san go léir atá sa gceangal ach amháin stíl dá mhalairt a bheith sna bhéarsaí roimis – dul an phróis a bheith orthu, aidiachta ar ceal, insint an scéil chomh lom san. Ach sa gceangal féin, féach níl an gléasadh san le fáil ach an oiread. Níl, mar ní gá é. Déanann teocht an ghutha atá inár gcluais gach ní atá riachtanach. Ach bí deimhin de ná déanfadh ach amháin ullmhúchán ceart a bheith déanta cheana ina chomhair ag an bhfuaire agus an loime agus an easpa ornáideachais, agus fós ag an ndul san na croinice, atá sna bhéarsaí eile.

Níor chuir an péintéir úd aduart ach aon spota amháin de dhath ar leith ar a phictiúir, agus bhí aige. Agus fé mar aduart níor chuir an file ach an ceangal, spota de dhath paisiúnta, lena raibh scríte aici, agus bhí aici. Ach cad a dhein an ceangal leis na bhéarsaí eile sin? Do chuir sé beocht i ngach líne díobh siar go dtí an líne tosaigh. (Bhuel, ná táinig beocht i ngach cuid de phictiúir an phéintéara freisin). Féadfaí a rá más ea i dtaobh 'Inquisitio 1584' go bhfuil trí cheathrú dhe scríte ar phlána fé leith ach go bhfaighimid an dán go hiomlán a bheith scríte ar phlána eile. Ach ní rud nua é sin – go mór-mhór i bhfilíocht na Gaeilge. Ach is le ceardaíocht a bhaineann sé i gcónaí.

Ní fheicim go bhfuil baol ann go dtiocfaidh meath ar an liric seo go luath, ná dearmad, mar níl aon iarracht den 'nuachtánachas' ann, ná den bhréag-ghastacht, ach ina n-ionad san saghas simplíochta atá uasal. Agus tá tréith eile ann a sheasóidh dó – ábhar nádúrtha. Is léir ar an gceangal nach uaithi féin amháin a labhrann an file ach uainn-ne féin go léir chomh maith; agus táimid buíoch di. Agus isé nádúrthacht an ábhair freisin a thugann thar n-ais chun cuimhne gach duine againn Baile an Fhianaigh eile. Cúig bliana fichead ó shoin do bhaineas féin amach an teampall beag briste a thóg Seathrún Céitinn agus duine eile i dTiobraid. Ceaptar gurb ann nó comgharach dó a cuireadh é – tá leacht dó i gceann de na fallaí. Thugas fé ndeara gurbh ar éigean a bhí rian coise fé dhéin an leachta san. Os cionn uaighe Thaidhg Ghaelaigh i mBaile Uí Laithnín do tógadh leacht sa bhliain 1910.[5] B'é an Canónach de Paor nach maireann ba mhó a fuair dua a thógtha. Nuair a chuas féin agus triúr eile ann leathdhosaen de bhlianta ó shoin fuaireamar an reilig go léir múchta ag fiántas fáis. Fear óg ón mball – chabhraigh sé linn teacht ar an uaigh, ach níorbh é a aimsigh í.

Nuair a chuireann liric i gcuimhne do dhuine eachtraí beaga a bhain dó féin isé nádúracht an ábhair an chúis, fé mar atá ráite agam; agus a fhios san a bheith ag duine tá slat tomhais aige chun a leithéid d'ábhar a aithint; mar ábhair eile – iad san a bhainfeadh file as an aer, mar adúirt Goethe,[6] níl de neart iontu dul i dtreis le substaint daonna an tsaoil seo.

Ach seachas an t-ábhar do bhí fórsaí eile ag cabhrú leis an bhfile – a greim féin ar an gculráid – nó cúlráidí, b'fhéidir. Déarfainn go bhfeicimid trí cinn acu – an chúlráid liteartha agus an chúlráid staire agus an log-chúlráid.

*   *   *

# 1800–1919[1]

The Macpherson controversy[2] was contemporaneous with the Whiteboy resistance.[3] In 1760, he began publishing his Ossianic poetry. Those Fenian lays which he was challenged to produce, and which with good reason he kept to himself, were then, of course, being familiarly recited at hearthsides in every province of Ireland, except in their towns and cities. They were part of the tradition. Neither their reciters nor their listeners had ever heard of Macpherson or the controversy.

For all that, his concoctions, based as far as the phrasing went mostly on Milton and the Old Testament, were to have their effect, not on the living language of course. Their publication accounts perhaps for Miss Brooke's *Reliques of Irish Poetry*, originals and translations.[4] She had honesty as well as courage. And worse translations have been produced in our own days. Of Miss Brooke we read: '. . . her last days were passed in solitude and semi-poverty in Longford, where she died of a malignant fever on March 29th, 1793.'* It is as if she had become one with those members of the Courts of Poetry which then were just after closing their doors. Like her, those singers always became poorer as they got older. It was from the labouring people she had first heard this poetry.

Due to her, to Macpherson, and to the labours of such men as Charles O'Conor,[5] there came towards the close of the eighteenth century a stir in historical, more or less Celtic, studies. In 1792, Dr. James MacDonnell gathered the traditional harpers to a congress in Belfast:[6] it is significant that it was not in Dublin. Some years later 'a confidential party' at Lord Edward Fitzgerald's house in Dublin decided 'that the English language should be abolished, setting themselves to the study of the Irish tongue.'[7] Robert Emmet also eagerly studied it. It is pitiful to read of the reactions of such generous-minded young men when, breaking with their familiar surroundings, they found themselves among the people. They were as far from

---

* For Miss Brooke and similar Language Figures, see *The Sword of Light*: Desmond Ryan.[8]

full understanding as were those young men of the Pale who due to the troubles of the Reformation found themselves in native countrysides, as Fitzsimon did when to escape imprisonment, he fled to the O Tooles and the O Byrnes of Wicklow.[9]

In 1808, some friends of Miss Brooke's set up the Gaelic Society. It had some scholars in it, for instance Theophilus O'Flanagan, a scribe in the Irish tradition, from Clare.[10] It set out to publish specimens of Irish literature, historical documents, etc. Other such societies were to follow. They were, in a sense, part of the Romantic Revival. They never lacked a certain amount of scholarship. If, however, one applied Dr. McDowell's significant test:* did these scholars ever contemplate the use of the language as the vernacular of the whole country, education and all? – one cannot help thinking that the question would have staggered them. Those societies never took any stock of the millions of their own people who then were living out their days in the Irish language, and in no other. 'Look there, look there!' cried old King Lear, but then what he wanted above all to see was that what his arms held was still living.[11] Those societies however looked elsewhere, creating a callous tradition.

In 1787, a pamphlet by Richard Woodward, Protestant Dean of Cloyne, denied that the tithes bore harshly on the people; among other matters, he urged the Government to bring the language into entire disuse.† There ensued a storm of controversy, Protestants, Presbyterians, and Catholics taking part. On the language question, a Daniel Thomas answered that 'to destroy the vernacular tongue is an attempt to annihilate the nation' since language is the distinguishing mark between natives of different countries.[12] It may be that this coupling of vernacular and nation as a concept may have appeared before; we confess we have not noticed it. Here, anyway, it was put squarely to the country in 1787; yet in every controversy from that day to this, one will come on all sorts of romantic generalisations which leave quite out of the question at issue, both the nature of a people's language and the nature of a nation. Daniel Thomas, as we have seen, struck the nail on the head: No native vernacular, no nation. The concept throws a wry beam of light on the well-meaning activities of such societies as we have mentioned; and gives us some idea of the harm done by O'Connell when he declared 'he could witness without a sigh, the gradual disuse of Irish.'[13] In his time the language was practically nothing but a vernacular. It was alive in a peasant mind, and nowhere else. And it was these very peasants who most worshipped O'Connell. He was one to be listened to. They must have translated his phrase into: keep Irish from the children. Only too well they did so in the years to come.

* *Irish Public Opinion*, 1750–1800: R.B. McDowell.[14]
† For this controversy, see *Irish Public Opinion*, 1750–1800: R.B. McDowell. p. 124.

O'Connell had been at school under English priests in France, and at an unfortunate time. Then he became a lawyer – a disastrous type of mind, as Burke saw, if circumstances are to be looked at not as isolated phenomena, but as phenomena deep-based in far-off reverences.

Actually among the people, his words did less harm than they might: the question was not perhaps being then discussed among the vast mass of them, Irish was still the speech all around them. There was, however, one particular class who, to judge by their attitude ever since, must have treasured every syllable of O'Connell's utterances on such matters. They were such town Catholics – every city and large town were still being run by non-Catholics – as were, almost stealthily, climbing the social scale. They were not the descendants of those who might, or might not, have taken pattern by medieval English officials or English churchmen: for in Dublin or Waterford or Cork, one does not come on the old oligarchical patronymics any longer: those town Catholics now often bear historic Irish names. Irish by nature, they had nevertheless adopted towards all native characteristics such attitudes as those un-Irish medievals might have left behind them, entrenched in merchandise or office. Moreover, the professions were now open to them: and they assiduously caught up professional views and mannerisms. However come by those town Catholics can only be pictured as silencing every twinge of national conscience with such sentences as flowed so callously from O'Connell's lips. 'I am sufficiently utilitarian not to regret its abandonment' (the language). 'A diversity of tongues is no benefit.' 'It would be of vast advantage to mankind if all the inhabitants of the earth spoke the same language.'[15] Even to-day in such classes, one might easily come on individuals who reckon such Benthamitish speciosities as these the very distillation of human wisdom.*

And in O'Connell's time the National School – the primary education system – was set up. All down the eighteenth century, the law of the land had presumed that the Catholic Irish people did not exist: such a presumption simplified legislative problems. The new Board of National Education simplified their own special problem by presuming that the Irish language did not exist. As a matter of fact, there were probably more people speaking Irish in 1831, when this scheme appeared, *than ever before.* It is true, of course, that now very many of them also knew English in some way or another, though there were probably still a million who knew no English whatever. The havoc wrought by that system of primary education has often been told. Archbishop MacHale, mostly on religious grounds, also perhaps

*  In *O'Connell Calling*: J.J. O'Kelly (Sceilg) we find O'Connell defended on the charge of hostility towards the language, but O'Connell's attitude towards it is not explained. Professor Denis Gwynn's *Daniel O'Connell* says, 'he had deliberately discouraged the old language in the conviction that English was more useful.' That admits O'Connell's Benthamism. Both books appeared in 1947.[16]

on national grounds, refused to touch it.[17] A fanatic? Yet if his way prevailed in education generally, generation after generation of Irish people could not since have grown up in utter unawareness that such a thing as Irish literature had ever existed – generations unable to name even one of the greater poets who ever wrote in the country's language. Could national ignorance go lower than that? Or national degradation?

And Catholic colleges were at the same time being set up which for all practical purposes acted on the self-same presumption as the National Board, as it was usually called, so far as the language and the nationality concreted in it were concerned.

Fortunately it was not to happen that the Whig Catholic class nor the Protestant Tories who then 'owned' the country were to shape out the destinies of the nation. Clio[18] had settled that it was rather that homogeneous mass, Whiteboys, Defenders and all, who with all their faults swear by Bentham only in the petty chaffering of the market place, were to do so.* To a man they came behind O'Connell, while the Whig Catholics held querulously aloof. And certainly O'Connell at the end of all left that mass more capable of discipline and more conscious of their strength in the various movements that were later to arise in Irish history. Yet it is also significant that his memory has had no spiritual influence or inspiration for those later movements. After-generations almost force themselves to admire him. In this, he contrasts with Davis who was no Benthamite.[19] Perhaps Davis had the good fortune to die young: his legend endures. He saw at least something of the connection between a language and nationality if he did not see it with the sharpness of a Daniel Thomas. Unlike Thomas, Davis found nothing wrong in the concept that a nationality could exist in two languages. Nevertheless, as Pearse pointed out, he was 'the first of modern Irishmen to make explicit the truth that nationality is a spirituality' – a view that has had immense weight in the fight for the language.[20]

Both O'Connell's utilitarianism and Davis's idealism seem however hardly worth recording in face of the disastrous famine that followed their

---

\*    Modern Irish history is the record of the revival of the Gaelic peasant. Against
     enormous obstacles – obstacles of deliberate social, political and religious oppressions,
     of indifference, of sheer misunderstanding, of fashionable economic theory – after the
     most appalling sufferings which culminated in a famine that destroyed or exiled half
     of a nation, the Irish peasant emerges his own and his country's master.
       *The Scots Tragedy*: – Colin Walkinshaw (1935), p. 142. To-day in Ireland the sense
     of such a victory is eclipsed in the vulgar aping of indiscriminate foreignism. That
     image of Albany's in *King Lear* seems terribly apt if only for 'nature' we read 'nation,'
     not a wry change since a nation is a perfectly natural thing:
       That nature which contemns its origin
       Cannot be bordered certain in itself;
       She that herself will sliver and disbranch
       From her material sap, perforce must wither,
       And come to deadly use.[21]

period – the Black '47. That scourge fell mostly, almost entirely indeed, on the four millions of Irish speakers. It was not the million deaths so much as the continuing emigration of living millions of others during the next half-century which broke the spirit of the people. In 1847, the population was the highest ever – and the countryside in spite of the rackrents, was alive with dancing, with singing and humble fiddling. After '47, what struck the visitor was the unbroken silence. That silence overtook the language.

Sir Henry Sidney's deliberate policy in the sixteenth century was to dissipate the big houses on which the language depended for cultural sustenance.[22] Worked out assiduously by his successors, the scheme succeeded. And now those colonists who had been given the lands of the big houses, by their want of consideration for the country that should have become their own, through famine dissipated the people in whose possession the language still was. There is the whole story in two simply chapters.

A sort of belated pseudo-Whiggery now possessed the towns and cities.[23] A generation, Catholic as well as Protestant, were growing up who did not know, as we have said, that Ireland had ever possessed a poet until Thomas Moore struck his lyre – in England.[24] And to such generations of Anglicised natives as these, it seemed that all the destinies of the ancient people were to be henceforth committed – that is, to generations dispossessed of even a memory of the twofold nature of that tradition which all along had strengthened the nation in reverence for the past – the literary tradition that was so much at one with the religious.

If it be urged that we have stressed this one point too frequently and too much, we answer: in what century? We have designedly kept before our mind those words of Professor Quiggin's:

> Up to the present (1911), works in Irish history professing to deal with the centuries under consideration contain little but a chronicle of the affairs of the English Pale. It may be expected that within a few years the great bulk of bardic verse will have been edited and translated.[25]

He adds that until then, no dispassionate history of Ireland from the Norman invasion to the Reformation can be written. That brings us to the middle of the sixteenth century. When Professor Myles Dillon, writing almost forty years later, tells us that the professional poets from the thirteenth to the seventeenth century were perhaps the most powerful secular influence in Irish society, he strengthens what Quiggin had said; and brings us to the seventeenth century.[26] Now what has been before our own mind is not so much the translatable points of information of historical importance that such literature contains as the structuring influence that this great mass of refined yet passionate verse itself had necessarily been having on the mind of the community century after century. Since there are little or no such translatable points to be come upon in a people's sculpture or architecture, is it to be maintained that a people's sculpture or architecture or music can tell us nothing of its creators' more real selves? – can not such arts, for instance, being interpreted, mitigate, if not contradict, the alien state-papers if native state-papers do not exist? Points of information have their importance no matter where come upon, but to take it that nothing else pertinent to our theme is to be come upon in an immense and various corpus of art is simply unthinkable. In our case native state-papers of the usual type do not exist: it remains, therefore, for us to build up a historical acumen that can take toll of quite other material to feel our way into the deeper past.

Our authorities then have vouched for the importance of the tradition down to the seventeenth century: if the poets were then the most important secular influence in the country, that tradition must have told on all levels of life. That tradition itself took a new way, as we have seen, when the bardic schools were shut: the common people took hold of it and made it their own. That achievement of itself is for us the most distinctively important fact in the whole story of the eighteenth century: one wonders if any state-paper urges it as such. It is also of vast importance in throwing light on the preceding centuries, for it could not have happened if they had not been what they actually were.

But in the nineteenth century only sparse fragments of that tradition survived the Famine; for the diaspora that resulted, as we have said, left Ireland a dumb soul that was no longer a distinctive creative being.

And yet the end was not come. It took some time, however, to discover how the few remaining sparks in the ashes might be brought together to light us to whatever of the tradition remained, unknowing itself, unknown of others, in hidden places, in unsifted manuscripts and in 'illiterate' peasants.

During and after the Famine a few solitary scholars were working on Irish texts in Dublin; and a few academic language societies were occasionally meeting. The Ossianic society[27] procured the services of O'Curry,[28] O'Donovan[29] and Standish Hayes O'Grady[30] – all men of character.* In 1876 was started the Society for the Preservation of the Irish Language – preservation is a terrifying word. And in 1879 the Gaelic Union started the *Gaelic Journal*, which lived on for many years. All praiseworthy, still more praiseworthy those unselfish workers, if only they had set themselves to discover where the living sparks really lay.

These societies and others more or less similar were hardly known to the ordinary citizens of Cork or Dublin, and still less to the speakers of the language in Donegal, or Connacht, or Kerry.

---

\* O'Curry especially – himself a living confirmation of so much of what we have been urging, the scholarliness that was intrinsic in the tradition itself.

Their organisers had heard of Philip Barron, but from him they had taken but little inspiration, not without some reason, for he had not been a success.[31] He was of an old Waterford stock, a speaker of Irish, a man of means. 'It was while he was at school that Barron had found that it was considered disgraceful in polite society to be ignorant of the history of any other nation, except one (Ireland).'* He had several useful ideas: the need for printed matter in Irish, for its use in the schools, for higher education in it. He built a small Irish college in which 'the ancient Gothic order had been adopted,' but he built it, Gothic and all, in an Irish-speaking district.[32] He spent his money on that and other schemes, not all so wise; and succeeded in interesting certain rich people in them. He was obviously a headlong enthusiast, and suddenly silence falls on himself and his schemes. Now, all this was as far back as 1835 – a dozen years before the Famine. The thing of importance is that Barron was conscious of the language as a living thing – to be fostered where it was and given a chance of growth. He was wise in that. Only one man in the country seems to have been wiser, and that was O'Donovan Rossa, the Fenian, who very courageously put his name in Irish over his shop in Bantry that he might induce his customers to use Irish in their business with him.[33]

Now this Fenian movement on which we have come, struck fire deep in the hearts of the people, though why it should do so is not very clear. Its leaders were arrested, were given long-term and even life sentences, but none was executed; their plans never came off – except in minor incidents. Perhaps the explanation of its appeal was that there was no ambiguity about its aim. It was separation. Fenianism was also fortunate in its name. An Irish scholar living in America, John O'Mahony, a revered member of the body, chose it.[34] It opened the whole book of living Irish literature to speakers of the language everywhere, for the heroic literature telling of Fionn and his companions was, as we have said, popular at Irish-speaking firesides, those firesides from which most of the Irish in America had gone there. It was this Fenian movement which brought the Famine Irish in America into politics – a significant event. It should be noted that its name meant nothing to the citizens of Dublin or Cork.

Though squelched, the movement never died. Yet, when its leaders gibed at newer movements as simply agrarian, they went very nearly quite astray. They were forgetting that it was the confiscation of Irish land which had led to all the manifold downfall of the previous three centuries. The people here, as often, led the leaders. It was the leaders, often town-bred, who gibed. The landsmen, farmers, labourers, and their relatives in the cities and towns, did not. The Land League against which the Fenians were gibing, must surely

---

* For a full account of this remarkable man, see *The Sword of Light*: Desmond Ryan, from which book we quote.[35]

have conducted its campaign in quite a different spirit, if those same Fenians had not stirred the country before it arose. Michael Davitt, who actually set up the Land League, was himself a Fenian on ticket-of-leave after seven years of imprisonment. He was the son of Irish-speakers, and himself an Irish-speaker. Ultimately that land movement, having in time abolished the alien landlord system, may yet, by restoring the Irish language to the Irish landscape, spiritualise such gains as Ireland has won, giving them human significance in the deepest sense of the word. In its actual working, however, the Land League injured the language, for it conducted its propaganda and all its business in English, bringing torrents of House of Commons oratory even into the heart of the Gaeltacht. (The very first meeting of the Land League was held in the Gaeltacht.)[36] At the same time it reconstituted the mass-homogeneity which was being disintegrated by Whiggism, unifying the community into a compact fighting force.

Not long after the start of the Land League, the Gaelic Athletic Association, which might easily have turned out a sports' association and nothing else, was set up. Fortunately its inspirer was Archbishop Croke, who saw that Irish nationality, in discarding its native games, was losing one of its vital modes.[37] He was as native-minded as MacHale, and equally attached to the language. From the beginning, the G.A.A. had known that its part was to restore certain beams of Irish nationality which had been eclipsed in ages of outlawry and famine. The extraordinary growth of this once humble enough association is really a measure of the vitality, engendered of the ages, that lies inert in, and accounts for, the still unbroken homogeneity of the common people. As the Association becomes richer and richer in these our days, it significantly becomes more aware of its affinity with the language movement. In spirit as in achievement it is not only unique but astonishing.

The Fenians, the Land League, the G.A.A. were all racy of the soil,[38] sprung from the proletariat and powerfully affecting it, that proletariat itself so different in mind from city-conditioned proletariats elsewhere. The last thing those foreign proletariats would picture themselves as is the residuary legatees of the nationhood of their own countries. It would not be true, at most only very partially true, if they did; though they might with every right protest that the middle upper classes in these same countries were being overweening when they claimed that position for themselves.

The word proletariat really means the men of no property – a phrase familiar enough. It means all those who must find some other way of assisting the State than by their wealth. From our men of no property have arisen in quite a short space of time, and almost sheer from the soil, what is now the very body-politic of Ireland – to wit our hierarchy, priesthood, parliament, professors, doctors, lawyers, civil servants, merchants, manu-facturers, not to say workers. In no country is the body-politic absolutely homogeneous, all of one grain. So too with us. But even when the Six-County parliament is no more,[39] our general description of our body-politic may be allowed to stand as correct enough for large considerations. It is that body-politic which will decide willy-nilly whether the future Ireland is yet to become what Switzerland has recently been, wrongly let us hope, described as, merely a going concern – a contrivance that works smoothly and is possessed of much technical skill – it has produced an excellent copy of the Book of Kells and could doubtless produce also an equally excellent copy of the Ardagh Chalice.

If our community make such a choice, then Ireland will be no more than an enlarged replica of any of its medieval towns – a trading station and no more. They, it will be remembered, failed ever to produce a single distinctive work of art, so far as anyone knows. How could they when they had no roots? What a strange consummation, what an anomaly – an Ireland without roots!

Fenianism, the Land League, the G.A.A. were all conscious of the importance of the past. Such names as John O'Mahony, Rossa, Croke, Davitt, all Irish-speakers, assert it.

If only in that dreadful nineteenth century, our educational system from top to bottom had been like-minded with them, how different an Ireland would now be in existence! And if at present we are all conscious of this, it is really the movement that was to follow those others we have been praising must be thanked for it. That movement was, of course, the Gaelic League.

As those preceding movements were influenced, each by what went before, so with the Gaelic League. Since its traffic from the start was directly with the language, not as an 'old antiquity,' but as a living thing, it saw the situation almost at once: those movements were trying to restore the national being, but at the same time our educational schemes were succeeding in gradually eliminating it. That system from top to bottom was still de-Irelandising Ireland.

The Gaelic League was founded, as everyone knows, by Dr. Douglas Hyde, Eoin MacNeill, Fr. Williams, S.J., and a few others in 1893. From his boyhood, Dr. Hyde, though a Protestant, had been going about with the Irish-speaking Catholic peasantry in the Roscommon countryside. They almost adopted him. He became a collector of their folk-lore,[40] their songs, a scholar, a professor, and in his very old age, President of the new State.* His mind was essentially creative. He was tactful and full of humour. Eoin MacNeill, the other most outstanding founder of the Gaelic League, was the son of Irish-speaking farming stock in Antrim, one of the Six Counties. He

---

* He was President of the Gaelic League for twenty-two years. The President of the Irish Republic at present, Seán T. Ó Ceallaigh, was Secretary of the Gaelic League for some years.

became a very famous professor of Irish history, Minister of Education in the new State – it was he who founded the Irish Volunteers – later known as the Irish Republican Army (I.R.A.). His mind was keen, almost sardonic.

The Gaelic League took some time to establish itself; it grew slowly until Mr. D.P. Moran, a journalist who had worked in London, started and edited a weekly paper called *The Leader* which, certainly in no very dainty fashion, did succeed in getting the younger generation to understand that flag-waving, House of Commons oratory, 'greenary' in general, harps, shamrocks, blackthorns, fairies and Celtic Twilight had nothing to do with Irish nationhood, whereas the language had everything.[41] Then the Gaelic League began to sweep the country. And yet, in any one place, it was difficult to be come upon. A branch of the Gaelic League meant primarily a class or a few classes in which the language was being taught – the teacher, hardly ever paid, in most cases was himself a student of the language, and often not much ahead, in knowledge of the language, of those he taught. Young men and women who had already put in their day's work, were the students, as we may note when we find a Frenchman writing thus of what might be seen almost anywhere in, say, 1906:

> But the stranger is most forcibly struck when he attends some Irish class in a poor quarter in Dublin, or even of London, and perceives how serious, deep and infectious is the enthusiasm of the crowds, young and old, clerks and artisans for the most part, with an 'intellectual' here and there – who are gathered together in an ill-lit hall. To these, there is no doubt that the thought of learning a language, and above all, of learning a language other than English, would never have occurred at other times, but now, after their day's work, they sit with an O'Growney in their hands, with shining eyes, and strained looks, greedily listening to the lesson, following with their lips, *con amore*, the soft speech of their teacher. Evidently here are people who have been transformed to the core of their being by this somewhat severe study, and by the importance of the role which they wish to play and which in fact they do play.*

'Transformed' – it is the right word. If at present the world knows of an Irish Republic, it is due, primarily, to those young men and women who sat week after week in those years in ill-lit halls – or sheds – with an O'Growney in their hands. Yet to look upon such classes, that reflection is the very last that would then cross one's mind, though it is a fact that Pearse

---

* *Contemporary Ireland*: L. Paul-Dubois (1908), p. 410. The text book used in such classes was *Simple Lessons in Irish*, by Father O'Growney, an earnest worker in the movement who died young.[42]

some years after 1906, perhaps seven or eight, used these words: 'A new junction has been made with the past: into the movement that has never wholly died since '67, have come the young men of the Gaelic League .... I have said again and again that when the Gaelic League was founded in 1893, the Irish Revolution began.'*[43]

In a pamphlet *From a Hermitage* (1915) Pearse reckons up with chances for rebellion. From the last page here are a few lines:

> In the third place the young men of Ireland have been to school to the Gaelic League. Therein it seems to me lies the fact which chiefly distinguishes this generation from the other revolutionary generations of the last century and a half .... We have known the Gaelic League and 'Lo, a clearness of vision has followed, lo, a purification of sight.' Our country wears to us a new aspect, and yet she is her most ancient self.[44]

In scores of books written during the last twenty-five years, confirmation of Pearse's opinion can be come upon. In the light of the fact that the Gaelic League, or shall we say its idea, has provided the nation with a sovereign state, its other achievements are not worth mention – its founding of a national literature in Irish, its forcing of the language into schools, colleges, and the National University, its vast publication scheme carried out without assistance from any government. These and kindred achievements are trifles if weighed against the setting-up of a sovereign state, for surely it has been noticed that languages die only when their fostering state is broken. As a matter of fact, languages do not die natural deaths at all: they are killed by violence, usually, if not always, by imperial violence.

For the first time since 1169, the Irish language has a state behind it. To say this is equivalent to saying that everything has changed for it, just as everything has changed for the languages of India, Pakistan, Palestine[45] – and indeed for the whole world.

---

\* Yet as far back as 1887, words even more pregnant perhaps with insight were written about the ancient language and those who serve it, written, curiously enough, by one whose grandfather was a Captain of Yeomanry at New Ross in 1798 – Lionel Johnson: –
   The speech that wakes the soul in withered faces,
   And wakes remembrance of great things gone by.
The lines explain everything that has happened since 1893.[46]

PART TWO

Representing Ireland

# Mr. Yeats in Cork[1]

It was rather piteous that Mr. Yeats should have as his audience here last Thursday night the members of the Literary and Scientific Society.[2] I am sure he would have spoken more warmly, more vividly, if he had an audience of younger people – younger, of our own time, and hence more likely to be interested in the things dear to the lecturer's heart. I was sorry that it was not to the Gaelic League he was talking – not that the Gaelic League might be edified, but that the speaker might have felt more at home. Mr. Yeats is very hard on the 'printed book'; the 'spoken word' alone is capable of mixing up literature and life. Well, Mr. Yeats talking to the Literary and Scientific Society was dealing with 'printed books'; talking to the Gaelic League, young, enthusiastic, agog for ideas, he would have found himself breathing the electric, nervous atmosphere of the 'spoken word'. Such, at any rate, has been the experience of other lecturers.

Mr. Yeats himself must have felt this during his lecture. If he did not, he came, without doubt, to know the fact at its close, when one of the leading members of the society stood up and asked the lecturer how he intended to bring his ideals of a National Theatre about. Now, imagine that! There is a society in Cork founded on the same principles as the National Theatre in Dublin;[3] it has produced some of the plays connected with the Dublin society; it has two plays written by Mr. Yeats himself. I can guarantee that the number of the members of the Literary and Scientific Society that was present at these performances was a most insignificant number; I am informed that it might reckon up to a half-dozen, but personally I would not put it so high. And I am just as sure that the coming Christmastide performances of the society will receive from these 'intellectuals' the self-same support. In Russia, at the present day, the 'intellectuals' are credited by many with having a good deal to do with the revolution; there is no fear that our local 'intellectuals' here will ever come to handling dynamite; no, not even the dynamite of *living* ideas.

There is no necessity to follow the lecture. We all now pretty well know the ideas of the National Theatre (too big a name, we are afraid, for the Abbey Street Theatre, but handy as a label). Mr. Yeats told the story of the rise of the Norwegian Theatre,[4] incidentally referring to the struggle it had with the 'intellectuals', the cosmopolitans, native to the soil. He referred to the spirit that was at that time capturing the mind of man, the spirit of realism – itself an outcome of the rapid progress of physical science. Now, realism was shrinking, and taking its place was the spirit of religion, spirituality, in a word. Literature was again looking into the mind of man, into his heart and dreams, instead of peering at his actions and revolving their motives. Ireland being an essentially religious country was likely to fall in with this movement of the mind of Europe in such a way as few other countries could. Evidently Mr. Yeats is not at one with those thinkers who believe that Ireland is bound to go through an experience of scepticism for the same reasons as drove most other European countries through the ordeal. He went on to explain how every art-movement is a 'going back' at the beginning; we would prefer to say that these art-movements to which he referred were struggles to get on to rails which had been left in more or less vicious moments. And then he said some nice things about folk-literature and folk-art – very nice things, but to our mind things that must, alas! be said with a sigh, always with a sigh, and never with a hope. Of course, he spoke of the art of the dramatist as he conceived it. There was much talk of being true to the internal rather than to the accidentals of the external – most of which tallied with our own beliefs, but there is not much use in discussing it – this kind of talk meaning so many various things in various mouths.

He concluded by asking for questions from those who didn't understand, with the result we have stated. Yes, but a young man not, we should say, a member of the society, then got up, and rather severely and justly, we think, criticised Mr. Yeats's crowd for identifying themselves with some plays of Mr. Synge.[5] His objection was – that these plays were not Irish plays inasmuch as they misrepresented the Irish peasant. Now, in answering, we think Mr. Yeats juggled, and fell into literary heresy. He gave a brief account of the plot of Mr. Synge's play, *The Well of the Saints* – two blind peasants, married, are persuaded by the neighbours of their mutual good-looks; a saint coming their way restores their sight; they behold the mutual ugliness; quarrelling ever more as a result until, as a punishment, they are again struck blind. Think, said Mr. Yeats, commenting on the play, of the splendid dream these peasants had while blind – the splendid dream of each other's beauty, the splendid dream of life. Think, say we, answering, of the very sensual dream of life they must have had, if their dream was a matter of bodily beauty. Were not the minds of the two peasants known to each other by all the senses except one? – they spoke to each other day after day, they touched and kissed and yet they knew each other so ill that the appearance of their countenances, not being regular, turned love to hate. Our idea is that the dramatist stayed his hand before he had got to his drama at all. The drama would be in showing the triumph of mind over matter. Give the peasants their sight; grant the shock; then let God do His work; let the past years, with their loves and their trials, let these speak as undoubtedly they would; let the mere physical world fade before the memory of the love of the darkened years, and the knowledge that, in spite of the physical, such things could again be, until the peasants welcomed blindness once more lest the bodily infirmities should ever, as in the first shock, overthrow their love again. Here was a drama! – how did the man stay his hand?

Excusing this play, Mr. Yeats said that the peasants were not typical peasants – that there was no necessity why a dramatist should select typical peasants. We think this heresy. Now, there are average peasants and typical peasants. Mr. McManus gives us the average peasant;[6] Mr. Colum gives us the typical peasant.[7] The shallow writer of short stories gives us the mind of the average peasant, the mind that speaks in the barber's shop, and in the current language of the day; the poet, because of his imagination, gives you the mind that sits silent in the barber's shop (though the man may speak), and that will but seldom talk in the language of the hour, his characteristic quality, rusticity, having seldom occasion to speak at all. His rusticity is from age to age, seldom changing. We accordingly believe that the poet does write down the typical peasant. To take it as a guide that it is not necessary to do so, what is it but to change Shakespeare's saying – 'Hold the mirror up to nature,'[8] into 'Hold the mirror, not up to nature, but up to nature's freaks!' This, we believe, is what Mr. Synge has done.

* * *

# The Peasant in Literature[1]

Much of the literature produced in Ireland of late years has been about the peasant. Some of it is in the Irish language; most in the English. The language side of the question is not what I wish to consider here.

No, this surely is a good sign, for we are in the main a nation of peasants. I knew a provincial paper of ours which once a year produced a 'literary' number; that number used to be written by the staff – well, it was very little of the peasant you would find in these special numbers, for the editor, sub-editor, and reporters on that provincial paper never looked at all at life as it went on around them. But this, all this, was in the olden time long ago. The paper has since grown so immensely important that it now buys its literary numbers at so much per yard – a half-crown, I think.

In our colder moments what do we think of all that peasant literature we have been producing these late years? How much of it do we keep by us, knowing that we shall return to it?

Very little, surely. But, then, a nation's body of literature is of slow growth; and, if our years have certainly added a few enduring pieces of work to our national treasure-trove, as I think they have, we ought to be satisfied. *Riders to the Sea* is surely the outstanding piece of work so added; but there are certain poems by Padraic Colum, notably 'The Drover,'[2] and certain short stories in Irish by Padraic Ó Conaire[3] that none of us would wish to see blotted away. And, of course, there are others – other plays, other poems, other stories – which in point of value come only a little short of those named. So that it may be taken that we have been doing something. Unlike the staff of that provincial paper I have mentioned, we have at least begun to look at life as it goes on about us.

It is surely true that many people have been writing about the peasants who haven't it in them to create literature. They have often met with a nine days' success; but this is explained by the fact that peasant literature was for a short time quite in fashion. These people knew the peasant; they had lived with him; they could report him truly – no, they could report him literally. Such writers were often Irish speakers, and their tales were often written in Irish. Their stories are very real in the non-essentials and very untrue in the essentials. Even so, they were valuable; every scrap written about the country folk by those who had lived with them was valuable to some degree. But a great amount has also been written by those to whom the peasant was a sealed book. Such writers, of course, went to books instead of to the fields. They probably succeeded in catching most of the meagre pennies that were to be had for this kind of literature. Their work had no value whatever.

To write literature about peasants must be always difficult. Put yourself in imagination in a farmyard or in the kitchen of a farm house, or in a potato garden; note the sameness of mood in the onflow of the life around you; measure the bourns of the farmer's, the labourer's, mental horizons; remark how stripped of pageantry are the few ceremonies that break in upon the daily toil – to do all this is to reckon up the difficulty of putting the little human colony of an Irish hillside into literature. Surely whoever would undertake to do so must have the fairy gift, must have genius. That, in Victor Hugo's phrase, is a promontory into the unknown;[4] and certainly it is not of the *known*, the mere essentials, whether of speech or business, native to these meagre surroundings that the web of beauty is to be woven. One may lack the gift of vision and yet achieve something stirring or picturesque or pleasing if one seeks a subject elsewhere – among adventurers or kings or warriors; but within the narrow and plain-coloured walls of the farm-house if, by aid of that rare gift of vision, one be not prepared to go out along that promontory into the unknown, discovering light and faiths and charities where all seems so drab and sordid and hard – if one be not capable of this his labour is vain. And it is so rare – the gift of insight, of seeing into the life of things!

Yet if one has it, the ground we are thinking of – Irish peasant ground especially – ought to yield rich harvests. If it is not virgin soil, neither has it by any reckoning been exhausted. In the essentials it may be more fruitful than pampered pleasances: the peasants' faith in unchartered worlds being so much more intense than the unrealised half-beliefs of the merely bookish. The peasant, equally with everyone else, stands at the conflux of two eternities; but who else realises it as he does? But the gift of insight is necessary to see this other worldliness colouring his every thought whether he rises up or lies down or goes about his fields. The very writers who are up in arms if poet or dramatist make a peasant mean or murderous or cowardly are often those who paint the peasant as if his beliefs were as superficial as those of the characters in magazine stories.

It will be found that whatever of value in literature of this genre we have been given of late years has been the work of men of vision. 'Impassioned contemplation' was Pater's phrase with regard to Wordsworth's genius[5] – impassioned contemplation! – there's the magic word.

\* \* \*

# Review: *The Tent and Other Stories* by Liam O'Flaherty[1]

The poet sang

> Deeper their voice grows, and nobler their bearing,
> Whose youth in the fires of anguish hath died – [2]

and we agree with him. But even long after youth is over, those self-same fires may rekindle themselves: like temptation, they cease only when the heart ceases. And always, in age as in youth, one emerges from their chastening ordeal with some deepened tone in the voice and some added stateliness in the pose. We have recovered a sense of values tenderer than those that use and wont had taught us unconsciously to live by. In our quickened sensibility we shrink from flashiness, from loudness, from the barbaric joy of giving pain. We have put off the Old Man.

Can it be possible that in the nation it is all different? That when the nation has had its spiritual conflict, brother thinking it right to shed the blood of brother, father that of son, son that of father – the nation, when the crisis is over, emerges cross-quartered, piebald, half-swaggering, half-dancing, loud-voiced, wanton, yet, strangest effect of all, full of the muck-rake wisdom of the world! Strange phantom! Its cry is that there must be no more nonsense, no more inhibitions – except perhaps courage, steadfastness, charitableness and gentility.

During the seven years from 1916 to 1923 the Irish nation went through a spiritual crisis so intense that only quite a small number of its individuals was not called upon to share in it. The intensity was to be measured not so much by the sacrifices made as by the spirit in which they were made. The death-words of boys, as well as the testimonies of brave enemies who saw them die, are on record. But who that lived through those years needs to be reminded of that spiritual crisis, its intensity, its high-mindedness? It was such a crisis as in an individual could not do otherwise than induce that nobler bearing and that richer voice which the wise poet noted and set down. Yet in the nation has been induced only that strange fantastic cross-quartered, piebald, worldly-wise-man attitude we have spoken of before. And one repeats the query: why should the nation differ so much from the individual? the people from the person?

If one should doubt that this is true portraiture of the national being as the fires and buffetings of revolution have fashioned it, we can but say, take up and read. Take up the novels, the plays, the polemical writings, the reminiscences that have been written in Ireland within the last three or four years when one, at last, got a chance of writing the real truth of things, and then say if the portraiture is true or false, is against the burden of these books or in agreement with it. These novels have been sent all over the world, the plays have been staged in alien capitals, the polemical writings reviewed and commended as the last word in frankness, in depth of feeling, in heroic truthfulness. These are the famous books. Other books may have been written, published, and thrust aside, or may have been written and never published at all, not being according to market-place requirements; but who is courageous enough to suggest that these shy and hesitating voices may be the true voice, the true record, of the new Ireland that has indeed emerged from all the pother? Why, to suggest as much is to declare that Ireland, the nation, is not sure of itself, looks about timidly, asks itself what is real, what is unreal, and is unable to lift its voice above the timid song of the tit-lark. Can this be true? Furthermore, to suggest as much, is to suggest that all those loud-voiced books that have gone screaming through the world are spurious, are notorious, have in them neither the depth of art nor the courage of art, nor the truth of art. To hold such views is indeed to be heterodox, for – a phenomenon not often witnessed – those screaming books we are thinking of have been crowned not only by the highest-browed critics in the country but by the editors of metropolitan and provincial newspapers, and magistrates have quoted them from the bench!

Mr. Liam O'Flaherty has written such books. They have been ridiculously over-praised, like all the other literary or quasi-literary work in which the voice of the newspaper was given an utterance a wee bit finer. Do we need anything so badly as a few upright critics who will have some sense of responsibility? Such critics as we have, have they no standards? Do they really think that the crude is good art? Or that Mr. Liam O'Flaherty's efforts at curdling the blood, as in *The Informer*,[3] are anything else than the cheapest form of melodrama?

His present book, *The Tent*, has stories in it that hitch on to *The Informer*, that from which the book takes its name, for instance, or 'Civil War,' or 'The Terrorist,' or 'The Sensualist,' and one or two others. They are really the weakest things in the book. When they do not in their crude accumulating of shock shell make us smile they simply leave us cold. If the mind returns to them at all, it is simply to think how easily they might be bettered. But these after all are only a small part of the book. His studies in animal life are always interesting, and the objectively-written end of 'The Wounded Cormorant' is one of the few pages which really infect the mind with its own feeling. There are then his stories of priests and their ways – perhaps the crudest of all. An artist must respond to his material; and wilfully to see only the externals of the Irish priest is simply misdirection of energy. Only in one story, the simplest of all, do we experience the reverberations that arise in the spirit when life, the inner, is reached. It is the story 'Mother and Son.' A mother is in great anxiety, her wildish son not having returned from school at anything like the usual time. At last he does come, and the mother instead of thrashing him, as she had intended, simply cuddles him, and thrusts the task of punishing him on to the father, who is not at home. That intention the boy dissolves in his mother by telling her of a big black horse that he has seen in the sky. We feel that the mother and son are indeed flesh of the same flesh; and we feel the little soul groping for a way in life, his mother's way – all softness, and his father's way, his father who has told him that he must never be afraid. The little story is tenderly and beautifully told; and the author of it has the root of the matter in him. He will presently give over trying to freeze the blood with whirling adjectives – the very wrongest way; he will learn that an artist who doesn't respect the material he deals in, who doesn't almost shrink from it, for it is Life itself, mysterious and majestical – is just a bungler and no more.

\* \* \*

# The Literature of Collapse[1]

One wonders if the Literature of Collapse – such as has been in the making among us ever since the Treaty was signed,[2] exhibit everywhere the same characteristics. It would be an interesting thing for some calm and wise

Irishman to examine for us the literature that has grown up in Germany since 1918. Doubtless he should have to make some allowance for the difference that must always exist, even in periods of collapse, between the expression of the mind of a free people and that of the mind of a people not free; but this distinction made, one wishes to know if Germany is having its P.S. O'Hegartys,[3] its Sean O'Caseys[4] and the others.

After the fever of midsummer, the cloudless August harvestings, how one welcomes those calm Corot-like days of October![5] One sinks into the mood of them and rests; and as Thoreau tells us of himself that after a long day of quiet idleness, even of suspension of thought, he often felt he had made growth somehow, was renewed, was different,[6] so in the long slow twilight of an October day one may at last begin to lift a head, to feel that back of all things, or under the earth somewhere were stirrings towards a future burgeoning; and then the welcoming of the future, and the feeling of quiet preparation for it in all things – *that* becomes the secret of living. But there are people who will not be still even how stilly the atmosphere is: where does Lamb remark that the sound of a saw on a warm summer day harrows one?[7] Sawing is a thing that must be done; but those frenetic people who will saw when we all would give ourselves to the healing powers of quietness and memory! They are perverse. They stand on their heads. They waggle their brains at us – brains too lively, too skittish. And we do not listen, do not take notice. Then they scream. They will shock us out of our quietness. They will do violent things, go cross-gartered, if necessary. Is it all courage? All wisdom? But then wisdom so seldom screams and courage is so seldom blatant.

Are these everywhere the notes of the literature of collapse? Everywhere is it crudely coloured? Does it scream? Is it skittish? Cattish? Is it perverse? One wishes to know.

These notes surprise one, for, as hinted, one who had not lived through such periods – and we have seen a few – would not expect them. He would rather expect some flux of consideration, some flow of gentleness, some slow old measures, some slow old tunes; he would forget that spent forces have always required stimulants; that they hanker after the old excitements, that they will not so easily turn over a new leaf and throw off the old man. It is not easy to confess yourself for spent. These notes then surprise one. The other leading characteristic of such literature – reaction – should not surprise one. The world of the average man, the commercial world, whose only care is to put money in its purse, suburbia, with its pleasurings on quiet lawns, the selfish self-maintaining world – all that is rudely knocked about when the nation makes up its mind that the time has come to make real its traditional dreamings. All that complacent world passes then through a miserable time; and, the national adventure over, in its own shrewd if cowardly way will, in the phrase of the day, get its own back. It begins to get its own back when the guns are put away! Curiously enough – and this is not what one would look for – it finds poets, publicists, writers of all sorts ready to assist it! The trumpets which sing to battle are reversed, are now blown through the wide end. Yes, surely reversed, for nobody can speak of the ideals of the daily press, of the average middle-aged man with a stake in the country, as worth fighting for. That all, or nearly all the novels, the plays, the pamphlets, the sermons – an odd one might be literary – should move in the same plane as the daily paper's leading article, which is the expression of the non-adventurous mind of the materialist – all that might be foreseen if one asked oneself in the very height of endeavour what the aftermath would bring us in the way of literature; but that the dress – the purely literary cut of its jib, should be so cinematic, violent, crude, feminine, cattish, mean – this is the more interesting aspect of the discussion: it is for this one would, if one had the chance, take up the literature of another people who also had suffered collapse, who also had signed treaties at the point of the bayonet – just for this, to see whether these are the characteristics really native to such literature or whether they are merely the notes of collapse in a school of literature already unstable with the push and drag of counterwrestling slavishness and protest? Are they the notes of collapse in general or simply the notes of the colonial mind in collapse?

In his book *The Victory of Sinn Féin: How It Won it, How It Used it: Secrets and Sidelights*, Mr. O'Hegarty opens his twentieth chapter thus: 'Of all the impostures with which the Anti-Treaty Party is made up, perhaps the most shameless and loathsome (after that of de Valera) is that which Miss Mary MacSwiney has so persistently and sedulously foisted on the country – the imposture of herself as a "Sea-green Incorruptible."'[8] Now this book, like every other line in all this new literature, takes for its motto *Nil nisi verum*,[9] with, on the other side of the swing-sign, 'The Truth, The Truth: in God's name and the Devil's' (Carlyle).[10] But holding the above quotation in mind one can scarcely refrain from asking does Truth in God's name really demand such cattishness for its propagation? Again, like every other line in that new literature, the purpose of the book is towards truth, honesty, self-reliance and hard work on the part of the people – to quote the publisher's not unfair announcement. Well, these also have been the notes of every leading article ever written since the days of Queen Anne. But this latter characteristic of the book does not interest one so much as the way in which we are all to be made self-reliant, honest, truthful and able workmen. It seems there is no way except the goad, the sting, the nettle, the taunt. And is not this the temper of the whole mass of this new work? Its creators see small. They see perverse. In *The Shadow of a Gunman* a poet plays the coward. Poets have – even in our own time, our own land. But really the trumpets that sung to 1916 and all that followed, one seems to recollect that they took whatever was going in the way of executions, hunger-strikings, imprisonments as well as the rest. One protests, for the simple reason that the poet in the little play is there as poet, as a type. If a dramatist uses a type, the type might be typical, if only for safety's sake (it is allowable to recommend safe virtues to those of the reaction). In Bernard MacCarthy's novel *Covert* only one of the very minor characters is mentioned as being a member of the Gaelic League: he is also an idiot.[11] One fails to find any reason why the Gaelic League is [to] be dragged in unless this sort of literature cannot be written except one looks at thing[s] through the wrong end of the telescope. Of course Mr. MacCarthy may have seen or known an idiot who was a Gaelic Leaguer, just as Sean O'Casey really saw a Tricolour in a tap-room.[12] The association of idiocy with the Gaelic League and the Tricolour with tap-rooms is a matter not worth mention, perhaps, but one sees in the two things just two words in an ever-increasing volume of words which the historian must later on school himself to read backwards if the real temper of the time described in its pages is to be come upon. In the whole of Liam O'Flaherty's *Informer* there is, unless we are mistaken, only one semi-colon. A writer has of course a perfect right to fling out all the instruments of the orchestra except the big and little drum, if he so choose. But we have been so rattled with all sorts of percussion instruments for the past couple of years one wishes that those very vigorous new writers would realise that the word in our heart is: Please, don't get on with the work, if you must make such a noise about it.

Is there no way of preaching truth, of striking down shams, of inculcating the doctrines of the daily press, except frenzy and crude colourings and snapping and snarling and percussion instruments?

*   *   *

# On Anglo-Irish Literature[1]

I

Of Synge as a portent in Anglo-Irish literature we can have no clear idea unless we have formed for ourselves some general view of that literature as a whole.

In our youth and even later it used always to be spoken of as Irish literature; and this custom old-fashioned folk have not yet given up: to them Thomas Moore's *Melodies* are still Irish Melodies. Generally, however, literature written in English by Irishmen is now known among us as Anglo-

Irish literature, while by Irish literature we mean the literature written in the Irish language and that alone; to have outsiders become familiar with the distinction is simply a matter of time.

Irish literature – the great mass of writing which for us began to exist, say about 1,200 years ago, and which is being still added to – is adequately covered by its description. It is Irish. It is as Irish as Greek literature is Greek or Russian literature is Russian. But what are we to say of Anglo-Irish as descriptive of that literature which had no existence until towards the end of the eighteenth century? Is that as Anglo-Irish as Greek literature is Greek? If a stranger, say a Russian, become acquainted with this literature, he will not of course ever think of troubling himself with such a question, he will not think of saying: But is this Anglo-Irish literature at all? for of course he accepts it as such. Before such a thought can strike him he must in some way have come to know this country, its people, the virtue that is in them. One will not therefore expect enlightenment on such a question from the Russian or any other outsider, least of all from the Englishman; and among ourselves, where it is habitual bodily to take over and use whatever is current in English thought, the question has not been raised. What has been discussed is whether this literature may justly be described as Irish – ridiculous argument to those who know what Irish literature is, whereas by taking the narrower question, whether it can fittingly be described as Anglo-Irish, we may clarify our ideas of the literature such as it is, and consequently our idea of Synge's place in it.

The answer to the question: Is there an Anglo-Irish literature? must depend on what regard we have for what Synge spoke of as collaboration – without perhaps taking very great trouble to explore his own thought. The people among whom the writer lives, what is their part in the work he produces? Is the writer the people's voice? Has there ever been, can there be, a distinctive literature that is not a national literature? A national literature is written primarily for its own people: every new book in it – no matter what its theme, foreign or native – is referable to their life, and its literary traits to the traits already established in the literature. The nation's own critical opinion of it is the warrant of life or death for it. Can Anglo-Irish, then, be a distinctive literature if it is not a national literature? And if it has not primarily been written for Ireland, if it be impossible to refer it to Irish life for its elucidation, if its continued existence or non-existence be independent of Irish opinion – can it be a national literature?

To ask ourselves such natural questions is to become at once aware that this literature differs in many ways from the literature of every normal people. If we ask such questions about any other literature – English, French, German, the answers are straightforward; they are what one expects. Every new book written by an Englishman in English is written primarily for his own people; English life and English literature as a whole lie behind it; the

English cosmos is the tree from which the book, like a ripe fruit, has dropped; and English opinion decrees life or death as its portion.

If we ask ourselves by what standards of criticism is French literature clarified and guided, the answer is at hand. So of German literature, of Russian. But to ask ourselves what standards of criticism help the growth of this Anglo-Irish literature, is to be puzzled. When one examines the matter closely one finds that in periods of national exaltation, when the spirit of the land is quickened by struggle, then, as if suddenly aware of the deficiency, Anglo-Irish literature makes an effort to develop a body of criticism of its own. As soon however as the struggle is over, this literature once again becomes a free agent; once again begins unduly to reflect movements and fashions in literature which do not take their rise in this country, which have nothing to do with the mental life of this country, fashions which never in the least degree become acclimatised in this country – as French or English fashions become acclimatised, say, in America; and not alone does it make use of its freedom from any incipient national literary tradition to forage where it will, to take on what colour it will, but once again definitely shows itself scornful of the judgement of this country, such as it may be, shows itself indeed utterly provincial in its overwrought desire to be assessed and spoken well of by the critics of another people. It is therefore not normal, for a normal literature while welcoming the criticism of outsiders neither lives nor dies by such criticism. It abides the judgement of its own people, and by that judgement lives or dies. If this literature then be not a normal literature it is not a national literature, for normal and national are synonymous in literary criticism.

To take another test: a normal literature is written within the confines of the country which names it. It is not dependent on expatriates.* The literary annals of almost every people will, of course, once in a while give account of their expatriate writers. In these cases the expatriation is hardly ever a life sentence, and expatriation itself is a rare phenomenon in the history of the literature. How different with us! Expatriation is the badge of all the tribe of Anglo-Irish literary men; and in nearly all cases it is a life sentence. It has ever been in vogue, and is still as bad as ever, or, it may be, worse. Even as I write, who knows if one other – we still have one or two left – may not have taken ship for New York, Paris, or London? Where to-day are those wild geese of the pen: Padraic Colum,[2] E.A. Boyd,[3] Joseph Campbell,[4] Lyle Donaghy,[5] J.B. Fagan,[6] Frank Harris,[7] Ethel Colburn Mayne,[8] Geoffrey Phibbs,[9] Thomas MacGreevy,[10] J.H. Cousins,[11] Gerald O'Donovan,[12] John Eglinton,[13] Stephen MacKenna,[14] Eric Dodds,[15] Conal O'Riordan,[16] Alfred Percival Graves,[17] E. Temple Thurston,[18] Monk Gibbon,[19] Con O'Leary,[20]

---

* This word must serve, although of course it is not the right word to apply to such writers as, for instance, Swift, Goldsmith, Shaw – writers for whom Ireland was never a *patria* in any sense.

Austin Clarke,[21] James Joyce,[22] D.L. Kelleher,[23] James Stephens,[24] Lord Dunsany,[25] Seumas MacManus, Sean O'Casey, Patrick McGill,[26] W.P. Ryan,[27] Shane Leslie,[28] L.A.G. Strong,[29] Robert Lynd,[30] St. J. Ervine,[31] C.K. Munro,[32] George Moore,[33] G.B. Shaw,[34] Liam O'Flaherty – others?* Here without any searching into the matter is a list of over thirty names: it would be impossible to make a list quarter as long of home-staying writers. Furthermore it is to be noted that whereas most of those expatriate writers live by the pen there are hardly more than one or two of the home-staying writers who do so; so that in a way we have no home-staying *writers* at all!

Why our writers have to go abroad is obvious: a home market hardly exists for their wares. Now unless one can show that the demands of the alien market are on all fours with those of the home market, how can this literature be Anglo-Irish? How can it be a national literature? The question is not: Can expatriates produce national literature? but: Can expatriates, writing for an alien market, produce national literature? For our literary expatriates differ from those of other peoples. Ibsen lived in Rome, in Munich; but he wrote for no alien market.[35] Turgenev lived in Paris, but it was for Russia he wrote.[36] So of Rolland,[37] of Unamuno,[38] of Ibanez,[39] of many others. At the present time a colony of American writers, pleading the lower cost of living, make their home very foolishly in Paris; it is however for America they write. Those expatriates then are not like ours, for whom practically no home market exists. In no sense do our expatriates write for Ireland as Ibsen wrote for Norway or Turgenev for Russia. Some of them, of course, have cut away their own land as summarily as Henry James did his.[40] Shaw, Ervine, Munro, others, are of this class. They however are not the type. The typical Irish expatriate writer continues to find his matter in Irish life; his choice of it however, and his treatment of it when chosen, are to a greater or less extent imposed on him by alien considerations.

A foreign critic, that Russian we have instanced, knowing that more of our people live outside than within our shores, would naturally imagine that our expatriates find their market in the larger Ireland beyond the seas. But, flatly, they do not. That greater Ireland does not know even their names. Indeed the strange thing is, and how piquantly strange it is, those few of the Irish abroad who keep abreast of the fortunes of Anglo-Irish literature in the world, are those who most likely have severed all except academic connections with Ireland itself. They are not those who hasten home to do their bit when an insurrection is on; they do not contribute to the funds of any political group in Ireland, and their contributions to Irish cultural establishments are so rare that we can remember only one or two in our

---

* This list is probably not quite accurate. Sometimes an expatriate writer returns and remains for a little while. The name of W.B. Yeats is not included as it is not his habit to spend the whole of any year abroad.

lifetime. Such exiles as these are above the battle. They are those who, in the United States, fling the taunt 'professional Irishman' at those whose efforts in the past have made such vast difference in the political status of Ireland. To all this it will be replied: They have cut off from political Ireland but not from cultural Ireland. The statement seems comprehensive until one reminds oneself that Ireland's culture for them, in almost all cases, consists of little else than this very literature we are considering.

Anglo-Irish literature then, as the phrase is understood, is mostly the product of Irishmen who neither live at home nor write primarily for their own people. Furthermore the criticism by which it is assessed is not Irish, nor even Anglo-Irish. These facts admitted, the foreign critic would recall how powerful are the moulds of a literature, how tyrannously, when once established, they shape out the subsequent individual books although these may come to be written under altered conditions and even in newly-discovered lands. That foreigner would reason thus: Anglo-Irish literature is a homogeneous thing, first fashioned in Ireland for Ireland, pregnant of Irish mind, of the genius of the isle. Those expatriate writers are Irishmen, he would continue, steeped in the traditions of this literature: its idiom is their idiom; its thoughts their thoughts; expatriation, it is true, may be having some distorting effect on the moulds, but native moulds are not easily changed, hardly ever shattered: the literature then that those expatriate writers, helped by these moulds, produce, is Anglo-Irish literature.

The foreign critic in reasoning thus would be certain he was right; we know he would be wrong. He would be taking for granted that this expatriation is a new thing; that the moulds of the literature were laid before it began; that there was a time when Anglo-Irish was a normal literature, written at home for the homeland. Of course there never was such a time. The moulds are not native to us for they were never fashioned at the bidding of the people of this land: in their making the intention, whether willing or unwilling makes no difference, was not to canalise some share of Irish consciousness so that that consciousness would the better know itself. The intention was rather to discover some easy way in which the strange workings of that consciousness might entertainingly be exhibited to alien eyes. Expatriation is not of to-day, nor of yesterday. It has been a chronic disease from Goldsmith's time, Steele's time,[41] Sheridan's time,[42] Burke's time,[43] Moore's time, Prout's time,[44] Wilde's time,[45] to our own time of Shaw, Joyce and Moore. Expatriation is, therefore, an older feature in this literature than the very moulds of it. The moulds can have been fashioned only by expatriate hands, and such expatriates as we have described: writers who did not labour for their own people. From the beginning then though we may think of this literature as a homogeneous thing, we cannot think of it as an indigenous thing. Its moulds therefore cannot have been fashioned to express the genius of Ireland in the English language. If in later years certain writers tried to do this, as some have tried, the unnatural homogeneity of these moulds proved their greatest enemy, so inflexible they have ever been.

II

We know the outlines of the history of this literature. Its earliest moulds cannot be distinguished from those of contemporary English literature. Later, it certainly did develop somewhat different moulds, which can be distinguished. These second-period moulds we may speak of as Colonial moulds. The earliest writers never thought of themselves as cut off from English life or letters; the Colonial writers felt they were; they frequently protest that they are as truly English as the English born in India, as those who have gone thither: their writing at all is often an effort to keep in communion with their kind. Their books may be all regarded as an account of this strange country they are condemned to, written not for their brothers and co-mates in exile – not even for them! – but for their kinsfolk in England. Maria Edgeworth's *Castle Rackrent* is the best specimen of this style of literature.[46] No other book did as much in the creation of what was to prove the most favoured of the moulds which subsequent writers were to use. This Colonial literature was written to explain the quaintness of the humankind of this land, especially the native humankind, to another humankind that was not quaint, that was standard, normal. All over the world is not that the note of Colonial literature? The same note is found everywhere in Kipling's Indian books. From Edgeworth's *Absentee* to *John Bull's Other Island* is a far cry, yet in Shaw's play we have the same theme, with some variations of course. In between, what scores of books have been written in which an Englishman is brought to Ireland and is taken around while a current of comment is poured in his ear, not that he may really understand what he sees, but that he may know that what he sees is only the scum of the milk: he may be a bit of a fool, this Englishman, but still he is normal; he is not one of a lesser breed; and it is really his unsuspecting normality that makes it necessary for the guide to hint that things even more strange lurk unknown to him in the background. In this way the writer can also prove his own intimate acquaintanceship with the life of a strange land and a stranger people. Instructed through history, through the poetry written in Irish by the quaint ones in the background, what an exhibition of crass obtuseness that assumption of intimacy now appears to us!

It was natural for the Ascendancy folk of this second period to write in this Colonial manner, for what are all their books but travellers' tales? It is true that often the traveller was born in the strange land he must write of, but then his father was a traveller if he himself was not, or his grandfather or great-grandfather – and why not take after one's kind? But it is also true that similar books were written by native-born Catholic Irishmen whose forbears had not come out of England. *The Collegians*, by Gerald Griffin, is an example.[47] In this we have an Englishman to whom the quaintness of the folk is exhibited with the accompanying stream of comment, exactly in the Colonial manner. This normal Englishman is really the symbol of the public for whom the book was written; and the writer of it, Gerald Griffin, may be taken as the type of the non-Ascendancy writer who under the stress of the literary moulds of his time wrote Colonial literature.

In Ascendancy literature the leading theme from the start has been: the decline and fall of the Ascendancy 'Big House.' Maria Edgeworth started this hare also, and the hunt still goes on. Within the last few years we have had *The Big House of Inver* by Somerville and Ross,[48] and *The Big House* by Lennox Robinson;[49] and in perhaps every decade of years, from Miss Edgeworth's time to our own, one can discover a book with the self-same theme. Synge, in his simple way, unaware that this was the leading theme in Anglo-Irish literature, thought that he had discovered the theme for himself; he writes: '.... and if a play-wright chose to go through the Irish country houses he would find material, it is likely, for many gloomy plays that would turn on the dying away of these old families.'* It is as well he himself never wrote such a play, for he had no feeling for history, and the theme is historical, the recognition of which fact makes the moderns, like Mr. Lennox Robinson, treat it very differently from the older writers, like Maria Edgeworth. Sweet are the uses of adversity! Castle Rackrent falls from generation to generation because the family had lost their virtue, but Mr. Robinson's Big House falls because the whole Ascendancy had lost their virtue.

This difference between *Castle Rackrent* and Robinson's *Big House* or Somerville and Ross's *Big House of Inver* – the sense that in telling of the fall of one 'big house' they are describing the fate of the whole Ascendancy, teaches us that this Ascendancy literature is not impervious to the teaching that comes with the passing years. For all that, *The Big House of Inver* is quite as much written for the English people as *Castle Rackrent* was, more than a hundred years before.

The strain of literature just described forms the mass of Anglo-Irish literature – if it be correct so to describe it. It is all written for their motherland, England, by spiritual exiles. Personally many of those writers would deny this description of themselves, but it is their works and not themselves we are to go by. It is not however to be thought that all the books which make up this mass of Colonial literature are all equally colonial. Many of the writers did it more naturally, like Sir Andrew Ague-cheek,[50] and we can readily segregate the more Colonial from the less Colonial books by asking does the book live by English or Irish suffrage? *Castle Rackrent* for

* *In Wicklow and West Kerry*, by J.M. Synge.[51]

instance lives by English suffrage, but Gerald Griffin's *The Collegians* lives by Irish suffrage. Again, the work of Somerville and Ross lives mostly by English suffrage; while Carleton's work – written quite obviously under Ascendancy influence – lives by Irish suffrage;[52] and so one may go through the list.

III

The end of a boat is wreckage, says the Irish proverb, and certainly the end of an Ascendancy is downfall. When we meet truly Colonial work written in our own day, like that of Somerville and Ross, we feel ourselves in the presence of a survival: for just as Ireland has won far from the flamboyant political oratory of forty years ago, so too we are winning away from the shameful literary tradition of the Prout, Maginn,[53] Lever,[54] Lover[55] school of writers. For very many years past, Anglo-Irish literature has been sitting between two stools: when the land is under the stress of a national movement the literature makes an effort to seat itself on the truly Anglo-Irish stool, – the writers make an effort to express their own land; but when it is again at peace, the literature returns to the Colonial stool – an attitude that pays better – with less work besides, for to 'explore' your own land for the foreigner, as Donn Byrne did,[56] is far lighter work than to express it to itself, as Charles Kickham attempted to do, however clumsily.[57]

Those who know of this literature only through modern specimens of it should recollect that these have all been written in a period of national revival: while writing those specimens the writers were sitting on the Anglo-Irish rather than on the Colonial stool. All the work done for the Abbey Theatre from its beginning to 1922 may be reckoned as Anglo-Irish literature, for, whether good or bad in itself, it made an effort to express Ireland to itself. Naturally the writers of plays that were to be performed in Ireland, in a national theatre moreover, were under *geasa*[58] to keep close to the national consciousness; and in general all the work done in this period – with some exceptions, the work of Somerville and Ross, for instance – is free from the Colonial strain: much of it is freakish, much of it written under the domination of English literary fashions, yet one does not feel in it that Ireland is being exploited for the foreigner. But then it was nearly all amateur work, indeed 'prentice work; and one cannot help noticing that in recent years, the national movement having temporarily collapsed, such of its writers as had reached the professional standard, so to speak, have, quite in the old manner, turned their eyes on the English or American markets. The work, mostly amateur, done for the Abbey Theatre between 1902 and 1922 was for Ireland's self; it was, *in intention*, genuine Anglo-Irish literature, but more than that one cannot say. We must not be waylaid into thinking that because it shed for the nonce its Colonial character it became genuine Anglo-Irish literature, or that because the world accepts it as Irish literature, it may really turn out to be Anglo-Irish literature, or that because it is neither quite English nor quite Irish it must be Anglo-Irish. Obviously to no Irishman is it as Anglo-Irish as Greek literature is Greek or Russian literature Russian. It may best be described as 'something escaped from the anchorage and driving free,'[59] a craft that thinks no harm of the kindly port it is registered in – let us be thankful! – but prefers for all that to keep its eyes, more especially in these later years, on the foreign merchants who are to purchase its wares. It may be that it is no more than an exotic branch of English literature.

One cannot expect an outsider to agree that a certain literature is exotic just because he is told as much. The native of the isle who tells him so is aware that it is not enough to say to him: Take up and read! For how is the outsider to know what is or what is not exotic to the genius of both the Irish and English peoples? If indeed he be acquainted with other exotic literatures – that of the old New England school for instance – he may be asked if this literature of ours has not the same airs and graces – the same scorn of native criticism, the same ineptness in dealing with the material around it, the same leaning towards the fanciful, the same scorn of the homely? The Irishman looks in the face of his own people, hears them utter themselves with intimacy, knows what is deep in them, what is merely fleeting, has old-time knowledge why they are such and such; knows finally, in some queer way, his own consciousness, has discovered in his heart some guidance to the matter at issue: aware of himself thus advantaged, as with those reasons which the intellect knows not of, the Irishman feels it in his bones that Ireland has not yet learned to express its own life through the medium of the English language. If he be a literary Irishman he knows that whatever moulds exist in this literature are not the inevitable result of long years of patient labour by Irish writers to express the life of their own people in a natural way. If he be not a literary man he can but feel that something is wrong. But how bring it home to the outsider that all this is true?

I recall being in Thurles at a hurling match for the championship of Ireland. There were 30,000 onlookers. They were as typical of this nation as any of the great crowds that assemble of Saturday afternoons in England to witness Association football matches are typical of the English nation. It was while I looked around on that great crowd I first became acutely conscious that as a nation we were without self-expression in literary form. The life of this people I looked upon – there were all sorts of individuals present, from bishops to tramps off the road – was not being explored in a natural way by any except one or two writers of any standing. And even of the one or two, I was not certain, their efforts being from the start so handicapped. It was impossible to feel that one could pose such Anglo-Irish writers as the world knows of against that multitude. To use the American phrase, the writers would not belong. One could not see Yeats, Æ,[60] Stephens, Dunsany, Moore, Robinson, standing out from that gathering as natural and indigenous interpreters of it. On the other hand there seems to be no difficulty in posing Galsworthy,[61] Masefield,[62] Bennett,[63] Wells,[64] against corresponding assemblies in English. Those writers do belong. They give the crowd a new significance: through them we may look with better eyes at the massed people of England. The crowd equally deepens the significance of the written word: what stranger, learned in English literature, recollecting it, would not be glad to find himself in their midst, viewing them, listening to them? He might surely well forget the footballing.

Some one here may say that literature is not a mirror of the mob mind. But one does not think of such English writers as we have named as mirroring the mob mind, nor of its being mirrored by the writers of an earlier day – Meredith,[65] George Eliot,[66] Dickens,[67] Thackeray.[68] We are not thinking of the crowd as such, but as an assembly of a number of the nation's individual souls. Those English crowds are 100 per cent. English; and the writers who best express the individual souls that make them up are 100 per cent. English.* It was never otherwise, it never will be otherwise. The writers in a normal country are one with what they write of. The life of every other people they gaze upon from without, but the life of their own people they cannot get outside of. That is why they belong. The position they thus occupy in the life they deal with has no resemblance to the position occupied by the world-famous Anglo-Irish writers in the life they are supposed to deal with.

IV

We have said that one or two living writers may be excepted from this general condemnation – for instance, Padraic Colum and T.C. Murray.[69] They have come not from the Ascendancy but from the people. And yet even in the case of these, which is equivalent to saying in the case of all, one may well be doubtful, the difficulties in creating genuine Anglo-Irish literature are so immense. It seems indeed an almost impossible task.

The difficulty is not alone a want of native moulds; it is rather the want of a foundation upon which to establish them. Everywhere in the mentality of the Irish people are flux and uncertainty. Our national consciousness may be described, in a native phrase, as a quaking sod. It gives no footing. It is not English, nor Irish, nor Anglo-Irish; as will be understood if one think a while on the thwarting it undergoes in each individual child of the race as he grows into manhood. Though not quite true, let us take it that the Irish-

---

* At this point it may be well to recall Rupert Brooke's: 'If I should die'.[70]

born child is as Irish in his instincts, in his emotions, as the English child is English: the period of education comes on: all that the English child learns buttresses, while it refines, his emotional nature. Practically all the literature he reads focuses for him the mind of his own people; so also does the instruction he hears. At a later stage if he come to read a foreign language he seizes what he reads in it with an English mind. He has something of his own by which to estimate its value for him.

How different with the Irish child! No sooner does he begin to use his intellect than what he learns begins to undermine, to weaken, and to harass his emotional nature. For practically all that he reads is English – what he reads in Irish is not yet worth taking account of. It does not therefore focus the mind of his own people, teaching him the better to look about him, to understand both himself and his surroundings. It focuses instead the life of another people. Instead of sharpening his gaze upon his own neighbour-hood, his reading distracts it, for he cannot find in these surroundings what his reading has taught him is the matter worth coming upon. His sur-roundings begin to seem unvital. His education, instead of buttressing and refining his emotional nature, teaches him the rather to despise it, inasmuch as it teaches him not to see the surroundings out of which he is sprung, as they are in themselves, but as compared with alien surroundings: his education provides him with an alien medium through which he is henceforth to look at his native land! At the least his education sets up a dispute between his intellect and his emotions. Nothing happens in the neighbourhood of an English boy's home that he will not sooner or later find happening, transfigured, in literature. What happens in the neigh-bourhood of an Irish boy's home – the fair, the hurling match, the land grabbing, the *priesting*, the mission, the Mass – he never comes on in literature, that is, in such literature as he is told to respect and learn. Evidently what happens in his own fields is not stuff for the Muses! In his riper years he may come to see the crassness of his own upbringing, as, doubtless, T.C. Murray and Padraic Colum see it; but of course the damage is done: his mind is cast in an unnatural because unnative mould. So does it happen that the Irishman who would write of his own people has to begin by trying to forget what he has learnt.

If it be so, and it cannot be otherwise, with T.C. Murray and Padraic Colum, men sprung from the people, sharing their national memory in all its ramifications, what chance of expressing the people of Ireland have those writers who, sprung from the Ascendancy, have never shared the Irish national memory, and are therefore just as un-Irish as it is possible for them to be? In the case of writers sprung from the people, what creates the difficulty is the over-whelming prestige of English culture in all Irish scholastic systems, and therefore in Irish life generally. Accepted as the only one possible, that culture, not rooted in their own emotional nature, as a national culture would be, puts their emotional nature out of action, or, at the least, drugs it with a sense of its own impotence. In the case of writers sprung from the Ascendancy their emotional nature differs from that of the Irish people (differs also of course from that of the English people) and such as it is is also doubtless thrown out of gear by the educational mauling it undergoes. They therefore are doubly disadvantaged. To become natural interpreters of the nation they need to share in the people's emotional background; moreover they need to become possessed of a culture based on that emotional subconscious. In the case of the writer sprung from the people all that is necessary is a mental equipment fitted to shape the emotional content that is theirs, as well as the nation's, into chaste and enduring form.

V

If this reasoning is right we now know why that crowd of 30,000 human souls I saw in Thurles – a crowd with a national tradition behind them – are still left unuttered in literature. And we may in the light of such reasoning begin to understand curious traits in the literature as it exists, traits that show it to be exotic, not national, not normal, not natural.

A national literature foretells the nation's future. Eighty years ago, sixty years ago, Prout, Lever, Maginn, Lover, others, were accepted by the English-speaking world as the genuine voice of the Irish nation. One wonders if any foreign critic thought it worth his while to forecast the future of this nation in the light of their pages. How interesting now to come on such a forecast! The Irish peasant, with no national assets in his possession outside his own knowledge that he was the native of the isle, during that period fought for the soil of Ireland, and by his own grit and courage, became possessed of it. Not only does he now possess the soil; he also fills the highest offices in the country, in Church, in State, in Learning – everywhere. This the literature of Lover and his compeers hardly promised. Extinction rather than distinction was what it threatened, laughing, 'with foreign jaws,'[71] as it did so. The future conquest of the soil was part of Irish consciousness: if it were not, the thing could not have come to pass; and anyway those of us who have read Irish poetry know that it has for many centuries been one of the deepest things in Irish consciousness; our 'national' writers however either were not aware of it, or, aware of it, could not or would not give it utterance. Yet this literature, so little at one with the national consciousness, is called variously Irish literature and Anglo-Irish literature! And no school of criticism has arisen in Ireland to warn us that if this literature in the future is to be more trustworthy, its creators must not go the way Prout and the others travelled; indeed by laughing 'with foreign jaws' at the 100 per cent. type of Irishman, such critics as we have urge the young writers on to the selfsame disastrous road. If Maginn and his fellows were absorbed in the Irish scene, had to write of it for native eyes and not for London drawing-rooms, they could not but have felt that already the disintegration of the Ascendancy in Ireland was setting in. The literature they produced is typical of Anglo-Irish literature in the mass. We do not say that now and then that literature does not send forward-struggling beams; what we assert is that of all living literatures its message has been most often and most utterly belied by what the years have brought to pass. It has always failed to speak the secret things in the nation's soul. Only at rarest moments does it penetrate the superficialities of Irish life; so that one does not wonder if the foreigner who browses on its 'glamorous' pages picture us as given over either to a wild whirl of fox-hunting and rioting, or as spell-bound by fairies that troop nightly from our prehistoric ruins, moping out an existence not wholly in this world nor quite beyond it.

VI

The paucity of even good, not to say great, fiction in this literature has been frequently noticed. Of that better sort of novel, which is little else than an impassioned study of the reactions of individual souls to their social environment, scarcely a single example is to be had. But from what we have been finding out about this literature, its lack of grip on the emotional background of the people, is not this easily understood? How could it be otherwise, if, more than any other form in literature, the novel, for its writing require a thorough intimacy with not only the scene itself and the people themselves but with all that gives one little world a distinctive vitality? The whole topsy-turvy scheme of Irish life makes against this. If we take up the first Anglo-Irish story to hand we can find no Irish homeliness in it: we may discover an attempt at the idyllic – watery gruel! Homeliness being beyond the knowledge rather than the power of the writers, they take refuge in the freakish, the fanciful, the perverse. Brilliancy often results; and it is strange, yet significant, that the more utterly expatriate the writer the more brilliantly his pages shine, Sheridan, Prout, Maginn, Wilde, Shaw – those who most summarily dismissed the claims of their own people, being the most brilliant of all. What is the explanation? 'Something escaped from the anchorage and driving free,' – that line already quoted from Whitman may help us.[72] Given an acute mind, given also an upbringing in Ascendancy circles, or adoption into them, or assumption of their ways, with their tradition of insolence, cynicism, recklessness, and hardness, what other note could be looked for from them when they had been received into a people among whom the very word 'home' is like a holy work – a people who in their native land are anything but insolent, cynical, hard, or reckless? The brilliancy of such writers is often described as Irish, whereas in reality it may be due to that disparity of intellect and emotion we have already mentioned. Into the English field of emotion, that world of homeliness, they have no entry; they are the creators of literature in which collaboration can have no part, and Shaw or Wilde attempting to do for England what Ibsen did for Norway or Chekhov for Russian,[73] or what Molière did for France,[74] is really matter for a Shavian[75] comedy.

Mr. Shaw has described himself as the faithful servant of the English people; is it not a strange thing that servitude to a stranger should eventuate in brilliancy? Yet is it not an old and a constant theme in literature? – the jester, just because he is not one of ourselves, is privileged to loosen his tongue – only that the jester in literature has a secret sorrow in the background, as if to preserve the natural roundness of life – heart as well as brain. All those writers were, as much as Mr. Shaw, servants of the English people: one wonders if their desertion of the land that most required their services was not their secret woe? From Prout's bitter gibing at O'Connell – that great if imperfect figure – one thinks it may have been so; that his secret sorrow should have expressed itself not in tears but in tauntings of one who did lay his gifts at his country's feet, must not surprise us, since the jester must find an unusual way.

VII

The three great forces which, working for long in the Irish national being, have made it different from the English national being, are: (1) The Religious Consciousness of the People; (2) Irish Nationalism; and (3) The Land.

Now the mentality of that crowd of 30,000 I looked upon in Thurles was chiefly the result of the interplay of these three forces. To let one's mind, filled with this thought, rest on that crowd, scanning the faces for confirmation of it, and then suddenly to shift one's thought on to the mass of Anglo-Irish literature, is to turn from solid reality to a pale ghost. For, for instance, who can name a novel dealing adequately with their religious consciousness? Yet this religious consciousness is so vast, so deep, so dramatic, even so terrible a thing, occasionally creating wreckage in its path, tumbling the weak things over, that when one begins to know it, one wonders if it is possible for a writer to deal with any phase whatever of Irish life without trenching upon it. To adopt the convention of Anglo-Irish literature, that is, either to leave it out, or to substitute for it the wraith-like wisps of vanishing beliefs that still float in the minds of a tiny percentage of the people, is to cut out the heart of the mystery. So firm is the texture of that consciousness that one may sometimes think that only about Irish life can a really great sex novel be written in these days; for the subject can have no great attraction for the serious artist except where the moral standards are rigid, and the reactions transcend the lusts and the shiverings of the mortal flesh. (Mr. James Joyce has gone astray – although that very texture we have spoken of nearly succeeded in holding him fast). We may perhaps know that genuine Anglo-Irish literature has come into being when at every hand's turn that religious consciousness breaks in upon it, no matter what the subject, as it does in the Greek plays – comedies as well as tragedies – or as it does in mediæval art, grotesques and all.

As for Irish nationalism, how can normal countries understand it? If one cannot live in Ireland long enough to have it penetrate one's being, driving one although quite a foreigner to take sides, as has so often happened, the only other way to get to know it is to learn the Irish language and read the poetry in it; for such is the nature of Irish nationalism that it demands sincerity, intensity, style for its utterance, in other words, poetry. We who have lived in Ireland in recent years, who have seen what we have seen, need no further instruction to believe that prose is no medium to express it in, no more than it was for the Jews in their ancient captivity. Like all forces, it wrecks as well as saves. We here are not concerned with the wisest way of dealing with it; we would only point out that it is one of the deepest things in Irish life, searching into the souls of men, drawing sanction, as it does, from hundreds of battlefields, slaughterings, famines, exoduses, as well as from hundreds of heroic lives and the piety of verse. Yet in the eyes of the world, taught of what the world calls 'Irish' literature, that force is a thing for derision, fitted rather for comic than for serious treatment in literature. What a curious message for 'Irish' literature to deliver to the world – as if a fishmonger should cry out rotten fish! Topsy-turvy cannot sing, it seems, except in a cracked voice. A stranger, one fancies, could from the pages of Conrad[76] gather a truer idea of the nature of Irish nationalism than from the heaped-up books of this literature the world knows of. One may be sure we are come upon genuine Anglo-Irish literature when, as with the force just spoken of, that spirit of Irish nationalism expresses itself almost in every page, no matter what the nature of the expression may be, direct or indirect, heroic or grotesque, or perverse, but not alien-minded.

Of the Land as a force in Irish life, we may, the better to contrast it with the same force in English life, recall that according to the late Sir William Butler, there have been no peasants in England since Queen Elizabeth's reign.[77] Overstatement or not, to-day in England only six per cent. of the people work on the land, whereas Ireland, in a sense, is a peasant-ridden country, fifty-three per cent. of the people actually working in the fields. It will then be understood that when under the domination of a national movement, certain writers in Ireland began to deal with this force in their novels and plays, they undertook pioneer service to their country. It also will be understood that while from certain Continental schools of literature they learned a little, from England they learned nothing. It was a doubly new experience for writers such as these, first to have to fend for themselves without help from England, secondly to find they had hitched their wagon to a living force. What wonder that those of them who most deeply sank themselves in their subject wrote far above their accustomed pitch? Darrell Figgis with his *Children of Earth*;[78] T.C. Murray's *Birthright* and *Autumn Fire*;[79] Seamus O'Kelly's *Wet Clay*;[80] Padraic Colum's *Castle Conquer*;[81] Lysaght's *The Gael*[82] may be taken as evidence of this. The Land then is a huge force in Irish life. It is not however as universal in it as the other two; one cannot therefore predicate its breaking in upon every page, yet one can understand how when true Anglo-Irish literature comes to be written, if ever, for a long time the Land must lie behind the literature in some such way as the freeing of the serfs lies behind Russian literature – with political rather than social affinities. Only after long years will those political memories drift from the consciousness of the Irish people.

These forces exist in all countries; in Ireland they have however been so hardened and sharpened, given, by centuries of onslaught, such momentum, that only such other countries as have also been or are still enslaved can feel with any fitting comprehension the intensity they have now acquired. For one who has come earnestly to know them, to recognise them in the build, the attitude, the eyes of our men and women – how visibly portrayed they were in those faces in Thurles! – it is impossible for such a one to take seriously such Anglo-Irish literature as exists. So measured against life itself, as it were, it has not begun to be.

VIII

We may be reminded that a good critic, the late Rev. Stopford A. Brooke, having examined Anglo-Irish poetry, named the notes of Religion, of Nationality, of the Peasant as chief among them* – the very notes we have been naming as having had most to do with making the Thurles crowd into what they appeared and into what they were. Therefore, it seems, it is not right to say that these notes are absent in Anglo-Irish literature.

All Anglo-Irish literature, including what is being written to-day, may be divided into two kinds – the literature of the Ascendancy writer and that of the writer for the Irish people. Roughly, the first kind includes all the literature that lives by foreign suffrage; the second, all that lives by native suffrage. It was in the second class that Stopford Brooke discovered these notes. One is therefore driven to the conclusion that the second class is true

* *A Treasury of Irish Poetry in the English Tongue.* Introduction by Stopford A. Brooke.[83]

Anglo-Irish literature, since in it we find reflected the face of the people of the land. But this sort of Anglo-Irish literature is hardly ever heard of outside Ireland, and this one does not greatly deplore, for it is not intrinsically good. Such of us as know how these native notes are to be come upon in Irish poetry, never without artistry, intensity, sincerity, style, have no desire to find the world at large experiencing them in the poems of Davis, or Charles Kickham, or even Mangan.[84] These and all their fellows Mr. W.B. Yeats might not hesitate to call 'bad popular poets,' and he would be right. Yet it is these bad poets, in spite of their deficiencies, that somehow, in our poverty, carry the message that is in Ireland's heart. The emotional content in them is sterling; their mental equipment, with its lack of self-criticism, was not, however, strong enough, keen enough, to shape the message into beautiful song. Only seldom is their work not mediocre, and it is never really good. Yet it lives on; and entirely by Irish suffrage. And this happens because its emotional content, as has been said, is right; and Ireland – the Ireland that counts – almost entirely educated, up to the present, in the Primary school, – does not see its defects of form. This popular literature probably bears the same relation to the Irish consciousness of our time as the more intense, more sincere, more polished poetry in Irish bears to the Irish consciousness of the eighteenth and previous centuries, when education was of a different brand.

In this submerged underworld of Anglo-Irish literature then, loose in texture, superficial, and most unnative in its forms, as it is, it was that the critic discovered those three notes to be of importance. In the world-famous literature the critic may perhaps also discover the same three forces, or rather ghostly echoes from the noisy smithy in which they work; but that they were, and are, the deepest factors in the national consciousness of Ireland he certainly never could discover from its pages.

If one then holds that Anglo-Irish literature has scarcely begun to exist, one may ask: Whether is this unsophisticated popular literature, with its Irish message, or the exotic poetry that Ireland, the Ireland that counts, cares so little for, the better foundation to build upon? Does it not seem that this simple poetry, close to the ground, clumsily endeavouring to recapture the notes that beat, pulse-like, in the nation's heart, is capable of being refined, of being intensified, of being carven into shapely forms? Whereas one may well wonder if the all too sophisticated alien-minded poetry of the 'Celtic Revival' school, dead tired as it is, weary of staring at is own airs and graces in the mirror, is capable of further growth. Says Mr. Yeats very truthfully, almost as if he were thinking of this:

> Nothing but stillness can remain when hearts are full
> Of their own sweetness, bodies of their own loveliness.[85]

Such hearts and such bodies, one fancies, are not to be tempted to the adventure of further growth, which so often means pain and disfigurement. If one approach 'Celtic Revival' poetry as an exotic, then one is in a mood to appreciate its subtle rhythms, and its quiet tones; but if one continue to live within the Irish seas, travelling the roads of the land, then the white-walled houses, the farming life, the hill-top chapel, the memorial cross above some peasant's grave – memorable only because he died for his country – impressing themselves, as the living pieties of life must impress themselves, upon the imagination, growing into it, dominating it, all this poetry becomes after a time little else than an impertinence. It is not possible to imagine it as the foundation of a school of poetry in which those three great forces Religion, Nationalism, the Land, will find intense yet chastened expression.

As with the poetry, so with the prose. *Knocknagow*, one of the few books which have furnished living figures to the Irish consciousness, as the *Pickwick Papers*[86] has to the English or *Père Goriot*[87] to the French, is of this submerged Anglo-Irish literature. It is a book unknown except to the Irish; and again one is not sorry, for, when all is said, it is only good in parts, and not great anywhere. The emotional content here also is right; the mental equipment, however, that shaped it but was not hardened by culture and discipline. And it may be taken as the type of many other such books, Carleton's – than which it is more popular yet not at all as good – the Banims'[88] and those of others. So that the same question arises: Is the development of this prose literature, in which under-educated Ireland discovers its own image, the way for Anglo-Irish literature in the future, or shall the alien market decide for ever the way of it?

As regards this bulk of popular poetry and popular prose, there is this further to be said: if a foreign student wish to come on Irish history and on Irish life generally as mirrored in imaginative literature, him one must direct towards it and not towards the Anglo-Irish literature that the world knows of. The years as they arrive do not belie its message, which is enough to approve it as of the Irish consciousness. It is obviously the result of collaboration, always unconscious, between writer and people. And the foreign student will find in it the interplay of these great forces – Religion, Nationality, the Land, expressed, clumsily it is true, yet naturally, and without obligations to alien markets; whereas in the world-famous sort of Anglo-Irish literature, of which the Irish people know so little, he will discover that some of those forces are scarcely to be felt at all, and that none of them is expressed naturally with any such intensity as is integral in the force itself.

IX

Having now looked at the humble literature in English that, unknown to the world, finds shelter and affection in Irish homes; and looked also at the literature that goes out from Ireland to the literary world, it is time to bring our conclusions together. The underworld literature is infantile; yet one feels that if ever a school of genuine Anglo-Irish literature emerge, it will grow rather from that literature than from its more famous, very distant relation above in the drawing-room. It is against the insolence of this still Ascendancy minded literature we would argue. Our complaint against it is that the mass of it cannot be held up to Irish life as interpretative of it; that its writers do not adhere to Irish life, as English writers to English life or French to the life of France. We complain that the three great forces that work their will in the consciousness of the Irish people have found little or no adequate expression in it, that its genius is set against any sympathetic interpretation of them as a trinity of forces which interplay each one with the two others. We complain that it has thrown up no body of criticism adhering to itself, anxious to assess its value and to place its writers.* We complain that it does not foretell our destiny, that it is, contrariwise, surprised with what the years bring to pass. We complain that in it is to be observed a disparity between the emotional and the intellectual background of the writers; that such writers of it as were, like Griffin and Prout, initiates of Irish consciousness, using Ascendancy moulds, went astray; and that those others, not initiates of birth, took no trouble to become so, nor made any use of such intellectual equipment as they possessed, sometimes admirable in itself, for the high purposes of art – the shaping out into chaste and enduring form of a genuine emotional content, personal to themselves but conscionable to the nation. Finally we complain that all those writers would have written quite differently if extramural influences, such as the proximity of the English literary market and the tradition of expatriation, had not misled them from the start. Whether these extramural forces can be withstood as long as England and Ireland speak the same language is another question.

X

The traits of this literature have been so seldom examined, are so little understood, that without some such study as this just made, we are not aware that Synge, as a portent in its annals, could be treated of. Those to whom his work is already known, begin, perhaps, to see why we may quite

---

* There are really only a few books on the matter – and only one of them really helpful: *Ireland's Literary Renaissance* by E.A. Boyd.

justly speak of him as a portent. Here, by one stroke, to show how he stands apart from all his fellow Ascendancy writers, it is but necessary to state, that he, an Ascendancy man, went into the huts of the people and lived with them.

\* \* \*

# The Playboy of the Western World[1]

### I

We have now come to *The Playboy of the Western World*. It is Synge's most famous piece of work, so famous indeed that one can hardly deal with it without becoming entangled in legend. To grow is of the nature of legend. 'There were riots in Dublin when this play was first produced,' and the foreigner, not knowing these for words out of a legend, sees, in his mind's eye, a tumult-ridden city, with chargings and counter-chargings in its streets and squares. Both inside and outside the Abbey Theatre during the first few performances of the play there certainly were squabbles and protestings, but to speak of them as riots is to use the very accents of the Playboy himself. Mr. Padriac Colum writes of the first performance:

> I remember well how the play nearly got past the dubiousness of that first-night audience. The third act was near its close when the line that drew the first hiss was spoken, – 'A drift of the finest women in the County Mayo standing in their shifts around me.' That hiss was a signal for a riot in the theatre. They had been disconcerted and impatient before this, but the audience, I think, would not have made any interruption if this line had not been spoken. Still, they had been growing hostile to the play from the point where Christy's father enters. That scene was too representational. There stood a man with horribly-bloodied bandage upon his head, making a figure that took the whole thing out of the atmosphere of high comedy.*

Mr. Yeats takes up the tale:

---

\* *The Road Round Ireland*, by Padraic Colum.[2]

On the second performance of *The Playboy of the Western World*, about forty men who sat in the middle of the pit succeeded in making the play entirely inaudible. Some of them brought tin trumpets, and the noise began immediately on the rise of the curtain. For days articles in the Press called for the withdrawal of the play, but we played for the seven nights we had announced; and before the week's end opinion had turned in our favour. There were, however, nightly disturbances and a good deal of rioting in the surrounding streets. On the last night of the play there were, I believe, five hundred police keeping order in the theatre and its neighbourhood.*

The protest made with such heat was two-fold. It was religious. It was nationalistic. And only such outsiders as have lived in countries where an alien Ascendancy, for two centuries or more, have been casting ridicule on everything native, can really understand it. Do not psychologists tell us that if an occurrence, which causes us mental pain, is repeated, every repetition brings not only its own particular amount of pain but brings, as well, recollection of our former sufferings from the same cause, that is, brings more than the amount of pain intrinsic in the event. The *Playboy* incident, then, was not unrelated: it awakened within the national consciousness ancestral disturbances. The new protest was portion of the old. Wherever there is an alien Ascendancy there is such an attendant protest, perennial, and on occasions quickening into noise and violence.

As to its cause and its nature, we may find instruction in these words:

If an Irishman of any distinction be found a blackleg, a knave, a traitor or a coward, there arises a certain mirth in the discovery among strangers of all kinds, especially the English, as if they were glad to light upon an example in that nation of what is a pretty general rule in most countries at this time of day. But where they dare joke upon it, the single blot is imputed with great gaiety to that whole people. Thus all Ireland is made answerable for the faults of every one of her children, and every one of these bears the whole weight of the country upon his shoulders. Therefore, the Irishman must, in his own defence, and that of his whole country, be braver and more nice in regard to his reputation than is necessary for any other man to be. If there is any mistake or crime in his conduct, not only he but his whole country is sure to pay for it. All this is owing to the calumny dispersed, time out of mind, by the tongues and pens of two neighbouring nations, in order to justify their own barbarous proceedings in regard to that unhappy people.

* *Plays and Controversies*, by W.B. Yeats.[3]

Will it be believed that these words were written two hundred years ago? They are to be found in a letter from Chevalier Wogan, an Irish soldier of fortune abroad on the continent, to his friend Dean Swift.* They contain the simple truth. To sit among the audience in the Abbey Theatre when one of, say, Sean O'Casey's plays is on the stage, is to learn how true it is that the single blot is, *with great gaiety*, attributed to the whole people. To remain silent in the midst of that noisy gaiety, even to fling brickbats about, protesting against it, is, one thinks, to avoid the deeper vulgarity.

The protest attending on an alien Ascendancy's callous caperings is, of course, always most active in the period of national revival. In 1907, when *The Playboy* was first produced, the Irish revival was rapidly gathering momentum – we who were then fairly young murmur when we recall the period, 'Bliss was it in that dawn to be alive,'[4] – and therefore Ireland's young men were become, perhaps, oversensitive where the representation of the native Ireland was concerned. Religion and nationality are not separable in Ireland. If in any piece of work there occur not only incidents which reflect, or seem to reflect, on the native Ireland, but also words and phrases which hurt the religious consciousness of that Ireland, then the offence of that piece of work is reckoned, in such periods, doubly gross, and not deserving of any fine consideration or afterthought. So was it with *The Playboy*.

It is too easily taken for granted by those who have since written on the whole matter that the protest was without foundation: that they who made it simply wrote themselves down barbarians. These superior people forget that the play is not now given the same representation as then; nor are all the offensive phrases spoken: the fact is they are usually all omitted. When the play was broadcast from London† not only were such phrases as offended in Dublin omitted, but many others as well, for instance, 'I wouldn't be fearing the looséd kharki cut-throats, or the walking dead,'[5] a sentence which the English censor also cut out when the Abbey company took the play for the first time to London. If, therefore, there are motes in the eyes of the Irish people, there are whole beams in the eyes of the English people. Then we fortunately have an outsider's account of the impression a performance of the play in Paris made on those present – a literary audience we may assume:

> Les acteurs qui ont joué à Paris il y a quelques années une traduction du *Baladin* n'ont pas semblé comprendre tout ce qu'il y a de délicatesse et de poésie profonde dans l'âme fruste de ces simples et leur langage savoureux. Ils ont poussé à la caricature et ont fait du *Baladin* une farce brutale et dégoûtante, sous prétexte que les personnages étaient des paysans. C'est que, lorsque nous représentons les paysans au théâtre, en

* *The Life of Chevalier Charles Wogan*, by J.M. Flood.[6]
† January 19th, 1928.

France, nous en faisons de fades soupirants de bergeries, vêtus de velours et de soie, et la houlette enrubannée – ou bien des lourdauds ridicules. Notre théâtre est un théâtre de salon, la France ce connaît pas le payson. En Irlande au contraire, le théâtre est presque tout entier paysan et, en vérité, c'est un art solide et profond que celui dont les racines sont fixées dans la terre et dont l'âme est celle du peuple.*

The actors seem to have given the play in somewhat the same way as it was first given in the Abby Theatre itself. Now, it will be admitted that the Irish people had many urgings, ancestral voices among them, towards protests that neither the French nor the English could scarcely realise, yet these peoples also, as we have seen, even if silently and through other channels, made their protest. They have not, however, been called barbarians for doing so. Of the protest in America it is better to take no account. Mr. Shaw felt called upon to write a pamphlet on it for the comforting of his own and England's soul: it was the pseudo-Irish who protested! They would, one must think, have proved themselves real Irish if they had done quite otherwise from what their brothers in Dublin had done!

The protest, at any rate in Dublin, was inevitable. The natural, the inevitable, needs no apology. The fault lies not in the native Ireland but in Ascendancy Ireland, which has played the game of literature not for its own eyes, such as they have been and are, but for English eyes, not expressing Ireland to itself but exploiting it for others. Had Ascendancy Ireland treated Ireland fairly, serving up, without any ulterior motives, in literary form, the life of the country, had Ireland been long accustomed to see its own life so served up, so looked at and commented on, honestly from many standpoints, always, however, from indigenous, that is, natural standpoints, *The Playboy*, instead of being greeted with outcry and passion, would have been taken for what it was worth.

In it Synge probably did give way to a desire to shock his audience; yet of this one cannot be quite certain. It may be that he expected a Dublin audience to look at the spectacle of the play as a purely folk audience in the West, self-contained and not conscious that their neighbour in the next seat in the theatre was English-eyed, might conceivably have done, for Synge was simple about many things, and was amorous of the honest insensibility of the folk consciousness. For that sensitiveness, that touchiness, if one likes, our history has induced in us, he had but little feeling: the 'harrow of sorrow' is a common phrase in Irish poetry, and a harrow reduces to fineness. As for our religious consciousness, he was not quite unaware of it, it is true; was sometimes even touched by it – if also, at other times, estranged – but certainly he never became initiate of it. Knowing of this dullness of his to

---

* *L'île des bardes*: Simone Téry.[7]

what is ever almost too alert, too quick, in our people's consciousness, we are able to conceive that he could honestly think the audience would enjoy the play even as he himself would enjoy it if another pen had written it. And his bearing in the theatre during the first performance falls in with this view of him. He is said to have remarked that it would be necessary to establish a society for the preservation of Irish humour. For humour he had an Anglo-Irish stomach, which, remembering Swift, and Lever, and Lover, and Maginn, and Prout, and George Birmingham,[8] and Sean O'Casey, and Somerville and Ross, and St. John Ervine, and Dr. Gogarty,[9] one thinks must be as strong, if not as naïve, as the folk stomach in all lands. On that night some of the pressmen questioned him on the play, and he answered them that certain incidents in it were improbable, that the whole thing was extravaganza. This admission his admirers at the time regarded as calamitous; and Synge himself in a short and very curious letter to the Press immediately withdrew it.

> *The Playboy of the Western World* is not a play with a 'purpose' in the modern sense of the word, but, although parts of it are, or are meant to be, extravagant comedy, still a great deal that is in it and a great deal more that is behind it is perfectly serious when looked at in a certain light. This is often the case, I think, with comedy, and no one is quite sure to-day whether Shylock or Alceste should be played seriously or not. There are, it may be hinted, several sides to *The Playboy*.*

This is an honest letter. An artist makes a play and afterwards analyses his own impulses in doing so; when Synge wrote this letter he was only beginning the analysing process. Far more illuminating, however, is this passage in a personal letter of his to a friend, written about the same time:

> It isn't quite accurate to say, I think, that the thing is a generalisation from a single case. If the idea had occurred to me I could and would just as readily have written the thing, as it stands, without the Lynchehaun case[10] or the Aran case.[11] My story – *in its essenc*e ('essence' underlined four times) is probable given the psychic state of the locality. I used the cases afterwards to controvert critics who said it was *impossible*.†

Extravaganza, of course, was not the right word. Dionysiac would have served him better, meaning by that word the serving of the irresponsible spirit of the natural man.[12] Between extravaganzaic and Dionysiac there is a

---

* *John Millington Synge*, by M. Bourgeois.[13]
† *John Millington Synge*, by M. Bourgeois.[14]

difference, but not a world of difference: if one adds sufficient champagne, so fizzing up the mixture, one thinks the Dionysiac becomes straightway extravaganza; and *The Playboy* is drenched in poteen, which is, of course, the champagne of the Western World. We therefore cannot hold that his admission that the play was extravaganza makes any great difference. His view not only of art, but of life, was naturalistic; he had no subtler philosophy; the daemon within us must be served, as even Martin Doul and Mary Doul, illiterates though they are, come to understand through the very teaching of life itself.[15] What have we in *The Playboy*? Christy Mahon haphazardly becoming conscious that by serving the daemon within him he has become 'master of all fights from now.'[16] Except his *Riders to the Sea*, Synge's entire work is an apology for the daemonic in life. Not for a moment do we think he intended *The Playboy* as a satire on the people of the West. Rather is it his tribute to them, his thank offering that, among them, the daemonic had liberty to strike out, to caper on the sands, to tumble about, even outrageously. This was for him the real spirit of the place, its psychic state. But one had to search it out.

> Yet it is only in the intonation of a few sentences or some old fragment of melody that I catch the real spirit of the island, for in general the men sit together and talk with endless iteration of the tides and fish, and of the price of kelp in Connemara.*

Those who rail against *The Playboy* take it as Synge's picture of life in the West, a satirical picture. Prosaic themselves they want the *endless iteration*, whereas what Synge offers them is really the flash in the eyes of a young fisherman singing a passionate Irish love-story in the Irish manner, which is to say, with an intense concentration on the matter sung and no thought at all of the vulgar exploitation either of his own voice or his own personality. Were Synge to deal with any other *stratum* of life, the life of his own Anglo-Irish circle for instance, or the life of Paris or London, he would equally have sought out the daemonic urge in the heart of it. He would have given us his dramatisation of the psychic state of that place, as he had read it; than which no man can do more, we, of course, understanding that no two readings of a psyche can ever be the same. In England he could take no interest, holding that life had been too whitened there to be of use to the dramatist. We may imagine he would not have found himself fully contented with any family or tribe or city or nation in the world unless that community, few or many, had, without any qualification, created the daemon within them sole arbiter of their destines. He went sorrowing through life because no such community was to be found. He thought the lack of sophistication among the people of

* *The Aran Islands.* (i.)[17]

the West, their open-air adventurous life, their instruction at the mouth of the winds, at the strong hands of the ocean, at the eyes of the stars, their living close to the earth – that all these circumstances had fattened in their midst the roots of the golden bough of life, and kept it evergreen and flourishing. In such places life was really lived, was natural. In cities and towns it was put upon by laws and regulations as well as a multiplicity of institutions: it was strangled by them, so de-energised as to be incapable of blossoming. His choice of Mayo was therefore so much flattery of Mayo: had it contained a whole population of *Playboys* he would have hailed it as a bit of heaven itself! His early detractors did not understand this. His wild phrases were held up to obloquy, as if he had intended them for considered pronouncements! In reality they were his equivalent for the flashing eyes of Connacht. Synge would distil the poetry of the place into something rich and rare; his detractors, however, looked for glossy photographs of the people with their Sunday clothes upon their backs.

Remembering that the Dionysiac is the spirited and not the spiritual, it is patent that he whose quest it is will come roughly up against the people's religious susceptibilities, for their religious susceptibilities are the very flower of their labouring to keep the daemonic in check. The quester would have them be what they have always been trying not to be. In his headlong pursuit, Synge became altogether irresponsible; the cheapest thing, the most regrettable thing in *The Playboy* is the quite unnecessary flinging about of holy names and religious allusions. We are not forgetting that the religious consciousness in the Irish people overflows into curious channels; that it is to be met with in the most unexpected associations; yet Synge not only overdoes his painting of this abundance, but overdoes it clumsily and without either cause or effect. One regrets he did not himself take the advice old Mahon gave his son, the Playboy: 'Leave troubling the Almighty God.'[18] Of this perhaps somewhat slapdash abundance in the people's religious consciousness he probably became aware when reading their Irish poetry, but in the poetry the challenging phrases usually seem nothing less than forced from the singers. And naturally we come on them in the serious rather than in the humorous lyrics. They have always a striking effect, which is exactly what they have not when Synge makes use of them.

It must be allowed that every artist is partial towards the daemonic. It is the principle that opposes the mechanical, the theoretic; it is the Greek mistrust of professionalism; it is in everyman the root of honest laughter; it is in everyman the mirror of nature, answering its moods; it is the fount of heroism, it is the very colour of life itself – as ineffable as is the spirit of music; wherefore, of course, artists as such, who never will rank themselves on the side of the cut and dried, are taken by it. Yet for all that, the greater artists have never shown anything but the deepest reverence for what Goethe used to call the earnest conduct of life,[19] which, at its best when the daemon suffuses it with warmth, becomes mere chaos when the daemon overlords it with no regard to any of the other powers within us. By so much do the greater poets differ somehow from the little terrible fry of the Bohemian *cénacles*, fanatics for theories, whether they know it or not. Synge obviously fell short of the great artist. Occasionally in his essays we find honest testimony from him to the necessity for this earnest conduct of life, and Mr. Yeats tells us he insisted that an artist, as well as anybody else, should provide for his family. Apart, however, from *Riders to the Sea*, all his art is so much laudation of one especial attribute of life, the spirited, rather than of the totality of life itself, multiple spirit as it is. Obviously, for all that, it would be quite unjust to rank him with those of the artistic *cénacles*: he didn't like them; he would have given a score of them for an Aran fisherman or a Wicklow tramp. His mind was more many-sided, therefore, than his art; he had not learnt how to master and shape forth all that he had received into it from life. But he was always ripening, which, of course, does not mean that each successive play was better than the last. Quite honestly, he expresses in *The Playboy* his idea of Connacht; yet one could show from his own essays that he knew and deeply felt other forces and other currents in the consciousness of the people. If he wrote *The Playboy*, he also wrote *Riders to the Sea*; and Shaw's flippant description of him as the Playboy himself is about as wrong as it could be. He was never a Playboy, not even while Christy Mahon was tumultuous in his brain. Molière was known as the Contemplative; and the name does not misfit John Synge by much.

Is there any reason, then, why we should take sides as between Synge and his scandalised audience? Both were honest, both consistent. If, playing the small boy, Synge did in places throw out a phrase to make them jump in their seats, they, probably knowingly and unjustly, decided to hiss at everything in the play since they had begun the rumpus at all. The critics who in cold bold, and with forensic attitudinising, took sides seem to us to be far more erring than either Synge or his protesting audience.

II ·

The story of *The Playboy of the Western World* is so full of twists and turns that it takes some time to tell it, not a good sign of a play. The scene is a country public house, a shebeen. It is nightfall. Pegeen is in possession. Her father, Michael James, and the neighbours are setting off to pass the night at a wake across the sands. There enters a 'queer fellow,'[20] – a slight young man, very tired, frightened, and dirty. This is Christy Mahon whom, later, we are to know as the Playboy. Stranger as he is, they all stare at him. He hints the police may be looking for him: is it a safe house? He tells them in covered phrases that he cannot recall any person, gentle, simple, judge or jury, did the like of him. He leads them on. Him they lead on, until at last in a sudden impulse of bravado he informs them that a week ago last Tuesday he killed his father in a quarrel. The glamour of this romantic story seizes on them all; he is made pot-boy to the house. Michael James, the owner of the house, and the neighbours set off towards the wake, leaving Pegeen, Shawn Keogh, who is soon to marry her, and Christy Mahon behind them. Shawn Keogh, whom the Playboy has eclipsed, Pegeen soon gets rid of: then she has Christy Mahon to herself. Their pleasure in each other's company is spoiled by the entrance of Widow Quinn, whom Shawn Keogh has sent to spy on the Playboy. But her, too, Pegeen gets rid of. In the end, Pegeen leaves the Playboy for the night, going into another room. As he examines the comfortable bed she has arranged for him he soliloquises: 'Well, it's a clean bed and soft with it, and it's great luck and company I've won me in the end of time – two fine women fighting for the likes of me – till I'm thinking this night wasn't I a foolish fellow not to kill my father in the years gone by.'[21]

The second act is merely a piece of contrivance: there is nothing inevitable about it. We see Christy next morning receiving visits from the young women of the neighbourhood, whom the romantic story, even at second hand! we are to believe, has bewitched, just as it bewitched the men the night before. Widow Quinn subsequently enters; and, still later, Christy's 'murdered' father himself! Christy, in the nick of time, hides himself, leaving Widow Quinn the task of setting his father on the wrong track as to his whereabouts, for it is in search of his son he has arrived at the shebeen.

In Act III. we have the Playboy entering into competition with the local athletes and defeating them all: we are to understand that the sudden realisation of manhood, which Pegeen's infatuation for him has brought to him, enables him to do so. Victor, laden with prizes, he returns to her from sports; and there follows the rather famous love scene between them. Unfortunately, just as Christy is, as he himself would have said, mounted on the stars of luck, his father enters once more, spoiling everything. Pegeen turns against Christy – he is obviously a liar, he has not killed his father at all! Maddened, Christy chases his father out, and this time, we are to understand, really kills him. Now, having made his boasting true, he expects Pegeen to receive him with open arms. But she tells him there is a great difference between a romantic story and a dirty deed in your back yard – which statement, of course, is Synge's apology for the comedy, and indeed an explanation of its idea. But the father survives this second killing also. Once more he enters, this time to drive his son home before him. Christy however is no longer the 'dirty stuttering lout,'[22] and it is he who drives his father out before him, like a heathen slave. Pegeen too he treats with disdain. He has attained.

III

The sources of *The Playboy* are interesting. In the *Aran Islands* we come on this passage:

> He often tells us about a Connacht man who killed his father with the blow of a spade when he was in a passion, and then fled to this island and threw himself on the mercy of some of the natives with whom he was said to be related. They hid him in a hole – which the old man has shown me – and kept him safe for weeks, though the police came and searched for him, and he could hear their boots grinding on stones over his head. In spite of a reward which was offered, the island was incorruptible, and after much trouble the man was safely shipped to America.*

Some years after the storm aroused by Synge's play, Professor Ó Máille searched out the details of the whole incident on which the play is based, and whoever wishes may now find the whole legend set out, names and all, in the Professor's book: *An Ghaoth Aniar*.[23] Although Synge's version of the story is thus partially true, the incident itself was tragic, as one might expect, and not humorous. Reading of it in Professor Ó Máille's book, the curious thought strikes one that the man himself who, having killed his father, found refuge among the people until he escaped, may have looked on Synge's drama with his own eyes, when the Abbey company took it to America. He would then have been something more than seventy years of age.

As with Synge's other plays, not only do we find the fable itself in his note-books, but in them also we come on phrases, speeches, and records of incidents which, tightened up somewhat, we are familiar with in the play. In the play we have: 'What's a single man, I ask you, eating a bit in one house and drinking a sup in another, and he with no place of his own, like an old braying jackass straying upon the rocks?'[24] Here, recorded in Synge's note-book, is the same speech as it fell from the mouth of old Mourteen: 'Bedad, noble person, I'm thinking it's soon you'll be getting married. Listen to what I'm telling you: a man who is not married is no better than an old jackass. He goes into his sister's house, and into his brother's house; he eats a bit in this place and a bit in another place, but he has no home for himself; like an old jackass straying on the rocks.'[25] Such a speech one can imagine Synge as repeating to himself, with great delight, for many days after he had come upon it. In the play we have horse-racing on the sands, and in his book on Wicklow and Kerry, we have such a scene fully described. The extent to which he depended on what he had seen and heard is an indication of his distrust of what was theoretic and merely invented.

* *The Aran Islands*. (i).[26]

## IV

*The Playboy* is too fantastic, comes not easily enough within our common experience of life, to form part of the tradition of great comedy. Admitting that spirit is an unaccountable thing, miracle-working, that it dazzles with swift wings, drugs with unwonted perfumes, yet the falling of a whole countryside at the feet of a self-declared parricide simply on account of his gamey heart and his fine bit of talk, is an assumption to which we cannot give more than grudging acceptance. The readiness with which the people in the play swallow down what we cannot look at, antagonises us; and this antagonism is kept alive by constant reference to the supposed crime. From our difficulty in accepting the scheme of *The Playboy*, we may learn that the scarcely possible is not half so comfortable a basis for comedy as the almost probable; and the whole *Playboy* scheme is hardly even scarcely possible. We are all the time engaged in coercing our minds not to engage in argument against the proposition before us. Skipping this weakness we find much brain-work in the play. The point of it is the continuous upgrowth of Christy Mahon's character from nothingness to full manhood. And this 'upliftment' is due almost entirely to his meeting with Pegeen; she, however, we are to remember, is, like the others in the shebeen, drawn to him by the glamour that the great adventure of killing his father has thrown around him. Later on of course we learn from her own lips that it is not the deed itself that wins either her, or the others, it is Christy's telling of the tale, the fine bit of talk. As on a chart we can follow the Playboy's upgrowth. He was a quiet poor fellow with no man giving him heed, he tells us; only the dumb beasts in the fields were his friends (John Synge is remembering his own boyhood). To Pegeen he is only a soft lad; she treats him to bread and milk! To Widow Quinn he appears as one fitter to be saying his catechism than slaying his da. To his father he was only a dirty stuttering lout, one who spent his days fooling over little birds he had, finches and felts; one who'd be off to hide in the sticks if he saw a red petticoat come swinging over the hills. In one place the Playboy remembers his own past, and Pegeen comforts him:

> 'What call have you to be that lonesome when there's poor girls walking Mayo in their thousands now.' 'It's well you know,' Christy answers grimly, 'what call I have. It's well you know it's a lonesome thing to be passing small towns with the lights shining sideways when the night is down, or going in strange places with a dog noising before you and a dog noising behind, or drawn to the cities where you'd hear a voice kissing and talking deep love in every shadow of the ditch, and you passing on with an empty, hungry stomach failing from your heart.'[27]

Next to this passage, one of the most pleasing in the play, let us place his words when he knows he has won Pegeen's love:

> 'Let you wait, to hear me talking, till we're astray in Erris, when Good Friday's by, drinking a sup from a well, and making mighty kisses with our wetted mouths, or gaming in a gap of sunshine, with yourself stretched back unto your necklace, in the flowers of the earth.'
>
> Pegeen (*in a low voice, moved by his tone*) 'I'd be nice so, is it?'
>
> Christy (*with rapture*) 'If the mitred bishops seen you that time they'd be the like of the holy prophets, I'm thinking, do be straining the bars of Paradise to lay eyes on the Lady Helen of Troy, and she abroad, pacing back and forward, with a nosegay in her golden shawl.'[28]

Always then we are looking at the Playboy striding forward, until, at the close, when his father would assert his authority over him, crying out: 'Come on now.' Christy answers: 'Go with you, is it? I will then like a gallant captain with his heathen slave. Go on now and I'll see you from this day stewing my oatmeal and washing my spuds, for I'm master of all fights from now.' His astonished father can but gape, exclaiming: 'Glory be to God!'[29] Christy's upgrowth is the strong spire of meaning in the play, if we may use Mr. Galsworthy's phrase.[30] In it, therefore, we have one more working out of the old theme that Dante knew of, that Goethe declared openly:

> The indescribable, here it is done,
> The woman soul leadeth us upwards and on.[31]

– only, of course, the plane of the spiritual, in which the great ones were at home, has been exchanged for that of the spirited. Writing a comedy, as Synge was, some such difference was to be looked for, because comedy is, as Aristotle pointed out so long ago, the imitation of ignoble actions,[32] an opinion that might be dwelt upon by those who write of *The Playboy* as if it should pass the same tests as a treatise on morals.

Christy Mahon himself is the only character that changes and grows; once it is seen for what it is, the graph of his progress is so direct as not to be interesting. Synge's sense of the psyche of place was always more subtle than his sense of the psyche of any man or woman, and of his men and women Christy Mahon is one of the simplest. One easily exhausts him. It is only when he triumphs, when he drives his stormy parent like a heathen slave before him, that he becomes fit material for great drama. For Christy Mahon lacks an abundant background within himself. He is poverty-stricken where Martin Doul is opulent. And Pegeen Mike, the only other character in the play who has a leading part, is, in background, even still more poverty-stricken. Indeed her background is to be found in theatre-land rather than in the Western World. She is the commonest thing in Synge, pert, bright-eyed, quick-witted, efficient in love-making as in bar-tending. She is the stock figure in amateur play-writing; and amateur actors revel in her type, because they know what to do with any such. Widow Quinn is a thinner Mary Doul, she is a Mary Doul who speaks for effect. This feeling is all over the *The Playboy*. From the Playboy himself downwards, every person is speaking for effect, an unwonted fault with Synge. Even Michael James does it, although his speech where he gives his blessing to the young pair who, one at either side, support him while he makes it, is indeed as rich as it has a right to be. So, too, one relishes old Mahon, with his pride in the atrociousness of the wound his son inflicted on him. His 'Glory be to God!' at the end of all is one of the best things in the play, far truer than Christy's carefully modulated cadences.

The two of these, old Mahon and Michael James, live, each of them, openly and unashamedly the life of the natural man. They care for nobody. They drink their fill and speak their fill, while the spirit we behold assuming sway over Christy makes of him 'a likely gaffer' – 'master of all fights from now.'[33] In the book *Wicklow and West Kerry*, Synge describes the simple people from beyond Dingle as revelling in the gaudiness of a travelling circus: a wet night did not prevent them from measuring out long miles of rough mountainy roadway to witness it. The bedizenment of the *Playboy*, the scorn of half-tones, the splashes of crude reds and yellows and apply greens, the efflorescences, the flaunting of such daemon as is either callously heroic or outrageously comic – it recalls somehow the travelling circus, posters and all. Poetry, Synge held, must become brutal again to find a way out. So too, he believed, must comedy.

V

It is the florid diction of the play that infects our mind somewhat as might the high colours of the circus-poster. Perhaps only those not gone far in the twenties take that diction to be quite successful. Except for the great difference in their characteristic themes, the associations that cling about them, Francis Thompson would perhaps strike us similarly;[34] he, as well as Synge, depended on not so much the 'little more' as 'the wasteful and ridiculous excess' to lift us beyond the prosaic.[35] Mr. T.S. Eliot quite correctly points out that Elizabethanism was 'a verbal even more than an emotional debauch';[36] and Synge in *The Playboy* outdoes the Elizabethans. Those selfsame Elizabethans seem to have gradually replaced Racine,[37] and indeed French drama in general, in his affections. His rhythms in *The Playboy* are more obtrusive, more rotund than in the earlier plays, as the incidents are more bustling – the whole aim is at excitement, tension, surprise. The excess of colour in his work we owe to his affection for the Elizabethans as we owe the daring, as also the homeliness, of his imagery to the Gaelic songs of Connacht, many of them truly folk songs. But both Elizabethans and Gaels had an instinct that told them that neither rapture nor intensity nor ecstasy ran to headlong verbalism. They knew when to rein in. They felt, and more especially the Gaelic poets felt, that the measure of intensity produced is in inverse ratio to the volume of the verbiage employed. In so far as you trick out your sentences with geegaw adjectives you diminish the effect the sentences produce: it is as if you were to wrap your hammer head about with webbing; let the webbing be as variegated as it may, the heart is taken out of the blow struck. Gaelic equivalents are to be found for many of Synge's most characteristic phrases, more especially for such of them as refer to religion, but the Irish phrases are always far swifter in their effect, far more effective: the hammer head is bared and strikes homes hard and true.

> Mallacht Dé do'n té sin
> A bhain diom mo ghrádh.[38]

> The curse of God on him
> Who snatched my love from me.

says the Gael, striking the nail on the head. Synge would have decorated both the curse and the beloved one, muffling the blow. There is in *The Playboy* a straining after terrible things, with not much more than a mush of colour and sweet sound resulting – a curious failure for one who would have the timber rather than the flower of poetry in his work. Adjectives, he should have known, always beat about the bush and give us time to set up defences. The Irish poets on the other hand show us no quarter, for it is not words that come hurtling against us, but the things for which the words stand – that is how it feels. With Synge, although taught of them, it is always words, words, words; and sometimes very feeble words. We do not recollect any Gaelic original for: 'Aid me for to win her, and I'll be asking God to stretch a hand to you in the hour of death, and lead you short cuts through the Meadows of Ease, and up the floor of Heaven to the Footstool of the Virgin's Son.'[39] Yet, if original there is, one may be quite certain it produces an altogether different effect. Instead of the overwhelming intensity aimed at, the passage quoted has the whine of the beggar in it, whose aim it is not to make an end. One feels the tension of the mind slackening as the words flow on and on. It is like something one would find in Sean O'Casey at his worst, or is it his best? And there is hardly a page in *The Playboy* that is not stuffed with such long-winded figures, some of them, it is true, exhibiting the excess of his strength; most of them, however, exhibiting nothing more than a disturbing mannerism. Now, mannerisms, as soon as we know them for such, have an uncanny power of instantly chilling the mind; and all Synge's own interest in his puppets, his liking for them, his own innate warmth of feeling, is scarcely powerful enough to sweep up alive through those ever recurring tricks of phrase and cadence. Even while reading these word-spinnings, one suspects their efficacy as an element of dramatic technique; in the theatre itself one cannot help wondering at their ineptitude. They become thus a double distraction. Whetting our appetites, they aim at the ultimate, and achieve nothing more than the moderate, losing half their breath in calling attention to themselves.

This desire of his to go 'beyond the beyonds' accounts for his frequent introduction of phrases with religious allusions in them: if we are to challenge anyone let us challenge God himself! Still less does this obvious phrase-making of his achieve when he draws upon the religious consciousness of the people. That consciousness was, as we have before explained, *terra incognita* to him: he knew it only dimly, could realise it only superficially. And if we would finally satisfy ourselves as to the truth that intensity in literature is to be achieved only by getting rid of the sense of language, getting back to the thing itself, we have only to compare his refashioning of some Irish phrase or sentence with the original. Thus Synge has: 'When you'll feel my two hands stretched around you, and I squeezing kisses on your puckered lips, till I'd feel a kind of pity for the Lord God is all ages sitting lonesome in His golden chair.' The original we find in the lines of the well-known 'Una Bhán':

> B'fhearr liomsa bheith ar leabaidh lei 'ga sior-phógadh
> 'Na 'mo shuidhe I bhflaitheas i g-cathaoir na Trinóide.[40]

> I'd rather be ever kissing her on a couch
> Than to be sitting in heaven in the Chair of the Trinity.

This is not a good example to illustrate the difference between love poems in Irish and Synge's idea of them; nobody would think of quoting the lines to illustrate any trait in these songs; what strikes us about them in general is that whenever the nameless singers go beyond the beyonds they find themselves truly driven to it: their songs seem to have been no more made for a public than Beethoven's last quartets. Synge's phrases are literary; from that feeling we cannot escape; but how far from that feeling we are when we find 'Uch, Mac Muire na nGrás dom shaoradh' (O, may the Son of Mary of the Graces save me!) in the well-known 'Snowy-breasted Pearl'[41] or when we come, in Liam Dall Ó h-Ifearnáin's perfect lyric: 'Pé i nEirinn í', on

Cé sheolfadh Aon Mhac Dé im' líon
Ach stór mo chléibh?

Whom did the Only Son of God direct into my net
But my heart's treasure?

   Synge's phrases, then, seem not alone watery to us who know the
originals, but very often strike us as being also absurd. Every Catholic knows
that no Connacht peasant, drunk or sober or utterly lost in ecstasy, could
have used them, no more than drunk or sober or gone in our five wits, we
could find ourselves asserting that two and two made five. Knowledge
imbibed at our mother's knees is not to be put away from us so easily; yet to
utter themselves as Synge's peasants sometimes do, such knowledge they
must have forgotten; as we ourselves must forget it, if we would accept such
a phrase as: – 'Oh, St. Joseph and St. Patrick and St. Brigid and St. James,
have mercy on me now!'[42] Such passages remind us that Synge's idea of the
religious consciousness of the people was that of the outsider; for in that
consciousness there is a vast chasm between the attributes of the Almighty
and those of the saints.


                                  VI

There is a world of difference in feeling between *The Playboy* and *The Well of
the Saints*. In *The Well of the Saints* we are, as it were, in a strange and distant
land, yet our constant surprise is not so much the strangeness of it all as the
familiarity of it all. The people, we are sure, have undergone bewitchment:
they have all become a little 'natural.' They move to a slow music,
processionally. Let us remind ourselves as often as we may that the whole
matter is absurd, that these people are quaintly ridiculous, yet they continue
to move on gravely, in a sort of stricken quietude, scarcely ever laughing and
but rarely smiling, undisturbed by our presence. They sojourn in a removéd
ground. They are at a distance from us: we mistrust the clearness of our sight.
But our gazing at them, our overhearing of them, has been an experience: we
have had not only holiday but unique holiday. Quite different is our feeling
towards *The Playboy*. For all the rather outlandish lingo and topsy turvy
evaluing of life in it, we experience far less sense of distance, of strange
voyaging. It is a bustling scene we have happened upon: the people bounce
against us: we know them for folk who have dressed up very well indeed; yet
we are sure we have met them before, many of them, Pegeen most frequently
of all, on the 'boards.' One tires easily of the rough and tumble; contrariwise,
again and again we find ourselves drawn back to those pieces of literature
where the whole event seems to be kept at a distance from us. In such cases

the writer has organised a little world of his own. We wish to go back into it, for something whispers us that due to our own inattention, perhaps, we assuredly did not bring the last time we were there as much with us as we might have done; this time, we delude ourselves, we shall get closer to the passionate hearts of the citizens. How curious a thing it is that atmosphere, mood, is the most inexhaustible element in literature! When we have satisfactorily encompassed a thought or a set of thoughts, we find ourselves enriched for ever more; but to the book or play where we find them, unless it have in it more than these thoughts, we had better not return; if we do so we shall find it a little cold. In those strange books, however, where thought is but one of the elements, those strange books that are self-centred, self-lighted, as from within, Musset's plays,[43] for instance, we shall always find some new instruction, some further stimulus: they grow in depth it seems not only with our growth, but a little more than it, so that we once again feel that we are leaving them incontinently, as indeed we shall leave life itself. *The Playboy* has its own atmosphere; as compared with *The Well of the Saints* it is, however, a commonplace atmosphere, commonplace even in its surprises. One easily fathoms it, easily exhausts it; only small passages in it entirely grip us when we return to it after voyaging elsewhere.

At first glance the play seems to be more typical of Synge than anything else he wrote. It is of course the piece that made him famous: the word 'playboy,' has gone abroad throughout the English-speaking world; every other day this man is described as the playboy of American politics, this other as the playboy of English letters, and so on; while Synge himself is of course, for many, the Playboy of the Western World – that, and no more. Yet there is less of Synge's self in this play than in any other thing he wrote. He was a brooder by nature; his mind was a wandering star, free, through want of purpose perhaps, of many orbits. When, however, that wandering star had had its orbit fixed, its path determined, with a terminus assigned, doubtless it travelled faster than before and, it may be, glowed the brighter for the speed. This brilliancy, however, if such we reckon it, hardly compensates for the more varying tints it exhibited, the choicer atmospheres it drew with it, when it wandered hither and thither, unfolding its own self, revealing its own self hail-fellow-well-met, in leisurely contact with sympathetic phenomena round about. The scheme of *The Playboy* was very definite. That very definiteness of itself, by too-hard focussing of the powers of its creator's mind, may have hindered that mind from revealing itself with such fullness as we have found it doing when it had permission to linger and, shutting its eyes, as it were, to draw riches from its own resources. The fact is, Synge never met in life either the Playboy or Pegeen Mike – neither in Aran nor in Wicklow, in Kerry nor in Mayo. He found the scheme and he created his types to suit it. And paradoxical as it may appear, because he invented them all out of his own brain, they remain apart from his own self – a thing that always happens: it would seem we must find ourselves in others if ourselves we would project on the vision of others. If we create a *Playboy*, all out of our own brain, it is as if we kneaded a homunculus between our fingers – the figure may be very dainty, very charming, but it has length and breadth, height and depth, with a birthday recorded in the annals. If, however, we meet in Wicklow, or elsewhere, a Martin Doul, and try earnestly to realise him in all his amplitude of nature – why, we lose ourselves, we use ourselves up in the effort; there is not enough in ourselves of love, of knowledge, of experience, to encompass him; we are conscious of lacking means fittingly to project that one affectioned figure on the consciousness of others. We may, therefore, understand how much thinner *The Playboy* is than *The Well of the Saints*. In the depth of Synge's being there was a well-toned music: it found its provenance in the sense of loneliness, in the consciousness that beauty had but little time to stay, love itself not even so long, that old age was upon us almost before we knew, that the grave was the end of all. This undersong that was Synge's very self, breathes here and there in *The Playboy* – there is the passage already quoted where Christy tells of his lonely wanderings, with a dog noising before and a dog noising behind, beholding others deep in love, himself uncompanioned – but truly not more than a hint of his inner self is to be found in it, whereas he is everywhere in *The Well of the Saints*. *The Well of the Saints* is therefore lit from within, and is a strange region, ineffable, unique; to travel in it is to be refreshed. *The Playboy* is contrived: we encompass the trick of it; we can see all round it. In comparison with his other plays we may speak of it as stagey, if indeed it be almost nature itself when compared with the dramas that were being written in England, and in other English-speaking counties, at the same time.

In only one way does it show progress: it is more obviously the work of a playwright. The acts are not complete, each in itself, as in *The Well of the Saints*; they flow over, not only inviting conjecture, but half-directing, half-waylaying it. Act I. is a good well-articulated piece of dramatic writing: it opens well, and continues well, the line of interest rising right through. Act II. has too much padding in it. The only essential point in it is the entrance of the Playboy's father, and one does not understand why this entry could not have been kept back until Act III. thus reducing the play to two acts. Act III. is a good, bustling act, alive from beginning to end, even if a little repetitious. It is full of matter: the sports on the sands, the return of Michael James from the wake, the real wonder of old Mahon that his son could achieve such heights of manhood, the love scene between Christy and Pegeen, the turning of the tables on the father, the swift ending. However much we may sigh for the aloofness of *The Well of the Saints*, *The Playboy* has more of the feel of legitimate drama in it, no slight recompense.

One quality, which is the very seal of creative genius, it shares with *The Well of the Saints*, as indeed with all his plays, it is homogeneous: all the men and women in it, even if none of them be as rich tempered as he or she might be, draw sustenance from the same impulse of creation: their little vessels of being have all been filled at the same fount, wherever in the Western World that fount may be. They differ from each other, each remaining the whole time harmonious with himself, yet all tread upon the same enchanted ground and are true children of it. Perhaps the Playboy's speech at the very end of the first act, where he half regrets not having killed his father long ago, is the only blunder in the play. It is the only passage in which the playboy is truly a playboy, consciously rogue. In the real sense of the term, a playboy lives by roguery, is conscious of it, is conscious too that to the initiated his roguery is an open book; is one moreover who enjoys not only his own roguery, but the sensations, half-looked for by them, that it excites in the initiated. Christy Mahon is no such playboy. If his words at the end of Act I. really give us his very self, if he is truly a rogue, he cannot but behave quite differently from what he does all through Act II. and Act III. A real playboy would not allow himself to be tied up by the simple Mayo men; he would, one thinks, rather have got them to tie up his father. Christy Mahon is an innocent rather than a rogue; and the play in which he is the chief figure is, therefore, not a piece of picaresque drama.

*The Playboy of the Western World* is a gaudy reckless spectacle; yet it was no small magic that raised it from the rather drab and meagre scheme of life of one of our poorest seaboards. In hidden places, and with the most crazy gear, the peasants there distil that potent spirit poteen which, Synge tells us, sends a shock of joy to the blood. No more, no less than that, did he ever wish this handful of living people to do for us.

* * *

# The Colonial Branch of Anglo-Irish Literature[1]

As to the name of the whole of this literature: Anglo-Irish, since it prevents confusion and makes for peace. Anyway it is accepted. You'll find a chapter in the *Cambridge History of English Literature* headed 'Anglo-Irish Literature.' And if some, resisting authority so eminently respectable, still persist in calling it Irish literature, let them beware of Dr. Gogarty, who rages when a Punic name falls on his ear.

As to the future of this literature: it lies in the bosoms of Hobbs and Nobbs, and Nokes and Stokes.[2] Not certainly in the bosom of Paddy McGinty (friend of mine, friend whose judgement goes with me – Mr. O'Faoláin asserts it,[3] though Mr. O'Connor is kind enough to say that my books, like his own, are read by those who have reached the Turgenev standard:[4] having said which Mr. O'Connor invites me to weep with him tear for tear in our unfrequented booth).

What remains to be discussed? Swamped by English culture, or not swamped? The bookshop long since has settled that question for me. Not for Mr. O'Connor. Bless you, not English culture but international fills our bookshops! he cries, lifting his eyebrows. I reply: International literature in English, which is to say that brand of it England chooses.

But I think 'most people' (arbiter chosen by Mr. O'Faoláin, highbrow), will agree that you can cut from the bookshop all that is international in it without sensibly disturbing the pattern. Trash! Mr. O'Connor calls the lot, international books and all. I agree. But there must be trash. 'Most people' will have it so. Then why not green trash? Cabbage green or shamrock green, which is more Hibernian, though I'd prefer to either, the green that the poet (joker!) saw in the eye of 'Gile na Gile' – *rinn-uaine* –[5] perhaps because there's a little in my own. Red trash in the English book-shop, I therefore look for, green trash in the Irish, yellow in the Chinese; and nobody swamped. I'm afraid I am old fashioned enough to trust still the judgement of the whole world in such matters, which holds that to swamp history and geography beneath alien history and geography is sheer waste of mindstuff, local and imported. It seems therefore that I make headlong for the normal; and I do, even if it lie at the end of 500 years or 1,000 years, of dreary inhibitions (the figures are Mr. O'Faoláin's, exact thinker), and I don't feel like doing anything else. So inclined, I cannot but agree with Mr. O'Faoláin when he says, though I don't like the abashed way he says it: 'There is a good deal in this idea about literature being based on national life.'[6]

But he also says 'Nationalism should be kept out of criticism',[7] and really I am afraid to go on, for putting his two brains together, his right and his left, we as critics are bidden not to look at the foundation of things! It is right to add that in Mr. O'Faoláin's article the two statements are separated by threequarters of a column, and if one doesn't give a jot about definitions or anything else, one can say in that much space such a heap of things off the tip of the tongue that it is difficult to keep track of them all. But whether we accept Mr. O'Faoláin's two statements taken together or one by one, or accept only one of them, it will not help us (and so we can quit him, for the nonce anyway). Because what all the pother is really about is: What bases itself on a *strangled* national life? And I answer, only for the purposes of this discussion, however: That bifurcated literature in English which Irishmen have been writing for something over a hundred years. The bifurcation is not a matter of Right and Left, as Mr. Murray seems to think, for a nationhood that is not strangled can throw up literature so divided, whereas only strangled nationhoods throw up literature bifurcated in the way Anglo-Irish literature is. Let's look at each branch. One is small in bulk, inept for the most part, but natural. Here and now we need say no more about it, except to describe it as an effort of the *strangled* consciousness to express itself without asking sanctions from the *strangling* consciousness. The other branch, I submit, craves sanctions from that source. And gets them, but only on conditions, implicit or explicit. For instance, Mr. Frank MacManus points out that that literature ignores the philosophy that goes with the Faith of the Irish people.[8] There is no denying it. Further, it not alone ignores but attacks, usually by derision, the philosophy of the nationhood of the Irish people. In my book on Synge I lay specific charges at the doors of this literature. This just mentioned is put thus: 'We complain that it does not foretell our destiny, that it is, contrariwise, surprised with what the years bring to us.'[9] It is no more natural for Irish writers to ignore or deride the forces in the national consciousness than for the writers of other countries. If those two charges, not to mention others, are justified, then the literature can be only little better than a simulacrum.

Others may be able to explain in some other way how such unreality as we find in this literature comes about. My explanation, for what it is worth, is the strangling 'except on conditions'. Usually the conditions are not explicit, but sometimes they are. I know it from an actual personal experience. 'We'll publish the book if *that* is omitted.' Not the actual words used, but the force of them. Mr. Ernie O'Malley knows it.[10] I cannot tell whether he feels about it as I do, but I honour England for insisting on calling the tune when she pays the piper. Let it not be taken that I am saying that every book published by England for Irish writers is of this branch of Anglo-Irish literature, and that every book published in Ireland is of the other. I do not know where *Knocknagow*, for instance, was first published.[11] But I do say that no writer who caters for the English fiction market can avoid sooner or later coming up against England's conditions. It is the tradition to accept them; and one walks by tradition very often without knowing it; so that it is quite possible that that tradition has often determined that a book or play should be of this branch of Anglo-Irish literature without conscious knowledge on the author's part of what is so shaping his book. When all is said and done this literature has even still the limitations that have always characterised Colonial literature. It has the feeling of Colonial literature in it: it changes, it grows recalcitrant, like Colonial literature, when the mother country becomes unduly exigent; and if the mother country doesn't keep it alive, it dies.

'I say,' Mr. O'Faoláin cries, 'Irish literature is absolutely Irish to-day!'[12] Absolutely; Couldn't be more Irish! His words are hysterical. And he's rather hard on his predecessors of yesterday. For they cried the same cry; and it was accepted for truth by great numbers, especially by our 'educated' classes.

> During those years of my boyhood and youth in Ireland Charles Lever was by far the most popular novelist. His stories were everywhere welcomed as pictures of Irish life. They were welcomed, not merely for their genuine humour, their unfailing vivacity, and their power of invention, but also for their faithful portraiture of typical Irish character. Yet I can well remember that while we boys and girls in our Cork set were enthusiastic admirers of *Charles O'Malley* and *Harry Lorrequer*, we were frequently asking each other whether any of us had met with such personages as in Lever's novels were understood to be found in every town and village? I am compelled to add that not one of us could say that he or she had ever met even one such person in the Irish life with which we were acquainted.

The passage is from Justin McCarthy's *Irish Recollections*.[13] So that the same cry must have been cried by the Mr. O'Faoláins of that day. Let's hope that none of the younger writers will be foolish enough to argue: 'But we are not Levers. We are Gaels. We know Irish. We know the Irish people; we are of their flesh, of their spirit.' It was almost natural for Lever and his fellows to accept England's terms. Those terms not having appreciably changed, nor likely to change, I cannot see how the future of this literature is not laid up in the bosoms of Hobbs and Nobbs and Nokes and Stokes, Browning's names, as everyone knows, for the popular writers of England, those who get away with it, and so set the pace. But there are writers in England, and critics, and ordinary people, who feel how strange some of this literature can be: 'No English playwright could afford to write this play about English people, and I have no means of knowing whether such plays about the Irish by an Irish playwright are ever produced in Ireland, and if so what happens to them or him.'

This is Mr. James Agate on *Paul Twyning*.[14] Mr. Agate is not a pro-Gael, he is not very squeamish. It seems that things happen in a country with a strangled consciousness that are incomprehensible to the inhabitants of a normal country.

Mr. Murray points out how this question of what is national literature turns up in every generation.[15] Some of us think it will continue to turn up as long as Ireland tries to express itself in a language over which she has not full sovereign power. If we were as far from England as America is, and were in numbers equal, not to say greater, and in wealth as secure as England is, then we could take any of our local dialects of English, the Kiltartan of Mrs. Mulligan's,[16] and make a national language of it, fitting it to our own mind, so creating such literary moulds as we needed. Nothing could prevent it from becoming a native language for us, we having sovereign power over it. As things are we cannot do this. We are anchored here, side by side with England; we are also a nation, even if our nationhood is strangled; and these two facts explain why we must get on with the work of putting Irish on top if we wish to express ourselves adequately and naturally. It is either that or, eventually, the extinction of a national consciousness. Fortunately the day when national consciousnesses refuse to be extinguished is come upon the world.

\* \* \*

# Jack B. Yeats Once More[1]

No, too much has not been written about the Jack B. Yeats exhibition.[2] The promoters have been thanked, certainly not thanked too much. To establish such a precedent as they have done, is obviously an outstandingly good deed. To those who placed the works so happily upon the walls (no small task ever) a word of praise is also due. I have found myself unwittingly feeding my eye on a grouping here and there without taking stock of any particular picture in it. Perhaps some few other words may also be said, for the evaluing of such an exhibition – an artist's mind in its most significant moods unveiled before us – is not so simple, while the implications in that evaluing may be far-reaching. The vital fount from which this refreshing and spontaneous treasure-trove has issued would seem to be in a very special sense the discovery that the Irish scene in all its moods and tenses was worth while. That discovery was induced in Jack B. Yeats, as in so many others, by the national revival that roughly began in the opening years of this century. The mists lifted more and more, and as is so frequent in such recoveries began then to settle down again. Perhaps for twenty years they have been thickening and re-settling about us – disturbingly. There has been in those years far too much running about after strange gods. Writers in English and Irish have been doing it, painters too, architects, and others. The value of what has been wrought out under such influences is now being questioned. It seems to lack staying power. That much of it, if any, will have even any sort of public tribute paid to it twenty years hence seems unlikely. Surely only a well-sprung, resilient, hardy and daring native culture could afford to take in such measures of heterogeneous foreignism as we have been taking in for twenty years (and with such assurance and wild words!). And our national culture at present, and indeed for long, long years to come, seeking, struggling anxiously, to come upon its own self! In our most fecund period, before the mists began to fall again, this groping of ours searched for the roots of the national being either in the heroism of our sagas, these so indubitably ours, or in that distinctive way of living, and praying and dying, which still survives, but less and less, in the far-off country places – a way not quite utterly forgetful either of those selfsame sagas. Both legitimate sources, and perhaps the only sources. Some of the pioneers worked in the heroic literature, others in the living tradition; few only were gifted enough to become happily intimate with both. Jack B. Yeats fortunately for him, and us, took to the country places. It is too facile to say that he had to, his genius shying at the magniloquent as at the academic. How do we know it did? If he had taken to the heroic with aplomb and youthful daring, wrestling with it long enough to test his powers; and then come from the fierce labour with more or less empty hands, we might be justified in assuming that he had not known himself. But he does not seem so to have tested his powers.

And it would equally be too facile to say that he chose the easier way. As if questing among living men and women, 'in their ordinary attire', as Whitman would have them,[3] behind their counters or at large in the fair, were simpler work than picking and choosing among sagas and legends, themselves in a way already picked and chosen. Life itself is never so simple as any representation of it, nor does it so easily deliver up its secrets. Has the life of our own countryside, except in the rarest cases, yielded anything of value to those who had come to it from Anglo-Irish surroundings? – people not unendowed, not untrained, unpractised. For all, life at large is more unseizable than life in history or song or fable; but for anyone from the Ascendancy side of our people, it must be still more obtuse and unreadable. They lack, almost naturally, one might say, that gift of mind which of all others is most necessary to the writer or artist who would find his matter in ordinary flesh and blood – tenderness; tenderness, which is the fine flower of reverence, that angel of the world. Come upon any ascendancy anywhere, either in history, or art, or life, and you come upon an established attitude towards all problems and questions: this thing can be done this way (usually the first at hand), and if not there is another in reserve; its name, main force. Either, because of the other, frustrates the spirit of reverence, out of which all art that is not artificial, springs.

Jack B. Yeats came from Ascendancy stock. One might with some assurance have prophesied of him forty or fifty years ago when he chose his path, that he would become, and continue to be, a seeker after the picturesque, the more outrageous the more attractive to him. To be such is not to be an artist at all, a creator, one seized upon by life for life's own ends. And more than likely the prophecy would not have been belied only that when Jack B. Yeats came to manhood those mists we have mentioned were clearing away, leaving an inviting sky and a fresh wind. He found his own country a new place, as did so many others; very picturesque, too, and takingly tatterdemalion at first glance; from the leaning towards which aspect of it he gradually, and only gradually, won free, his vision strengthening towards tenderness and grace. Indeed, it is only in his middle period that one comes upon in his work something altogether aloof from entertainment value, comes upon such overtones as sing sheerly to the spirit itself. The value of many of the pictures painted between, say, 1916 and 1927 is inestimable; the evocative power in them inexplicable. The artist who achieves such works as these can be recompensed only in terms of mute thankfulness. They are classic in the sense that Dr. Pádraig de Brún[4] pointed to in his address opening the exhibition. In them, of all the aids an artist may use to project his vision on the mind – values, colours, shapes, weight, textures – not one is used so overweeningly as to undo even slightly the stress of any of the others. There is no excess. Naturally in general the effect is quiet, the colours subdued, shell-like often in tint and texture. Yet quiet and all as in general they are, they win upon us more and more, enter in, and deeply search us, evoking from the depths of us tendernesses and intimations, judgements, too, sometimes against ourselves. In all this evocation, which, of course, is nothing else than the illumination of life itself, subject matter plays its part, its due part only, as is the way of classic art (which can take any subject, even what we call romantic, in its stride). Inactive, however, the subject matter never is, nor unvocal, nor limp: and there is no way of differentiating between what influence it is continuously exerting upon us, and what those other aids of their own intrinsic power are also exerting upon us at the same time, and continuously. Subject matter in such work and these aids – each a living force in itself – are harmoniously co-ordinated, as, again, is the way of classic art. So that in these middle-period pictures we have that nameless grace that can be impaired by a shade the more or a ray the less. It is because of this tensioned resilience that they are so powerfully evocative – powerfully, though not immediately so, perennially however, once they become ours.

One wonders if some of the last period pictures, on the other hand, those that have to be interpreted for us in words, would suffer appreciable disturbance if several additional shades and rays were added to them. Perhaps it is my own limitations that prevent me from finding them so evocative, or so magical in any way. One cannot help noticing tones that are exaggerated, noticing, too, sometimes a weighing of colour without an increase of substance. One must admit that an artist cannot help becoming impatient with a technique that he has mastered; but whether an artist should become impatient with the very nature of his medium when tried out on subjects that do not lend themselves to it at all, that is another question.

Among the latest pictures, however, are some as painter-like as ever, pictures one should like to live with. For instance, *A Dusty Road* (1940), the *Belle of Chinatown* – two in which the subject matter hardly counts at all, and *Farewell to the Sea* in which it counts for much. This last picture is quite summary in its statement, yet full of spirit, the poise of the figure masterly with a tender intimacy.

One does not wish to see national tributes become an annual event; one does think, however, that there is every reason for perpetuating so natural and so gracious a feature of the community's life. And Sean Keating would seem to be the next name on the list.[5]

PART THREE

The Nation and the State

# Their First Fault[1]

Many a lyric hangs for us like a rich cloud in the air: we are glad for its balance, its rich glow, almost for its aloofness. Or such a poem we may liken to a well-shaped vase on which the colours have run and fused into a pattern more subtle and moving than the artist's carefully-wrought design. Such a vase brightens a dark corner – it, too, is a glowing thing, self-contained and aloof from the stir and fretting of the hours. But then somehow it may happen that that haughty vessel or serene cloud suddenly, for all its self-poised aloofness, takes possession of us and flings us or raises us, not to those serene heavens where we pictured it as mocking at the fret of life, but right into the whirlwinds and quakings of life itself.

In Browning's *Paracelsus*, there is a lyric, 'Over the Sea our Galleys went,' which for me at least shone always for and in its own splendour – a rich thing, full of colour and movement, a superb piece of decoration. That and no more. And then that aloof piece of decoration seems suddenly not to have taken on life, but to have taken on some spirit over and above it, for what I feel is that it has flung me through its own power deeper into life than I should have ventured had that self-poised lyric never existed.

It opens:

> Over the sea our galleys went,
> With cleaving prows in order brave,
> To a speeding wind and a bounding wave —
> A gallant armament.[2]

In the galleys are adventurers out to find a better land. They are weary with the toil and with the long journeying, but still brave and with hearts for music and song. All that is theirs of value is with them: they have said farewell to all their past: it has long since fallen below the stars on the horizon. And so they sail.

On each deck is a stately tent:

> Where cedar-pales in scented row
> Kept out the flakes of the dancing brine:
> And an awning drooped the mast below,
> In fold on fold of the purple fine.
> That neither noon-tide, nor star-shine
> Nor moonlight cold which maketh mad
> Might pierce the regal tenement.[3]

What precious freight was enclosed in these central tents of perfumed cedar wood, on every deck? But the story goes on.

At last they spy out the dim shape of land.

> One morn, the land appeared! a speck
> Dim trembling betwixt sea and sky —
> Avoid it, cried our pilot, check
> The shout, restrain the longing eye![4]

But in vain the wiser pilot went amongst them, crying out his warnings:

> But the heaving sea was black behind
> For many a night and many a day,
> And land, though but a rock, drew nigh;[5]

And, though but a rock, that land enticed them to its barren bosom – them and their riches – them and their very soul. At last it is time for them to disclose the treasure within the cedar tents.

> So we broke the cedar pales away,
> Let the purple awning flap in the wind,
> And a statue bright was on every deck![6]

And then:

> We, shouted, every man of us,
> And steered right into the harbour thus,
> With pomp and pæan glorious.
> An hundred shapes of lucid stone!
> All day we built a shrine for each —
> A shrine of rock for everyone —
> Nor paused we till in the westering sun
> We sate together on the beach
> To sing, because our task was done;[7]

And then:

> When lo! what shouts and merry songs!
> What laughter all the distance stirs!
> What raft comes loaded with its throngs
> Of gentle islanders?[8]

And then:

> Oh, then we awoke with a sudden start
> From our deep dream; we knew, too late,
> How bare the rock, how desolate,
> To which we had flung our precious freight.

> 'The islets are just at hand,' they cried;
> 'Like cloudlets faint at even sleeping,
> Our temple-gates are opened wide,
> Our olive-groves thick shade are keeping
> For the lucid shapes you bring' — they cried.[9]

And then mark what they did next:

> Yet we called out — 'Depart!
> Our gifts, once given, must here abide:
> Our work is done; we have no heart
> To mar our work, though vain' — we cried.[10]

To the barren rock they clung – they and their precious freightage – although the islands of the temples and the olive groves were still at hand. And here is the comment on the whole thing:

> Nay, wait: all this in tracings faint
> May still be read on that deserted rock,
> On rugged stones, strewn here and there, but piled
> In order once.[11]

Then follows – mark what follows:

> The sad rhyme of the men who proudly clung
> To their first fault, and withered in their pride![12]

Such is some account of a lyric that had always existed for me as a rich cloud or a well-shaped vessel. Now! Now! It is with me night and day. Every voice I hear in the streets – they seem speaking in the very accents of the sad rhyme of this people who long since vanished from the face of the earth – leaving but faint markings on the bare rock which they would persuade themselves was worthy of their lucid stones.

* * *

# A Landscape in the West[1]

The landscape, as if consciously, piles itself up, slowly, slowly, gathering its strength from far off against the ocean. And to stand on the cliffs, to look down through the flights of never-resting, ever-screaming seagulls on the passion of the baffled foam beneath is to feel with the dull patient earth in thus massing itself against the tireless waves. A vast, dun-coloured, mournful landscape, that needed not, one thinks, those far-flung various ruins to help it sway our minds towards its own broodings.

One's thought is that it is the self-same elemental powers as here are never quiet that have made such lavish wreckage. But no. The ruins are not old, the earliest stone of all those broken walls was laid fresh into the earth not quite eighty years ago. Yet so dilapidated, so hoary even, their appearance now that one finds it hard to think that they easily might yet have not shed their first gloss and shapeliness, for what is eighty years in the life of substantial masonry?

The name of one man, long since dead, is written everywhere. Gaelic, yet the name of a family that for almost two hundred years before this son was born to the house, had turned its back on all things that speak native and not outland. If in earlier times the unbookish Normans became more Irish than the Irish themselves, in later times certain of the long-annaled Gaels became more Cromwellian than the upstart Cromwellians themselves. It is, however, the name of one individual, not that of the family, that is written in these ruins upon the wind-swept uplands. 'This was his house.' We turn out glance, piercing though the over-grown parkland, and, at last, half-emerging from the grey clustering trees we discover the stripped roof-timbers of a broken mansion. 'His stables.' It was in the days of coaching and large hunting parties he built them, and without stint he did so, for his pleasure was to surround himself with company from Dublin, from London. I could not say how many horses might not find stabling in them if the gales had not left them without rafter or slate. In a rough graveyard by the sea we come on a largish tomb. The iron railings are rusted, are giving; so, too, the shapely slabs, panels and plinths. This tomb he erected that a friend of his might be remembered. Grottos elsewhere we come upon, overgrown with briers. Of all his erections one only we remember as still remaining good and serviceable: it was a stone bridge that carried the public road across the river that flowed through his domain.

Those ruins do not lie close together; far apart instead, so far that one might live and die in the place without, perhaps, ever thinking of them all as so many words in one story.

Far-flung, for the whole countryside was his. Was he a child that liked to write his name on every page of the book he had paid for? Or was he like Harry Richmond's father?[2] – his weakness a warm effusiveness of mind and heart, a theatrical lavishness, one who did not know when to stay his hand, at least not while there were any spectators left to applaud his gesture.

It was really a force outside himself that took possession of him at a certain period of life, uplifted him, flooded his being with an unwonted warmth, gave him to see, as for the first time, the swarming peasantry from whom he and his had been drawing sustenance century after century. That force was the O'Connell movement at the time when Davis had heightened it with youthful passion and play of thought.

It is curious to think how, willy, nilly, a great movement flows in time into the cells of every heart in the nation. Even those who resist it to the end, who seem to become only more surly and stubborn through this resistance of theirs, even those will have their sense of life itself, its generousness, its ruthlessness, deepened, awakened. Not a living being remains so cloddish as before, for no such movement can attain vast proportions without absorbing into itself the generous instincts of those leading ones whose souls it expresses, in some such manner as they themselves, those leading ones, express the most generous instincts in the soul of the nation. A great national movement becomes in its ripeness like some richly endowed individual, one whose personality draws out from all those with whom he traffics whatever they have in them of warmth and courage.

Before this rich landowner gave way to the impulses that the stirring in the nation had excited in himself, he must have wrestled with his new thoughts on many a sleepless pillow. Service was not one of the tenets of the creed he had been taught in his youth. Yet it is this holy word, service, that all, or at least most of those ruins on the uplands speak to us. During a certain number of years it seems he could not do too much to assist his tenantry and beautify the landscape. He had become an idealist. Nevertheless, the memory of him that still abides in the district is that of one who rack-rented with the worst of his class! Strange! But I think it is the memory of the whole life of the man, not the memory of his few short years of warmth and generosity, that naturally enough remains in the thought of the people. He outlived, of course, the abortive rebellion, the imprisonments, the exilings, the national collapse. To that collapse I can see him yielding. I can see him packing once more for London, wondering, it may be, that he could ever, even for a day, have dreamed of living out his life on those dun-coloured uplands above the sea.

I have never troubled to trace the stepping-down of that family, down and down, until one cannot now recollect whether it may not have utterly faded away. The stepping-down cannot have been quite the same as in the case of a Cromwellian house; yet, perhaps, it is the smallness and not the greatness of the difference that would surprise us if we troubled to compare the downfall of both. The Cromwellians never really established contact with the mind of the Irish nation. Many of them, for all that, were touched by such national enthusiasms as in their days rose and fell; never, of course, as our Gael must have been when once his heart opened to generous moods and thoughts. 'Spirit of the Nation' – it was a great phrase in those years; and how he must have, as I have said, first struggled against that spirit! And then, having yielded ever so little, how alarmed he must have been to find it become so insatiable! He would drain bottoms, pluck the rocks from the hillsides, set the plough where plough had never been, build house after house, shed after shed, scheme unceasingly – unceasingly! – yet only still to find that spirit speaking in his ear: Is that all?

What did the Spirit of the Nation really require of him? That he should re-establish contact with the mind of his race. That, and no less. He, following his fathers, had gone far, as far as he could from such communion. And he might cover a whole province, instead of a whole countryside, with benefactions without getting back towards it the distance of a wren's flight. The Spirit of a Nation looks not at the gift but at the thought of the giver. Does that thought make for homogeneity, for the creation or the re-making or the strengthening or the perfecting of a self-contained national mind? For homogeneity is the very principle of nationhood; and to achieve it a nation ruthlessly casts out, using economics as an implement. And if this be not understood among us here in Ireland, where in the world should it be understood?

And so in time this pervert Gael came to be cast out, even as if he had never been anything more native than a Cromwellian of the Cromwellians whose fate it was never to come into contact with the national being at all.

It is a vast landscape, mournful, dun-coloured; beyond it the plane of ocean, with huge clouds above it, fading into nothingness before they are half-way from our right hand to our left.

\* \* \*

# The Book I am Writing Now[1]

The book I am writing now happens to be – God between us and all harm – a study of nationhood: my enemies will call it a boosting of nationalism. But then I have no enemies.

Of course what really needs to be written is a study of imperialism. It is doubtful if we here in Ireland – ordinary people – can write calmly or wisely about nationhood, for the simple reason that we have not experienced nationhood; we certainly have not experienced normal nationhood. We have no more experience of it than any Hindu or Moslem in India has; and therefore it is a bit of an adventure to write about it. It is also of course a bit of foolishness. Now, on the other hand, we have experienced imperialism. We obviously have experienced it in a way no Englishman has. What we might then say about it should be of use. A study of imperialism by an Irishman could be nothing else than a study of Ascendancy – alien Ascendancy – for a country might also of course generate a native Ascendancy. Russia would seem to have done so. I have never seen a study of Ascendancy – a study of how being part of an Ascendancy colours the mind of those who uphold it, as also of those others who suffer it. For instance a study of Spenser,[2] Swift, Castlereagh,[3] and such folk – lessening down into shorter chapters on Carson,[4] Sir Henry Wilson,[5] Lawrence of Arabia,[6] St. John Ervine, written for the one purpose of determining what such men had in common in their mental make-up – should prove an interesting book. And quite a useful book, for truth to say, it seems impossible to admit that any history of Ireland can have validity unless the writer of it comes to his task with a firm grip of Ascendancy psychology. Well, for some reason or other, it is not in fashion to write about imperialism. That must be why it is a study of nationhood that I am engaged upon. Sometimes I ask myself what it really is that I am engaged upon, for nearly all the dreadful sins that I see listed as being the outcome of nationalism appear to me to spring directly or indirectly from imperialism. Chesterton when he was a Little Englander – though indeed he was never anything else, to give him his due – once said that imperialism means just keeping people down.[7] Well, if people are kept down, they erupt in the long run. And I really think that it was not fashion, though powerful the sway of it, that has set me trying to riddle out why some should call nationalism what I take to be the result of imperialism.

Naturally I try for my own satisfaction to clarify the terminology. Everyone must have noticed how what is 'state' in one mouth is 'nation' in another, or indeed in the same mouth a few minutes after; and 'nation' may also mean nothing more determinate than the whole people. When I am feeling particularly malicious I resolve once again to make a little collection of examples of the misuse of the terminology used in such writings. And here I quote some simple words from an early chapter of this book I am writing:

> To speak of the state is to speak of the institutions through which government is carried on. Where there is a government there is a state.

No government, no state. If we allow ourselves to say that a nation came into being on a certain day (as one so often finds historians saying) we are mixing up nation and state; for nations do not come into being on any known date, while on the other hand states often do. Now, if a state comes into being on a certain date, what was there before that date in that particular country? It is surprising how many will answer the question by saying: why, the nation! Evidently then, there can be such a thing as a stateless nation. There can of course be no such thing. If one thinks that a nation can be stateless one is thinking that somewhere in the world there is, or has been, a civilised people without governmental institutions. Where is there such a people? How could there be? Obviously, as regards the relation of state to nation, it makes all the difference in the world, we hold, both to state *and* nation, whether the state is governing its own nation or another. We say both to state and nation, for it is normally taken to make a difference only to the nation.

So much for that quotation. It may be noticed that those simple folk who fancy that a nation can be stateless have not settled for themselves the apparently puerile question: which comes first, nation or state? – that is, in period of time. It is not at all a simple question. For it is really another way of asking which is the more elemental in nature. Again one may glibly answer: the nation; for in our mind the state is really an elaborate structure. Yet, is not the state brought into being by sheer necessity? I quote from my book another few lines:

> [...] Whichever comes first, and how anything could be more elemental than crude government is difficult to imagine, and whatever the relation between them may be, whether both are native – that is, both nation and state, or whether one, the state, is alien, they are always two organs of the one organism. They are complementary in somewhat the same way as man and wife, whether they get on well together at all. Are they not always influencing each other – whatever their origins and whatever their relation?

Now as these few quotations will remind us, it can be taken for granted that when the state is alien and the nation native, the relation between them cannot be too happy – or too helpful to humanity. We often find this question debated by writers who seem to forget that an alien state set over a foreign nation is not merely a state – that is, it is not merely an abstraction. It is a *nation*-state. That is, it has a nationality of its own: so that in such conditions, you have two nationalities in a country and one state – a very mixed combination. We say certain writers do not realise the situation, for they may often praise such a condition of things because they distrust the tendencies of the nation-state as a thing in itself. Do they realise, for instance, that each of the four states governing Germany at present is each a nation-state?[8] In saying this I am paraphrasing certain paragraphs in my book for the sake of brevity, in an attempt to indicate some of the questions that must arise in such a study.

Now, apart from the opposition that must obtain between nation and state when the state is an intrusion, many writers hold that nation and state are *always* opposed one to the other from their very nature. In my work I quote these words from Dr. Hilda Oakeley's wise and well-informed work entitled *Should Nations Survive?*. She says: 'There is the opposition between the organisation which, being equipped with power for definite purposes, takes power as its prerogative and essence, and the community exercising its freedom in developing the values of cultural life, whose growth is inherent in the historic society.'[9] My immediate comment is:

> Instead of Dr. Oakeley's word – 'opposition' – we should prefer to use 'tension' – such tension as is more natural to civilised than to savage man. For the continuing normal function of state and nation finds sanction in the very nature of civilised man – the functioning of the state is man's nature as citizen, the functioning of the nation is man's nature as civilised human being. Man as citizen will cherish the state, for its collapse may mean death for him and his; while man as a civilised human being will not allow the nation to be scanted by the state, because such scanting must mean an impoverishment of what his spirit needs for full activity.

[...] Elsewhere in my book I make reference to those who, though not in so many words, take the state as a sort of engine controlled by the nation: they say it expresses the nation. This is of course to make of the nation a scapegoat. I quote:

> Anthony Trollope was a postal official;[10] as a bye-product he turned out quite a number of novels. But of course to know really what Trollope was we have to turn to the archives of the English postal service: in these we come on the man as expressed in his really useful work, not in his novels. But some might prefer to seek for Trollope in the pages of his novels. Or, why not seek an expression of him in both? If the state is the expression of the nation, of what is that repository of art, music, architecture usually called 'national' an expression? If it is not an expression of something it is nothing; and no one has ever taken it that the art-work of a people is merely the expression of the souls of those who actually created it. To think of seeking in statehood

alone an expression of the national being – in its rules and regulations, its armies and navies, its code of laws, its methods of law-making – is, it seems to me, to reduce the mind of man to a very simple common denominator indeed; for all these activities are conditioned by a prosaic actuality – by a sense of what is useful here and now. They do certainly express as much of the whole national being as the archives of the English postal service gives us of Trollope's being. What they express is useful. Only it seems to us that to interpret what they do express we must call to our assistance those 'nationals', poets and suchlike, who it seems spend the bulk of their time in fashioning out negligible bye-products. The fact would surely seem to be that the state expresses man the citizen and the nation man the spiritual being [...]

\* \* \*

# The Struggle Between Native and Colonist[1]

The story of one of the most historic resistances known to mankind should be worthy of being based on something deeper than politics. That story is the struggle between native and colonist.

As I hinted the other week in my review of Dr. McDowell's *Public Opinion in Ireland, 1801–1846*,[2] the question of how history should be written is at present a very live question. It is a perfectly general question and, therefore, no final answer is to be looked for. Our question as to the writing of Irish history is on a quite different plane, in as much as it refers only to a particular case – our own.

We may take it as obvious that every country should write its own history for its own people. In any case, that is what usually happens. That it should happen so is of the nature of things. Against the nature of things it is vain to struggle.

In January, 1910, the late Canon O'Leary, an t-Athair Peadar, wrote these words in a letter to the Vincentian, Father Patrick Walsh, who was then issuing very useful little editions of Irish songs under various names:[3]

I remember a long time ago hearing a remark from a student in Maynooth when I was a student there. The remark came at the end of a discussion about national self-respect: 'Every nation,' said he, 'has something to point to and to be proud of. We have not a single thing to be proud of.'

It is a pity that an t-Athair Peadar did not say where that particular student had come from. I'd wager he came to Maynooth from a town of a fair size or from a city. He might, however, have come from a one-horse town on the edge of the Gaeltacht.[4] But from the countryside proper he hardly ever came, and certainly did not come from the Gaeltacht itself.

When I say he probably came from a city, I am thinking of my own case: I might have made that remark sixty years ago. When I say that he certainly did not come from the Gaeltacht, I am thinking of what I came upon there when I first came to know it forty-four years ago. I was then thirty-one.

### WRITTEN BY ENEMY

I shall not elaborate these conclusions, except to say that that particular Maynooth student was probably, by his home and school surroundings, as much estranged from the Irish tradition as I was: he was probably also a bookish creature with such incipient conceit as that type develops.

At any rate, he seems to have come to the questioning stage. He had not, we may be sure, come as far as questioning the whole orientation of the mind of our writers of Irish history – practically all of them.

For I cannot think of any country in the world where so strange a type of youth could have come to manhood so dumbfounded unless he had been brought up on the history of his own country as written by its hereditary enemy.

Is not that our position almost still? – although, of course, quite a number of events have happened here in the sixty years I have been referring to – events of such weight and concussion as must have made their own rough impression even on the popular mind without any intervention of interpreters or historians.

What really are our histories except the story of the struggle of the English State to maintain its position in our midst?

And this is true of the best of them. It is even true of the excellent books left to us by the late Prof. Curtis – his history of Ireland, his works on medieval Ireland, and his other minor studies.[5]

Because Edmund Curtis took the trouble of learning Irish and developed a love for its literature, he gives relatively more space to the Irish side of the various stages of our history than any of his professional predecessors.

For all that, it is not unfair, I think, to include him among all the others, that is, among those whose work, taken by and large, gives us the story of the struggle of England to maintain its grip upon our liberties.

## THE NEW PATTERN

After all, are not all such books based primarily on the State papers of the enemy? Are not nine-tenths or even more of the authorities consulted by them written themselves after the self-same fashion?

One might notice how often those special paragraphs or even chapters which deal with the Irish side of the struggle begin with a conjunction – 'meanwhile –' or 'on the other hand –' or 'if only –' or 'after all –' or frankly 'now, if we turn to the other side . . . .'

If this be so, and of course we see that we are taking the matter in a very general way, is it not fair to say that the Irish paragraphs are simply tacked on to the main story?

And that that main story is apparently very authoritatively based on the written document and the State papers of the enemy.

Is it not then true to say that such few Irish State papers as do happen to make an appearance are most frequently only such as have fortuitously remained fastened in English files, preserved for what reason one can only conjecture?

It is the pattern of such books which is wrong. The story of Ireland from 1169 to 1922 is the story not of a lawful government in trouble but of a continuing struggle between native and colonist: on such terms the struggle has been resolved.

It follows that the orientation of our future school of historians should be the reverse of the orientation of that school whose work has been before our minds.

It should express itself in such terms as we natively have a right to expect. It happens also that the world at large outside England expects it not to be otherwise.

Our historians surely have their work cut out for them. But already they are aware that the idea of what history is is changing, that the State paper is somewhat at a discount, that the political side in future will no more be the be-all of history.

To be aware of such a change is not without its comfort.

The story of one of the most historic resistances known to humankind should be worthy, one thinks, of being based on something deeper than politics.

Because up to this it has in general been so based it could happen that a full-grown young Irishman could utter the extraordinary words that lodged themselves so deeply in the memory of a citizen of the Gaeltacht.

\*   \*   \*

# A Story of Two Indians[1]

Towards the ending of our struggle for freedom in the 'twenties, Margaret O'Leary, who was afterwards to produce some well-written and well-observed novels,[2] wrote me from Glengariff to say she had come on an Indian there who was inquiring into Irish ideas; she was sending him on to me.

After a day or two he arrived. He was well-made, lithe, personable, frank; and was immaculately dressed. He was a law-student from Cambridge. In those days such as he – representatives, not official, of half the suppressed nations of the world – sought us out, some of them falling from the sky, it would seem. And always they were wistful about, and generally hopeless of, their own particular case.

Before we had seated ourselves, my visitor took up a book from the table and, unbidden, began to read aloud a full paragraph.[3] I was rather taken aback, not knowing what he was after.

But I could not help noticing that his English was perfection's own self: it was more immaculately dressed than his own person. It really was the matter of language that had prompted the act.

Nevertheless, it was our struggle that had brought him across the sea. He talked and questioned as a law-student might be expected to do. He already knew a good deal about us. He wanted to know everything.

On his part he had much to tell of his fellow-Indian students in Oxford and Cambridge, how they would swarm up to London and 'demonstrate' when some pretentious Anglo-Indian Indian was billed to appear at some public function, his mouth stuffed with fine phrases about the solidarity of the Empire.

They were really in a privileged position. During the war they had been kept in safe-keeping in England. And they took toll of it.

## 'POOR INDIA!'

However, what I have to say of my visitor falls under two points. First, I noticed that he always referred to his own country as 'Poor India,' to our astonishment.

And so always it was during his stay in Cork, where he met with all the various types that made up the movement. 'Poor India!' they'd answer. 'Aren't there millions, hundreds of millions, of you there to make matters right?' He'd shake his head, and murmur once more: 'Poor India,' as if millions meant nothing more than individuals.

And yet, in the end, it was the millions made the difference. And to say so is not to lessen Gandhi's greatness by one iota.

My second point requires a different approach. Having gone everywhere round about and seen all that was to be seen, and having himself made a public speech at a rebellious *aeriocht* held in the shelter of Blackrock Castle on the Lee below the city, the time was come for him to depart.

And so he invited almost all those he had been meeting with to a farewell party in a central hotel – and he certainly did us proud.

Then there was some singing. If I remember right none of the songs was in the English language. At last, he himself was called upon.

He started on a then-popular concert-song. He was immediately stopped: had he nothing of his own?

As a matter of fact, he had not. He made several attempts. He got nowhere. His education had brought him to that . . . . And there's my second point about him.

GAELIC INDIAN

All this happened quite a long time ago – more than thirty years, but it all came back to me on a little journey I made lately from Youghal's dilapidated bridge to Cork City. Just as we were about to start, into the bus swarmed a half-dozen or more Indians, young men, young women. They were in holiday mood.

One was photographing everything. Another sat beside me – a young man of about twenty-two or so. We had a few words together – the hot day, the full bus. Then there was silence.

Suddenly he turned his face swiftly to mine and said: 'Do you speak Gaelic?' As swiftly I turned to him: 'Yes.' The next thing I heard was 'Cionnus tá tú?' spoken quite naturally, quite correctly. He had dozens of phrases, and he was anxious to add to them.

Before we parted at the city's bus office he had rehearsed at least half-a-dozen and written them down – the sounds, that is to say, in what I took to be the Hindustani script. Of the scenery we passed through he took not the slightest heed.

No, he wasn't a scholar. Nor was he a student. He was an engineering apprentice in a Coventry factory.

It was from his fellow-workers there, young men from Ireland – the new Ireland – that he had picked up the phrases – there, and in a hospital (from the nurses, presumably).

He told me that he and others had been sent from Calcutta and were to return there when they had put in six years; he had served three already.

He understood Ireland, I should say, much better than my Cambridge student of thirty and more years ago. I did not ask him whether he had forgotten the songs of his own people. I should hazard he had not. He took pride in telling me that in fifteen years Hindustani was to be the official language of India – 'official' was the word he used. It is a more useful word in this case than national. For national is a word of no precise meaning.

### THE NEW AGE

Now, what has brought it into my mind to write all this was an announcement I had listened to, that a new state was to be set up in India – in fact, several new states – and their limits were to be fixed according to the language spoken in the area.

A start was to be made with the speakers of Urdu – a language with a literary history of five or six centuries. The announcement spoke of these new states as linguistic states.

Truly a new day is dawning on the world. Even in little things one may notice it. Fifty years ago no young Indian working in an English factory would have bothered his head to pick up fragments of any language outside English: it was not done.

Nor would any young Irish speaker working in the same factory have dared to utter a word of his own people's language. That certainly was not done.

Little things these. But that notion of Linguistic States is no little thing.

It is little less than a challenge to that devastating uniformity which mankind's conquest of physical forces is threatening the world with.

### GOD SPEED THE TONGUE!

* * *

# What is a Nation?[1]

Dipping into an Indian book, Daniel Corkery asks – What is a Nation?

Lately I described how a law student from Cambridge, an Indian, on entering my room, immediately took up a book and from it read a passage aloud.[2] That book was Macaulay's *Reviews and Essays* – a book calculated to give an elocutionist every chance.[3] In my mind, however, that student connects himself more closely with another book – *Nationalism*, by Sir Rabindranath Tagore.

For, before he left me that evening, I had got him to write his name on a flyleaf in it. I am now looking at it. He added his address. It was: National Liberal Club, Victoria Street, London, S.W.

That book appeared in 1917, as my older readers may remember. They will certainly remember that its author, who had received the Nobel prize in 1913, threw back his title at England after Dyer's slaughter of hundreds of unarmed Indians at Amritzar in 1919.[4] Such a man should, one thinks, be able to discuss Nationalism.

What he discusses under that name is, however, only that bugbear imperialists parade throughout the whole world to blind the world from peering too insistently at their own doctrine and its effects, that is, at Imperialism.

On page nine he writes: 'A nation, in the sense of the political and economic union of a people, is that aspect which a whole population assumes when organised for a mechanical purpose.'[5]

'Political and economic union,' 'Organised for a mechanical purpose' – what has a nation as such to do with such labels? Surely what they attach themselves to is not the nation but the state.

It was as a protest against such false conceptions as these terms indicate that Pearse used, if he did not invent, the descriptive phrase – 'the spiritual nation.'[6] It was a useful phrase. It is still useful. But a nation does not need to be described as spiritual for it is never anything else. One might as well use such phrases as 'a human man,' 'a spiritual man.'

The state's business is, in part, to act and think politically, as also economically, and to organise mechanically when necessary – always acting and thinking for its own safety and improvement. The nation knows no such business.

The Indian poet again, on page 110, asks: 'What is the Nation?' and answers: 'It is the aspect of a whole people as an organised power.'[7] And almost immediately he tells us what a price it pays for being such. 'But this strenuous effort after strength and efficiency drains man's energy from his higher nature, where he is self-sacrificing and creative.'[8]

In saying this, he thinks he is condemning the nation, the nation as such. From what we have just been saying, is it not, however, obvious that it is the state he is condemning, in as much as it is the state, and not the nation, that tries to gather power to itself? It is the nation that is self-sacrificing and creative. A state is never self-sacrificing or creative.

Indeed, without noticing it, he is in many other places also finding it necessary to posit in the state (which he miscalls the nation) ideals set ever against itself in some degree.

These ideals, however, he never sees as a people's natural concept of itself as a community, existing, as such, in the plane of memory, will and understanding, a higher plane than that of mere physical existence, in which also as a community it has to make do. Without seeing it, he is always happening on this higher plane. Thus on page eighty-eight, we find: 'We must admit that there is a living soul in the West which is struggling unobserved against the hugeness of the organisations under which men, women and children are being crushed . . . .'9 Now his expression 'living soul' equates itself exactly with Pearse's 'spiritual nation.'

Understanding however, if we take the trouble of doing so, the inexactness of his terminology we can find many wise statements and judgements in his pages. He stresses the fact that a submerged people can learn nothing, properly speaking, from its oppressor: 'If you compare England with Germany or France, you will find she has produced the smallest number of scholars who have studied Indian literature and philosophy with any amount of sympathetic insight or thoroughness.'10 And perhaps I cannot do better than finish with this wise counsel: 'We, in India, must make up our minds that we cannot borrow other people's history, and that if we stifle our own we are committing suicide. When you borrow things that do not belong to our life, they only serve to crush your life.'11

PART FOUR

# Contemporary Reception

# A New Chapter of History: *The Hidden Ireland*[1]

Whether Mr. Corkery set himself the task of giving us a chapter of literary history or of social history, or yet a volume of literary criticism, it is not easy to say. He has given us none of those things, but something that is far better.

What survives of our Gaelic literature has far too long been the spoil of the grammarian and the philologist. The poet has been a subject for all who would compare his dress with the garments of to-day, would praise the tailoring or expose the patches, but would never once give thought to the man and the soul and the spirit.

## A PROUD INHERITANCE

Mr. Corkery concerns himself in this book only with the Munster poets of the eighteenth century. He could have chosen no better period for his study. For that age, when the Gaelic nation was an outlaw, when the stress of the long struggle was forcing it with relentless severity to break with its traditions, gave us men who in the fields and the hovels of Munster created for our literature the most superb examples inherited by any people of music conveyed in language.

The message of the poets was not always weighty, their thoughts not always deep; but the music of their words, begotten of an unequalled delicacy of ear, will stand for all time as one of the proudest heritages of the Gael. Our pride will be the greater and our pardon for shortcomings the more generous when we view that poetry as the work of an outlawed tribe, deprived of earthly goods and denied education; as the creation of farmers and labourers who could take up the pen only in hands wearied by the plough and the spade.

## A DYING POET

Where else but in Gaelic Ireland of the eighteenth century could one picture a dying, poverty-stricken peasant take his leave of life with such a gesture as that of the lonely Aodhagán Ó Rathaille:

> Stadfad-sa feasta, is gar dom éag gan moill,
> Ó treascradh dreagain Leamhan, Léin, is Laoi;
> Rachad-sa a haithle searc na laoch don chíll,
> Na flatha fá raibh mo shean roimh éag do Chríost.[2]

Mr. Corkery views those poets not as the grammarian might, but as the student of history, of a nation's spiritual struggle, and of a people's inmost heart, should. If he is over-severe in his condemnation of Lecky's failure to touch upon the story of the hidden Ireland of the eighteenth century it is because he can measure the mineral richness of the veins and seams whose very existence Lecky did not even suspect. He is scornful, too, of those who would teach us that all that was great and historical in that age had its origin and end in the doings of the Planters' Parliament; but we can excuse his vehemence as being the reaction against a fashion that would have us accept the days and achievements of Grattan's Parliament as the Golden Age, the period of supreme inspiration in Irish history.

### A NEW LIGHT

His book is one that can be read with profit and pleasure not only by those whose minds are steeped in the wells of Gaelic literature but by those who have as yet only caught a passing glimpse of its rivulets. He shows how the general history of the period influenced Gaelic thought, how it diverted the currents of literature from the natural course.

It may, perhaps, be objected that he has allowed Aodhagán Ó Rathaille and Eoghan Ruadh and Merriman to overshadow their contemporaries more completely than their merits would justify; that he passes too rapidly over Seán Clárach and Seán Ó Tuama and Piaras MacGearailt; and that he has ignored Liam Dall. But one cannot judge the enthusiast as one would the detached critic; and who that approaches the study of Irish letters does not become the lover, ceasing to be the critic? The story of Irish literature in the eighteenth century is an absorbing chapter in our history, full of pathos and of tragedy. The merit of Mr. Corkery's achievement is that he has tried to shed a new light on its pages, to make it a human study. It is a merit that carries one headlong over his minor faults of criticism and evaluation.

* * *

# Gaelic Poets of Munster[1]

So much has been claimed for the Gaelic poetry of the eighteenth century, and so little done to show us its merits, and thoughtful people who do not know the native language, but are anxious to know about its literature, have sought in vain for a trusty guide to translate the best of this poetry for them and explain and interpret it. A few of the more famous poets, such as Aodhagán Ó Rathaille, have been edited for the Irish Texts Society[2] and the Gaelic League, but truth to tell, the bald and literal translations which are given in these editions are seldom inviting or calculated to convince modern readers that this poetry *is* poetry. Now at last Mr. Daniel Corkery, already known as a man of letters, a Gaelic scholar and a student of European literatures, has given us a long and careful analysis of the work of the Gaelic poets of Munster, who, writing in the period that began with the Treaty of Limerick and ended with the Repeal movement, proved to be the last, and in some ways the greatest, masters of the poet's art in Irish.

Mr. Corkery's book is fascinatingly written, and the subject makes it all the more fascinating. It seems to us head and shoulders above any prose work in English that we have seen dealing with the more modern Gaelic literature. His enthusiasm and personality inform the whole book, but this in no way impairs its critical value; for in other fields – as, let us say, Homeric studies – we take for granted that the author is to be in love with his subject if he is to make us in love with it, too. The mass of stuff – biographical, social, literary – which Mr. Corkery has brought together in this most interesting book makes it one that the historian must read, as well as the enthusiast for Gaelic literature. The author claims for his book that it is a supplement – one of many which are needed – to Lecky's famous volumes on eighteenth-century Ireland, and this claim can be allowed without disparagement to a great name. Lecky certainly left almost untouched that side of his subject which we may call the Irish-speaking peasantry and common people of eighteenth century Ireland – 'The Hidden Ireland,' Mr. Corkery calls them – who, in the main, had not a single leader to represent them and whose thoughts, hopes and dreams were of necessity obscure to the English-speaking rulers of the country. On the other hand, it is to be remembered that in Lecky's time the Gaelic side had scarcely been worked at by people acquainted with the old language, and that, if Irish scholars had done their duty by the native records, Lecky certainly would have utilised their researches.

The poems and songs of such poets as Aodhagán Ó Rathaille, Eoghan Ruadh Ó Súilleabháin, etc., make then 'documents,' and very human 'documents,' for understanding the Irish history of their time. Nevertheless, the historian will not find anything very definite in them. Although the grievous pressure of land-laws and penal statutes provoked much of their verse, in the main the poets seemed to aim at leading the people away from present sorrow by pictures of the good old days when Ireland was under native lords, or of the glorious times that would come if James Edward or Bonny Prince Charlie should come into the Crown. They sang to ease their own hearts and the hearts of their listeners at once.

Mr. Corkery shows us how the poets of eighteenth-century Munster, though poor and without patrons, save for a few of the surviving Gaelic and Norman gentry in the 'big houses,' formed a true poetic craft, maintaining that craft at a high level, keeping up 'poetic schools' in various places, such as Charleville – or Rathluirc, as it was then – and existing in such numbers that almost every parish in Munster could claim a local poet of its own. Mr. Corkery gives many translations of their work. After producing much that is incontestably high in inspiration and a great deal that has poetic merit, these schools came to an end about 1827; and it is pretty clear that Daniel O'Connell, himself an Irish speaker and an old Irish chieftain, by his constant use of English for public purposes and his avowed contempt for Irish, did more than any man of his time to hurry the old language into its rapid decay.

We may conclude with a word on the poetic merit of Mr. Corkery's Munster bards. Ourselves, we feel that Aodhagán Ó Rathaille in some four or five lyrics is incontestably one of the world's great lyric singers. Other poems such as Donagh MacNamara's 'Bán-chnuic Eireann Oigh' or 'Fair Hills of Holy Ireland' are truly noble;[3] but other specimens here given of the Munster poets need explanation, analysis and understanding of their time and tradition; and so we can but commend readers to Mr. Corkery's book, which will convince us, if anything can, that the last native Gaelic singers were poets, indeed.

* * *

# A Book of the Moment: Gaelic Poetry under the Penal Laws[1]

Lecky said that to write the history of Catholic Ireland under the Penal Laws a man must draw upon the annals of France, Austria and Spain; and it is true that during the eighteenth century all the best Gaelic blood sought a career overseas, leaving at home a mass of people gradually being driven down to serfdom, not even peasants in the proper sense, for they had no secure tenure of the land. Yet Lecky knew about this underlying stratum of people, the part of Ireland in direct contact with the soil, only what he could read in English. Now comes along another Irish writer, not merely able to read Gaelic, but imbued with the spirit of a culture that has its roots very far back, long centuries before English was a language; and he is able to show us that in the darkest hours *mens agitabat molem,*[2] an intellectual life quickened the muddy lump. The moral of Mr. Corkery's book is that Gaelic Ireland in the eighteenth century had a future, because it retained conscious connexion with its past. Two earlier volumes by him, collections of short stories and sketches, throw much light on the Ireland of our day. Whoever wants to understand the struggle of 1919–21 ought to read *The Hounds of Banba* and learn how it looked to Sinn Féin.[3] But this new work of literary study, though it was nothing authoritative or final about it, illuminates Irish history in its continuity. Mr. Corkery has in rare measure the gift of sympathetic interpretation, which excludes rancour, and other forms of narrowness. He can put things in their right place; his vision is at no point limited to Ireland. But the case that he makes, to my mind successfully, is that Irish literature has to be judged by its own standards, and not by those which the Renaissance imposed. The point of special interest about Irish poetry is that it was a public institution with a social character; it was essentially the product of schools. And he shows us the pathetic attempt of Gaelic Ireland, when it had become one obscure mass of peasantry, to preserve this institution – an instinctive effort to perpetuate what was most characteristic in the life of the race.

For, so long as there remained one unit of the loose knit fabric of States which made up Gaelic Ireland, poets were maintained at the public cost. Mr. W.F. Butler in his book on the Irish Confiscations quotes the letter of some English statesman marking down 2,000 acres which the Maguires of Fermanagh set apart for the upkeep of their poets and chroniclers, 'persons that merit no respect but rather discountenance from the State.'[4] After the Ulster Plantation the last trace of Gaelic rulers was gone, but Mr. Corkery brings out very well that for more than a century the Big House with its hospitality to some extent made good what had been the tribal provision. The schools, however, did not and could not last as long as that, and the schools were the essence of the bardic tradition. Naturally, when poetry was a paying trade, men tried to keep it in the family; apprenticeship was rarely granted outside the family pale, and the craft imposed its own technical rules, most difficult of observance. Since they were accredited official poets, it lay with them to admit or reject; and both in diction and versification there was evolved an elaborate pedantry. But there was also definitely imposed the idea of style. Nothing in the world could be less like folk-song than the poetry of Gaelic Ireland in the sixteenth century. In the seventeenth, when the bard was no longer official, buttressed up by many conservatisms, but depended upon individual patrons, he must please or starve; and Mr. Corkery quotes poems to show how grudgingly these experts consented to write what – so at least they said – nobody could fail to understand. Neither did they think that the bounty of their patrons was adequate to their deserts and their needs; but they still had possible patrons to look to when Aodhagán Ó Rathaille was born, in the reign of Charles II. He saw the final overthrow of Catholic Ireland, and lived on far into the penal days; but he wrote to the end as an aristocrat for aristocrats – survivor of an order which took rank with the nobles, writing the praise and deeds of great princes and great families; and flinging his heart into passionate revilings and passionate lamentation of the changed Ireland.

O'Rahilly was perhaps the last of those who might be called professional poets: he had been trained in some survival of a bardic school, and was immensely erudite in genealogy; and he looked to live by patrons. The typical poets of the penal days grew up when poverty was the native portion of Catholic Gaeldom and every man of them had his trade. Most were schoolmasters, clever boys who had got Greek and Latin and English in a hedge-school, and set up on their own. But others were farmers – one or two even gentlemen farmers – and one at least was a publican, 'Merry John O'Toomey' of County Limerick, who hung up a signboard with a hearty quatrain on it, to say that any wandering bard would be welcome, even though he lacked pence. The public-house, it may be added, 'went broke.' But few of the poets ever had anything to lose. They were peasants, as a class; vagabonds often, about as virtuous as Villon. Yet the art which they practised was not a peasant art: it was academic. The schools were dead, the race of poet-professors was extinct; but the instinct for the school survived, and they invented the Court of Poetry. At the summons of the leading poet of a district they would assemble, in the Big House, if one were hospitable, in the chief poet's barn (they called him the Sheriff) if it were good enough, or, failing these, in the tavern; and there by rush lights, in the turf smoke, they would listen to the verses which this man or that, perhaps a passing visitor, had composed. In several places the Court had its register, a volume in which approved pieces were inscribed. There was no question of print. All this literature has been preserved, only in manuscript or by memory; not a few pieces have come down only by word of mouth, transcribed in these last years from the dictation of some mountainy man who could neither read nor write. Yet there were masses of it. Of all the poets the most typical is the most popular – Eoghan Ruadh Ó Súilleabháin, born about 1750 near Killarney, who set up a high school at eighteen and before he was twenty was ejected from it for trouble about a girl. Then he turned 'spalpeen,' or wandering spade labourer, on the roads with his fellows: and so it went on for years. Now and again he would set up a school; but always there would be trouble of one sort or other. At one big house he was employed as a labourer; some one wanted a letter written and the red-haired ploughboy volunteered: the letter went off in four versions – Greek, Latin, English and Irish. He was promoted then to tutor in the household, and there was more trouble – bad trouble, seemingly, for the safest way out was to enlist. He took to the sea and was in Rodney's fleet that defeated Grasse: wrote an English poem in praise of Rodney that brought him to the Admiral's cabin. There he was asked what he wanted, and he said, 'My discharge,' and was told he would not get it. But he slithered somehow into the army, and out of the army by creating footsores on himself, and so back to schoolmastering in Kerry, where he died of a drinking bout after fever at the age of thirty-six. Even to-day his exploits and his fame are a legend throughout Munster.

They were not all quite so disreputable. Pierce Fitzgerald, one of the most notable, was a man of substance, so respectable that he changed his religion to save his property for his children: we have his poems apologising. But a couple of others – Red Donagh MacNamara and Andy Magrath, 'the Jolly Pedlar,'⁵ also became Protestants, for a while anyhow, to get the price of a drink. Macnamara, who had been put out of a school, even denounced to the magistrate the man who succeeded him in that illegal and contraband occupation. Yet this choice blackguard wrote (in Hamburg of all places, for he was a seaman also) the most beautiful of all eighteenth-century Gaelic lyrics, 'The Fair Hills of Ireland.'

I cannot pretend even to understand their poetry for the most part, still less to judge it. But Mr. Corkery is manifestly keenly appreciative of literature in many kinds, and he derives delight from these verses. The rest of us may remember that long education is needed to enter into a literary tradition which is alien to our own. Anyone can enjoy Homer – but Pindar? For that matter, anybody can enjoy French prose, but how many Englishmen really feel as a Frenchman does about much of what by French standards is the best French poetry? In any case, the abstract value of this literature to the literary critic is not the question: my point is that from 1700 to 1800 there was in the province of Munster (where Gaelic culture survived strongest) a continuous production of elaborate verse having on it all the marks of a school. The typical form was the *Aisling* or Vision, a theme that recurred, like the Crucifixion, in Italian painting. There was the description of Erin, the beautiful damsel, poverty-stricken, ragged and oppressed, and the picture of the promised deliverer – a Prince from over the water. Jacobite poetry, but how unlike the Scots! Mr. Corkery knows that well. The 'intimacy, the warmth of feeling, the directness of expression,' are far from the Irish poems. 'Bonny Prince Charlie' was a living man for Scotland: to Ireland the Stuarts were 'far away people.' But, as Mr. Corkery says: – 'On the other hand, Ireland is in all the *aisling* poems; and the only lines in them that strike fire are those of her sorrows – her princes dead, her strongholds broken, her lands in the possession of churls, her children scattered across the seas.'⁶ We shall not understand rightly the Ireland whose filth and misery Swift described, Berkeley pitied, Young surveyed, and Maria Edgeworth made living and comical, until we realise that pride survived under all that squalor: –

'Tis not the poverty I detest
Nor being down for ever,
But the insult which follows
That no leeches can cure.[7]

So the wastrel sailor of Rodney's fleet put it in a verse. The Ireland that was down then has in our days struggled to its feet – for good or ill. This book is one of the things that teach us to envisage rightly what has so often been regarded as a prolonged *jacquerie* or rising of the serfs against their masters. 'The Hidden Ireland' was an Ireland that did not regard itself as naturally or historically servile: its poets probably did more than any other class to preserve its sense of right to freedom; and it is only justice that Ireland of to-day, with full opportunities to justify its pride of race, should recognise her debt to these obscure torch-bearers.

In the meanwhile, our debt to Mr. Corkery demands that one should say how much curious and interesting social history, in his pictures of the bardic schools, and how much acute literary criticism, especially concerning the effects of the Renaissance on European literature and art, has been passed by without the least mention, in this review of a really notable and valuable book, which is also most likeable.

\* \* \*

# The Other Hidden Ireland[1]

Professor Daniel Corkery's book, *The Hidden Ireland*, has kept Irish literary and historical criticism in a ferment ever since its appearance nine years ago. It challenged that version of late Irish history which was set forth by Lecky and followed by almost all later writers, at home and abroad. In effect, it said: Lecky described only the shell of Ireland; he ignored the real national life and culture; from him the real Ireland was hidden; he saw only the Ascendancy. Prof. Corkery drew a majestic picture of the secret Ireland of the Gael. His art convinced readers for whom the actual historical *data* long had been available in duller books. However, he did not tell the whole story of the Gaelic side of Irish history, neglected by Lecky and others who wrote before the revival of Gaelic studies. He dealt only with Munster, and Northern Gaels have resented his slighting treatment of Gaelic themes outside Munster.* He shewed as little sympathy for the Anglo-Irish as Lecky shewed for the Gael. If Lecky was partial, so was he. To dismiss Anglo-Ireland as unworthy of a Gael's study, however, is hurtful to Gaelic interests, seeing that a large part of Gaelic and Catholic thought was expressed, during two centuries, in English. The task of the just historian is to depict Irish history with the Gaeltacht as the core, but also to dissect the anglicised sphere, recovering whatsoever belongs to the nation and dis- carding only what is alien through and through.

Justly to understand Anglo-Irish history, we must make a bold departure from accepted opinion. We may find that there is a 'hidden' Anglo-Ireland as well as a 'hidden' Gaeldom [...] Let the case be summarised in propositions.

(1.) Both Gaelic writers, like Dr. Corkery, and Anglo-Irish writers often err by surveying only a section of the true historical field. The identification of Gael with Catholic is plausible in a study of Jacobite Munster, but it collapses at once if we survey the whole Gaelic field from Kerry to the Hebrides. The schism of the sixteenth century cut geographically across the Gaelic world. Scotland and that part of Ulster which was infiltrated, not planted, became Protestant even before the plantation of Ulster. On the other hand, a big non-Gaelic population in Leinster remained Catholic. Hence, we find Gaelic Protestants and non-Gaelic Catholics at the very outset of the period.

(2.) Three big Plantations followed, which affected the racial map of Ireland in all the provinces. It is a fact that English planters were assimilated in three provinces. Those planters who were not assimilated were the Ulster planters, who were mainly Scottish (*i.e.* Gaelic) by blood. The last plantation, that after the Williamite war, was that which produced the phenomenon of Ascendancy.

(3.) There was much more intermarriage between the races and creeds formerly than in recent times. This we may see by the absorption of Cromwellian settlers, the anxiety of Protestant writers, the tales of abductions, also by Anglo-Irish pedigrees, few of which, save in the landlord class, fail to shew repeated crossing with the old race during the century before Emancipation, and even after. The recovery of Catholic discipline after Emancipation was the main check on mixed marriage, now almost extinct, to the great benefit of religion and domestic peace.

(4.) Not merely was the black and white cleavage between Gall and Gael less distinct in former days as to blood, but community of occupation brought the two together more than now. Old-fashioned rural life made parishes

---

* 'The book has one very serious fault – the treatment of the Ulster poets. Corkery's criticism of Lecky might well be applied to his own work on the subject.' – Rev. L. Murray in Introduction to *Amhráin Sheumais Mhic Chuarta* (1925).[2]

self-contained. In field and fair, the Protestant minority (even if pure English as to blood) could not but pick up the language of the majority.*

(5.) The general knowledge of Irish by Protestants throughout rural districts, which resulted from these factors, can be demonstrated. We might take poets Comyn in Clare and Fitzgerald in Waterford county, so well described by Dr. Corkery,[3] as examples of Protestants who were indistinguishable from their Catholic neighbours in Gaelic culture in the Penal days. Farther back, the dispute among Protestant prelates in the seventeenth century as to whether services should be conducted in Irish[†] shews how considerable was the use of Irish among the Protestants of the seventeenth century. Bishop Bedell[4] wanted Irish-speaking clergy and Irish prayers for existing congregations, whereas the anglicising party (which prevailed) wished to spread the English language. The tone of the difference shews that Bedell's desire was not simply for Irish as a proselytising agency. Already, moreover, a Protestant version in Irish of the New Testament had been made by Bishop Daniel (Uilleam O Domhnaill),[5] and we have the testimony of Stanihurst[6] that, in Elizabeth's day, Irish was 'gaggled' throughout the Pale. Down to the proselytising movement of the nineteenth century there was a certain slender thread of Protestant Gaelic activity, as when sermons by Tillotson[7] and other Protestant divines were translated, in despite of the official policy of anglicisation. When John Wesley brought Methodism to Ireland,[8] his followers soon found the need for preachers in Irish if they were to reach the Protestant common people, neglected by their prelates in Ireland as in England; Gaelic preachers were appointed and it is recorded how one of these addressed troops in Bandon in 1798 in Gaelic after failing to make himself understood in English – they were Scots. As for the Presbyterians, they were largely Gaelic-speaking when they came from Scotland, and they remained so till a late date. Everyone knows the tale of how their Dr. Neilson (author of an Irish grammar published in 1806) was arrested in 1798, after preaching in Irish in County Down, on suspicion of treason.[9] A predecessor of John Mitchel's father in Newry was a Gaelic speaker from Scotland; he used to go down into County Louth to preach to a Gaelic-speaking congregation near Dundalk. Until seventy years ago a course of Irish was part of the training of Presbyterian clergy. When Cardinal Logue[10] was a young curate in Ballybofey, he was the cordial friend of the Rev. Mr. Steele,[11] a Presbyterian clergyman who preached on alternative Sundays in Irish.

These notes shew that there certainly is a *stratum* in Anglo-Irish history when the Protestant people were largely Gaelic-speaking, and in some places predominantly so; that they were interpenetrated with Gaelic influences and

---

* The small-holding districts of the Ulster border and the Donegal Gaeltacht shew to this day a community of occupation and of speech.

† Dr. Douglas Hyde's *Literary History of Ireland* gives typical *dicta*.[12]

largely by Gaelic blood. Some might claim that Irish Protestants, by rights, are as un-English as the Scots. Suffice it here to make the modest claim that their history never can be written justly until the Gaelic *stratum* has been explored, instead of ignored. Obviously, it must have left a great mark on the Anglo-Irish mind. To some of us an intangible kind of evidence is strong: I mean the rhythm of natural speech. No Englishman can write a ballad in the 'Irish mode,'* but it is a matter of common experience that Irish Protestants have the very accent in their popular verse.† Gaelic ancestry is manifest here to such a critic as MacDonagh. A scrutiny of popular Anglo-Irish writings, as distinct from works that bear the classical discipline of the University of Dublin, would be fruitful. What would we not give to recover those ballads which Goldsmith wrote in student days, indulging a racy genius that he restrained in his formal literary work! Traces of the Gaelic *stratum* in Irish Protestantism are found, not merely in the Anglo-Irish accent, however, but in Gaelic letters. One of the errors in modern criticism is to assume that everything found in Irish is *ipso facto* a Catholic production, an expression of the true Irish spirit, as if everything in good English from Milton to Mitchel should be regarded as the voice of England. In truth, Gaelic literature, although overwhelmingly Catholic, does contain some works of a diverse mind [. . .]

We may make bold, perhaps, to claim that Anglo-Ireland could have become completely Gaelic as it became completely English if, from 1700 to 1750, the balance had not been turned by certain factors.

One factor was emigration. It might be objected to the theory of a big Protestant Gaelic *stratum* that it left disproportionately small traces; but this takes a different aspect when we read of the enormous emigration of Protestants throughout the eighteenth century.

> 'For nearly three-quarters of a century,' writes Lecky,‡ 'the drain of the energetic Protestant population continued, and their places, when occupied at all, were occupied by a Catholic cottier population . . . . The famine of 1740 and 1741 gave an immense impulse to the movement, and it is said that for several years the Protestant emigrants from Ulster annually amounted to about 12,000 . . . . They went with hearts burning with indignation, and in the War of Independence they were almost to a man on the side of the insurgents.'

In a word, the typical Protestant common folk emigrated in such vast numbers as to change the complexion of Anglo-Irish life.

* Thomas MacDonagh, *Literature in Ireland.*[13]
† Witness such extravagances as 'The Night before Larry was Stretched,' and some Orange ballads even.
‡ *History of Ireland in the Eighteenth Century*, Vol. I. Chap. II.[14]

The second factor was the official policy of the Protestant Church and the University of Dublin, its adjunct. As we have seen, the very men who most wished to create a national Church used that institution to discourage the use of the national language. As for the University, it was founded expressly for the propagation of the English culture in Ireland; and if we do find one of its earliest professors an O Huiginn,* a scion of a bardic house, he was engaged because he would be useful in the work of Anglicisation. In the seventeenth century, the University, like Ussher[15] himself, was not unfriendly to Irish historical studies. In the eighteenth, however, its distinctive bent was settled unmistakingly for Anglicisation and classicism. Swift and Berkeley were both the greatest and most typical of the *alumni* of Trinity College, Dublin. Nay, but their genius became its very *genius loci*. From them Trinity learnt to pride itself on a 'hard intellectual light.' Their philosophy may be traced in all the most characteristic sons of Trinity since their day – Swift's scepticism, Berkeley's subjectivism, the classical detachment from the living nation which we see in both. Trained in Trinity, the leaders of the Irish Protestant Church almost all have borne the mark that Swift left on the Anglo-Irish spirit. An Ussher might be a 'fundamentalist' Protestant, with a bias towards rigorism; but, since Swift, Irish Protestant leadership has been virtually Modernist. A religion thus detached from traditionalism could not but tell against the racy old Gaelic culture. The creator of Gulliver, who saw the world as a cruel phantasmagoria, could not love the things to which the Gael was loyal; the author of a subjectivist philosophy could not encourage the blunt Gaelic realism. Their disciples were alien to the Gaelic spirit. Hence educated Protestantism tended steadily to the detachment of its people from the old life.

It was among the common folk, so largely swept away by emigration, that the strain of Gaelic tradition lingered faintly, and racy Irish sympathies persisted. When a patriotic movement appeared in Protestant Ulster, in revolt against the Ascendancy, it was natural that Gaelic ideas should reappear. So we find the United Irishmen of Belfast publishing a Gaelic magazine in 1795; and the Corkman, Thomas Russell, on becoming librarian there, takes up Irish studies together with other Protestant patriots.† In the house of the Protestant Dr. James MacDonnell, in what now is Belfast's main thoroughfare, Gaelic poets, harpers and scribes meet with the comrades of Wolfe Tone, among them Whitley Stokes,[16] who financed an Irish dictionary and was the forbear of a grand family of Gaelic scholars; and the doctor himself is lamented in a Gaelic elegy in 1845. The Gaelic tradition, in fact, pouring in from the Glens, nearly captured Protestant Belfast, with a Scottish tinge; it was the political *débâcle* that prevented the

---

\*  Cf. *The Poems of Tadhg Dall O Huiginn*, Introduction by Miss E. Knott.[17]
†  *Gaelic Literature Surveyed*, Appendix.[18]

uprise of a Protestant Ulster Gaelicism, corresponding to the Gaelicism of the Highlands. We observe, among the United Irishmen of the North, a strong sense that the Irish language is as much theirs as any other part of the Irish heritage, and their remarkable devotion to it, and to traditional music, refutes the now popular theory that they were merely subversive revolutionaries under French influence [. . .]

The upshot of all this is that to identify *Catholic* with *Gael*, as it is bad religion, so it is bad history. It is a sort of Irish Nazi-ism. The Catholic body in Ireland always, since the first invasion, has included non-Gaels in high places; St. Patrick himself was no Gael; Catholicism and racialism are mutually destructive. On the other hand, whereas the Gaelic world once was a unit in blood, speech, tradition, faith, from the South of Ireland to the North of Scotland, a big part fell away from the Faith, and the character of its members was transformed. Religion, as we know, transforms the type where the blood is identical; in contiguous Scottish parishes you may see Calvinistic dourness contrasting abruptly with the Catholic way of life, as if different nations met there. The anglicisation of leaders was the agent by which the division was brought about, as when clans followed their chiefs in Scotland into Presbyterianism, and the Anglicisation of the Irish Protestant Church buttressed it against pervasive Catholicism [. . .]

To ask Protestants, or Anglo-Irish folk, to take up Gaelic studies is not to demand more of them than a due pious interest in their own antecedents. The complete boycott of Irish things, even on the census paper, which Lord Craigavon's[19] Northern Government practises, is unhistorical as well as illiberal; perhaps, for this very reason, it will fail, since the call of the blood must assert itself in the Ulster Protestants some day. All penal action against Irish culture is a mark of the inner fear that it will conquer – one does not penalise Esperanto!

In all countries, truth in history is the greatest of healers. We who desire spiritual reunion must wish that the Anglo-Irish will cease to rest on the political *Anglo* and will give its due place to the historic *Irish*, or Gaelic, in their past. To do this will be for the community to follow the path of so many individuals, back to the position where the roads divided and beyond which there lies the happier unity, spiritual peace.

\* \* \*

# An Irish 'Provincial'[1]

> Only for the fact that there was a nationalistic movement in the land
> when Synge returned to Ireland he would never have come to write
> *Riders to the Sea*, no matter how often he visited the Aran Islands, nor
> how long he stayed in them. His success is testimony to the necessity
> for such movements in every country situated as ours – that is,
> unprotected against the overflow of a stronger and richer neighbouring
> tradition . . . . Unless we learn to know ourselves, to stand on our own
> feet, we shall never achieve self-expression. Unless a writer sinks
> himself in the heart of his own people he will never, let his own gifts
> be what they may, accomplish work of such a nature as permanently
> satisfies the human spirit.[2]

In these words Mr. Daniel Corkery closes a study of Synge.

Those who are familiar with Mr. Corkery's *Hidden Ireland* will be quite
prepared for his dismissal of the whole Anglo-Irish literary movement as a
manifestation of 'provincialism,' but not even all of these will be in
agreement with him. The national movement affected others as it did Synge
– there can be little doubt now that the plays of the long list of Irish
dramatists and playwrights were written primarily for their own people.
Whatever may be said about the 'expatriate' novelists and poets, who, as it
must be agreed, wrote primarily for an external public, the men who wrote
plays during the past thirty years in Ireland had their eyes on the stage of the
Abbey Theatre or its forerunners. Most of these playwrights, including Mr.
Corkery himself, made their most potent appeal to an Irish audience, and, in
point of fact, only a very few of them have made any appeal at all to the
audiences of other lands. Irish plays in English are no more appreciated or
understood in England or America than they would be in Scandinavia or
Holland, and such a play as *Cathleen ni Houlihan* moves an Irish audience in
a manner in which it could not hope to move an audience in any other land.[3]
It is not ignorance of history only that prevents that play from its utmost
emotional appeal outside Ireland; it is the fact that Yeats created Kathleen
out of 'the heart of his own people.'

> 'Anglo-Irish literature . . . . as the phrase is understood,' says Mr.
> Corkery, 'is mostly the product of Irishmen who neither live at home
> nor write primarily for their own people . . . . The intention, whether
> willing or unwilling makes no difference, was not to canalise some
> share of Irish consciousness so that that consciousness would the

better know itself. The intention was rather to discover some easy way, in which strange workings of that consciousness might entertainingly be exhibited to alien eyes.'[4]

When a writer is faced, as the writer in Ireland invariably is faced, with a community which reads very little, and even when it does read, is prepared to have its reading material prescribed because of qualities entirely outside the realms of literary art, what else may he do but appeal to alien eyes and an alien intelligence? Irish writers are faced with a triple kind of censorship: first, the censorship of those who do not read at all; second, the 'reserved list' of Library Committees; and finally, the Statutory Censorship Board.[5] The worst of these, of course, is the first, as it is the absence of a large reading public that compels Irish writers to seek readers abroad. The 'Reserved List' in Irish public libraries also would be found enlightening, and one Irish author has suffered under the Censorship Board. If we compel our writers to seek their readers in other lands, Mr. Corkery ought not to complain then that they are merely 'provincial.'

In order that Irish literature may be Irish, apparently, it will be necessary to have 'a succession of nationalistic movements, rising and falling, each dissolving into a period of reaction, of provincialism, yet each, for all that, leaving the nation a little more sturdy, a little more normal, a little less provincial than before.'[6] To our mind it would seem that the real 'provincial' in this matter is Mr. Corkery himself: Synge's art made his appeal universal, and Mr. Corkery may be thanked for having ranged him with those who exhibited his countrymen entertainingly to alien eyes.

\* \* \*

# Synge and Irish Life[1]

Surprise is necessarily short-lived, and the plays of Synge no longer affect us with the breathlessness of novelty. A slight reaction against the exuberance and wild colouring of his imagination set in shortly after his death. But the limitations of his strange genius have been recognised, and there has been no serious questioning of his individual place as a dramatist. Even his position in the Ireland of his day can be estimated, and the violent controversies which centred around his work are now almost a memory. The partisans who saw in his work either a travesty of Irish peasant life or an exact copy of island manners and customs: all these excitable disputants have disappeared like the Kilkenny cats through the excess of their own zeal. Time has justified the claims of art; and *The Playboy of the Western World*, once the trailing coat-tail of belligerency, is now accepted with affection and delight by popular Irish audiences. Professor Corkery, however, believes that there are still prevailing misconceptions which must be cleared; and his book is not only a serious critical estimate of Synge's work but an interesting attempt to show how far, measured by the standard of Roman Catholic orthodoxy, Synge failed to reflect the native mind of Ireland. The author is well-qualified to present what must appear to be a justifiable national grievance. He is Professor of English Literature at University College, Cork. His own stories and plays reveal the quiet and devotional strain in Irish provincial life. Furthermore, Professor Corkery is an authority on certain phases of Gaelic poetry.

Unfortunately for the sake of critical peace, Professor Corkery opens his book with a vigorous attack on the whole modern Anglo-Irish school. In these poets and playwrights he sees the natural successors to Lover, Lever and the ex-Jesuit Father Prout. The leaders of the Celtic Twilight school spring from an Ascendancy class: they are divided by birth and education, by political and religious differences, from the majority of the Irish nation. Their literary market had been an alien one, and they have amused or surprised the world at the expense of the Irish majority. The author of *The Playboy* might well seem the worst of the batch, for his work was the centre of controversy, the very bone of contention. Paradoxically enough, Professor Corkery singles out Synge as the great exception from his rule of condemnation. To some this might seem but another instance of the Irish spirit of contradictoriness: in reality, Professor Corkery is but showing that consistent logicality which has so often given rise to Irish 'bulls.' His reasons are clear and succinct. 'To show how Synge stands apart from all his fellow-Ascendancy writers, it is but necessary to state that he, an Ascendancy man, went into the huts of the people and lived with them.'[2] Impartial critics might regard the work of the modern Anglo-Irish writers not as an interpretation or an exploitation but as a creation. Reacting from the cultural and religious traditions of their own early environment, they found in the realms of Irish mythology, folklore and life wonder and surprise for themselves. Their work is a record of personal approximations and rather of sophisticated delight. English poets have become tramps or sailed before the mast, even novelists have 'roughed it,' in order that they might savour an existence different from their own. Synge's adventure in the 'huts of the people' sprang as much from a modern literary fashion as from an impulse towards wild simplicity. But Mr. Corkery sees in art an impersonal or mystic process. 'Collaboration with a given people in a given time and place has produced all the classics of literature.'[3] Again he tells us that 'collaboration really means the fertilising of the whole region of conscious ideas by contact with the self-ineffable, self-incommunicable qualities of the Unconscious.'[4]

Having set up this impersonal standard of art, Professor Corkery proceeds to examine Synge's work, and to discover how far the playwright succeeded as a collaborator with the Irish folk. Though Professor Corkery adheres to the older-fashioned methods of judicial criticism, his analysis of the plays is painstaking and acute. We may note, for instance, his excellent defence of *Deirdre of the Sorrows*. Many critics have regarded Synge's last play as symptomatic of a decline or change in his genius. Professor Corkery finds in it a deepening quality, a promise of fuller imagination. A personal preference for chastened expression causes Professor Corkery to rate this play and *Riders to the Sea* above the more highly coloured comedies. The exuberant language of the comedies is, in fact, almost distasteful to him.

The main purpose, however, of this book is to show how far Synge failed to express the religious consciousness of Ireland. The religion of the Irish peasant, as Professor Corkery remarks, 'is a mighty fact,'[5] but the fact was given no great consideration by Synge. This aspect of Synge's work has, of course, been frequently pointed out. M. Maurice Bourgeois says of his essays: –

> One would never suspect on reading these essays that the Irish country folk are Christian worshippers whose religious feeling is often carried to an absurd excess of superstition and almost to fetishism. To Synge the Irish peasant is a latter-day Pagan, on whose old-time heathendom the Christian faith has been artificially and superficially grafted.[6]

Professor Corkery points out that most of Synge's plays were comedies and that it would be unreasonable to search in them for piety. He is content to object to Synge's over-use of holy names and to point out examples of religious 'howlers' which the playwright made through lack of interest or carelessness. But even if Synge were temperamentally inclined towards piety, he was handicapped in his collaboration by nature and literary tradition. 'Of spiritual sensitiveness Synge had little. In that – one regrets it – he was at one with all the Ascendancy writers from Swift onward to George Bernard Shaw.'[7] Not only that: had Synge endeavoured to explore the religious consciousness of the folk, he would have been met by almost insuperable difficulties. 'We can easily conceive how instinctively the islanders would shrink from exposing to the gaze of such a one the dearest thoughts of their souls.'[8] In fact, Professor Corkery makes it quite clear in other passages that only those who are 'initiates' by birth can really comprehend the Roman Catholic consciousness of Ireland. Under such circumstances it is scarcely reasonable to blame Synge. Professor Corkery, however, admits that, despite all these obstacles, Synge in one play obtained a glimpse into the arcana of

Irish religious life. 'Greatly moved on one occasion, he achieved his masterpiece: *Riders to the Sea*. It is the unique example where an Ascendancy writer entered with any effective intimacy into the life of the Catholic Gaelic people.'[9] As *Riders to the Sea* is the only folk tragedy written by Synge, and as in this play he showed sympathy with the spiritual life of the folk, despite all the difficulties propounded by Professor Corkery we may be pardoned for believing that the argument of the book has been pushed too far.

But in his examination of *The Tinkers' Wedding* Professor Corkery makes his position clear. Synge, the 'rebel' against conventional life and institutionalism of every kind, acknowledged the natural piety of the folk, but he expressed indirectly his dislike of religious institutionalism – a dislike which is not to be found among the folk. *The Tinkers' Wedding* has never been produced in Ireland, and its effect on Irish susceptibilities has not been properly tested. A pair of tinkers who have been living in sin are suddenly smitten with a desire for the respectabilities of marriage. But the sight of the black-coated priest suddenly fills them with alarm: he seems to them to be a representative of law and moral order. He becomes the fowler with the net, but unlike wild birds the tinkers express their alarm a trifle too vigorously. Most English readers would be content to take the comedy for what it is worth, as a self-contained work of art. For the nonce they would be content to see a clergyman as he appears to the childish and wild mind of wandering tinkers. But Professor Corkery is emphatic in his attitude towards the priest as a mere *Possenfigur*.[10]

> No one reared in an Irish Catholic household would dream of creating a similar figure, unless of course he were a mere sensationalist, for he would know that such a character would not be accepted. Even variations must keep measure, and literature, and more especially dramatic literature, is a game played by two parties – the writer and his public.[11]

It is hardly necessary to point out that, had Synge accepted this definition, we should not even have had *The Playboy*.

Professor Corkery's condemnation of the modern Anglo-Irish school might cause one to believe that he is not without religious and political prejudices equal in vehemence to those which he has imputed to that school. But, believing that art is a collaboration, he is as severe in his condemnation of those modern Irish writers who by birth and upbringing are 'initiates' of the Irish religious consciousness of Roman Catholicism. Just as the Anglo-Irish poets and playwrights have reacted from their early environment, so these writers have reacted; among the elders one need but mention Mr. George Moore, Mr. Conal O'Riordan, Mr. James Joyce and Mr. Joseph Campbell. The same revolt may be noticed in all the younger Irish novelists of importance, such as Mr. Brinsley MacNamara,[12] Mr. Con O'Leary, Mr.

Eimar O'Duffy,[13] Mr. Liam O'Flaherty and Mr. Peadar O'Donnell.[14] Professor Corkery's method of dealing with these younger writers, who are questioning and exploring the orthodoxy of Irish life, is simple; he expatriates them. 'The typical Irish expatriate writer continues to find his subject matter in Irish life: his choice of it, however, and his treatment of it when chosen, are to a greater or less extent imposed on him by alien considerations.'[15] Literature in Ireland must, in fact, be co-extensive with the orthodoxy of the majority. Professor Corkery's refusal to face facts would be of no importance were it not probable that his views are symptomatic of the Ireland of to-day. His book will enable English readers to realise the difficulties against which modern Irish writers who demand mental freedom and the right to criticise the prevalent ideas of their country must contend.

\* \* \*

# Corkery's Synge[1]

Belloc wrote on the path to Rome.[2] I am writing this on the way to Lough Derg – shall I get there? – in fact these actual words are being penned in Dundalk Station. I have just now been admiring the Mourne Mountains, seen across the water. But my purpose is not to write of the things I see around me, but rather of Professor Corkery's book, his new book about J.M. Synge. At first sight, it seems a strange combination, one of the most native writers, writing about him who has been taken as their leader by the 'Ascendancy.' The word is Professor Corkery's, and he is careful to distinguish 'ascendancy' writing, on the one hand, from 'native' writing in English, from Gaelic literature and from the brilliant productions of the expatriated Irish cosmopolitans, such as Bernard Shaw and George Moore.

The truth is probably that though we rail at the whole tribe of ascendancy and cosmopolitan writers, we generally have a favourite or two among them. Personally I favour the poems, and not the politics, of Yeats, and the plays of Lennox Robinson (I place him much below T.C. Murray, however). I am willing to make a present of all that Synge, Æ, and Seán O'Casey ever wrote. I mildly admire one to two things by Lady Gregory. The rest of them are to me not worth mentioning.

Professor Corkery, whilst having no particular liking for Yeats or Lennox Robinson, or O'Casey, or, I fancy, even for T.C. Murray, gives his every vote for Synge. It is probably not much more reasoned a preference than my own liking for Thackeray and O. Henry;[3] but reasons in full are given here. Professor Corkery admits that Synge was one of the 'ascendancy' in the fullest sense, but will have it that he was saved from ascendancyism by his studies of the people, made while living among them. He admits, however, that Synge turned an absolutely blind eye to the religious sentiments of the people, and to this extent all his work is out of focus, that he succeeded in making men and women who, like the characters of Dickens, never existed, is admitted. All Synge's people are without conscience, and therefore practically without real character. They are said by people who know the Aran Islanders to have only a faint relation to the islanders, from whom they are for the most part drawn. They speak a marvellously vivid dialogue, a species of prose poetry, couched in a dialogue that never was on earth. The attraction of wholly non-moral people speaking this strange tongue caught the taste of Europe and made Synge famous in his time. O'Casey did much the same thing with the speech of the Dublin tenements in our own day. Opinion has now hardened on the fact that Synge's dialect is as false to life as the picture he draws. Men neither speak like Synge, nor act like Synge's characters in any part of Ireland. He was in fact something like Turner, the painter, a brilliant unrealist.[4] And we can scarcely complain of the originals being hurt by the caricature.

I remember an account of the first night of *The Playboy* I got from the late R.J. Kinahan, the barrister, just after it. Kinahan was brilliant, but rather a conventional man, quite ready to enjoy 'a good story' like most men of his type. He said that the play gave the audience the impression of being not anti-Irish, but anti-human; and, of course, we all know how the audience rose at the phrase about ladies in their night attire as detailed by Corkery. I saw the play much later, and was surprised there had been so much pother about it. *Riders to the Sea*, a much better play, I saw either the first night or soon afterwards. I remember it gave me the effect of a visit I had once paid to a dissecting room, but the man with me was greatly impressed. Corkery says that it is distinguished from Synge's other work by a glint of Christianity breaking through it, but the main theme is that the hopeless fight against the sea is as pagan a motif as anything in Synge's work and perhaps less obviously offensive. As a tragedy, however, it is certainly effective.

Professor Corkery is of course right in stressing the fact that Synge died young. Had he lived to share the political enthusiasms of the next ten years, getting some idea of moral values the while, he might have won more enduring fame. His is all the time the work of a young man, influenced by the anti-moral tone of his artistic surroundings; perhaps he was to some extent in revolt against the ultra-moral and almost Jansenist tone of his favourite author, Racine. For he was one of the very few English-speaking men who had a real appreciation for that writer.

Even those who may not be greatly interested in Synge will find much to attract them in Professor Corkery's volume. He writes frankly from a 'native' point of view throughout, and is prepared to incur the penalty of loss of publicity and practical suppression which such a view entails. I need not tell readers of this journal how such suppression is brought about. Thirty years' boycott and silence has been the result of our labours, and any man who is unwilling to sneak to ascendancy and anti-Christianity will meet the same fate, to be ignored and forgotten by his fellow-Christians. For the anti-Christian forces are, if anything, stronger in such matters, and have more influence among Christians than even in matters of jobbery. He who writes Christian and writes well will write for the Irish alone, and for a very small class among them. Such a man is Daniel Corkery. My congratulations, therefore, to the Cork College for having chosen such a man as its teacher of literature.

* * *

# Synge and Ireland[1]

In the pages of Mr. George Moore's *Hail and Farewell*, the English reader may learn much about the political and religious odds against which the new poetry and drama of Ireland had to struggle for independence.[2] The *Playboy* controversy has been forgotten by the world and Synge's plays have long ago won the affection of Irish audiences. But the freedom of the artistic conscience is still ungranted, and every succeeding writer of originality must fight his own cause. Mr. Corkery's book is the first essay in literary criticism which has come from Ireland in recent years, and it is disturbing to find that this distinguished writer believes in more than argument. Writing of Sean O'Casey's plays, he says: 'To remain silent in the midst of that noisy gaiety, even to fling brickbats about, protesting against it, is, one thinks, to avoid the deeper vulgarity.'[3] Mr. Corkery, who has just been appointed to the Chair of English Literature at University College, Cork, has undertaken to explain the grievance of the brickbatters. His own novels and stories have distinction: they accept and present Irish life in subdued and quiet tones. His orthodoxy is unquestionable, despite the fact that his recent study in later Gaelic literature, *The Hidden Ireland*, unconsciously upset a pious legend and caused a flutter in ecclesiastical circles. But if Mr. Corkery is a novelist of melancholy charm, as a controversialist he is vehement and unsparing. His book shows the difficulties against which younger Irish writers of liberal mind must contend.

Briefly, Mr. Corkery regards the entire Anglo-Irish school as an abnormal phenomenon. It was the attempt of a small Ascendancy class, Protestant in outlook and education, to express the life and emotions of the Irish Catholic majority for the benefit of a foreign public. The comicalities of Lover and Lever yielded to the depredations of poets who seized on the 'wraith-like wisps of vanished beliefs that still float in the minds of a tiny percentage of the people.'[4] Synge, of course, reacted against the Celtic Twilight: he bid adieu to 'the skinny Sidhe': but he tumbled too deeply into Red Dan's ditch.[5] Synge came nearer than his contemporaries to the mind of the folk, for he lived in remote glens and on islands, but his temperament was peculiar. Moreover, in common with all Ascendancy writers, he had 'an inherent lack of spiritual delicacy.'[6]

There is a clear case against Synge, for those who dislike naturalism, and no amount of tubbing will wash out the pagan dye of his genius. It is this feeling of paganism which Mr. Corkery dislikes so intensely. His study of the plays is careful and conscientious, though a trifle academic. He employs an elaborate critical apparatus that is unnecessary, for the limitations of Synge's method and overwrought style are immediately recognisable. He finds fault with Synge's free use of holy names and his cordial dislike of priests. But he admits that Synge, in his one early tragic play, *Riders to the Sea*, showed sympathy with and knowledge of the spiritual consciousness of the Irish peasantry as distinct from religious institutionalism. If Mr. Corkery demands more from the plays than Synge could give, we may, nevertheless, agree with his final summary:

> The creations of Synge's genius have now passed by, as in a frieze. They were all peasants, even if a few of them carried crowns upon their heads. When they laughed, the laugh was loud and coarse, as befitted their background, a country public-house or a tinker's ditch; when they sorrowed, the sorrow was unrestrained and wild: the glens were there to receive it .... Such of them as were beautiful were reckless; and those that were grotesque were not conscious of it. They never took thought of that beauty which 'lies in no secret of proportion.' The rapture of self-sacrifice, the quality of mercy, the joy of reconciliation, the relief of forgiveness they knew nothing of: strangely enough, for all of us, however circumscribed our days may have been, have experienced such revelation. None of these revelations, however, recurred to our memories while our ears were stretched and our eyes opened to what was afoot among those excited and excitable men and women.[7]

But Mr. Corkery's tardy acceptance of Synge's plays as a self-contained world of imaginative art is, in itself, a condemnation, for he regards art as a complete collaboration between a writer and his people. Catholic Ireland has already given us Mr. George Moore and Mr. James Joyce: the young native writers are equally in revolt; but Mr. Corkery banishes them all beyond the fold. The Irish sex novel, in particular, must be kept within rigid bounds and its writers must 'transcend the lusts and shiverings of the mortal flesh.'[8] The fact that a drastic Censorship of literature prevails in the Irish Free State, that educated Irishmen are searched at the ports of entry for books that 'incite passion,' suggests that the abnormal and humiliating conditions which Mr. Corkery confines to the Anglo-Irish class may be of wider extent.

* * *

# Daniel Corkery on Synge[1]

'Every great and original writer,' as Wordsworth and Coleridge agreed, 'in proportion as he is great or original, must himself create the taste by which he is to be relished; he must teach the art by which he is to be seen.'[2] Synge has, in no small measure, done these things, and it is time now for us, the generation that inherited his teaching, to stand away a little and study the man and the dramatist in the light of our own time.

It is, perhaps, because of the glow of homage and the cloud of dispraise that seem alternatively to be played over his name, that Synge is, to many of us, a figure never clearly seen. There is an element of astonishment, always, in reading or witnessing his work – surprise that is not more surprising, or wonder that it is so moving and true; a sense that here is a writer who knew the heart's secret of Ireland; a doubt, then, that some essence has eluded him .... Synge's thought appears to us as does a mountainy landscape coloured by a high sun, the shapes and outlines merged together and lost. Then the sun sinks; slanting, amber beams fall across it, and ridge and crest and hollow are clearly seen. That is what happens when we read Daniel Corkery's book.

It is criticism of an unusual kind, for it is sharply individual and yet communal too. Individual all honest criticism must confessedly be, for what mortal can pretend to regard another with an all-embracing, god-like gaze? It is one human understanding revealing, of another, not the whole, but so much, only, as the critic's own gifts and limitations enable him to comprehend.

### INDIVIDUAL CRITICISM

Criticism is most valuable, therefore, when the critic is one who knows, analytically, the things which the creative writer instinctively feels; who desires, in literature, that which the writer desires; loves, in humanity, what he loved, and has worked, much or little, in similar material at the same or a kindred craft; and if this is granted there is no one living better equipped than Daniel Corkery to be the critic of Synge. He is able, not only to appreciate with a fellow-country man's and a fellow-craftsman's pleasure, the things in which Synge excelled, but his imagination ranges over those regions where Synge endeavoured to travel and failed to find the way.

It is in discussing these shortcomings that the critic seems to speak a whole community's mind – with that suspicious and exacting vigilance towards an Anglo-Irish writer which the Irish people invariably display.

### WHEN SYNGE FALLS SHORT

The interesting thing is that no one is more conscious of that tendency in the Irish people than is Daniel Corkery; no one has ever described it so accurately and so subtly traced it to its source. He shows that our 'overweening sensitiveness about the portrayal of the national character' is an unfortunate necessity in Ireland as long as the Ascendancy tendency to ridicule everything native endures.[3] He writes as an Irishman to whom 'religion and nationality are not separable,' and as one of those who 'go to the work of a native dramatist to experience a focussing and a clarifying of all their own tangled thoughts, impressions, desires, ideals.'[4] And he finds Synge wanting, in that the Irish peasants of his creation are devoid of religious consciousness, 'are allowed to have only a child's gaudy idea of the spiritual,' are incomplete portrayals of people whose lives are lived in the awareness of the eternal – 'for whom the skies have not been emptied of their heavenly powers.'[5]

The whole chaotic problem of Anglo-Irish literature Mr. Corkery treats with an intellectual courage and discrimination that are tonic to the mind. His judgements on the writers – Maria Edgeworth, Thomas Davis, Gerald Griffin, Somerville and Ross, Shaw, Lennox Robinson, are searching, yet, one is persuaded, fair. All whom he names, except Padraic Colum and T.C. Murray, come in for a share of blame as 'scanting' the spiritual element in Irish life. Synge he regards as a 'portent,' and *Riders to the Sea* as 'the unique example where an Ascendancy writer entered with any effective intimacy into the life of the Catholic Gaelic people,' and finds in this play a quality lacking in all the rest of his work.[6]

INTENSITY

In his study of Synge, Mr. Corkery reveals some of that 'quality of intenseness and power of impassioned contemplation' which he finds in that tragedy.[7] He guides us in the exploration of the dramatist's shy and brooding personality, as Synge himself explored the people of the West. Thus guided, with wonder and excitement, we 'feel our way into his mind.'[8]

The language that still has growth in it, the command of 'unbookish words' which Mr. Corkery likes in his subject, he, too, may claim; and what life, what reality they give to his style! How instantly the imagination catches his meaning when he writes of 'the vexing criss-cross of daily life,' of life 'broken up, as ours is, with the hissing and snapping of opinions!'[9]

That immediacy is one secret, all through the reading, of the exhilaration produced by the book. Thoughts and moods of our own, hitherto dormant, gather themselves together and leap, at the critic's summons, into response. Reading criticism of this quality is a release from a burden of bewilderment and a lasting illumination of the mind.

\* \* \*

# Synge and Irish Literature[1]

Mr. Corkery's book falls for consideration into two divisions, into what he has to say about the work of Synge, and into his theorems and conclusions about Irish literature in English, or 'Anglo-Irish' literature, as he prefers to call it. Other commentators have written about Anglo-Irish literature, with the difference that they were using Anglo-Irish as an identifying label rather than as a definition. Mr. Corkery however, going beyond Ernest Boyd and Thomas MacDonagh, uses it as a definition. For him Anglo-Irish literature is not Irish at all – curiously enough, save Synge. And Synge is admitted to be Irish merely for use as a stick to beat all the rest, from Maria Edgeworth to Mr. Yeats. To most people the phrase Anglo-Irish literature means Irish literature written in English. To Mr. Corkery it means English literature written in an Irish dialect of English. This would be understandable and consistent if his position were that Irish literature can be written only in the Irish language. But it is not. His position is that it is not language but material that matters. Synge's material, in some unknown way, is better than that of Mr. Yeats, and therefore Synge is 'a portent' while Mr. Yeats is a minor English poet. Maybe it serves Mr. Yeats right for forcing Synge on the literary world as a genius.

I will come later on to Mr. Corkery's general theory about Irish literature, but it will be convenient first to get Synge out of the way. Mr. Corkery attempts, twenty-five years after the hurly-burly, a re-valuation of Synge, and many of his conclusions will not be quarrelled with by anybody, even though few people will arrive at them in precisely the same way. The amazing thing, considering his bias and his impatience, is that he puts Synge so high, higher for instance than I would. He finds *Riders to the Sea* 'almost perfect,'[2] *The Well of the Saints* 'the most Irish of all he wrote,'[3] *Deirdre of the Sorrows* 'a ripened artistry,'[4] defends *In the Shadow of the Glen*, mildly rebukes *The Tinker's Wedding*, says pleasant generalities about *Poems and Translations*, and has a high opinion of the Aran and Wicklow essays – 'Sometimes I have the idea that the book on the Aran Islands will outlive all else that came from Synge's pen.'[5] Even for *The Playboy* he has only very mild reproof.

Mr. Corkery is under the very great disadvantage, in dealing with Synge, of starting out with a theory. His theory is that Synge is the only 'Ascendancy' writer who became a Nationalist (culturally, not politically), that he lived with the people, put himself *en rapport* with their consciousness, and that his writings are the result of that. Having adopted that theory to start with he must necessarily make the best of his exemplar and belabour all the other 'Ascendancy' writers, which he does. He tells us that the Irish language was the key to it all. But in Synge's case it does not seem to have been the key. He learned Irish at Trinity. Mr. Corkery, in chronicling that, permits himself a cheap sneer at Trinity. But he utterly fails to realise the significance of it to his own argument. Synge learned Irish, and so little did that fact open up his consciousness to Ireland, so little did it move him, that he promptly left Ireland and became what, in other people, arouses Mr. Corkery's contempt 'an expatriate.' He went to the Continent to study music, just as Goldsmith went there to play music. And he stayed there, wasting his time on music, and reading French poetry, until Mr. Yeats said to him 'Give up Paris, you will never create anything by reading Racine, and Arthur Symons will always be a better critic of French literature. Go to the Aran Islands. Live there as if you were one of the people themselves, express a life that has never found expression.'[6] Mr. Corkery quotes this, but is so engrossed with his theory that he misses the significance of it. Synge went, and he found in Aran what he had been looking for, material suitable to his peculiar gift and temperament.

Synge was a dark, silent, shy, sensitive, solitary, and brooding spirit. He was aloof and abnormal, with an affinity for the vagrant and the primitive. He found in Aran and in Wicklow the material which freed his impulse to write, and the fact which makes his writing so much better than others is the fact that he had a better intellect. To read Mr. Corkery, one would imagine that material and –isms were the things that made a writer.

In *Riders to the Sea* Synge was handling a theme which is at once simple and universal and the natural mould of which restrained and disciplined his exuberance and his riotousness, and it is the only work of his where these qualities of his are disciplined. It is easily first in his writings. *The Well of the Saints*, I agree with Mr. Corkery, is his next best writing. There is more of the abnormal Synge in it and it is by that more a lesser piece of writing. Parts of it are undisciplined, exuberant and riotous. Of *The Tinker's Wedding* there is nothing whatever to be said, nor of the *Poems and Translations*. *In the Shadows of the Glen* is a tragedy turned into a comedy difficult to accept. Daniel Burke is real, but neither Nora nor Michael Dara nor the tramp is – with their mists and their mountain ewes and Patch Darcy. A play might have been made of it if the tragedy of the original story had been kept. *Deirdre of the Sorrows* seems to me to be, on the whole, a failure. It is not that there is not vigour in it, and force, but that Synge's language and treatment do not suit the theme. *Deirdre* is a heroic tragedy and should be told either in poetry or in heroical prose. Mr. Synge has made of the characters modern men and women.

Now look at *The Playboy*. His fame as a world dramatist Synge owes altogether to it, or rather to the accident that it caused a riot and a controversy. *Riders to the Sea* and *The Well of the Saints* made no noise amongst the critics, but the row's the thing, and those who made the disturbance at the first performances made Synge famous. *The Playboy* holds the boards as an extravagant comedy, and Mr. Corkery's chiding of one or two expressions in it is very mild. No critic now would defend it as a serious play. But it must be remembered that Synge wrote it in order to shock the sensibilities of the Irish people, or at the best deliberately put in things for this purpose, and that at its first performances Christy Mahon was played by W.G. Fay[7] as a moral degenerative, by the express directions of the author. Later productions, with Fred O'Donovan[8] as Christy, turned it into the rollicking extravagant comedy we know. The truth about the *Playboy* is that Synge wrote it while he was smarting at the coldness with which *The Well of the Saints* was received, and that when he was rehearsing the play his comment was 'Now I've got something to shock them' [I have this on the authority of the late Frank Fay.[9] And indeed it is much to be desired that W.G. Fay should put down somewhere his recollections of this and other things].[10] Not that there is not good stuff in the play. There is. Christy and Pegeen, seriously treated, would have made a good play, but the 'Widow Quins' and the 'Shawneen Keoghs' are perilously like caricatures.

Somebody said that Wilde was the Lord of language, and somebody else went one better and said he was the slave of it. Synge certainly was. He created out of the living rural Irish speech a literary language of great lyrical beauty, and it ran away with him. Parts of *The Playboy* are little else but language. He wrote one masterpiece. He was an artist of talent rather than of genius, even though he did achieve one masterpiece. Outside that one masterpiece, which handles finely a universal theme, he was unable to resist the fatal attraction which the abnormal, the exceptional, and the bizarre had for him. Mr. Corkery puts him too high.

Now for the general theory. It is, in a nutshell, that only an Irish Catholic Nationalist can write Irish literature. Others possess 'certain inherited prejudices as well as an inherent lack of spiritual delicacy.'[11] But Mr. Corkery goes even further. Even an Irish Catholic Nationalist can only write Irish literature under certain conditions, he must write out of certain material – otherwise he is, in effect, an 'Ascendancy' writer. Mr. Corkery thus defines for us the material out of which, and out of which only, Irish literature can be written: – 'The three great forces which, working for long in the Irish national being, have made it so different from the English national being, are: (1) The Religious Consciousness of the People; (2) Irish Nationalism; and (3) The Land.'[12]

On this basis he examines and rejects everything before Synge – Griffin, Banim, Carleton, Lever, Lefanu,[13] everybody down to Sean O'Casey who, we are gravely told is 'an ascendancy writer.' Kickham is damned with faint praise. Of Synge he writes: 'Greatly moved on one occasion, he achieved the shedding of these prejudices, and wrote his masterpiece: *Riders to the Sea*. It is the unique example where an Ascendancy writer entered with any effective intimacy into the life of the Catholic Gaelic people.'[14]

Need I say more on this than that this theory of Mr. Corkery's is wrong-headed and damnable. It is carrying bigotry and intolerance into literature. It is a denial of the Irish Nation. It is prejudiced and, in the real sense, ignorant. Mr. Corkery specifies 'Irish Nationalism' without having the faintest understanding of what it is. He quotes with approval Turgenev's 'Russia can do without us, but we none of us can do without Russia'[15] and he forgets a saying by a great Irishman 'Ireland cannot afford to do without a single Orangeman.'[16] The principles of Irish Nationalism have been often stated. They were stated by Swift, by Tone, by Grattan, by Mitchel, by Parnell, by Griffith, by Pearse. They have never been seriously challenged. The Irish Nation includes all the people of this Island, Catholic and non-Catholic, Gael and Sean-ghall, native and 'ascendancy.' An Irish national literature must include all of them, and an Irish 'cosmos' – word beloved by Mr. Corkery – must include all of them.

Mr. Corkery appears to be under the impression that people write for the purpose of expressing their race-consciousness or their religious con-sciousness, or to serve their people, or something else like that. They don't. They write to express themselves, and the value of their expression is not measured by their material but by their workmanship. The difference between *Riders to the Sea* and *The Racing Lug*[17] is the difference between a great artist and a minor one – the material is the same. The same thing may be observed if one compares Ibsen with Edward Martyn,[18] or any good Abbey play with its imitations. Further, the artist is selective and creative. He selects such of his material as suits him, and he shapes and alters it to suit him. He creates something out of raw material. Take, for instance, Mr. Corkery's own novel *The Threshold of Quiet*. The people in it have the accents and the lineaments of Cork people, but there are no people in Cork so grey, supine, dejected, and spineless as these people are. Yet the novel is a fine novel. What Mr. Corkery did was to take a small piece of raw material, which is at his door, re-shape and remould it, and out of his own artistry and a silly phrase of Thoreau's[19] make a thing of beauty. Every artist does that. The greatest literature does not come out of any of Mr. Corkery's three essentials, or out of all of them, but out of the artist's own consciousness. If you go to the trouble of examining great literature, you will find that the greatest of it deals with individuals, and not with causes, types, sociologies, -isms, or any of the things which in other countries correspond to Mr. Corkery's three essentials for this country. *Clayhanger*, for instance, which is about people, is a greater novel than *The Man of Property*, which is about types.[20] While poetry is the greatest of the divisions of literature, and love poetry, which deals altogether with people and not at all with types or causes or -isms, is the greatest poetry.

For my part I think that work done by an Irishman, in an Irish setting and with an Irish background, whether done in Irish or in English, is Irish literature, and I should use the term 'Anglo-Irish' only as a convenient label, if it be used at all, and not as a definition. Maria Edgeworth, and Griffin and Carleton, and Banim, and Allingham,[21] and Ferguson,[22] and Lever and Lover, are all Irish literature, as Irish as Mr. Corkery himself. They are, naturally, imperfect, and they have to be judged against the background of their time, but they make, even the worst of them, an attempt at an Irish expression in English. English has become, in the course of time, a mother language here and we can, and do, express ourselves in it in a distinct and unmistakable way. We hope eventually to get back to Irish. But in the meantime and as things are we are expressing ourselves in English, and the feeblest beginning of that expression is as Irish literature as if it had been written in Irish. It may all, from William Molyneux down,[23] be only a transition, but it stands, and for the greater portion of the period it is the only expression Ireland has.

Mr. Corkery refers somewhere to 'race' as being the important thing in moulding a literature. Is it? Is it not rather geography? Climate, physical configuration? Has not this Island taken all the races that have come into it and changed them into something which is Irish in the broad sense, and not wholly Gael or Gall or hybrid? And has it not, moreover stamped its imprint even on those not born here at all who have come and lived here for a few years? Is it not the fact that those Irishmen who have written English literature have written stuff which is distinct, with qualities which English literature as a whole has not got? While Englishmen who have lived here have imbibed something which changed and strengthened them. Arthur Griffith, in his most exalted moments, used to claim Spenser, holding that he would never have written *The Fairy Queen* were it not for his residence here, and Congreve,[24] who was educated here with Swift, and, in modern times, there is no doubt that it was Ireland which released the genius of Trollope. There is a certain hardness, a realism, a brilliance, and a facing up to facts, which appears in the work, for instance, of such men as Sterne[25] and Swift and George Moore and Shaw, which has no basis at all in English literature. It comes out just as clearly in those Irishmen who have written in the last thirty years of intense national consciousness – Colum, Murray, Boyle, O'Duffy, MacNamara, O'Casey for instance – as it does in the work of those who wrote at an earlier date and are scorned by Mr. Corkery as 'Ascendancy' writers, and modern 'expatriates,' like Moore and Shaw. You can say that there is an Irish soil, and an Irish climate, and an Irish atmosphere, which are a potent moulder, not alone of men's bodies but of their minds; or, if you are mystically inclined like myself, you can say that there is a spirit of Ireland, an Irish National Soul, always trying to express itself through whatever population exists here, a Soul which is equally indifferent to religion and race. Bury this Island a mile deep in poison gas, and repopulate it with any race you like, and if you and I, reader, and Mr. Corkery could come back in a thousand years we would never know that there had been any catastrophe.

I throw the net wide, then. I claim as Irish Literature Molyneux, and Swift, and all those from Maria Edgeworth down to O'Casey whom Mr. Corkery abolishes, and I claim as Irishmen of Letters Scotus Erigena,[26] and Berkeley,[27] and Sterne, and Hamilton, and Wilde, and a multitude of others. I deny *in toto* Mr. Corkery's theories and propositions, explicit and implicit.

If one surveys at the present moment, the work of all those writers who are, in Great Britain, in America, and in Ireland, writing in the English language, one is left with four outstanding names, four names that seem reasonably certain of surviving – Mr. Yeats, Mr. Moore, Mr. Shaw, and Mr. Joyce. So far as Mr. Yeats is concerned, only a person applying the Nelson touch to criticism could write of him as Mr. Corkery does. The whole of Mr. Yeats's work is Irish Literature of the highest order. Not alone is he the greatest living Irish poet, but the greatest poet Ireland has ever produced. Everything he has done has been done with the touch of a master. *John Sherman*,[28] written in any other Nation, would be as famous as *Under the Greenwood Tree.*[29] We have been for twenty years acclaiming dramatic masterpieces at the Abbey, only to realise with *The Words on the Window Pane* what a masterpiece really is like.[30] Now look at Mr. Moore. His early novels are practically unreadable, though *A Drama in Muslim* is of value as an Irish study in manners. He began to write with *The Untilled Field* and *The Lake*, both Irish and *The Lake*, especially, being the first hint of the perfection of his mature style. *Hail and Farewell*, purely Irish, crowned him, and from that he has gone from strength to strength. Are *Heloise* and *Aphrodite in Aulis*, books of his which are not Irish in subject,[31] to be ruled out for that reason, although the whole strength and equipment of him are Irish? Is *The Shaving of Shagpat* English literature?[32] Is *Under Western Eyes*?[33] Is *The Ring and the Book*?[34] Now come to Mr. Shaw. Mr. Corkery, having called him an expatriate and all that, sneers at him as 'lacking in spirituality.'[35] On the contrary he is full of it. It is not alone all over *Saint Joan* but it is in all his plays. He is accused of writing *John Bull's Other Island* for the English market. It happens to be the only play of Shaw's which he wrote for a particular market. He wrote it for the Abbey Theatre, specifically and particularly for his own people [and it was praised by Arthur Griffith]. He is sneered at – because *The Apple Cart* is produced first in Polish[36] – as writing international literature. Shaw's plays are international in just the same sense as *Riders to the Sea* is international, that is they deal, like it, with themes which are universal. But Mr. Shaw, if he is full of spirituality, is not its slave. And his mordant ironism is essentially Irish. While Mr. Joyce is not alone Irish, but Dublin Irish. Everything he has ever written reeks with Dublin. If ever any writing came out of a cosmos Mr. Joyce's comes out of an Irish cosmos.

There are a couple of references to Æ which I would like to say a word about. In two places Mr. Corkery quotes gleefully Synge's reference to 'The Skinny Shee,' in a sort of glancing sneer at Mr. Russell.[37] Mr. Russell is not an outstanding literature genius, like Mr. Yeats. He is a painter, a poet, a journalist, a philosopher. But the thing which he is most of all is a thing which Mr. Corkery does not at all apprehend – a flaming and unique personality, a personality which he has squandered in a dozen ways in Ireland's service. His place is not with the poets as such but with the prophets and trumpet voices. If a great deal of his prose is not Irish literature, then neither is Emmet's speech from the Dock, Mitchel's *Jail Journal*, nor Pearse's *Ghosts*.

I think this book is a bad book and a mischievous book. There is hardly a critical opinion expressed about Synge with which one can agree for Mr. Corkery's reasons. There is hardly a critical opinion expressed about anyone else which is not superficial or flippant or unsound. The book, in fact, is not a book of criticism but a book of propaganda. Some time ago Mr. Corkery made the statement in public that 'What Ireland needs is Catholic Literature,' made it to an audience which, as he was well aware, not alone was not interested in literature but actually disliked and was suspicious of literature, an audience which meant by Catholic Literature a pietistic formalism which is neither Catholic nor Literature.[38] The present book is written in the same mood.

* * *

# Correspondence: The Heart Has Reasons[1]

Dear Sir, – A tag is occasionally a very useful thing, particularly when the tag carries with it the name of some great man, Pascal, for instance.[2] So with Mr. Hendrick and his 'heart whose reason is unknown to reason.'[3] If people whose hearts trouble them in this way would only ask themselves, as Pascal certainly would have asked himself, whether the fault lay in their hearts or in reason, what a deluge of drivel we poor reason-led mortals would be spared! In the present instance Mr. Hendrick is troubled by symbols, and 'such is the poverty of language that we can find no words to give expression to these hidden symbols.'[4] A striking admission surely! Language, which followed Dante into the life to come, cannot follow Mr. Hendrick into the labyrinth of his own reason. Again, has it struck Mr. Hendrick that the fault may lie not in language but in his own reasoning faculties?

Two eminent examples of this muddy thinking – if it were not that an Irishman is absolutely devoid of sentimentalism, I should have called it sentimentalism – occur in this last issue of *The Tribune*. First by long odds comes Mr. Hendrick's article. After this comes Mr. Corkery's 'Landscape,' otherwise an earnest and a beautiful bit of writing. They are alike only in this, that their authors are both wailing after something; Mr. Corkery after The Spirit of the Nation (the capitals are his), and Mr. Hendrick after those symbols which, inscrutable, so he tells us, to reason, and inexpressible to language, he first refers to as rains, then as winds, then again as storms, and finally as 'spiritual symbols that have been nourished and strengthened by the winds and the rains of tradition.'[5] Well, as Pascal did not say, 'what a piece of work is man!'[6]

But Mr. Hendrick's 'symbols,' like a Victorian novel, are dignified with a purpose. Those wild people who wish to preserve our Dominion status are gravely informed that they have mistook the 'purpose' of what he at last condescends to speak of as 'a storm' – at this point I failed to discover whether he was speaking of symbols or street-ambushes, but I know it must be one or the other. That a storm, being the work of natural forces, cannot have a purpose is beside the point; and, now that a perfectly natural calm has succeeded a perfectly natural storm, without the storm's having attained its 'purpose,' the only course open to us is to begin the storm all over again.

That, briefly, is the logic of the thing, and an extraordinary bit of logic it is. Indeed, of this reason reason knoweth nothing, and the less it knows of it, say I, the better.

Then comes Mr. Corkery, a very Oisin, weeping after The Spirit of the Nation. Were I in the mood to be merely satirical I need only requote that tag again and again in its original capitals to achieve my purpose. But I am not in the mood to be satirical, because to balance an intangible, invisible, inexpressible, rainy, windy symbol with a very noble sentiment would be to prove myself lacking in a sense of proportion. I understand what Mr. Corkery desires and I respect that desire, although I believe that with him feeling has outrun understanding. His incursions into mediævalism, like the incursions of Professor Stockley[7] into mediævalism, seem to me to be expressions of the mind left high and dry; no longer rowing, they would have the river stop that they may not be outdistanced. Mr. Corkery is speaking now of what he calls a 'pervert Gael.' 'He would drain bottoms, pluck the rocks from the hillsides, set the plough where plough had never been, build house after house, shed after shed, scheme unceasingly – unceasingly! – yet only still to find that spirit speaking in his ear: Is that all?'[8] Mr. Corkery would have us believe that until the man makes his peace with The Spirit of the Nation that work will go for nothing.

I do not believe it. I do not believe that the spirit of the nation, any more than the spirit of the Catholic religion, is a permanent and unchanging thing. I say that if his people did not accept this man and his work, whatever his beliefs, whatever his tradition, his people did not prove themselves worthy of him, and if they be poor as a result, they have gotten only what they have deserved. A nation, sir, is only a nation while it is absorbing life into itself, while it is absorbing individuals into itself.

I am not so foolish as to imagine that we can have a nation without the national tradition, that is to say, without the sum of what we have learned, but neither am I foolish enough to think that without our national tradition we cannot have a 'bus service. To think so would be to think falsely and to pervert every standard of judgement.

The truth is that we need our national tradition in the making of our national philosophy. It is not that tradition is itself a philosophy, for what is it but the sum of certain experiences? It is the reaction of intellect to these experiences which counts.

A last word for Mr. Hendrick. After the storm comes the calm; after the hysteria of the idealist come the low and heartbreaking sobs of Mr. O'Casey. Intellect comes between, and art, and industry. Mr. Hendrick is a relic of the storm, high and dry, with little learning. Mr. O'Casey, it would seem, is also by now a relic, and when we have left him, too, behind us . . . .

\* \* \*

# Correspondence: Have We a Literature?[1]

Sir, – Your contributor seems to be sadly at sea about the meaning of Seán O'Faoláin's articles on the study of Irish. Surely even a person who had failed to notice Mr. O'Faoláin's contributions to other periodicals would not so grievously miss the point of his complaints on the texts used in University College! These texts are admittedly not literature: no one of the authors prescribed could be called an artist: several of the books one might almost say are the work of illiterates. A. de B. answers that they 'are of first-rate value for students who are strangers to the Gaelic tongue';[2] of course if our University intends to cater for students who are strangers to the Gaelic tongue there is no more to say. The universities, then, are not as Seán O'Faoláin and myself foolishly imagine they should be, places of higher learning: they are mere elementary schools. But, even so, A. de B. does not seem to be quite sure of himself: he defends the reading of a book like *Solus an Ghradha*[3] by stating that French students in their leisure hours improve their knowledge of French by reading Pierre Loti.[4] I am at a loss to know whether this is persiflage or ignorance: Loti is the greatest of modern French stylists whose work is known all over the world: Pádraic Óg Ó Conaire's books, so much as I have seen of them, are infinitely worse than the worst of English magazine stories.

As to the main point of A. de B.'s article – 'Have we a Literature?' (by the way, I thought Mr. O'Faoláin's articles were written to show we had a literature) – as to this the answer is obvious. A. de B. says the literature of the eighteenth century is of great literary importance. Mr. O'Faoláin says not. Since none of A. de B.'s friends have succeeded in making it of any importance, since there is not to my knowledge any beautiful or desirable book of eighteenth century poetry, the discussion is obviously Mr. O'Faoláin's. Now, if one should say of the classic poetry that it was of no literary importance, there is always *Dánta Grádha* for answer. What would A. de B. have us read?

I am afraid that the Gaelic Leaguers, A. de B. and his friends, are quite incapable of distinguishing good from bad and they can get nobody to take seriously their opinion on what is good and bad. Who could accept the opinion of a man to whom Loti and the modern Irish authors are one? I quote from A. de B.: 'Let the poets of the people – that prolific school, with its remarkable verbal dexterity, its versatility and its living charm – be given simply a just place. These poets will then rank in Irish letters as the Elizabethan and Cavalier lyric poets rank in English.'[5] There you are! The very worst period that Irish produced will rank with the very best that English produced! Quite simple. All one has to do is to refer to Mr. Corkery and the thing is done.

Now, A. de B. writes a great deal of tosh about Mr. Corkery's *Hidden Ireland*. Listen to this: 'The principles illustrated by quotations from the Munster-men in a single century hold good over a larger scope of time and space, and it remains for other critics to apply these principles in detail to other schools.'[6] What in heaven's name are the principles Mr. Corkery has enunciated? Has he enunciated any? Are we to apply to the lyric poetry of the early centuries the theory that they are mediæval poetry? I hope not, and I would advise any critic who dreams of it to ask himself first whether the *Agamemnon*[7] has not about as much connexion with mediæval thought and imagination as 'Liadain and Curithir.'[8]

The truth is that Mr. Corkery's book is valuable not for its principles but for its enthusiasm. It has restored a historical balance which to us was maddening in its onesidedness: it has enabled us to look at one period of our disastrous history with a serener eye. The unfortunate thing is that it is not being praised for its real merits, but for qualities it does not possess. It does not set up literary standards, but since Irish-Ireland has come to that stage at which it realises its own nakedness, realises that beside the mature art which the Synges and the Russells and the Yeatses have produced, its O'Laoghaires and O'Conaires are the most insignificant scribblers, for this reason it will invent standards, invent anything that will restore its complacency. The Ireland which expressed itself in literature is, I believe, with Seán O'Faoláin, a great Ireland, but I am afraid it is still a hidden Ireland.

* * *

# Ireland Reads – Trash![1]

Is Ireland culturally swamped? Of course it isn't! Whatever may have swamped Ireland, it is not culture, English or any other sort. My friend, Professor Corkery, complains that the booksellers' windows are a sad sight because only a dozen books in them will have been 'written for Ireland or about Ireland.'[2] I could understand a man complaining that booksellers' shops were inadequate in comparison to those of foreign countries, that they were so few, that, outside Dublin, they were practically non-existent; that those which do exist sell little but trash. I can not understand the man who would console himself with the thought that the trash was 'written for Ireland or about Ireland.' I could not do so, nor, I am certain, could Professor Corkery.

The fact of the matter is that good books sell good books. Serious Irish writers get a poor show in their own country, because serious foreign writers are not read. The people who read Chekhov and Turgenev will read Daniel Corkery and Frank O'Connor, and there aren't, worse luck, enough of them to make it worth their while. Ireland imports eight hundred thousand novels, says Mr. MacManus. That means little or nothing. Three or four good public libraries would circulate as many in a year. Assuming that the average cost is something like two shillings (it is probably less), one can calculate the infinitesimal sum spent per inhabitant on fiction. And of this eight hundred thousand books it would be safe to say that seven hundred and fifty thousand are detective stories, cowboy stories, love stories. They are not novels; they are light entertainment, relaxation, dope. They have as much relation to literature as the cigarette in my fingers. They are not English; they are international. You will find them streaked all over French and Italian bookshops. They might as well be anonymous for all they contain of any culture. And now the Gum is giving them to us – in Irish![3]

It is the same with the cinemas, the dramatic societies. They have no cultural existence. Whether the stuff we see originated in Dublin, London or Hollywood doesn't matter a straw to anybody but economists. What does matter is that we do not see the fine things.

Ireland badly needs a cultural swamping. When I was growing up I read everything – English, French, German, Russian, Italian – that I could get from the local library or from my friends. So did Professor Corkery. So did Mr. MacManus. In time we made of them something that was our own. That is how nations, too, develop. A growing organism needs to be fed and better too much than too little. Ireland is a rapidly growing nation, and intellectually it is dying of starvation. Frankly, I am exasperated when I hear people dispute about the proportions of the starvation diet it feeds on. I have often felt, seeing a library van leave fifty books in a country parish, that if only one could leave fifty books in every house, there might be some hope. I have rarely visited a parish without meeting one or two men of outstanding natural intelligence who could have made something fine of themselves if only they had been given a chance.

To give these men a chance you must have not only abundance but variety of reading. That, I feel, is where the various censorships do so much mischief, because by the time they have assured themselves that literature does not contain harmful or subversive ideas, they have reduced it to a dead level of meaningless platitude. All that escapes is usually the trash I have spoken of. For some mysterious reason no one ever wants to censor that. For my own part, I had far rather read a dangerous book than a dull one. Ideas are born of the clash of ideas. A growing organism can absorb far more than people think and turn it into excellent nourishment.

I do not wish to be taken as quarrelling with the principle of censorship. But in practice it requires men of more than ordinary intelligence, whose values are ones that are generally recognised and whose judgements are to a great extent predictable. The judgements of the present Censorship Board are far from predictable. As Mr. MacManus says, they sometimes appear to add eccentricity to arbitrariness.[4] One effect of that, which has not been commonly realised, is that it makes it impossible for any Irish publisher to publish the works of those writers whom Mr. MacManus refers to as 'The Left Wing Group.'[5] The banning of even one book, such as Seán O'Faoláin's *Bird Alone*,[6] would be quite sufficient to bankrupt a small publisher, and it seems to me a most mischievous thing to make it impossible for the Irish writer to publish at home. Already he has been too much tempted by the English market, but this perpetuates that old bad state of things which compelled him to publish abroad because there was no market at home. Now the market at home is coming, but he will have to go abroad because no one will dare to publish his work here.

I throw my hat at the question of nomenclature. To enquire whether a book is 'Irish' or 'Anglo-Irish' or 'Colonial' or whether we find 'reflected in it the face of the people of the land,'[7] or whether it is the sort of book 'Irish people will take to their hearts,'[8] to ask if it is 'representative' – all this without considering whether it has any merit as a book seems to me the same sort of folly as enquiring the proportion of Irish books read by a man who hasn't enough to read. 'Irish' or 'English' are handy words for people who have to classify books; it may add an additional flavour to be told that a good book is typically 'Spanish,' but 'Irish' and the rest of them have absolutely no critical significance. Having in my youth made the mistake of damning all the writers I disliked as 'Anglo-Irish' and convincing myself that then and there I had disposed of them forever, I now abjure the hateful error, and beg the other contributors to this symposium not to repeat it.

* * *

# Synge[1]

## I

Since the plays of John Synge were first produced in our Theatre we have seen a revolution. In those days Synge was the wicked man, the foreigner, the atheist, the traducer of the Irish people. Now, thanks to the work of

Professor Corkery, *Synge and Anglo-Irish Literature*, he has been accepted as almost an Irish writer. If he did traduce the Irish people it was unconsciously. As a Protestant, he couldn't know better!

Professor Corkery's thesis is that there is no such thing as what he calls 'Anglo-Irish' literature. In Synge and one or two others there is an approximation to it; that is all. 'The three great forces', he says, 'which, working for long in the Irish national being, have made it so different from the English national being are: (1) The Religious Consciousness of the People; (2) Irish Nationalism; and (3) The Land.'[2] He then goes on to say that the mentality of a crowd of 30,000 he had seen at a hurling match in Thurles 'was chiefly the result of the interplay of these three forces' – apparently unaware that the mentality of any crowd or any man is chiefly the result of things far less subtle, and forgetting that later he will say that 'if Irish life differs from English life ... that difference is due to a quality of intenseness in Irish mind, there racially or else induced by whole centuries of suffering ....'[3]

But it is on the first ground that he dismisses the poetry of Yeats. 'It is not possible', he says, 'to imagine it as the foundation of a school of poetry in which these three great forces, Religion, Nationalism, The Land, will find intense yet chastened expression.'[4] And in so far as Synge remained a Protestant and alien to nationalist, Catholic ideas, he too failed as a writer.

One thing stands out from this judgement; the fact that Corkery considers literature a purely representative thing. For him the artist's justification is as a parliamentary deputy of literature. What three things in the early history of nineteenth-century England does Keats represent? Professor Corkery does not say.

Nationality, like period, like family, like sex, like bodily make-up, like vocation, like class, is something we cannot escape. It is one of the things that condition us. Keats, if you wish, is representative of the male sex, consumptives, the lower middle classes, doctors, post-revolutionary Europe, disappointed lovers, Protestantism, and England. And if he is representative of one then he must be representative of all. But that is what your middle-class critic will not see. He must have his cake and eat it – a determinist artist but only up to a point, because if he once admits that an artist is representative of more things than one he surrenders his case, and admits by implication that the artist is representative of nothing: is only an individual soul, is in fact nothing but an artist.

II

That does not mean one dismisses the Irishness of Synge, Lady Gregory or Yeats. All were proud of it, bragged of it as one brags of family; Synge, recovering from an operation, was heard to say, 'These damned English! They can't even swear without being vulgar'. Their books and plays are entirely different to anything that came before them; Corkery's attempt to lump Yeats with Anglo-Irish writers whom he doesn't like is as big a failure as his attempt to reconcile Synge with Irish writers he does like.

What is it that makes these three stand out from all the writers before and almost all those after them? Not their representative quality, for that, as I have said, is not a literary quality. Not their flight to the people, because that is only part of the story.

One thing I would have you notice is the audacity of all three. Now, one of the distinguishing marks of the border-line literature, the books and plays of which we express our doubt if they are really Irish; the work of the Shaws, the Moores, the Joyces, the Sheehans,[5] the Corkerys, the Somervilles and Rosses – is the author's refusal to fight. The orthodox because it would be wrong to fight, the others because it would be foolish to fight. Shaw and Joyce go away because they cannot be bothered to stay at home and fight out elementary things. Ten years ago an Irish playwright told me he did not care to fight for principles which had been established in Europe five hundred years ago. I wonder if he would say the same thing now.

Why did Yeats, Lady Gregory, and Synge choose to do their work in Ireland where every obstacle would be put in their way? Why did they choose to write for the theatre which in itself is a challenge to the mob? I suggest that the reason was a philosophy common to all three, though it originated with Yeats. That philosophy holds that nothing is settled, that everything must be created anew, that there is no such thing as progress, and that all utopianism is a curse. Ideas that run counter to the whole middle-class conception of life. We know that Yeats loathes the optimism of the nineteenth century, but even if we didn't we could deduce it from the existence of this theatre.[6] And in the same way we can deduce that the majority of Anglo-Irish writers are typical of the middle-class attitude, do believe in progress, and that Ireland is five hundred years behind the rest of Europe. Even Professor Corkery believes it!

Now I suggest to you that nationalism alone could never have created this theatre; apart from the fact that I believe myself nationalism never created anything. It needed this philosophy that everything must be created anew to send a man back from Paris or London to work out his destiny in a provincial town. And Yeats and the others wrote for the theatre because the theatre is still the purest of the arts; it is the only art in which everything must still be relevant, even if the relevance is only that of form. But Yeats's theories go deeper than that. If civilisation and literature grow old and impure, the language of civilisation grows old and impure with them. Acting, which is the sign language of civilisation, grows impure. Philosophy and religion, the mental languages, grow impure. So this literary movement of ours, if one surveys the plans of its founders, was to be an attack on middle-class civilisation, on literature, on acting, and finally, because inescapably, on philosophy. In each case the method was the same; it was the method of the religious reformers – asceticism.

Middle-class civilisation is full of things which to the ascetic eye are disgusting. We find it in literature in the form of opinions, notions of right and wrong like those we shall shortly see Professor Corkery handing about, sensibility and humanitarianism, uplift and long novels. We find it in the theatre in the form of loud-speakers, wind machines, properties, scenery, cycloramas,[7] and lighting sets; in acting as pathos, characterisation, and restlessness. It is everywhere and never sees anything directly; it is like a great barrier between man and the vision of his end; it fusses about the difference between Celt and Saxon, Indian and white, rich and poor, Protestant and Catholic. It is all the time explaining, defining, and one abstraction gives birth to another, because when Mr. Corkery has explained to us that the Irish mind differs from the English in its Religion, Nationalism, and Land, it is quite open to a Communist to come along and give us a completely different set of abstractions, and when Mr. Forster has written his *Passage to India* it will be someone else's turn and he will give us the Hindu instead of the Mahommedan point of view, equally relevant.[8] Yeats, the propagandist of the Irish theatre, is much less a nationalist than an ascetic who asks his fellow writers to take a vow of poverty, to write no word which is not living speech, to express no thought, as he says in praise of Synge, which does not belong as much to yesterday as to today. He would have them ignore middle-class art and philosophy and go back to the sources of all art and all philosophy: myth, saga, and primitive life.

He made many converts: a rich amateur like Martyn, a society novelist like Moore; but their zeal did not last. Martyn revolted against the English language only because he was a propagandist of Irish; and the society novelist, after writing a group of rural tales, transfigured by the maudlin righteousness of the reformed drunkard, relapsed into gossip. The best of the converts was his brother, whose paintings are still a Franciscan sermon against the self-indulgence of representation. His most remarkable were the very simple; the actors who for long years after the original impulse was past, preserved the rigid discipline, the noble poverty of gesture and speech.

That philosophy was his great gift to Synge and Lady Gregory. I do not know if he gave it knowingly, because he has made so many mistakes that I feel he may not be altogether aware of it himself. But they adopted it, modified it, gave it back to him in new forms, and to see how three such disparate personalities recreate in their work the same simple set of ideas is a study in criticism.

The borrowing, of course, is not all on one side. With Synge, dialect suddenly appears in Yeats's poetry and alters the whole texture of it. All three are preoccupied with language, and set about eliminating from their style all impure words of literary association; Yeats spends days on rooting out the word 'strife'; Synge ingenuously boasts that in *The Playboy* he has used only one or two words he has not heard among country people; Lady Gregory sets up the ideal of 'thinking like a genius and writing like the common people'.[9]

'Tragedy', says Lady Gregory, 'must be a joy to the man who dies';[10] in one phrase abolishing all the art of accident, all humanitarian literature, because it is impure. But she might have found the idea in Yeats's *King's Threshold*:

> Poetry is the scattering hand, the bursting pod,
> The victim's joy among the holy flames.[11]

'I showed Lady Gregory a few weeks before her death a book by Day Lewis', says Yeats. 'I prefer', she said, 'those poems translated from the Irish, because they come out of original sin.' She prefers original sin because it is original and therefore not corrupted by thought. Yeats takes up the idea in a poem, 'What theme had Homer but original sin?'[12] When Synge heard an English producer was to stage *Deirdre*, he said gloomily, 'He'll turn it into "The Second Mrs. Conchubar"'.

All take a pride in reducing everything to an ultimate simplicity. Yeats never carried out his idea of rehearsing his players in barrels to keep them still, but Lady Gregory rehearsed them with plates on their heads. She makes her Sarsfields and Brian Borus and Devorgillas speak like the cottagers of Kiltartan, and reduces a comedy to the quarrels of two old men in bed or an outlaw and a policeman sitting back-to-back on a barrel; while Synge makes the aristocratic characters of his most noble tragedy talk like the islanders of *Riders to the Sea*.

In this he reveals a certain class bias which is common to all three. They are virulently anti-middle class. Moore quarrels with Yeats's statement that the middle classes have produced no art; but what concerns Yeats is that it is the middle classes who have produced most of the muddle and fuss. In the simplicity of the world there was only the lord and the peasant; in the theatre the two are interchangeable; it is the middle classes who will not blend, and probably all would have been furious with Shaw for interpreting both peasant and aristocrat in terms of the middle classes. It is the middle class which stands as a barrier between the poor man and aristocrat; they ignore it in their work.

Synge innocently defines the theory in his *Aran Islands*. 'Their way of life', he says, speaking of the islanders, 'has never been acted on by anything much more artificial than the nests and burrows of the creatures that live round them, and they seem, in a certain sense, to approach more nearly to the finer types of our aristocracies . . . than to the labourer or the citizen, as the wild horse resembles the thoroughbred rather than the hack or the cart-horse.'[13]

I must apologise for the digression, but it is necessary in order to explain why none of them conforms to Corkery's three canons of Religion, Nationalism, and Land. Now we can easily see why; engaged on this task of reducing everything to its ultimate simplicity, 'the profound and common interests of life' in Synge's phrase,[14] they had no business with middle-class formulas. So that Corkery's reproaches to Synge for his lack of spirituality, his refusal to recognise Catholicism, are really beside the point. One must understand that, up to a certain point, these are men working to a theory, experimenting with the economics of literary poverty. People still recount as a good joke that Synge thought of an historical play dealing with the Rebellion of '98, the characters in which were to be two women, Catholic and Protestant, quarrelling in a cave with a yeoman as protagonist. It is very much the idea of a man working to a theory, and the theory envisaged not the sort of Irish literature Corkery asks for, an Irish literature taken over from European literature, with all the complexity of European life involved, but a new literature which should be Irish merely because it couldn't be anything else.

The three were laying the foundations of a house. Wisely or unwisely is a different matter. Sometimes it seems to me the house is laid out on too grandiose a scale and that it may never be finished; which may explain why, since the death of Synge, the site has remained vacant, and why so many tin shacks have been built on it in the course of years – but that is another story [. . .]

* * *

# Irish – An Empty Barrell?[1]

'Language is but the instrument conveying to us things useful to be known.'[2]

We are reviving Irish because we are proud of it. If there was no reason to be proud of it we would do better to let the dead rest: and if it were alive – that is to say, were being spoken – and we had no reason to be proud of it, we should do properly in flinging it aside as our forefathers flung it aside in the eighteenth century after it had become divorced from its intellectual content.

But Irish has an intellectual value – not as a trainer in mental gymnastics: Swedish or Pali[3] or Chinese or Mathematics are as good for that – but as the inheritor of the most beautiful and amazing mass of poetry in any European language north of the Danube. This mass of poetry, only becoming known by slow degrees, will be of the greatest value to the world when fully known, and must in time astonish and intrigue the artists of Europe. But it is a poetry that began to decline from the early seventeenth century and was a corpse by 1700. Apart from this poetry, Irish has no other content worth the mention, though it is of course indirectly the guide to a most interesting and unique social organisation. To enjoy and profit by this content the Irish we know and teach is of little use. Even if every child in the schools could speak with fluency the colloquial Irish that is being taught to-day, he could never, without great pains and more serious study than the average man has time for, enjoy the subtle beauties and strange philosophy of our literature. Consequently the work in the schools to-day does tend towards making of Irish-speaking children so many empty barrels prodigal of sound – of sound and fury signifying nothing.

Let us consider the position under the heads of the three stages of education: primary to university.

Think, first, of the position of an English child in an English school and you will at once get a conception of the injustice being done to Irish education. The highest achievements of his race in literature and language are within easy reach of the boy from Camden Town or Highgate from the moment he enters fourth standard. Blake, Keats, Shelley, Wordsworth, Shakespeare – they all combine from the very beginning to give him standards that will last him a lifetime, to educate him, to intellectualise him. Being for him not a difficulty but a joy, because of their excellence and their nature, they teach him much and rapidly. The novel, drama, poetry – whole centuries of achievement – are at his disposal. Language is for him essentially an instrument conveying things useful to be known. But the child in Limerick or Kilkenny? First of all, the same treasures are his, too, and what literary education he has, or ever will have though Ireland spoke Irish from end to end (unless the education authorities change their entire outlook in the immediate future) he will get from these same English sources. If that be so there seems to be but little use in reviving Irish. For it is not that Irish has not a literature as entrancing and as valuable – I personally believe it to be more valuable and entrancing – but that it is so long, now, since Irish literature had its day that none but the mature scholar can enjoy it. And this not merely because its language is difficult, though that is so, too, but because it came out of a civilisation to which the approach is slow and arduous, and is the expression of a genius and a philosophy all our own. But the preparation for this content is to teach Irish in the most colloquial way possible: more than that to decry the teaching of Irish as a literary language – by analogy, no doubt, with modern methods of foreign language teaching that have nothing in the wide world to do with Irish whose content can only be reached by handling Irish strictly and constantly as a literary medium. One may, or may not, reach Lamartine[4] and De Musset by a colloquial handling of French: it depends on the time and the teachers and the conditions. (Recollect our Irish schools with four classes at different work in one room under a single teacher.) But one will never reach Villon or the Roman de Roland in that way. So one may reach the decadent drivel of the eighteenth century in Ireland by the present slap-dash treatment of Irish, but NEVER the content that makes Irish worth our pride. Taught without its content, and without preparation for its content and without respect for its content, Irish does but one thing only for our children. It wastes their time.

The eighteenth-century content is not, in any case, reached until the secondary school. Before that, though an English child has such unsurpassed poetry as Blake's 'Tiger',[5] or such good introductory material as 'The Piper of Hamelin',[6] all the Irish child can feed on is things that have lived in a sort of becrutched Saint Vitus's dance after the eighteenth century and the famine, mere folk-prattle of no intellectual value. As for the eighteenth century stuff itself, it must be the considered opinion of any man with an ounce of critical acumen and an unprejudiced mind that it is on the whole so far beneath the level of such poetry as the two little things I have named from English literature, as to be, in considered words, worthless in itself, and if taught as good literature and held up for admiration, a most pernicious standard to set up before the minds of children. For the children will learn to make comparisons as they grow older, and come to deride what they have been taught as a fair representative of Irish literature – thus defeating one of the main purposes of the revival – and they will come also, and I think with some justice, to contemn the people who have been fooling them from the teacher's rostrum and the educational departments of the State.

I am aware that there are critics who have praised this decadent stuff, and their praise has been most harmful. It has gulled to a sweet satisfaction the enthusiasts for the revival, and since enthusiasts are at all times a force, it is unfortunate that they should rather be encouraged in their ignorance than guided to a realisation of the true facts and set to work to Ireland's profit rather than, as at present, to her harm. Mr. Corkery's book on the 'Hidden Ireland' of the eighteenth century is typical: it has come at an unfortunate time. It is as if England, in a position like to ours, suddenly discovering her literature, produced as her first book of literary criticism a volume crowning with bay poetasters since swept off to their rightful corner by the overwhelming mass of her true greatness. It is possible that Mr. Corkery knows the trifling worth of his materials, but to the enthusiasts his volume is become as a bible and the eighteenth century as the holy-land: it is a piquant reflection that was intended to do good and has actually succeeded in doing more to retard Irish education than three centuries of foreign rule.

The situation is a pitiable one. Here in the one-time home of learning, under a native government, we are in a position almost identical to that of Europe before the rise of the Humanists. Then Europe taught the classics in so barbarous a fashion – omitting the content in short – that nobody but an Irishman of the year 1926 could appreciate it: for we teach Irish without regard for the literature too. One might hope that the Universities, at least, teach the content that gives Irish its sole value; for if they do, then the teachers have it and they may in time, if the authorities change their tactics, hand it on in some way to the schools. But the Universities (because one is entitled to expect most from them) are in the most wretched condition of all. I picked up, while writing this, the list of readings in Irish literature for the degree of Bachelor of Arts in one of the constituent colleges for a recent year [...]

It might be argued, though I should argue very strongly to the contrary, and I imagine every educationist would agree with me, that these books were good enough for beginners at a language. But will any man dream of suggesting that for students there are more than two books on this entire list that are worth even the three hours of a midnight train journey? As literature, which they purport to be, the bulk of them are incredibly ridiculous, and, as a sample, the last book on the list is undoubtedly one of the trashiest yellowbacks that it has ever been my lot to read.[7] And this is Irish as taught in the Universities!

Let us remind ourselves of the true value of Irish, according to which it will either live – or die though ten governments wasted money on its revival. It is its intellectual content: it has such a content, for it was not for nothing that scholar-critics like Meyer and Pokorny[8] thought it worth the devotion of a lifetime. Its great poetry is capable of inspiring any set of artists that Ireland may produce, and of deepening the lives of serious students just as well as English or French or German could hope to do. If the one school of writers – the Anglo-Irish – that this content has already inspired should now continue to flourish, and if a school more directly influenced by the past should also spring up, the result cannot but be fruitful for both Ireland and Europe. But what hope is there that such a Gaelic school can ever make contact with the hidden resources of our national genius while the language which is the key to them is treated in this way from infant-school to university? Here is futility with a vengeance: like empty barrels the children speak their insignificant Irish; at best the growing student learns something of a literature that he will come to despise; and the student of the universities fattens his brains for three mortal years on material that must kill his critical faculty ere he swallow it, or else, if he refuses to lower his intellect to the level of his professors, fail him in his examinations. A trained teacher of Irish, he returns to the schools to deceive his pupils in turn, to kill their critical judgement as his own has been killed while in their desks, and to stultify their intellect or his own in a round of barrel-rapping.

What is wrong is simply this: we are not clear as to what we can and cannot attain in the fight for the revival of Irish. We are not at all clear as to our objective: the result has been that our efforts have been aimless, and, as I hope I have shown, for the greater part of no avail.

* * *

# Correspondence: The Spirit of the Nation[1]

Sir, – I think it well that Frank O'Connor has answered Mr. Corkery's article on the 'Spirit of the Nation,'[2] and well that he chose to answer it passionately, for it would appear that the writer of the article is more likely to respond to an appeal to his heart than to his head. His point seems to be that hard work in the confines of the nation is useless to the nation and to the worker unless 'breathed on' by the spirit of the nation: unless, that is (I make bold to translate) the worker realises that there is a national tradition and works in it.[3] Mr. Corkery is quite correct in saying that any country is the richer and the more stable for having and recognising its national tradition, but he does not appear to realise that the national tradition of A may not be the national tradition of B; in the meantime, while our national tradition is being definitely formed by the hard work of men like Horace Plunkett, and Æ, and the gunmannings of Michael Collins and Rory O'Connor, and the visions of W.B. Yeats, and the idealism of Mr. de Valera, and the cutting up of Ardnacrusha by Siemens-Schuckert,[4] and the mild efforts of the Gaelic League, and the publication of a weekly paper in Cork,[5] and the quiet efforts of craftsmen of all sorts throughout the country, is it fair of Mr. Corkery to cry from high Olympus that all these people can achieve nothing until the five others besides Mr. Corkery himself have put the one-and-only, the real brand of national tradition beyond fear of further breakages? Neither Mr. Corkery nor anyone else of those I named is the custodian of the national tradition: in the first place, as he says rightly, it is not an intact tradition at all, but rather the makings of a tradition and the makings in our hands; and I have sufficient faith in my own generation, which is not Mr. Corkery's generation, to believe that we shall and in our time make a better tradition for the Ireland of our day and future days than has ever entered the type of mind that Frank O'Connor has attacked. As a matter of fact I should not be surprised to find that the national tradition as Mr. Corkery sees it and as Frank O'Connor and I see it, differs only in that the one having come out of a memory of an Ireland of long defeat is a narrow

tradition fearful always for its own safety, and the other coming out of an
Ireland of fight and conquest is a wide tradition that like the Ireland of the
middle ages spreads its arms to the ideas of every country in the world.


* * *


# The Emancipation of Irish Writers[1]


[. . .] I once heard of a man who wished to found a Society for the
Emancipation of the Irish Intellect, and who was asked, 'Whom will you have
in your Society for the Emancipation of the Irish Intellect? No doubt, to begin
with, you will have George Russell?' Whereupon he glared angrily and said,
'How can I have a man like George Russell in a Society for the Emancipation
of the Irish Intellect? Why, the man is a – why, he isn't even a Protestant!'[2]

Now, our friend of the Society for the Emancipation of the Irish Intellect
is not so rare a bird as he may seem, nor so foolish as he sounds. He was
merely voicing a feeling, common enough among intelligent Irishmen of to-
day, that our people are not expressing themselves freely, either in literature
or in life, to which is added, or rather, in which is implied, the feeling that
these depths left unexpressed in Irish literature can only be expressed in a
satisfying way after some awakening in the people themselves.

It is an attitude, like many such in Ireland, which derives its appeal from
its historicity. We have an extraordinary habit here of making discoveries
fifty years after we should have made them, and then of continuing to act on
them fifty years after we [should] have stopped. For such a discovery as this
is exactly the discovery we should have made around 1850 or 1875, and
actually was made by some Irishmen, quicker-witted than the rest, around
1900. Mr. W.B. Yeats was born in 1865; Æ, in 1867; John Millington Synge,
in 1871; Mr. T.C. Murray, in 1873 [. . .]; Mr. Daniel Corkery, in 1878;
Padraic Colum, in 1881, and so on.

But it is true that to make such a discovery is one thing and to act upon
it another. And it is also true that a literature such as ours – or, indeed, the
mere beginnings of a literature, for Anglo-Irish literature as it stands is
nothing more; it takes hundreds of years to establish a literature – progresses
by a process of perpetual discovery, by an endless tidal movement of
tradition rising to its triumph and ebbing to its decay until a revolt swings it
forward once more to a new flood. So that it is not only fitting but well that
a literature should often be examined in its course, its tides often recharted,
lest it find itself sinking on the ebb when it thinks itself rising on the flow.

Unhappily, here in Ireland for the last twenty years or so, these growls of dissatisfaction are all we have got, and nobody could call them criticism, and nobody can but distrust their frequency. Nobody can but feel that they are dictated less by an interest in literature than by other interests, such as politics, that have little to do with literature. And one distrusts them, also, because of their pretense to the spontaneity of a national sentiment, when one knows that they are in fact merely catchwords repeated from the papers and periodicals, debating societies and political clubs of the bourgeois intelligentsia. And one fears them for another reason, that makes one sympathise with them even while one distrusts them – one knows that they are inevitable in a period such as ours, inevitable and unreliable as the judgements of a youth raised to sudden position and power. He is insecure and self-conscious in his new status, overcritical and dogmatic in the effort to sustain the rôle. Patience, forbearance, understanding are the last things one expects from such a period. It is a period in no way helpful to literature.

Thus, a characteristic criticism of the type to which I refer, comes from Professor Daniel Corkery in his book on *Synge and Anglo-Irish Literature*. Here the charges are varied: Irish literature has adopted literary fashions not acclimatised to Ireland; it is scornful of the judgements of the people, and there is no native criticism (two charges which rather mark one another out); Irish writers are not interested in the life, political welfare, or cultural establishments of their people; we do not write for our own people but for England; we have never foretold the future of our country; in short, we do not 'face the facts of the Irish scene' – do not, in other words, express adequately the fullest depths of the national character.[3] 'The three great forces,' Professor Corkery sums up, 'that work their will on the consciousness of the people – Religion, the Land, Nationalism – have found little or no adequate expression in' Anglo-Irish literature.[4]

Now, as I have already observed in passing, this critical attitude is of recent origin, and it is applied to a literature which is also of recent origin. And that is something which even the critics themselves do not seem to realise. Yet you cannot do justice to any literature unless you make yourself aware of your own relationship to that literature. And the relationship here is that this criticism is the criticism of the revolutionary mind applied to a literature written in a revolutionary atmosphere.

Irish prose literature has hardly yet as much as begun. In what has been accomplished we may observe two main divisions, however – divisions which may be completely altered by the light subsequent developments throw on what we are doing.

We must divide prose literature into pre-1916 and post-1916. To begin with we have work from such writers as Canon Sheehan, Katherine Tynan,[5] Edith Somerville, George Moore, Gerald O'Donovan, Seumas O'Kelly,

James Joyce, James Stephens, Daniel Corkery. These might be further divided, if you so wish, though it is not essential, into writers (very few of these names) who wrote before the actual Irish literary revival had got under way. Canon Sheehan, for example, is not in the same literary atmosphere as George Moore – he was a writer who received no help from his contemporaries. Indeed, at the beginning he had none. After these writers come a different generation; at any rate, a different atmosphere surrounds them. There are Eimar Duffy, Con O'Leary, Brinsley MacNamara, Liam O'Flaherty, Austin Clarke, Peadar O'Donnell, Frank O'Connor, L.A.G. Strong, Kate O'Brien,[6] and others. And no criticism should fail to distinguish between these two main divisions.

To illustrate what misjudgements may follow from a failure to observe this distinction, take Professor Corkery's conclusion that the three forces working on the Irish consciousness, Land, Religion, and Nationalism, have been inadequately treated in Irish literature. Thirty years before Mr. Corkery made this discovery, Professor Stopford Brooke and Mr. T.W. Rolleston edited an anthology of Irish verse, in the introduction to which they listed the three notes almost constantly sounded in that verse, and they are those three notes that Mr. Corkery finds absent from Irish literature. What has happened is plain. Mr. Corkery, being of the later school of criticism, has formed his opinions of Irish literature on its later, more modern school, and in the later, more modern atmosphere of the revolution. Brooke and Rolleston published their book in 1900, with an enlarged edition in 1905. Whether their opinion would equally well apply to the period since then I cannot tell. But it is plain that Mr. Corkery's opinion cannot apply to the period before 1905, and whether or not it is correct for later periods, he should have made clear to himself and to his readers that it has not the same relevance to any period but his own.

It has, in fact, (correct or astray) only a partial relevance to his own period, for as a creative writer Mr. Corkery is of the pre-1916 school, though as a critic he belongs to the post-1916 school, the politically minded critics of the revolution. It is not George Moore, or James Stephens, or Seumas O'Kelly, or even James Joyce, who arouses feelings of anger in modern Ireland – not even Synge, for Synge is now acknowledged. It may be that the poetry of Mr. Yeats or Æ does not meet with the approval of the moderns, but that I cannot say; and in any case, it is hardly credible that a dissatisfaction with two poets, even poets of influence, could arouse a prejudice against an entire literature. It is patent that this modern dissatisfaction is roused by the work of such writers as O'Casey, O'Flaherty, MacNamara, O'Donnell, Clarke, O'Duffy, Frank O'Connor, and myself, who have touched the national consciousness on the raw. And the sins of these few writers are visited on the head of Anglo-Irish literature. It is time that was made quite clear, and time our critics realised what they are doing.

In a word, they are approaching not merely a section of a literature from a nationalistic or political standpoint but all literature. One notices at once in Mr. Corkery's statement about Land, Religion, and Nationalism that the critic has not gone to the literature to see what it does speak of. He goes rather to politics and sociology to see what it might speak of. When Brooke and Rolleston found these notes in Irish literature, it was an intelligent and wise criticism, because, in the first place, the examples were there to illustrate what was meant, whereas Mr. Corkery can offer no exemplars for whose literary merit he could care to vouch, and, secondly, the earlier critics are content to allow literature to choose its own materials and make no suggestion that it ought to have treated them in some other way. It is an odd type of criticism which would dictate to an artist as if he were a building contractor.

But, postponing for the moment disbelief in this attitude to literature, one has to observe how superficial this type of criticism is, even according to its own theory. Of what help is it to an artist to suggest to him in the vaguest terms of sociology or politics certain aspects of Irish life with which he might deal? Of what use to speak of Land, for example. I can understand that to a social reformer or a politician it might be a magical word, and it might even appeal to a writer like Mr. H.G. Wells, interested less in human beings than in social processes. But to anybody else it represents merely a cause which might produce certain effects, a certain atmosphere, certain situations, certain psychological characteristics, and these are undoubtedly things in which any novelist would be deeply interested and about which he would be glad to talk until the cows come home.

But does your politically minded critic make haste to advise discussion of psychological effects? Never. The greed that follows on land hunger, for example, the cruelty, the inhumanity, the brutality – we observe no critic suggesting that Irish literature should give these things adequate expression. One can well imagine what our young man of the Society for the Emancipation of the Irish Intellect would say to a book dealing with these – 'Oh, no! no! what we want is books dealing with the pleasant and finer qualities of life on the land.' And, I hasten to agree, there would be a great deal of right on his side, and no novel failing to hold an even balance between qualities could escape the censure of being superficial. But the point is that while the novelist could foresee a nice discussion as to what is not only normal but possible and bizarre – for even the bizarre as well as the possible is the prerogative of the artist – our critics are lazily content to talk vaguely about the most obvious social phenomena under the impression that this is literary criticism.

But the truth of this matter is that the modern Irish reader, from whose mind things nationalistic and political are inseparable, and who will not be content until he gets what he would call a full and sincere interpretation of

Irish life, is simply asking what he is not entitled to ask of literature. Judged according to his standard what would British readers think of Mr. Shaw, Americans, of Mr. Mencken?[7] What chance would Molière get in the Ireland of the day? And one can feel that Falstaff – at any rate, the Falstaff of the second part of *Henry IV*[8] – would get as short shrift as Joxer.[9] While as for Pope,[10] Defoe,[11] Dryden,[12] or a novel like *Wuthering Heights* – ![13]

And here I am leaving out of account altogether the extreme Celtophile critic in whose mind Irish life is idealised according to a literary convention, idealised, romanticised, and even at times sentimentalised. To such a critic Mr. Joyce's Leopold Bloom must be a hard nut to crack – Mr. Leopold Bloom frying the entrails of fowl for his wife's breakfast while she sags the wires of the spring bed with her heavy body.[14] Not Irish, would such a critic say? To which one replies wearily, perhaps so and perhaps not, but it is literature. And really beyond that you cannot go. You may blame literature for being poor politics, or politics for being poor literature; but in the first case, you are a bad critic and in the second, a bad politician, and in either case, a traitor to your calling.

[. . .] I have said that nobody can ask a writer to interpret Irish life sympathetically if the writer does not want to. And that we of the post-1916 period are unsympathetic, as a rule, there can be no denying. But the question we must now ask ourselves is whether that lack of sympathy with 'certain facts of Irish life' has impaired our sympathy for any other facts and so impaired our artistic integrity. Has our lack of sympathy with certain aspects of Irish life produced a lack of sympathy with humanity?

Admittedly, the professed satirist must take sides, at least in the degree that such a writer as Dryden takes sides. Whereas the novelist or the dramatist who takes sides does so under no compulsion of technical necessity and does so, in fact, at great risk. It is a byword in appreciation of the greatness of Balzac or, better still, Shakespeare, that they held the balance of life so evenly between their characters, good and bad, that it is next to impossible to define their own attitude to their people. They are the greatest who seem to compass all life and balance all life, and yet leave us questioners of life at the end. They have detachment without loss of emotion; passion without loss of justice; judgement without loss of sympathy.

I think it almost inevitable that the integrity of the modern Irish writer should be impaired. Attacked on every side by political prejudice, national enthusiasm, pietistic evangelism, he has to fight tooth and nail for his vision of life. He has to preserve a constant effort of will to retain that consistency between belief and creative action which may be said to define integrity. For to correct the balance of life is the writer's way of achieving a balance of truth. No writer worth his salt could live in such an atmosphere of self-delusion and self-esteem as this atmosphere of modern Ireland without desiring to correct the balance of truth in his art. And if in the stress of that fight he loses something of the wholeness of the vision at which he aims, I think the last person who should chide him is the deluded man he is trying to save [...]

* * *

# Daniel Corkery[1]

[...] The book on Synge [...] contains the application to Anglo-Irish letters of the historical attitude outlined in *The Hidden Ireland*. The Introduction sums it all up, and is a marvellous piece of special pleading, though written in elusive English that is often vague and sometimes quite meaningless. In sum (according to this point of view) Anglo-Irish Literature, since 1900 in particular, is 'astray' as an interpretation of Irish life, gives 'no adequate expression' to the forces 'that work their will in the consciousness of the Irish people,' and – a typically suggestive but unprecise sentence – its practitioners did not 'use such intellectual equipment as they possessed,': 'sometimes admirable in itself, for the high purposes of art – the shaping out into chaste and enduring form of a genuine emotional content, personal to themselves but conscionable to the nation.'[2] Writing for an English market ('keeps its eyes on the foreign merchants who are to purchase its wares') it has been 'misled' from the start.[3] In brief, Anglo-Irish literature is not an adequate interpretation of Irish life.

To illustrate this Corkery takes a hurling-match at Thurles, a crowd of thirty thousand country and town folk, and says,

> It was while I looked at that great crowd I first became acutely conscious that as a nation we were without self-expression in literary form. The life of this people I looked upon – there were all sorts of individuals present, from bishops to tramps off the road – was not being explored in a natural way by any except one or two writers of any standing.... One could not see Yeats, Æ, Stephens, Dunsany, Moore, Robinson, standing out from that gathering as natural and indigenous interpreters of it. On the other hand there seems to be no difficulty in posing Galsworthy, Masefield, Bennett, Wells, against corresponding assemblies in England .... Those English crowds are 100 per cent. English: and the writers who best express the individual souls that make them up are 100 per cent. English .... The writers in a normal country are one with what they write of.[4]

To those who have accepted Anglo-Irish literature as literature this will sound painful. To those who approach it as the expression of a high-hearted Nationalism it will be (and was) a trumpet-call. With a little alteration it would equally well trumpet encouragement to all Nazis, Fascists, Communists, and every other type of exclusivist for whom the essential test of literature is a political, racial, or religious test. All a Nazi need do, to make that passage personally gratifying, is to put for 'Yeats, Æ, Stephens, etc.' – Ludwig,[5] Feuchtwanger,[6] Toller,[7] etc., with 100 per cent. Teuton in his mind and a meeting at the Munich Spielplatz instead of Thurles.

One may pass over the disingenuousness of Corkery's choice of lyric writers from the Irish group (Yeats, Dunsany, Stephens, Æ) instead of O'Donnell, O'Connor, O'Casey, and such like as possible interpreters of the 'mob'; and of Naturalistic writers from the English group, Bennett, Wells, Galsworthy. He is, after all, fighting here for a propagandist idea and may be forgiven a little sharp practice. But one does not so easily forgive his suggestion that 'the writers who best express the individual souls of England' are Bennett, Wells, Galsworthy. Not because they may not but because one knows well that Corkery sincerely thinks these writers very small beer: one knows that his spiritual affinities are writers like Musset and Turgenev, the feminine lyrists; that, if anything his own romantic image of life is far nearer to that of Yeats and Stephens, than to Bennett and Wells: that he is being disloyal to himself as an artist in trying to make his theory fit. And that is unforgiveable.

Of course, the fact is that *The Old Wives' Tale*,[8] or *The Country House*,[9] or *The New Machiavelli*[10] do not interpret an English cup-final crowd at Wembley. To ask art to do things like that is to socialise it, and that precisely is what Mr. Corkery's nationalism means – the nationalisation of culture.

That is the core of the weakness of this approach. It is not a critic's approach. It is a politician's, and clearly one cannot find any common ground for discussion under such conditions unless one agrees on the nationalistic premises. That the emotional content of, let us say, *The Portrait of the Artist as a Young Man* is genuine, Corkery will not admit! He says Joyce is 'astray!'[11] He suggests of Stephens that his idyllic picture is 'watery gruel.'[12] He has a good word, but not complete approval, for T.C. Murray and Padraic Colum, but for nobody else. That O'Casey is 'conscionable' to the nation he does not admit, because O'Casey satirises Nationalism![13] But, one leaves the position in disgust, – it is an impossible attitude which cannot allow a man to satirise what he honestly thinks deserving of satire. It is a position which leads Corkery into more than one baseness, more than one disloyalty [...]

\* \* \*

# Let Ireland Pride – In What She Has[1]

Would it not sound odd if one asked, Is France swamped culturally?[2] It would, because we all know France produces its natural quota of culture.

So do we. More than our quota. The only trouble is that our finicky critics refuse to accept it. They say – 'Oh, yes, Ireland produces culture alright.' They have to say that, because the list of names honoured by as good critics as Mr. de Blácam or Mr. Corkery (But outside Ireland – 'A man is never thought a prophet, etc.') is impressively long. But they add – 'Only it is not Irish culture – not native – not racy of the soil.'

Most people stare at this statement in amazement. They say, 'But, after all, when we go to the Abbey it seems to us that we are in a place where the whole thing reeks of Ireland. And take, then, Peadar O'Donnell; and Yeats; and, at the very least, O'Flaherty's *Famine*, and his short stories, and *The Martyr*; and *Hail and Farewell*, nobody but an Irishman could have written it; and O'Connor's *Guests of the Nation*; and Austin Clarke; and Higgins' poems about the West;[3] and scores of other poets and playwrights? Not native! Not racy!'

'No!' growls Cassandra. 'No! No! Ireland is a nice country, a good, holy, happy, flawless, merry country. These fellows often poke fun at us. Just as that scoundrel Molière did at the French – he should have been censored; and that ruffian Swift at the English, and Sterne, and just as Rabelais did – they nearly got him, and serve him right, too. And the English and Americans praise these fellows. That shows there must be something wrong with them. No, they are not Irish! We won't have them!'

The fact is that people who, like de Blácam and Corkery, refuse to take pride in our literature, do not really want literature at all. They want their own particular brand of literature. They are exclusivists.

They are in the best of company. Goebbels and Hitler are laying down precisely the same excluding law for Germany that de Blácam and Corkery want to lay down for Ireland. The whole lot of them say, in effect – '*You* write what we want or you can get out.' (Mr. de Blácam says so precisely in his article of last week – he says some of us are 'writing what the nation does not want.').[4] Isn't that a nice intelligent attitude for a man of letters?

Supposing the nation went Communist and said to Mr. de Blácam: 'You write what the nation wants or get out,' what would he say?

He would say what every self-respecting man or artist must say to anyone who takes up a Hitlerian attitude. He would reply: 'We will write what we honestly feel to be the truth, and we will not get out. This country is our country just as much as yours. Our conception of nationality is just as sound as yours. You may gag us. You may side with the big battalions. But you will do so as a renegade from your own loyalties, and you will play false by the nation in the end by trying to steamroll it into a level submission to the ideas of a few men.'

And de Blácam would say that rightly.

Mr. Corkery displayed this nationalistic complex in its extreme form when writing last month in *Ireland To-day*: –

> 'If there ever does come into existence a corpus of literature fittingly named Anglo-Irish literature' – oh, those definitions: – 'it will have been built up by such books as our people, through very affection, keep from fading away. If a novel . . . is merely glanced at by the people of this country it may prove to be quite an excellent novel, but a piece of Anglo-Irish literature it is not likely to turn out.'[5]

'It may be an excellent novel . . . .' You see Corkery doesn't care about that very much. The thing is that it must be of the Hitler brand. (Pure Aryan for Hitler. So out on his neck goes the Nobel prize winner, Thomas Mann.[6] And out go a score of others with him.) Pure Irish for Corkery. And out on his neck goes W.B. Yeats, another Nobel prize winner, and a score of others with him?

For you see – following Corkery's reasoning (which is also de Blácam's) – if Paddy MacGinty 'scarcely glances' at W.B. Yeats – which is more than he usually does – then W.B. Yeats, though he may have been a Fenian as a young man, a friend of John O'Leary,[7] a poet who sang Ireland's wrong, a defender of Casement,[8] or what not else, must now – because of Paddy MacGinty – go and nationalise himself elsewhere.

But if the people (that vague word) through ignorant affection for some cheap popular writer should preserve him – as, for as long as we have been English-speaking, the people have preserved plays like *The Colleen Bawn*[9] – then is that a bit of native literature?

To be sure, Corkery is thinking in centuries, and if we could all live to be 500, or see 500 years ahead – his appeal to popular taste might be helpful.

*Might! Only might.* For it is not popular taste that preserves great literature but the insistent praise of men of discrimination who mould public taste. What, in England, for example, has preserved *Tristram Shandy*? Who has preserved Congreve, whose *The Way of the World* is the most perfect comedy ever written?[10] Not Paddy MacGinty, or John Smith, but the discriminating few. Vox Populi,[11] in letters, is but the echo of what some highbrow said yesterday.

There is, of course, a good deal in this idea about literature being based on national life. We all agree on that. Ireland has had many men who wrote what was based on no kind of life – neither here nor there. Men like Dick Millikin,[12] the Corkman to whom is attributed the 'Groves of Blarney', or Thomas Parnell.[13] Dick wrote a poem in three cantos called *The Riverside*.[14] Every river in the world gets a mention in it. But the Lee might never have flowed at his feet for all the impress it made on his magnum opus. He is forgotten to-day. Much as Moore's *Lalla Rookh* is forgotten.[15] Deservedly. It was divorced from life.

But when Irishmen of our times have begun to feed on Irish life, avidly, packing it into their books, this question about literature based on life becomes purely academic. I say Irish literature is absolutely Irish to-day. Mr. de Blácam says not. Who is to judge?

[...] Ireland has to-day as fine a literature (in English) as any country in the world in proportion to its size: a National theatre famous over the world; a body of poets and novelists to match any land. Yeats is as good an Irishman as Corkery; O'Flaherty as de Blácam – read his *Famine* if you doubt it – as fine a historical novel as *Knocknagow* and incomparable as literature. But will *Famine* be read? Not if de Blácam and Corkery can damn it with faint praise.

Ireland needs to pride in what it has. It needs critics who will praise or blame its literature on its merits *as literature*. That is all we ask [...]

Nationalism should be kept out of criticism. It puts a premium on a bitter self-righteousness, encourages purely destructive comment and I have constantly seen it produce dishonest judgements in the interest of precon-ceived ideas.


\*   \*   \*


# King of the Beggars[1]


[...] There were many successors to Ó Bruadair, and as time goes on the distinction between poet and peasant vanishes, for the 'poet' is not now supported by rich and intelligent patronage, but has to work like any other man for his living. The songs heard in the cabins of the eighteenth century were composed over the spade-handle by men who were job-gardeners like the northern poet Art MacCooey,[2] or day-labourers like Eoghan Ruadh Ó Súilleabháin, or composed over the rent-collector's ledger by a Pierce MacGhearailt, or into the mouth of a postman's bag by a Tomás Ruadh O'Súilleabháin[3] – a protégé of Dan O'Connell.

What they brought in the way of distraction to the people from 1700 onward is the subject of that unique book *The Hidden Ireland* by Daniel Corkery; as he pointed out, such men might be addressed by any foreign traveller without being recognised as the lineal descendants of the old bardic line, the proud possessors of an aristocratic tradition of literature. Here, however, it is not the literary value of the work of these men that is in question. We are interested only in the light these semi-popular songsters throw on the political thought of the people who heard them, and presumably applauded them on occasion, even as they were doubtless occasionally comforted by them in the midst of lives so exiguous as to be miracles of endurance.

From this point of view it is correct to speak of them as 'semi-popular' because their songs reveal a division in Irish life in the eighteenth century which has, hitherto, hardly been recognised at all; a division identical with that we have already observed in the sympathies of Ó Bruadair. For one thing it is patent that these singers did not, at the beginning of the century, think in the least of a popular audience, however willing they were, equivocally, to be supported by popular sympathy. Ó Bruadair has shown how that naturally occurred; how the old order was chained by its memories to a wish-fulfilment concept of reality. His contemporary, who lived on in 1730, O'Rahilly, has likewise, in all his work, but two main ideas – that the Stuarts will return, and that the old patronage will return with them. But so long as that patronage of the nobility comes back there is not a line to suggest that O'Rahilly cares two pins what will happen to anybody else [. . .]

One tries to defend him and his tradition, perhaps, by saying that this is, after all, a convention and nothing more. But what does that mean? It means either that these semi-popular poets had nothing to say to the people that was related to their real political and social condition; or else it means that the people were themselves living in a conventional attitude of mind, asked for and desired no realistic songs, had no wish for a faithful image of their appalling conditions – were, in one word, sleep-walking. Either conclusion means that four million helots, of whom Chesterfield said that they were treated worse than Negroes,[4] and for whose masters Lecky had no milder word than 'Anti-Christ,'[5] were living in a state of political obfuscation, not indeed ripe for a realistic political leader, but badly in need of one.

Actually, however, there is no reason whatever to suppose that the people ever heard these conventional poets reciting their conventional poems, or if they by chance heard them, heeded them. Why should they? The whole tenor of these poets' complaints is that their poems are not heard or heeded. They constantly bewail the passing of a time when bookish men did hear, heed, understand, and reward [. . .] That cry is one of the commonest among these hapless men whose songs, so late, so out of tune with the times, are like the troubled cries of birds nesting in a wintry season.

Such conventional verses have never been gathered from the mouths of people as have been the later, more simple songs that came home to their hearts and their lives from singers who had learned, in accepting the inevitable, the first lesson in political wisdom. These later singers did not so much write as sing, however mournfully, and they sang with more verve and more truth, like O'Rahilly's successor Seán Clárach MacDomhnaill, whose verses reflect the realities of that eighteenth century so well in the lines,

Atá mo chóraid gan fuithin
'S mo chuingir gan féar gan fás . . . .

My cattle are shelterless,
My team without grass do not thrive.
My people are in misery
With their elbows out through their clothes.
The pack is after me
At the command of the law.
My boots are in bits
And I haven't a copper to pay to repair them . . . .[6]

From that, to go back to another of O'Rahilly's elegies, this time on one
O'Callaghan of Clare, is surely to go back from intelligence to somnam-
bulism. Here, again, it is the friars, and the clerics, and the bards who have
lost. Here, again, the dead hand of the past is trying to write on a page that
has been already scarred and blotted by brutal conquest. While his people
are, like those wretches whom the American traveller, Asenath Nicholson,
found in Omey, living in burrows in the sand;[7] or, as a hundred travellers
found them, starving in windowless, chimneyless hovels that they shared
with their lean beasts, O'Rahilly is fantastically listing, over and over, the
glories of O'Callaghan's house, glories in which we do not find, once, a
homely detail, a thing we could take as a fact, one item to make us feel that
we are not being taken by the hand into a complete dream-world.

He goes fondly through his list – wines; viands; coverlets; sweet odours
'from the breath of the trumpeting bands'; airs played on harps; 'the wise and
learned reading histories,' and there we get, again, a glimpse of what really
matters to O'Rahilly – 'books in which there is an accurate record of each
great family that rose in Europe'; and then the list goes on, waxlights,
soldiers, silver goblets, speckled silks, satin garments, 'invalids drinking
mead,' heroes playing chess . . . all from a patron whose line has been traced
back, in verse after verse, through Phœnix, Mercury, Pan, Ceres, Cairbre,
Lugh, Ionnadmhar, Adhamar, Mogh Corb, Cobhthach, and five and fifty
more until we come to Noah, Magog, Methuselah, and, lastly, Adam.[8]

Well, indeed does Professor Corkery say in *The Hidden Ireland* that 'from
the view of history the value of such verse is inestimable,' though not exactly,
or solely, as he has measured it.[9] Its value is rather a negative value. Its value
is to underline the one thing with which we are here properly concerned –
that chasm which was breaking apart the old world from the new, Gaeldom
with all its irreality and make-believe from the modern democratic Ireland
that, in the torment of slavery, presently opened its bloodshot eyes to a
realisation of the state to which all that old Gaelic make-believe had reduced
it [. . .]

# Notes

## Preface

1 Aodh de Blácam, 'The Other Hidden Ireland', *Studies*, 23.91 (Sept. 1934), 439. (See p. 186.)
2 Including *The Irish Times, The Irish News, The Times Literary Supplement, The Spectator, The Daily Telegraph, The Standard, The Manchester Guardian, The Leader, Glasgow Herald, The Irish Press, The Dublin Magazine, and The New Statesman.*
3 See Patrick Maume, *'Life that is Exile': Daniel Corkery and the Search for Irish Ireland* (Belfast: Institute of Irish Studies, 1993), 140.
4 Seán Ó Tuama, 'Daniel Corkery, Cultural Philosopher, Literary Critic: A Memoir', *Repossessions: Selected Essays on the Irish Literary Heritage* (Cork: Cork University Press, 1995), 247.
5 Others include 'Le Pinson', used mainly in his contributions to educational journals, 'Richard Mulqueany' and 'Neuilin Siubhlach'.
6 See Maume, *'Life that is Exile'*, 51.
7 According to Patrick Maume, Corkery's acquaintances, particularly in later life, recall him on occasion speaking contemptuously of women and their intellectual abilities. See ibid., 101.

## Introduction

1 See Frank O'Connor, *An Only Child*; Seán O'Faoláin, *Vive Moi!*; and Seamus Murphy, 'Mr. Daniel Corkery: An Appreciation'.
2 The Gaelic League was founded in 1893 by Douglas Hyde, Eoin MacNeill and others. Its objectives included the revival of the Irish language and the preservation of Irish literature, music and traditional culture.
3 Irish Ireland is a generic term for the forms of cultural nationalism that developed during the 1890s and the first decade of the twentieth century. Those who adhered to the Irish Ireland philosophy believed that Ireland should follow its own traditions in all aspects of its culture, including language and literature.
4 Lord Mayor MacCurtain was shot dead by disguised RIC men in front of his wife and children in 1920. Later that year, Lord Mayor MacSwiney, who had been sentenced to two years' imprisonment for possession of seditious documents and a numerical cipher code issued to the RIC, died while on hunger-strike.
5 Declan Kiberd, 'W.B. Yeats: Endings and Beginnings: A Review Essay', *Éire-Ireland*, 32.2 & 3 (Summer & Fall 1997), 87.
6 Louis M. Cullen, 'The Hidden Ireland: Reassessment of a Concept', *Studia Hibernica*, 9 (1969), 47. In a Postscript to a later pamphlet edition of this essay, Cullen distances himself from some of his harsher criticisms of *The Hidden Ireland*. See Louis M. Cullen, *The Hidden Ireland: Reassessment of a Concept* (Mullingar: Lilliput Press, 1988), 47–54.
7 Terence Brown, 'The Counter-Revival: Provincialism and Censorship, 1930–65', in Seamus Deane (ed.), *The Field Day Anthology of Irish Writing, Vol III* (Derry: Field Day Publications, 1991), 90.

8  See Patrick Maume, *'Life that is Exile': Daniel Corkery and the Search for Irish Ireland* (Belfast: The Institute of Irish Studies, 1993); See Colbert Kearney, 'Daniel Corkery: A Priest and his People', in Jacqueline Genet (ed.), *Rural Ireland, Real Ireland?* (Gerrards Cross: Colin Smythe, 1996).

9  Breandán Ó Buachalla, 'Ó Corcora agus an Hidden Ireland', *Scríobh*, 4 (1979), 113; Seán Ó Tuama, 'Dónall Ó Corcora', *Scríobh*, 4 (1979), 107.

10  Seán Ó Tuama, 'Dónall Ó Corcora', 101, 106.

11  ibid., 102–3, 101.

12  Ó Buachalla, 'Ó Corcora agus an Hidden Ireland', 114–15, 116.

13  ibid., 116.

14  ibid.

15  Cited in ibid., 110.

16  Seán Ó Ríordáin, Gaeilge Sinsear, RTÉ, 1977.

17  Seán Ó Ríordáin, 'Do Dhomhnall Ó Corcora', *Eireaball Spideoíge* (Dublin: Sáirséal agus Dill [1952]; 1976), 51.

18  ibid., 52.

19  Paul Delaney, 'Becoming National: Daniel Corkery and the Reterritorialised Subject', in Aaron Kelly and Alan A. Gillis (eds), *Critical Ireland: New Essays in Literature and Culture* (Dublin: Four Courts Press, 2001), 46.

20  ibid., 48.

21  Declan Kiberd, *Inventing Ireland* (London: Jonathan Cape, 1995), 558.

22  Terence Brown, *Ireland: A Social and Cultural History, 1922–1985*, revised ed. (London: Fontana Press [1981]; 1985), 57.

23  Daniel Corkery, *The Hidden Ireland: A Study of Gaelic Munster in the Eighteenth Century* (Dublin: Gill & Son [1925]; 1941), xi.

24  ibid., 273–8.

25  ibid., 3, 105, 198.

26  Daniel Corkery, *A Munster Twilight* (Cork: Mercier Press [1916]; 1963), 65, 71.

27  See Seán Ó Tuama, 'Dónall Ó Corcora'; See Patrick Walsh, 'Daniel Corkery's *The Hidden Ireland* and Revisionism', *New Hibernia Review*, 5.2 (2001).

28  Daniel Corkery, 'The Struggle between Native and Colonist', *The Irish Press* (30 Aug 1953). (See p. 169.)

29  Daniel Corkery, Chapter XI: '1800–1919', *The Fortunes of the Irish Language* (Cork: Mercier Press, 1954), 118–19. (See p. 95.)

30  ibid.

31  The restoration of voices from the past that have been written over and obscured has always been a fundamental part of the postcolonial project. This restoration has taken various forms, from Chinua Achebe's fictional depiction of a pre-colonial Igbo community in *Things Fall Apart* (1958) to Ranajit Guha's historical account of the nineteenth-century Indian rural poor in *Elementary Aspects of Peasant Insurgency in Colonial India* (1983).

32  Corkery, *The Hidden Ireland*, 84.

33  ibid., vi, vii.

34  Daniel Corkery, *Synge and Anglo-Irish Literature* (Cork: Cork University Press, 1931), ix.

35  ibid., 7–8. (See p. 117.)

36  ibid., 17. (See p. 124.)

37  ibid., 9. (See p. 118.)

38  ibid., ix.

39   ibid., 8, 8–9. (See p. 118.)
40   ibid., 6. (See p. 116.)
41   ibid., 27. (See p. 130.)
42   ibid., 14. (See p. 121.)
43   ibid., 15. (See p. 122.)
44   ibid., 19. (See p. 125.)
45   ibid., 14. (See p. 121.)
46   Maume, *'Life that is Exile'*, 117.
47   Daniel Corkery, *The Philosophy of the Gaelic League* (Dublin: Connradh na Gaedhilge, 1943), 9. (See pp. 77–8). Indeed, Corkery even began speaking dismissingly of his own English-language literary output at this point in time, referring to it as 'part and parcel of English literature'. Interview with Arthur Fedel. Cited in Maume, *'Life that is Exile'*, 124.
48   ibid., 8. (See p. 76.)
49   ibid., 7. (See p. 76.)
50   Salman Rushdie, 'Commonwealth Literature does not Exist', *Imaginary Homelands: Essays and Criticism 1981–1991* (London: Granta, 1991), 64.
51   Terry Eagleton, *Heathcliff and the Great Hunger: Studies in Irish Culture* (London: Verso, 1995), 269. For a more recent example of an extreme 'remaking' of English, see the vivid and idiosyncratic language employed by the Nigerian writer, Ken Saro-Wiwa, in *Sozaboy: A Novel in Rotten English* (1985).
52   Frantz Fanon, *Black Skin, White Masks* (London: Pluto Press [1952]; 1986), 30.
53   ibid., 18.
54   ibid.
55   ibid, 17–18.
56   Corkery, *Synge and Anglo-Irish Literature*, 15. (See p. 122.)
57   The daffodil(s) in question is to be found in Wordsworth's 'I Wandered Lonely as a Cloud', a poem that was assigned a central role on the English colonial curriculum. In Jamaica Kincaid's *Lucy*, the titular character describes how she was made to 'learn by heart a long poem about some flowers I would not see in real life until I was nineteen'. Self-negation is signalled in this novel when Lucy, having been forced to recite this poem to an approving audience, dreams that she is being smothered by 'bunches and bunches of those same daffodils'. Jamaica Kincaid, *Lucy* (New York: Farrar, Straus & Giroux [1990]; 2002), 30, 18.
58   Daniel Corkery, 'Ourselves and Literature: II', *The Standard* (13 Dec. 1930), 8.
59   For examples of Corkery's overuse of such terms, see 'On Anglo-Irish Literature', 'Mr. Yeats in Cork', 'A Landscape in the West' and 'The Colonial Branch of Anglo-Irish Literature'.
60   Daniel Corkery, 'Literature and Life: Was Du Ererbt', *The Irish Statesman* (13 July 1929), 372.
61   Corkery, *Synge and Anglo-Irish Literature*, 26. (See p. 130.)
62   Corkery, *The Hidden Ireland*, 28. (See p. 41.)
63   Corkery, *Synge and Anglo-Irish Literature*, 19. (See p. 125.)
64   Corkery's choice of elements was heavily influenced by Stopford A. Brooke, an Irish clergyman, whose Introduction to *A Treasury of Irish Poetry in the English Tongue* (1900) pinpoints nationality, religion and rebellion as the distinctive features of Irish literature.
65   Corkery, *Synge and Anglo-Irish Literature*, 20. (See p. 125.)
66   ibid. (See p. 126.)

67 ibid., 21–2. (See pp. 126–7.)

68 ibid., 22. (See p. 127.)

69 ibid., 19. (See p. 125.)

70 Brown, *Ireland: A Social and Cultural History*, 1922–1985, 67.

71 Seán O'Faoláin, 'The Emancipation of Irish Writers', *The Yale Review*, 23.3 (March 1934), 490. (See p. 228.) While recognising the antagonism that developed between Corkery and O'Faoláin, the reductive nature of the opposition established in Irish scholarship between a parochial and backward-looking Corkery and a cosmopolitan and progressive O'Faoláin should be noted.

72 Seán O'Faoláin, 'Let Ireland Pride – In What She Has', *The Irish Press* (2 April 1937), 8. (See p. 232.)

73 Kiberd, *Inventing Ireland*, 558.

74 Homi K. Bhabha, *The Location of Culture* (London and New York: Routledge, 1994), 173.

75 Benita Parry, 'The Institutionalisation of Postcolonial Studies', in Neil Lazarus (ed.), *The Cambridge Companion to Postcolonial Literary Studies* (Cambridge: Cambridge University Press, 2004), 76.

76 Simon During, 'Postcolonialism and Globalisation: A Dialectical Relation After All?', *Postcolonial Studies*, 1.1 (1998), 32.


PART ONE. THE IRISH LANGUAGE AND GAELIC CULTURE

*Russian Models for Irish Litterateurs*

1 Daniel Corkery, 'Russian Models for Irish Litterateurs', *The Leader* (27 May 1916). Corkery was not the only one writing at this point in time to extol the values of modern Russian novelists and to suggest that their writings might serve as a model for contemporary Irish-language literature. In a 1908 essay, Pádraic Ó Conaire had likewise argued that modern writers in the Irish language should look to the novelists of Russia. See Ó Conaire, 'Sean-Litridheacht na nGaedheal agus Nuadh-Litridheacht na hEorpa . . .', in Gearóid Denvir (ed.), *Aistí Phádraic Uí Chonaire* (Indreabhán: Cló Chois Fharraige, 1978).

2 Sir Walter Scott (1771–1832) was a Scottish historical novelist and poet. His works include *Waverley* (1814), *Rob Roy* (1817) and *Ivanhoe* (1819).

3 Alexander Pushkin (1799–1837) was a Russian novelist and poet who pioneered the use of vernacular speech in his writings. His works include *Boris Godunov* (1831) and *Eugene Onegin* (1833).

4 Mikhail Lermontov (1814–41) was a Russian writer, poet and painter. His works include the novel *A Hero of Our Time* (1839).

5 Nikolai Gogol (1809–52) was a Ukrainian-born Russian novelist, satirist and dramatist who is considered to be one of the founders of modern Russian realism. His works include *The Inspector-General* (1836) and *Dead Souls* (1842).

6 Egan O'Rahilly (Aodhagán Ó Rathaille) (*c.*1670–1726) was an Irish-language poet and scribe. In his poetry he lamented the demise of the MacCarthy chieftans. He is commonly credited with the composition of the earliest political *aisling* and poetical warrant poems. His best-known poem is the *aisling* 'Gile na Gile' [Brightness most Bright]. Daniel Corkery dedicated a chapter of *The Hidden Ireland* to Ó Rathaille's life and poetry.

7 Eoghan Ruadh Ó Súilleabháin (1748–84) was a labourer, schoolmaster and Irish-language poet. Daniel Corkery, who dedicated a chapter of *The Hidden Ireland* to Ó Súilleabháin's life and poetry, was accused by later Irish-language scholars of placing too much value on Ó Súilleabháin's poetry.

8 Pierce Fitzgerald (Piaras MacGearailt) (1700–91) was an Irish-language poet. Corkery provides an overview of his life and poetry in Chapter 10 of *The Hidden Ireland*.

9 Cathal Buidhe MacGiolla Gunna (*c.*1690–1756) was an Irish-language poet. His best-known work is 'An Buinneán Buidhe' [The Yellow Bittern], a poem about a bird that died while looking for water and is found with its beak stuck in ice. Corkery's play *The Yellow Bittern* (1917) is based on a story he heard about the death of this poet.

10 During the First World War, there was public and official support in Russia for projects that demonstrated that Russian culture was worth fighting for. The international fervour for all things Russian, including Russian literature, however, began just after the 1905 revolution, culminating in the 'Russian craze' of, approximately, 1910–25. English-language literary journals at that time contained a constant flow of commentary on Russian literature and continually called for more and better translations.

11 The Irish-language writer and journalist Pádraic Ó Conaire (1882–1928), who believed that a twentieth-century literature in Irish could best be achieved through literary internationalism, suggesting on a number of occasions that writers of Irish-language literature study the works of such authors as Chekhov, Hardy, Conrad and Hamsun. *Deoraidheacht* [Exile], one of the earliest examples of modernist fiction in Irish, is set in London and explores the impact of urban exile on Irish emigrants. Not all proponents of Irish-language literature were as enthusiastic about this 1910 novel as Daniel Corkery. In 1917, An tAthair Peadar Ó Laoghaire launched a successful campaign to have *Deoraidheacht* removed from the syllabus of the National University on the grounds of sensuality and perversity.

## The Modernisation of Irish Poetry

1 Daniel Corkery, 'The Modernisation of Irish Poetry', *The Leader* (13 Jan 1917).

2 Kuno Meyer (1858–1919) was a German scholar, distinguished in the field of Celtic philology and literature. On its publication, Meyer's *Selections from Ancient Irish Poetry* (1911) was acclaimed for its editorial scholarship and the sensitivity of Meyer's translations.

3 Canon Peter O'Leary (An tAthair Peadar Ó Laoghaire) (1839–1920) was an Irish writer and Catholic priest. His best-known works are his autobiography *Mo Sgéal Féin* [My Own Story] (1915) and his novel *Séadna* (1904). His modernisations of Irish-language literature include *An Craos-Deamhan* (1905), *Eisirt* (1909), *Bricriu* (1915) and *Guaire* (1915).

4 Robert Browning (1812–89) was an English poet and playwright.

5 Thomas F. O'Rahilly (1883–1953) was Professor of Irish at Trinity College, Dublin from 1919 to 1929. The text referred to by Corkery is the 1916 collection *Dánta Grádha: An Anthology of Irish Love Poetry of the Sixteenth and Seventeenth Centuries*.

6 Geoffrey Keating (Seathrún Céitinn) (*c.*1569–1644) was an Irish Catholic priest, poet and historian. His works include *Foras Feasa ar Éireann* [A Survey of Irish History] and the spiritual essay *The Three Shafts of Death*.

7 John Milton (1608–74) was an English poet, polemicist and civil servant. He is best known for his epic poem *Paradise Lost* (1667).

8   Oliver Goldsmith (1728?–74) was an Irish writer, poet and physician. His works
    include the pastoral poem 'The Deserted Village' (1770) and the novel *The Vicar of
    Wakefield* (1770).

### The Hidden Ireland

1   Daniel Corkery, 'The Hidden Ireland', *The Hidden Ireland: A Study of Gaelic Munster
    in the Eighteenth Century* (Dublin: Gill & Son [1924]; 1941).
2   George Townshend (1724–1807) was Lord Lieutenant (Viceroy) of Ireland from
    1767 to 1772.
3   William Henry Nassau de Zuylestein, 4th Earl of Rochford (1717–1781) was a British
    diplomat and statesman. From 1768 to 1775, he was one of the secretaries of state.
4   The Nagle family was wealthy, Catholic and Irish-speaking. Edmund Burke's
    mother was one of the Nagles, as was Nano Nagle, the founder of the Presentation
    order of nuns. Ó Súilleabháin is rumoured to have entered into a sexual relationship
    with the mother of the Nagle children he had been hired to teach.
5   W.E.H. Lecky, *A History of Ireland in the Eighteenth Century, Vol II* (London:
    Longmans, Green & Co. [1892]; 1913), 188–9. William Edward Hartpole Lecky
    (1838–1903) was an Irish historian and essayist. The final volumes of Lecky's *A
    History of England in the Eighteenth Century* were published separately as *A History
    of Ireland in the Eighteenth Century*, 5 vols.
6   Maria Edgeworth (1767–1849) was an Irish novelist and children's writer. Her
    works include *Letters to Literary Ladies* (1795), *Castle Rackrent* (1800) and *The
    Absentee* (1812).
7   Jonathan Swift (1667–1745) was an Irish satirist, political pamphleteer, poet and
    cleric, who was appointed Dean of St. Patrick's Cathedral, Dublin. Although he was
    reluctant to take up the post at St. Patrick's Cathedral as it involved returning to
    Ireland, Swift used his pamphleteering skills, once in Ireland, in support of Irish
    causes. His pamphlets include *A Proposal for the Universal Use of Irish Manufacture*
    (1920), *The Drapier Letters* (1724–25) and *A Modern Proposal* (1729). In *The Drapier
    Letters*, Swift, in the persona of the drapier addressing 'the Whole People of Ireland',
    observes that the English 'look upon us as a sort of Savage Irish, whom our
    ancestors conquered several hundred years ago'. He goes on to remind his English
    readers of their own 'savage' past: 'And if I should describe the Britons to you, as they
    were in Caesar's time, when they painted their bodies, or clothed themselves with
    the skin of beasts, I should act full as reasonably as they do.' Jonathan Swift, 'To the
    Whole People of Ireland', in Claude Rawson (ed.), *The Basic Writings of Jonathan
    Swift* (New York: The Modern Library, 2002), 332–3.
8   George Berkeley (1685–1753) was an Irish philosopher and Anglican bishop of
    Cloyne. His pamphlet *The Querist*, which was concerned with the economic and
    social situation in Ireland, was published in three instalments in 1735, 1736 and
    1737. This quotation is derived from the nineteenth query of the first instalment of
    *The Querist*.
9   W.E.H. Lecky, *A History of Ireland in the Eighteenth Century, Vol I* (Cambridge:
    Cambridge University Press [1892]; 2010), 166.
10  Ibid., 250.
11  Cited in ibid., 285. Corkery is referring here to Philip Stanhope (1694–1773), 4th
    Earl of Chesterfield, who was Lord Lieutenant or Viceroy of Ireland from 1745 to
    1746.

12   Samuel Madden, *Reflections and Resolutions Proper for the Gentlemen of Ireland* (Dublin: George Ewing, 1738), 67.

13   Jonathan Swift, 'A Proposal for the Universal Use of Irish Manufacture', in T. Scott (ed.), *The Prose Works of Jonathan Swift D.D., Vol VII* (London: George Bell & Sons, 1905), 26.

14   Alice Stopford Green, *Irish Nationality* (London: Williams & Norgate, 1911), 182–3.

15   Donnchadh Ruadh MacConmara (1715–1810) was a schoolmaster and Irish-language poet. His best-known works are 'Bán Chnoic Éireann Óigh' [The Fair Hills of Ireland] and 'Eachtra Ghiolla an Amaráin' [The Adventures of a Luckless Fellow], an account of a journey overseas to Newfoundland. Corkery discusses both of these poems in Chapter 10 of *The Hidden Ireland*.

16   Seán Ó Tuama (1706–75) was a publican and Irish-language poet. Corkery provides an overview of his life and poetry in Chapter 10 of *The Hidden Ireland*.

17   Brian Merriman (*c.*1749–1805) was a schoolmaster and Irish-language poet. His best-known poem is *Cúirt an Mheán-Oíche* [The Midnight Court], the principal themes of which are clerical celibacy, the plight of young women who can't find husbands, and the misery of a young woman who is married to an old man. Chapter 9 of Corkery's *The Hidden Ireland* is concerned with Merriman's life and poetry.

18   This might be the Cork-based lyric poet and satirist of the same name referred to by Edward O'Reilly in *A Chronological Account of nearly Four Hundred Irish Writers, with a Descriptive Catalogue of their Works* (Shannon: Irish University Press [1820]; 1970), ccxxxi.

19   William English (Liam Inglis) (1709–78) was a teacher, Augustinian priest and Jacobite poet. He is credited with a wide range of secular and religious verse, including a number of poems inspired by newspaper reports on the progress of the Seven Years War. Edmund Burke, who spent some time with his maternal family, the Nagles, as a child, was tutored by Inglis.

20   Micheál Ó Longáin (1766–1837) was a teacher, scribe, Irish-language poet and 1798 insurgent. His poem 'Buachaillí Loch Garman' laments Munster's failure to participate in 1798 and praises the 'boys' of Wexford for their part in the rebellion.

21   Arthur Young (1741–1820), commonly regarded as a pioneer of the Agricultural Revolution, was an English writer on agriculture, economics and social statistics. In his *Tour in Ireland*, he strongly urged the repeal of the penal laws and condemned the restrictions imposed on the commerce of Ireland. Young's discussion of language use in Wexford can be found in Arthur Young, *Tour in Ireland, 1776–1779* (London: Cassell & Co. [1780]; 1893), 179.

22   John Sevenson, *Two Centuries of Life in Down, 1600–1800* (Belfast: McCaw, Stevenson & Orr, 1920), 218.

23   De Bougrenet de Latocnaye, *A Frenchman's Walk through Ireland, 1796–7*, John Stevenson (trans.) (Belfast: McCaw, Stevenson & Orr, 1917), 54. This book was originally published in 1798 as *Promenade d'un Français dans l'Irlande*.

24   This phrase was actually directed against Valentine Browne by a fellow settler, William Herbert. See James Carmody, 'Story of Castle Magne (cont.)', *Kerry Archaeological Magazine*, 1.2 (April 1909), 73–4.

25   Young, *Tour in Ireland*, 170.

26   George Sigerson, *The Last Independent Parliament of Ireland, with Account of the Survival of the Nation and its Lifework* (Dublin: Gill & Son [1918]; 1919), xxi.

27   Sir Jonah Barrington (1760–1834) was an Irish lawyer, judge, historian and politi-
     cian. His best-known publication is *Personal Sketches of his Own Time* (1827–32).
28   William Carleton (1794–1869) was an Irish writer. His works include *Traits and
     Stories of the Irish Peasantry* (1830) and *The Black Prophet* (1847).
29   William O'Neill Daunt (1807–94) was an Irish nationalist politician and secretary
     to Daniel O'Connell. He wrote a number of books including *A Catechism of the
     History of Ireland* (1844). His diaries were edited by his daughter Alice and
     published in 1896 as *A Life Spent in Ireland*.
30   Maria Edgeworth, *The Absentee* (Oxford: Oxford University Press [1812]; 1988),
     146.
31   Michael Doheny, *The Felon's Track: or History of the Attempted Outbreak in Ireland*
     (Dublin: Gill & Son [1849]; 1920), 235.
32   ibid., 256.
33   Liam P. Ó Murchú (ed.), *Cúirt an Mheon-Oíche le Brian Merríman* (Dublin: An
     Clóchomhar Tta, 1982), 30.
34   Tadhg Dall Ua h-Uigín (Ó Huigín) (1550–91) was an Irish-language poet and the
     best-known member of the Ó Huigín bardic family.
35   Liam Dall Ua h-Ifearnáin (O'Heffernan) (*c.*1720–1803) was an Irish-language poet.
     Among his works is the *aisling* 'Caitlín Ní Uallacháin'.
36   Seamus Dall Ua Cuarta (Seamus Dall MacCuarta) (*c.*1647–1733) was part of the
     Airgíalla tradition of poetry.
37   Donnchadh Dall Ua Laoghaire (Ó Laeire) was a harpist and Irish-language poet.
     For further details, see Donncha Ó Cróinín (ed.), *Seanachas Phádraig Í Chrualaoi*
     (Dublin: Comhairle Bhéaloideas Éireann, 1982), 3–4, 36.
38   Turlogh Carolan (Toirbhdeallach Ó Cearbhalláin) (1670–1738) was a harpist and
     composer.
39   Georgiana Chatterton, 'Rambles in the South of Ireland', in Adam Waldie (ed.),
     *The Select Circulating Library, Vol II* (Philadelphia: Adam Waldie, 1839), 191.
40   Cited in An Seabhac (Pádraig Ó Siochfhradha) (ed.), *Seanfhocail na Mumhan*
     (Dublin: An Gúm [1926]; 1984), 34.
41   See John Churton Collins, *Jonathan Swift: A Biographical and Critical Study*
     (London: Chatto & Windus, 1893), 162. The practice was observed by Samuel
     Burdy, author of *The Life of the Late Rev. Philip Skelton* (1792).
42   W.R. Le Fanu, *Seventy Years of Irish Life – Being Anecdotes and Reminiscences*
     (London: Edward Arnold, 1893), 100.
43   William King (1650–1729) was Anglican Archbishop of Dublin from 1703 to
     1729. Much of his correspondence survives and provides an important historic
     resource for the study of the Ireland of his day.
44   Letter 443: 'The Archbishop of Dublin to Archbishop Wake, Upon the Same', in
     Henry Ellis (ed.), *Original Letters, Illustrative of English History, Vol IV* (London:
     Harding & Lepard, 1827), 328.
45   Anon., *The Groans of Ireland: In a Letter to a Member of Parliament* (Dublin: G.
     Faulkner, 1741), 3. Cited in Lecky, *A History of Ireland in the Eighteenth Century,
     Vol I*, 186.
46   Cited in Lecky, *A History of Ireland in the Eighteenth Century, Vol I*, 187–8.
47   Anon., 'A Ógánaigh an Chúil Cheangailte', in Douglas Hyde (ed.), *Abhráin Grádh
     Chúige Connacht or Love Songs of Connacht* (Dublin: Gill & Son; London: T. Fisher
     Unwin [1893]; 1909), 40. See also Seán Ó Tuama (ed.), *An Duanaire, 1600–1900:
     Poems of the Dispossessed* (Dublin: Dolmen Press, 1981), 302.

48 Art O'Leary (Airt Ó Laoghaire) (1747–73) was a captain in the Hungarian Hussars. Upon returning home to Ireland, he refused to sell his prize-winning horse to the High Sheriff of Cork, Abraham Morris, and was consequently proclaimed an outlaw. Under the penal laws, a Roman Catholic could not own a horse worth more than £5 and was obliged to sell a horse for no more than £5, irrespective of the animal's value, to a Protestant if asked to do so. O'Leary was tracked by Morris's men and shot dead. His wife, Eileen O'Connell (Eibhlín Dhubh Ní Chonaill), is said to have composed the poem *Caoineadh Airt Uí Laoghaire* [Lament for Art O'Leary], mourning his death and calling for revenge.

49 Seán Ó Tuama (ed.), *Caoineadh Airt Uí Laoghaire* (Dublin: An Clóchomhar Tta. [1961]; 1968), 41.

50 Seán Clárach MacDomhnaill, 'Oidhche Bhíos im Luighe im Shuain', in Risteárd Ó Foghludha (ed.), *Seán Clárach, 1691–1754* (Dublin: Oifig Díolta Foillseacháin Rialtais, 1932), 50. Seán Clárach MacDomhnaill was a teacher, labourer and Irish-language poet, who took on a leadership role amongst the poets of Munster. 'Mo Ghile Mear' [My Gallant Darling], a lament written after the defeat of Bonnie Prince Charles at the Battle of Culloden in 1746, is his most famous poem. Corkery provides an overview of MacDomhnaill's life and poetry in Chapter 10 of *The Hidden Ireland*.

51 De Bougrenet de Latocnaye, *A Frenchman's Walk through Ireland, 1796–7*, 116.

52 Anon., 'Cill Chais', in Ó Tuama (ed.), *An Duanaire*, 328.

53 Lecky, *A History of Ireland in the Eighteenth Century, Vol I*, 334.

54 Anon., 'Seán Ó Duibhir an Ghleanna' [John O'Dwyer of the Glen]. For the complete poem and a translation, see George Sigerson, *The Poets and Poetry of Munster: A Selection of Irish Songs*, 2nd Series (Dublin: John O'Daly, 1860), 110–17.

55 Edmund Spenser, *A View of the Present State of Ireland* (Oxford: Clarendon Press [1633]; 1970), 19.

56 See Lecky, *A History of Ireland in the Eighteenth Century, Vol I*, 285.

57 Young, *Tour in Ireland*, 190–1.

58 Alexander MacKenzie, *The History of the Highland Clearances* (Inverness: A. & W. MacKenzie, 1883).

59 Jonathan Swift, 'On the Causes of the Wretched Condition of Ireland', *The Works of Jonathan Swift, Vol II* (London: Henry G. Bohn, 1856), 159. The original reads as follows: 'we are become as hewers of wood and drawers of water to our rigorous neighbours.'

60 In Irish origin legends, King Milesius of Spain is the ancestor of the vast majority of the Irish Gaels.

*Eoghan Ruadh Ó Súilleabháin*

1 Daniel Corkery, 'Eoghan Ruadh Ó Súilleabháin', *The Hidden Ireland: A Study of Gaelic Munster in the Eighteenth Century* (Dublin: Gill & Son [1924]; 1941).

2 The MacCarthys were one of Ireland's greatest medieval dynasties. 'MacCarthy Mor' is the title given to the Chieftain of the MacCarthy family.

3 The Kenmare Estate, one of the largest estates in Ireland, was owned by the Browne family.

4 Cited in W.E.H. Lecky, *A History of Ireland in the Eighteenth Century, Vol I* (Cambridge: Cambridge University Press [1892]; 2010), 285.

5   Attica is an historical region of Greece that was home to such influential figures as the playwrights Sophocles and Aeschylus and the philosophers Socrates and Plato. Hymettus is a mountain range situated in Attica.

6   Bardic Schools provided an education for scholars of history, law and poetry.

7   Courts of Poetry were normally held in local taverns. The poets who attended read their poems aloud to one another for criticism and correction. Courts of Poetry, which were presided over by a judge or high sheriff, were a parody of the English court system.

8   Pádraig Ó Duinnín (ed.), *Amhráin Eoghain Ruaidh Uí Shúilleabháin* (Dublin: Gaelic League, 1901), x–xi.

9   ibid., xi.

10  ibid., xv.

11  Mercutio is a character in William Shakespeare's *Romeo and Juliet* who due to his clever banter, witty comebacks and sexually-charged language is perceived to be a reckless jokester.

12  Pan, in Greek Mythology, is the god of rustic music. Pan once had the audacity to compare his music to Apollo's and to challenge Apollo to a trial of skill.

13  Ulysses was the legendary Greek king of Ithaca and the hero of Homer's epic poem *The Odyssey*.

14  Pádraig Ó Duinnín, *Beatha Eoghain Ruaidh Uí Shúilleabháin* (Dublin: Gaelic League, 1902), 16.

15  Cited in ibid.

16  Corkery is referring here to Pádraig Ó Duinnín [Patrick Dinneen], editor of *Amhráin Eoghain Ruadh Úi Shúilleabháin* (1901).

17  Tobias Smollett, *The Adventures of Roderick Random* (London: Printed for J. Osborn, 1748)

18  John Masefield, *Sea Life in Nelson's Time* (London: Methuen & Co. [1905]; 1906), 123.

19  The *aisling*, or vision poem, is a poetic genre that developed in Ireland in the late seventeenth and eighteenth centuries, particularly in the region of Munster. In an *aisling*, Ireland appears to the poet in a vision in the form of a woman. The woman, often a goddess figure or 'sky-woman', may speak of a lover in exile, of strangers in her house, or of her hope that she will be rescued.

20  Ó Duinnín (ed.), *Amhráin Eoghain Ruaidh Uí Shúilleabháin*, 25.

21  George Brydges Rodney (1719–92) was a British naval officer. He is best known for his commands in the American War of Independence, particularly the victory against the French that Corkery refers to in *The Hidden Ireland*.

22  In 1781, Sir Charles Douglas (1727–89) was appointed Captain-of-the-Fleet for George Brydges Rodney. He was with Rodney on his flagship during the victory against the French at the Battle of the Saintes.

23  Français Joseph Paul de Grasse (1722–88) is best known for his successful command of the French fleet at the Battle of the Chesapeake, during the American War of Independence. De Grasse was defeated the following year by Rodney at the Battle of the Saintes.

24  Ó Duinnín (ed.), *Amhráin Eoghain Ruaidh Uí Shúilleabháin*, xvi–xvii.

25  ibid., xviii–xxi.

26  ibid., 34.

27  ibid., xxii.

28  ibid., xxiii. Ó Súilleabháin is said to have had a sexual encounter with a girl on his death-bed.

29  ibid.

30  The fifth chapter of *The Hidden Ireland* is concerned with *aisling* (vision) poems. In this chapter, Corkery briefly discusses part of an *aisling* poem by Ó Súilleabháin.

31  Ó Duinnín (ed.), *Amhráin Eoghain Ruaidh Uí Shúilleabháin*, 16.

32  ibid., 120

33  ibid., 116.

34  See ibid., 45–7.

35  ibid., 48.

36  ibid.

37  Denis Murphy, *Cromwell in Ireland: A History of Cromwell's Irish Campaign* (Dublin: Gill & Son, 1883), 428.

38  J.C. MacErlean (ed.), *Duanaire Dháibhidh Uí Bhruadair: The Poems of David Ó Bruadair, 3 Vols* (London: Irish Texts Society, 1910–17), Vol I, No. 5, verses 25–6. Dáibhidh Ó Bruadair (1625–98) was a seventeenth-century Irish-language poet, whose poetry charts the destruction of the Gaelic world. In 'An Longbhriseadh', for example, he laments Ireland's plight after the Treaty of Limerick and the flight of the Wild Geese. When his patrons, the Fitzgeralds, left with the other Wild Geese, Ó Bruadair was forced to find work as a farm labourer.

39  See John Milton, 'On the Detraction Which Followed upon my Writing Certain Treatises' (1645–6).

40  Corkery is referring here to the famous French poet François Villon (1431–?63).

41  Ó Duinnín (ed.), *Amhráin Eoghain Ruaidh Uí Shúilleabháin*, 61.

42  ibid., 74.

43  ibid., 73.

44  François Rabelais (*c.*1484–1553) was a French writer, monk and doctor, who is commonly associated with satire, the grotesque, and bawdy songs and jokes.

45  Ó Duinnín (ed.), *Amhráin Eoghain Ruaidh Uí Shúilleabháin*, 80.

46  ibid.

47  ibid., 85.

48  ibid., 83.

49  Ogham is an ancient linear script and the first known written language of Ireland. The script was supposedly inspired by the god of eloquence, Oghma.

50  Ó Duinnín (ed.), *Amhráin Eoghain Ruaidh Uí Shúilleabháin*, 105.

51  ibid., 106. Courts of Poetry employed both the language and forms of the British court system. Moreover, the 'warrants' associated with these poetry gatherings often contained legal phrases and English loanwords. In Chapter IV of *The Hidden Ireland*, Corkery outlined the practices of Courts of Poetry and criticised what he interpreted as their subservient mimicking of official law. The humorous nature of the 'warrants' written by Ó Súilleabháin and others suggests, however, that the origins of these Courts lay less in a desire to mimic that which is admirable, than to lampoon that which is not.

52  ibid., 2.

53  Robert Browning, 'A Grammarian's Funeral', *The Poetical Works of Robert Browning, 1833–1858, Vol II* (London: Hutchinson & Co., 1906), 610.

54  Ó Duinnín (ed.), *Amhráin Eoghain Ruaidh Uí Shúilleabháin*, 120.

55  ibid., 52. In Greek mythology, Hebe is the goddess of youth.

56   ibid., 40. In Greek mythology, Helen is the daughter of Zeus and Leda. Her
     abduction by Troy brought about the Trojan War.
57   The *Pléiade* is the name given to a group of sixteenth-century French poets, who
     sought to renew French poetry by drawing on Greek and Roman poetic forms.
58   Ó Duinnín (ed.), *Amhráin Eoghain Ruaidh Uí Shúilleabháin*, 16.
59   In a letter to his brother George, John Keats (1795–1821) referred to his poem
     *Endymion* as 'a test, a trial of my Powers of Imagination and chiefly of my invention
     which is a rare thing indeed'. See W. Jackson Bate, *John Keats* (Cambridge, MA:
     Harvard University Press, 1963), 169.
60   Ó Duinnín (ed.), *Amhráin Eoghain Ruaidh Uí Shúilleabháin*, 119.
61   ibid., 53.
62   ibid., 68.
63   In the poem 'Cailleach Bhéara' [Old Woman of Beare], the woman, who has entered
     a nunnery, bemoans the loss of past pleasures.
64   Jean-Baptiste Poquelin (1622–73), known by his stage-name Molière, was a French
     playwright and actor who is primarily remembered for his comedies.
65   Ó Duinnín (ed.), *Amhráin Eoghain Ruaidh Uí Shúilleabháin*, 72.
66   Alfred, Lord Tennyson, 'The May Queen' (1833). 'The May Queen', while enthu-
     siastically received by Tennyson's contemporaries, was, by the 1920s, considered by
     many literary scholars to be a prime example of sentiment turned into Victorian
     sentimentality.
67   Thomas F. O'Rahilly (ed.), *Dánfhocail: Irish Epigrams in Verse* (Dublin: The Talbot
     Press, 1921).
68   Ó Duinnín, *Amhráin Eoghain Ruaidh Uí Shúilleabháin*, xxxvii. Pindar (*c.*522–443
     BC) was the great lyric poet of ancient Greece. Robert Burns (1759–96) is widely
     regarded as the national poet of Scotland. Pierre-Jean de Béranger (1780–1857) is
     considered to be the national song-writer of France. Rudyard Kipling (1865–1936)
     was one of the most popular writers in English, in both prose and verse, in the late
     nineteenth and early twentieth centuries.
69   Ó Duinnín, *Beatha Eoghain Ruaidh Uí Shúilleabháin*, 50.

## The Philosophy of the Gaelic League

1   Daniel Corkery, *The Philosophy of the Gaelic League* (Dublin: The Gaelic League,
    1943).
2   Edgar Allan Poe, 'The Haunted Palace', in James A. Harrison (ed.), *The Complete
    Works of Edgar Allan Poe: Poems* (New York: George D. Sproul, 1902), 200.
3   'Kiltartanese' was Lady Augusta Gregory's term for the Hiberno-English dialect
    that was spoken in the parish of Kiltartan, Co. Galway. Gregory (1852–1932) drew
    on this dialect in her publications *The Kiltartan History Book* (1909) and *The
    Kiltartan Wonder Book* (1910). She also produced a number of collections of
    'Kiltartanese' versions of Irish myths.
4   Alfred Lord Tennyson, 'The Cup: A Tragedy', in T. Herbert Warren (ed.), *Tennyson:
    Poems and Plays* (Oxford: Oxford University Press, 1971), 703.

## Review: Cré na Cille le Máirtín Ó Cadhain

1   Daniel Corkery, '*Cré na Cille*', *Feasta* (May 1950). According to Patrick Walsh,
    Tomás Ó Muircheartaigh, president of the Gaelic League and editor of *Feasta*,
    proof-read Corkery's Irish-language contributions to the journal. See Walsh, 'Daniel

Corkery: Tradition and an Individual Talent', unpublished M.A. thesis, University of Ulster, 1993, 69.

2  Máirtín Ó Cadhain (1906–70) was a teacher, labourer, and Irish-language author of two novels and six collections of short stories. He was a member of the army council of the IRA and was interned in the Curragh during the 'Emergency' for his republican activities. *Cré na Cille* (1949), which is generally regarded as his masterpiece, was critiqued upon its publication by conservative elements within the Irish-language movement for its humorous portrayal of the intrigues and petty jealousies of an Irish-speaking community.

3  Máirtín Ó Cadhain, *Cré na Cille* (Dublin: Sáirséal & Dill, 1949), 142.

4  Hamlet says these words to Polonius in act ii, scene ii of William Shakespeare's *Hamlet* (*c.*1599).

5  Corkery is referring here to Thomas Babington Macaulay (1800–59). Macaulay – who was an essayist, poet, historian and politician – employed a journalistic style of composition characterised by the systematic use of short sentences.

6  Irish-language activists from the 1880s to the first decades of the twentieth century were engaged in an often acrimonious debate concerning the process by which a literary tradition that had been suppressed and largely oral for two centuries was to be restored. Some argued that the Irish-language literature of the Gaelic Revival should attempt to pick up from where the tradition had been ruptured in the seventeenth century, while others, including Peadar Ó Laoghaire, sought to root this literature in the contemporary spoken language.

7  John Dos Passos, *U.S.A.* (Harmondsworth: Penguin Books [1938]; 1966), 6–7.

8  ibid., 922.

9  For an informative overview of the differing views held by Irish-language activists on the literary worth of folklore and its value as a model for the prose fiction of the Gaelic Revival, see Philip O'Leary, 'Seanchuidhthe, *Séadna*, Sheehan, and the Zeitgeist', *The Prose Literature of the Gaelic Revival, 1881–1921* (Pennsylvania: Pennsylvania State University Press, 1994), 91–162.

*Review: 'Inquisitio 1584' le Máire Mhac an tSaoi*

1  Daniel Corkery, 'Dán Cruinn Beo: "Inquisitio 1584"', *Feasta* (Feb 1953). Máire Mhac an tSaoi (b. 1922) is a literary critic, translator and Irish-language poet. Her poetry collections include *Margadh na Saoire* (1956), *An Galar Dubhach* (1980) and *An Cion go dtí Seo* (1987). 'Inquisitio 1584' is an elegy for an executed sixteenth-century Irish chieftain.

2  Máire Mhac an tSaoi, 'Inquisitio 1584', in Seán Ó Tuama (ed.), *Nuabhéarsaíocht, 1939–1949* (Dublin: Sáirséal & Dill [1950]; 1974), 105.

3  Seán Ó Tuama's edited collection, *Nuabhéarsaíocht, 1939–1949* (1950) was seminal in introducing contemporary Irish-language poetry to the general public and in emphasising the modernist tendencies of such poetry. By giving so much space to their poetry, the anthology established Máire Mhac an tSaoi, Seán Ó Ríordáin and Máirtín Ó Direáin as the major Irish-language poets of the period.

4  Máire Mhac an tSaoi, 'Oíche Nollag', in ibid., 100.

5  Tadhg Gaelach Ó Súilleabháin (*c.*1715–95) was an Irish-language poet. His religious poems, which are his best-known works, were first published in 1802 as *Timothy O'Sullivan's Pious Miscellany*. His secular poems include variations on the *aisling* theme. *Pious Miscellany* was the most widely-read Irish-language publication in the period before the foundation of the Gaelic League.

6   See Johann Wolfgang von Goethe, 'Conversations with Eckermann', in G.W. Allen and H.H. Clark (eds), *Literary Criticism: Pope to Croce* (Detroit: Wayne State University Press, 1962), 141.

## 1800–1919

1   Daniel Corkery, '1880–1919', *The Fortunes of the Irish Language* (Dublin: Published for the Cultural Relations Committee of Ireland by C.J. Fallon, 1954).

2   Corkery is referring here to the controversy over the legitimacy of James Macpherson's Ossian poems. This cycle of poems, which Macpherson claimed to have translated from ancient sources in Scots Gaelic, was largely derived from the Irish ballads that Macpherson dismissed as corrupt modern imitations.

3   Whiteboyism, which was largely concerned with defending the land rights of tenant farmers, emerged in the 1760s.

4   Charlotte Brooke's *Reliques of Irish Poetry* (1789) was an anthology of Irish-language odes, elegies and songs, with English-language translations. The publication was in part a response to the Macpherson controversy, in that Brooke included in the collection the poems and songs of her locality which echoed those contained in James Macpherson's *Fragments of Ancient Poetry* (1760).

5   Charles O'Conor (1710–91) was a Catholic activist, Irish-language scholar, historian and antiquarian. He intervened in the Macpherson controversy with his *Dissertation on the Origin and Antiquities of the Ancient Scots* (1775), which claimed Ireland as the source of all Gaelic culture.

6   Corkery is referring here to the Belfast Harp Festival of 1792, a three-day event involving nine harpists that was organised by Dr James MacDonnell, Robert Bradshaw and Henry Joy.

7   See Ida Ashworth Taylor, *The Life of Lord Edward Fitzgerald, 1763–1798* (London: Hutchinson & Co., 1903), 198.

8   Desmond Ryan, *The Sword of Light: From the Four Masters to Douglas Hyde, 1636– 1938* (London: Arthur Barker, 1939), 57.

9   Corkery is referring here to Henry Fitzsimon (1566–1643), a Catholic convert who entered a Jesuit seminar at Louvain in the 1590s and returned to Ireland a number of years later as an ordained priest. He was imprisoned from 1600 to 1604 for his counter-reformation activities and, when condemned to hang in 1641 on suspicion of involvement in the rebellion of that year, he escaped to the Wicklow mountains before making his way to a Jesuit community in Kilkenny.

10  The Gaelic Society was founded with the aim of improving the general under-standing of the literature and antiquities of Gaelic Ireland. Theophilus O'Flanagan (1762–1814), a native speaker of the Irish language, was the first secretary of the Society. O'Flanagan edited the Society's only publication, *The Transactions of the Gaelic Society* (1808). He also assisted Charlotte Brooke in her *Reliques of Irish Poetry* (1789).

11  Lear says these words in act v, scene iii of William Shakespeare's *King Lear* (*c.*1603), as he holds Cordelia's dead body.

12  Cited in R.B. McDowell, *Irish Public Opinion, 1750–1800* (London: Faber & Faber, 1944), 124.

13  Cited in W.J. O'Neill Daunt, *Personal Recollections of the Late Daniel O'Connell, M.P.* (London: Chapman & Hall, 1848), 14–15. Daniel O'Connell (1775–1847) was an Irish nationalist leader who campaigned for Catholic emancipation and repeal of the Act of Union.

14 McDowell, *Irish Public Opinion, 1750–1800*, 23–4.

15 Cited in ibid., 14. Utilitarianism is a philosophy which argues that the right act or policy is that which causes the greatest good for the greatest number of people. It was expounded by the English philosopher and social reformer Jeremy Bentham (1748–1832) in his *Introduction to the Principles of Morals and Legislation* (1789).

16 J.J. O'Kelly, *O'Connell Calling: The Liberator's Place in the World* (Tralee: The Kerryman, 1947); Denis Gwynn, *Daniel O'Connell* (Cork: Cork University Press, 1947), 224.

17 John MacHale (1791–1881), a supporter of O'Connell, was appointed Catholic Archbishop of Tuam in 1834 despite strong government opposition. MacHale, a native Irish speaker, was an enthusiastic advocate of the Irish language, through which he often addressed his congregation. He opposed the plans for national schools and Queen's Colleges put forward in the late 1840s and succeeded in gaining the support of the church hierarchy for his strongly-held views against the education together of Catholic and Protestant children.

18 In Greek mythology, Clio/Kleio is the muse of history.

19 Thomas Davis (1814–45) was a poet, journalist and nationalist. In the early 1840s, he co-founded the *Nation* newspaper and assumed leadership of those who left Daniel O'Connell's Repeal movement to establish a new political group known as Young Ireland.

20 Pádraic Pearse, 'The Spiritual Nation', *The Murder Machine and Other Essays* (Dublin: Mercier Press, 1976), 64.

21 Colin Walkinshaw, *The Scots Tragedy* (London: Routledge, 1935), 142. Albany says these lines in act iv, scene ii of *King Lear* (*c.*1603).

22 Henry Sidney (1529–86) was lord deputy of Ireland from 1565 to 1571 and from 1575 to 1578.

23 The term 'whiggery' refers to the notion that our past and present are an inexorable march of progress towards enlightenment.

24 Thomas Moore (1779–1852) is remembered primarily for his *Irish Melodies* (1807–34), a ten-volume work consisting of 130 poems set to music arranged from 'traditional' Irish tunes. The *Melodies* earned Moore a substantial income and the unofficial title of national lyric poet of Ireland. Some commentators, however, viewed Moore's *Melodies* as debased Irish airs designed for an English audience.

25 E.C. Quiggin, *Prolegomena to the Study of the Later Irish Bards, 1200–1500* (Oxford: [s.n.], 1911), 32.

26 Myles Dillon, *Early Irish Literature* (Chicago: University of Chicago Press, 1948).

27 The Ossianic Society (1853–63) was founded with the aim of collecting and publishing poems and tales of Oisín and the Fianna, especially those in extant manuscripts in the Irish language.

28 Eugene O'Curry (1796–1862) was an Irish-language scholar who transcribed, edited and translated manuscripts. He worked for the Ordnance Survey under George Petrie and was later employed, with John O'Donovan, as a translator of Brehon Law manuscripts.

29 John O'Donovan (1809–61) was an Irish-language scholar who worked, alongside Eugene O'Curry, for the Ordnance Survey and as a translator of Brehon Law manuscripts.

30 Standish Hayes O'Grady (1832–1915) was an Irish-language scholar who started to compile a catalogue of Irish manuscripts contained in the British Museum. The catalogue, which was unfinished on his death, was completed by Robin Flower.

31 Philip Barron (*c*.1797–1860) was a Celticist and Hebraist who sought to sustain the Irish language as a spoken language by producing Irish-language publications that even the poorest could buy, and by establishing a college that taught through the Irish language. His magazine, *Ancient Ireland*, ran for five monthly numbers. His Irish-language college at Bunmahon, Co. Waterford closed shortly after it had opened.

32 Ryan, *The Sword of Light*, 129.

33 Jeremiah O'Donovan Rossa (1831–1915) was an Irish Fenian leader. Although he learned English in school, his family spoke Irish at home and he retained a life-long attachment to the language.

34 Following the Young Ireland Rising of 1848, in which he took part, John O'Mahony (1816–77), a Gaelic scholar, fled to France and then New York. While abroad, he was active in associations formed by Irish exiles to promote the cause of Irish freedom. In 1858, he co-founded the Fenian Brotherhood, whose name was inspired by the mythical warriors of the Fianna.

35 Ryan, *The Sword of Light*, 127.

36 The first mass protest meeting of the Land War period took place in Irishtown, Co. Mayo in April 1879. A second protest meeting, which Charles Stewart Parnell addressed, took place in Westport, Co. Mayo in June 1879. Out of these meetings came the Land League of Mayo. This was then absorbed into the National Land League with Parnell as its president and Michael Davitt as one of its secretaries.

37 Thomas William Croke (1824–1902) was Catholic Bishop of Auckland, New Zealand and then Catholic Archbishop of Cashel and Emly in Ireland. At the first meeting of the Gaelic Athletic Association, Croke was nominated as a patron. In his letter of acceptance, which was published in a number of newspapers to attract support for the new organisation, Croke spoke of the importance of culture, and in particular sport, to the national movement. This letter is often viewed as the unofficial charter of the GAA.

38 The phrase 'to create and foster public opinion in Ireland, and to make it racy of the soil' was first used by the Irish peer, politician and judge Arthur Woulfe (1739–1803). It was later adopted as the motto of *The Nation* newspaper.

39 Corkery is referring here to the first devolved government of Northern Ireland, the Stormont administration (1921–72). Northern Ireland consists of six of the nine counties of the Irish province of Ulster.

40 Douglas Hyde's first collection of folklore, *Beside the Fire*, was published in 1890. His other publications include *Love Songs of Connacht* (1893), *Religious Songs of Connacht* (1906) and *A Literary History of Ireland* (1899).

41 D.P. Moran (1869–1936) was editor of *The Leader* from 1900 to 1926. He was a vigorous advocate of Irish Irelandism and a strong critic of what he considered to be the sham cultural nationalism of the Celtic Twilight.

42 Louis Paul-Dubois, *Contemporary Ireland* (Dublin: Maunsel & Co., 1908), 410. Eugene O'Growney [Eoghan Ó Gramhnaigh] (1863–99) was a priest and an Irish-language activist. He was one of the founders of the Gaelic League and an editor of *Irisleabhar na Gaedhilge*. As part of his efforts to revive the Irish language, O'Growney published a series of lessons titled 'Simple Lessons in Irish' in the *Weekly Freeman* and

in *Irisleabhar na Gaedhilge*. These lessons, in which approximate pronunciation was placed after each new Irish-language word, were published in book form by the Gaelic League in 1894.

43  Pádraic Pearse, 'Oration on Robert Emmet', in Desmond Ryan (ed.), *Collected Works of Padraic H. Pearse* (Dublin: Pheonix Publishing Company, 1924), 72.
44  Pádraic Pearse, 'From a Hermitage', in ibid., 210–11.
45  Corkery is, in fact, referring to Israel here.
46  Lionel Johnson, 'Celtic Speech', in W.B. Yeats (ed.), *A Book of Irish Verse* (London: Routledge [1895]; 2002, 153.

## PART TWO. REPRESENTING IRELAND

### Mr. Yeats in Cork

1  'Lee' (Daniel Corkery), 'Mr. Yeats in Cork', *The Leader* (30 Dec 1905). William Butler Yeats (1865–1939) was a poet and playwright, whose works are associated with the Literary Revival.
2  The society referred to here is the Cork Literary and Scientific Society, which was founded in 1820.
3  Corkery is referring here to the short-lived Cork National Theatre Society, which was founded in 1904, as opposed to the better-known Cork Dramatic Society which he co-founded in 1908.
4  Yeats, who as a Symbolist believed that drama should speak to the eternal language of the soul as opposed to the everyday language of physical life, was opposed to the Naturalism of Norwegian theatre in which he could find no room for the soul and the beauty of life. The burgeoning dramatic movement in Norway was, however, part of Norway's quest for cultural independence and Yeats approved of the way that it had enabled Norway to escape Denmark's cultural shadow. See Michael McAteer, *Yeats and European Drama* (Cambridge: Cambridge University Press, 2010), 46.
5  John Millington Synge (1871–1909) was a playwright whose works include *The Shadow of the Glen* (1903), *Riders to the Sea* (1904) and *The Playboy of the Western World* (1907). *The Well of the Saints* (1905) is a bitter parable about a blind couple who prefer to become blind again rather than face the world of sight.
6  Seumas MacManus (1868–1960) was a storyteller, schoolteacher, historian, poet, novelist and prolific writer of popular short stories about Irish rural life.
7  Padraic Colum (1881–1972) was a poet and playwright. He wrote a number of plays for the Abbey Theatre, including *The Land* (1905) and *Thomas Muskerry* (1910). He is generally considered to have brought a much-needed 'peasant realism' to the Abbey.
8  Corkery is quoting from act iii, scene ii of *Hamlet* (*c*.1599). Hamlet, at this point in the play, is instructing the actors who will soon be performing in front of his stepfather.

### The Peasant in Literature

1  Daniel Corkery, 'The Peasant in Literature', *New Ireland* (4 Dec 1915). *New Ireland* was a nationalist weekly that ran from 1915 to 1922. It was suspended from October 1919 to December 1921, during which time it was issued under the name 'Old Ireland'.

2   'A Drover' was published in 1907 when Colum was twenty-six. The drover of the poem is driving his cattle eastward across Ireland to better land so that they can be fattened for the market.

3   Most of Ó Conaire's short stories were initially published in *An Claidheamh Soluis* and other newspapers. His short-story collections include *Nóra Mharcais Bhig agus Sgéalta Eile* (1909), *An Chéad Chloch* (1914) and *Seacht mBuaidh an Éirighe-Amach* (1918).

4   'Un génie est un promontoire dans l'infini.' Victor Hugo, *William Shakespeare* (Paris: Lacroix, Verboeckhoven et Cie, 1864), 317.

5   Walter Horatio Pater, *Appreciations, With an Essay on Style* (Rockville, MD: Arc Manor [1889]; 2008), 37.

## *Review:* The Tent and Other Stories *by Liam O'Flaherty*

1   Daniel Corkery, 'Review: *The Tent and Other Stories* by Liam O'Flaherty', *The Irish Tribune* (16 July 1926). Liam O'Flaherty (1896–1984) was a writer and revolutionary. He seized the Rotunda building in Dublin to set up a socialist state just prior to the establishment of the Free State and fought on the anti-Treaty side during the Civil War. His first book, *The Neighbour's Wife*, was published in 1923. Amongst his better-known publications are *The Informer* (1925), a psychological thriller that was turned into a film of the same name by John Ford, and the historical trilogy *Famine* (1937), *Land* (1946) and *Insurrection* (1950). His short-story collections include *Spring Sowing* (1924), *The Tent and Other Stories* (1926), *The Mountain Tavern and Other Stories* (1929) and *Two Lovely Beasts and Other Stories* (1948).

2   Matthew Arnold, 'A Modern Sappho', *The Poems of Matthew Arnold, 1840–1867* (London: Oxford University Press, 1922), 66.

3   *The Informer* (1925) established O'Flaherty as a major new writer. The novel, which is set in the aftermath of the Civil War, tells the story of Gypo Nolan, who informs on his friend and former comrade in return for money.

## *The Literature of Collapse*

1   Daniel Corkery, 'The Literature of Collapse', UC/DC 422, The Papers of Daniel Corkery, University College Cork.

2   Corkery is referring here to the Treaty that established the Irish Free State. In the Civil War that followed the ratification of the Treaty by the Dáil, Corkery was to take the anti-Treaty side.

3   Patrick Sarsfield (P.S.) O'Hegarty (1879–1955) was a civil servant, historian and biographer. His publications include *John Mitchel: An Appreciation* (1917), *The Indestructible Nation* (1918) and *The Victory of Sinn Féin* (1924). O'Hegarty, a member of the supreme council of the IRB, took the pro-Treaty side during the Civil War. His approach to Irish literature and culture was also quite different to Corkery's. He defended the Literary Revival, recognised Joyce's *Ulysses* as a masterpiece and praised O'Casey's *The Plough and the Stars*. Indeed in 1927, the same year as Corkery wrote 'The Literature of Collapse', a positive appraisal of Sean O'Casey's plays, written by O'Hegarty, was published in *The North American Review*. P.S. O'Hegarty, 'A Dramatist of New Born Ireland', *The North American Review*, 224.835 (Jun-Aug 1927), 315–22.

4 Sean O'Casey (1880–1964) was a playwright and revolutionary socialist. His Dublin trilogy – *The Shadow of a Gunman* (1923), *Juno and the Paycock* (1924) and *The Plough and the Stars* (1926) – are generally considered to be his finest plays. The first of these plays is set against the background of the War of Independence, the second against the backdrop of the Civil War and the third takes the Easter Rising as its setting. O'Casey, who broke with the Irish Citizen Army in 1914 because of the increasing rapprochement with the Irish Volunteers, condemns Irish nationalism in these plays.

5 Jean-Baptiste-Camille Corot (1796–1875) was a French landscape painter who, due to a group of hazy landscapes that he painted in Ile-de-France in the late 1820s, is often viewed as a precursor of impressionism.

6 Henry David Thoreau, *Walden; or, Life in the Woods* (Boston: Ticknor & Fields, 1854).

7 'A carpenter's hammer, in a warm summer noon, will fret me into more than midsummer madness.' Charles Lamb, 'A Chapter on Ears', *Essays of Elia* (London: Edward Moxon [1823]; 1840), 24.

8 P.S. O'Hegarty, *The Victory of Sinn Féin* (Dublin: Talbot Press, 1924), 106.

9 Nothing if not the truth.

10 Corkery is referring here to Thomas Carlyle (1795–1881), the Victorian essayist, historian and journalist.

11 John Bernard MacCarthy, *Covert* (London: Hutchinson, 1925).

12 This is a reference to act ii of *The Plough and the Stars*. The setting of this act is a public house, outside of which a political meeting is being held.

## On Anglo-Irish Literature

1 Daniel Corkery, 'On Anglo-Irish Literature', *Synge and Anglo-Irish Literature: A Study* (Cork: Cork University Press, 1931).

2 Colum emigrated to the USA in 1914.

3 Ernest A. Boyd (1887–1946) was a critic and author who wrote the first literary-critical account of the Literary Revival, *Ireland's Literary Renaissance* (1916). Boyd moved to New York in 1920 and worked on the editorial staff of the *New York Evening Post*, after which he became advisor on foreign literature to the publishers Alfred A. Knopf and Blanche Knopf.

4 Joseph Campbell (Seosamh MacCathmaoil) (1879–1944) was a poet and playwright, whose works are associated with the Ulster Literary Revival. His writings include the play *The Little Cowherd of Slaigne* (1905), and the poetry collections *Songs of Uladh* (1904), *The Rushlight* (1906) and *The Mountainy Singer* (1909). He moved to the USA in 1925, but returned to Ireland in 1939. While in America, he founded the School of Irish Studies in New York (1925), the Irish Foundation (1931) and the journal *The Irish Review* (1934).

5 John Lyle Donaghy (1902–49) was a poet. His poetry collections include *At Dawn over Aherlow* (1926) and *Wilderness Sings* (1942). Donaghy lived for some years in England and later in Co. Wicklow.

6 James Bernard Fagan (1873–1933) was an actor-manager and playwright who was born in Belfast and died in California.

7 James Thomas (Frank) Harris (1856–1931) was an editor, author and adventurer, who was born in Galway and ran away to the USA at the age of fifteen.

8 Ethel Colburn Mayne (1870–1941) was a novelist, short-story writer, biographer and literary critic who moved to England in 1905. Her writings include *Gold Lace*

(1913), *Bryon* (1912), *The Life and Letters of Anne Isabella, Lady Noel Byron* (1929) and *Browning's Heroines* (1913).

9    Geoffrey Phibbs (1900–56) was a poet and editor who was born in England, raised in Sligo and returned to England in 1929, where he famously became involved in a complex relationship with Robert Graves, Nancy Nicholson and Laura Riding.

10   Thomas MacGreevy (1893–1967) was a poet and critic who moved to Paris in 1926.

11   James Henry Cousins (1873–1956) was a writer, teacher and theosophist, who moved to England in 1913 and then to India in 1915.

12   Gerald O'Donovan (1871–1942) was a Catholic priest and novelist, who left the priesthood in 1904 and eventually moved to London. His best-known publication is *Father Ralph* (1913).

13   William Kirkpatrick Magee ('John Eglinton') (1868–1961), an essayist associated with the Literary Revival, moved to Wales in 1922.

14   Stephen MacKenna (1872–1935), translator of Plotinus, lived for periods of time in London, New York and Paris.

15   Eric (E.R.) Dodds (1893–1979) was an Irish classical scholar who spent most of his adult life in England.

16   Conal O'Riordan (1874–1948) was a novelist, playwright and managing director of the Abbey Theatre.

17   Alfred Perceval Graves (1846–1931) was a poet, folklorist and balladeer, who graduated from Trinity College Dublin in 1871 but spent most of his life in England. He is chiefly remembered as an anthologist and collector of Irish songs, and as the author of such lyrics as 'Father Flynn' and 'Trotting to the Fair'.

18   Ernest Charles Temple Thurston (1879–1933) was a poet, playwright and author of several anti-Catholic novels, including *The Apple of Eden* (1905) and *The Passionate Crime* (1915). He was born in Suffolk, raised in Cork and died in London.

19   Monk Gibbon (1896–1987) was a poet, novelist and teacher. He worked in Switzerland and England, as well as in Ireland.

20   Con O'Leary (1888–1958) was a journalist, novelist and playwright. While a student at University College Cork, he wrote two plays for the Cork Dramatic Society and became one of the Society's leading actors. After graduation, he moved to England and became a Fleet Street journalist.

21   Austin Clarke (1896–1974) was a poet, verse-playwright and novelist, who moved to London in the early 1920s where he wrote reviews for newspapers and worked as an assistant editor of *Argosy* magazine.

22   James Joyce (1882–1941) was a novelist, short-story writer and poet, who spent much of his adult life in Paris, Trieste and Zurich. Amongst his publications are *Dubliners* (1914), *A Portrait of the Artist as a Young Man* (1916) and *Ulysses* (1922).

23   Daniel Lawrence Kelleher (1883–1958) was a school-teacher, playwright, poet and travel writer. In 1915, he founded the cork-based Twenty Club, of which Corkery was a member.

24   James Stephens (1880?–1950) was a writer of novels, essays, short stories, poetry and criticism. His best-known work is his fantasy novel *The Crock of Gold* (1912). In 1922, Stephens moved to London, where, in the 30s, he became a popular broadcaster for the BBC.

25   Edward John Moreton Drax Plunkett, 18th Baron of Dunsany (1878–1957) wrote plays, novels, short stories and essays. He is primarily remembered as an author of

fantasy fiction. Plunkett was born in London, but lived for a while on his family estate in Co. Meath.

26   Patrick McGill (1890–1963) was a poet and novelist who was born in the Glen of Glenties, Co. Donegal, but emigrated to Scotland at the age of fourteen to pick potatoes. He served as a private with the London Irish Rifles during the First World War and is best known for a series of bitter novels about the war. He also wrote novels that described the life of migrant labourers. McGill spent the latter part of his life in the USA.

27   William Patrick Ryan (1867–1942) was a journalist, novelist, playwright and poet. He worked as a journalist in London, but returned to Ireland in 1905 to take up the editorship of the *Irish Peasant*, a Co. Meath weekly that he transformed into one of the leading Irish newspapers. In 1910, he returned to London where he continued his journalistic career. Amongst his publications are *The Heart of Tipperary* (1893) and *The Irish Labour Movement* (1919).

28   John Randolph ('Shane') Leslie (1885–1971), a relative of Winston Churchill, wrote verse, fiction, biography and history. He was born in London, raised in Co. Monaghan and died in Sussex.

29   Leonard Alfred George Strong (1896–1958) was a poet, short-story writer, novelist, critic and biographer. He was born in England and spent much of his later life there, but regularly stayed in Ireland as a child.

30   Robert Wilson Lynd (1879–1949) was an essayist, critic and journalist who, in 1901, moved from Belfast to Manchester and then to London.

31   St John Ervine (1883–1971) was a playwright, novelist, critic, biographer, social commentator and manager of the Abbey Theatre. Following the First World War, in which he lost a leg, Ervine, who strongly disapproved of nationalist non-participation in the war, moved to England where he worked as a drama critic for several newspapers.

32   Charles Kirkpatrick Macmullan ('C.K. Munro') (1889–1973) was an Irish-born playwright whose plays were popular in London.

33   George Moore (1852–1933) was a novelist and short-story writer whose works include *A Drama in Muslin* (1886), *Esther Waters* (1894) and *The Untilled Field* (1903). In 1873, Moore went to Paris to become a painter, but, finding his talent insufficient, moved to London and began to write. He returned to Dublin in 1901 and became associated with the Literary Revival. In 1911, he moved back to London where he lived for the rest of his life.

34   George Bernard Shaw (1856–1950) was a playwright, novelist and journalist who moved from Dublin to London in 1876. His writings include *Man and Superman* (1903), *John Bull's Other Island* (1904) and *Saint Joan* (1923).

35   The Norwegian playwright Henrik Ibsen (1828–1906) left Norway in 1864 and, for twenty-seven years, only returned for brief visits.

36   During the latter part of his life, Ivan Turgenev (1818–83), the Russian novelist, lived either at Baden-Baden or Paris.

37   The French dramatist, novelist, art historian and mystic Romain Rolland (1866–1944) lived principally in Switzerland for approximately twenty-five years of his life.

38   Miguel de Unamuno (1864–1936) was a Spanish essayist, novelist, poet and philosopher who was exiled from Spain in 1924 for opposing the military dictatorship of General Primo de Rivera.

39   The Spanish realist writer Vicente Blasco Ibáñez (1867–1928) moved to Paris at the beginning of the First World War.

40  The American-born writer Henry James (1843–1916) spent the last forty years of his life living in England.

41  Richard Steele (1672–1729) was an essayist and playwright who was born in Dublin but spent most of his life in England.

42  The playwright Richard Brinsley Sheridan (1751–1816) was born in Dublin where his father, Thomas Sheridan, was manager of Smock Alley Theatre. He left Ireland for England in 1759 to join his parents who had moved there some years previously.

43  Edmund Burke (1729–97) was an orator and political philosopher who was born in Dublin, spent much of his childhood in Co. Cork, and moved to London in 1750 to study law.

44  Francis Sylvester Mahony ('Father Prout') (1804–66) was a priest, journalist, poet and humorist who was born in Cork and lived for many years in Rome and Paris as a foreign correspondent for London journals.

45  The playwright Oscar Wilde (1854–1900) was born in Dublin but moved to England where he was imprisoned for 'gross indecency'. On his release, Wilde left England and spent the rest of his life in Italy and France.

46  *Castle Rackrent* (1800), Maria Edgeworth's first novel, was an immediate success. It tells the story of the decline and fall of an Ascendancy family and is humourously narrated by the family's servant.

47  Gerald Griffin (1803–40) was a poet, dramatist and novelist. *The Collegians* (1829), a novel of passion and murder based upon an actual case, is his best-known work.

48  Edith Somerville (1858–1949) and 'Martin Ross' (pseudonym of Violet Martin) (1862–1915) were novelists and short-story writers. Together they wrote three collections of comic stories about an Irish RM and five novels before Martin's death in 1915. Somerville insisted that Martin's name appear on subsequent publications. *The Big House of Inver* (1925) tells the story of the decline of the Ascendancy Prendevilles.

49  Lennox Robinson (1886–1958) was a playwright and theatre manager. Amongst his plays are two about the Ascendancy class, *The Big House* (1926) and *Killycreggs in Twilight* (1937).

50  Andrew Ague-cheek is a comic character in William Shakespeare's *Twelfth Night* (*c.*1601). Born into the rank of gentleman, he is a fool who is taken advantage of by those around him.

51  John M. Synge, *In Wicklow and West Kerry* (Dublin: Maunsel, 1921), 49.

52  William Carleton (1794–1869) was a novelist who was the son of Irish-speaking tenant-farmers. His writings include *Traits and Stories of the Irish Peasantry* (1830–3) and *The Black Prophet* (1847).

53  William Maginn (1794–1842) was a journalist and wit, who was one of a number of Irish expatriate writers based in London in the 1820s and 30s to propagate the figure of the 'stage Irishman'.

54  Charles Lever (1806–72), author of *Harry Lorrequer* (1840) and *Charles O'Malley* (1841), was a comic writer who is primarily known for humorous depictions of Irish manners and eccentricities that were designed to appeal to an English audience.

55  Samuel Lover (1797–1868) was a novelist and painter. His 1842 novel *Handy Andy* features an Irish servant man, whose language and antics provoked laughter and disdain in an English audience. Lover's name is often coupled with that of his contemporary, Lever, as an exploiter of the 'stage Irishman' myth.

56  Donn Byrne (1889–1928) was born in New York of Irish parents and raised in Armagh and Antrim. He wrote a number of sentimental romantic novels about

Ireland, the most popular of which are *Blind Raftery* (1924), *Hangman's House* (1925) and *Destiny Bay* (1928).

57 Charles Kickham (1828–82) was a poet, novelist and short-story writer. *Knocknagow* (1873), generally accepted as his finest work, has probably been reprinted more often than any other Irish novel. Indeed, the historian R.V. Comerford has estimated that at least one hundred thousand copies of the novel were published in Ireland alone. Comerford, *Charles J. Kickham: A Study in Irish Nationalism and Literature* (Dublin: Wolfhound Press, 1979), 209–10.

58 In Irish mythology and folklore, a *geis* (plural *geasa*) is a taboo, whether of obligation or prohibition, similar to being under a vow or spell.

59 Walt Whitman, 'A Song of Joys', in Sculley Bradley (ed.), *Leaves of Grass and Selected Prose* (New York: Rinehart & Co. [1949]; 1953), 151.

60 George Russell ('Æ') (1867–1935) was a poet, painter, playwright and editor. He was a close friend of W.B. Yeats and a mentor to aspirant Irish writers.

61 John Galsworthy (1867–1933) was one of the most popular writers of the early twentieth century. His works include the commercially-successful and critically-esteemed *Forsyte Saga* (1906–21). Galsworthy was the 1932 winner of the Nobel Prize in Literature.

62 John Masefield (1873–1967) is remembered as a poet who wrote about the sea and as the author of the classic children's novels *The Midnight Folk* (1927) and *The Box of Delights* (1935).

63 Arnold Bennett (1867–1931) was a novelist and playwright of huge popular appeal. Amongst his writings are *Old Wives' Tale* (1908) and *Clayhanger* (1910).

64 H.G. Wells (1866–1946) was an English author who is now best known for his work in the science fiction genre.

65 George Meredith (1828–1909) was an English novelist and poet. His writings include *The Ordeal of Richard Feverel* (1859) and *The Egoist* (1879).

66 Mary Anne Evans (1819–80), better known by her pen-name George Eliot, was an English novelist, whose works include *The Mill on the Floss* (1860) and *Middlemarch* (1871–2).

67 Charles Dickens (1812–70) was the most popular English novelist of the Victorian era. His writings are characterised by a concern with social injustice.

68 William Makepeace Thakeray (1811–63) was a nineteenth-century English novelist who was famous for his satirical works, particularly *Vanity Fair* (1847–8), a panoramic portrait of English society.

69 T.C. Murray (1873–1959), who was to become one of the leading Abbey playwrights, was initially encouraged to pursue a writing career by Corkery. In his plays, he attempted to portray the manners and speech of west Cork.

70 Corkery is referring here to Rupert Brooke's patriotic war poem, 'The Soldier', from Brooke's 1915 collection *1914 and Other Poems*.

71 Corkery is referring here to a phrase in Homer's *The Odyssey* and its interpretation by the Byzantine scholar Eustathius.

72 Whitman, 'A Song of Joys', in Bradley (ed.), *Leaves of Grass and Selected Prose*, 151.

73 Anton Chekhov (1860–1904) was a Russian short-story writer and playwright.

74 Jean-Baptiste Poquelin (1622–73), known by his stagename Molière, was a French playwright and actor.

75 The word 'Shavian', when used as an adjective, describes something that relates to, or is characteristic of, George Bernard Shaw or his works.

76 Joseph Conrad (1857–1924), born Jósef Teodor Konrad Korzeniowski, was a Polish novelist, who became a British subject in 1886.

77 Sir William Frances Butler (1838–1910) was an army officer, writer and adventurer who was born in Co. Tipperary and served with the British army in Canada, South Africa and Sudan.

78 *Children of the Earth* (1918), published under the pen name Michael Ireland, depicts the life of a rural community on an island off the west coast of Ireland.

79 *Birthright* (1910) was the first of Murray's plays to be performed in the Abbey Theatre. *Autumn Fire* (1924), which has a *Phaedra*-theme, was Murray's best and most successful play. In a previously-published article, 'The Genius of T.C. Murray', Corkery had praised the blend of naturalism, Catholicism and lyricism in *Autumn Fire. The Irish Tribune* (19 March 1926).

80 *Wet Clay* (1922) is a melodrama that features a returning American emigrant. O'Kelly's novella *The Weaver's Grave* (1919) is generally considered to be his best work.

81 *Castle Conquer* (1923), Colum's first novel, is set in an impoverished nineteenth century and features a trial for an agrarian murder.

82 Edward Lysaght's *The Gael* (1919) is a didactic novel set in the west of Ireland.

83 In his Introduction to *A Treasury of Irish Poetry in the English Tongue* (1900), Stopford A. Brooke, an Irish clergyman, pinpoints nationality, religion and rebellion as the distinctive features of Irish literature.

84 James Clarence Mangan (1803–49) translated German poetry, as well as writing poetry under his own name. His best-known poem is 'Dark Rosaleen', in which, in the Gaelic tradition of the *Aisling*, he sees Ireland as a beautiful and sorrowing woman. Mangan is now regarded as the most significant Irish poet of the mid-nineteenth century.

85 W.B. Yeats, 'Meditations in Time of Civil War' (1921–3), in Stephen Regan (ed.), *Irish Writing: An Anthology of Irish Literature in English, 1789–1939* (Oxford: Oxford University Press, 2004), 356.

86 *The Pickwick Papers* (1836–7), published initially in instalments, was Charles Dickens's first novel.

87 *Le Père Goriot* is an 1835 novel by French novelist and playwright Honoré de Balzac (1799–1850).

88 John (1798–1842) and Michael (1796–1874) Banim were brothers who together wrote a series of novels set in post-Union rural Ireland.

*The Playboy of the Western World*

1 Daniel Corkery, 'The Playboy of the Western World', *Synge and Anglo-Irish Literature: A Study* (Cork: Cork University Press, 1931). This was not Corkery's first commentary on the play. In 1910, following the Cork première of *The Playboy of the Western World*, Corkery strongly defended Synge and the play in a lecture he gave to the Cork Literary and Scientific Society. Indeed, *The Woman of the Three Cows*, an early Corkery play that was never staged, is clearly influenced by *The Playboy of the Western World*. It is notable, however, that Corkery's appraisal of *The Playboy of the Western World* in *Synge and Anglo-Irish Literature* is less positive than his comments on the play in his 1910 defence of Synge.

2 Padraic Colum, *The Road Round Ireland* (New York: Macmillan & Co. [1926]; 1930), 368.

3  W.B. Yeats, *Plays and Controversies* (London: Macmillan & Co., 1923), 193.

4  William Wordsworth, 'Book XI', *The Prelude* (New York: D. Appleton & Co. [1805]; 1850), 299.

5  J.M. Synge, *The Playboy of the Western World and Riders to the Sea* (New York: Dover Publications [1907, 1905]; 1993), 12.

6  J.M. Flood, *The Life of Chevalier Charles Wogan* (Dublin: Talbot Press, 1922), 146–7.

7  Simone Téry, *L'île des Bardes: Notes sur la Littérature Irlandaise Contemporaine* (Paris: Ernest Flammarion, 1925), 156.

8  George A. Birmingham was the pen-name of Canon James Owen Hannay (1865–1950). Hannay was a novelist and playwright, whose works were popular in England, but critiqued in Ireland for representing the country and its inhabitants from an Ascendancy perspective. Following the 1914 performance of his play *General John Regan* (1913) in Westport, a town in which he had served as Protestant rector, Hannay's effigy was publicly burnt.

9  Oliver St John Gogarty (1878–1957) was a surgeon, wit and poet. W.B. Yeats was an admirer of his poetry and for a while he was very good friends with James Joyce, who immortalised him as 'stately plump Buck Mulligan' in *Ulysses*. Amongst his poetry collections are *The Ship* (1918), *An Offering of Swans* (1924) and *Others to Adorn* (1939).

10  In 1894, Agnes MacDonnell, a landlady on Achill Island, was savagely attacked by her former land agent, James Lynchehaun. MacDonnell survived the attack but was left with substantial facial injuries. Lynchehaun was arrested and charged, but escaped custody and returned to Achill Island, where he was hidden by friends for three months. For further information, see James Carney, *The Playboy and the Yellow Lady* (Dublin: Poolbeg, 1986).

11  See p. 140.

12  Dionysus is the Greek god of wine, ritual madness and ecstasy.

13  Maurice Bourgeois, *John Millington Synge and the Irish Theatre* (New York: Benjamin Blom [1913]; 1965), 208.

14  ibid., 209–10.

15  Martin Doul and Mary Doul are the names of the two blind beggars in Synge's *The Well of the Saints* (1905).

16  Synge, *The Playboy of the Western World and Riders to the Sea*, 57.

17  J.M. Synge, *The Aran Islands* (New York: Cosimo [1906]; 2005), 49–50.

18  Synge, *The Playboy of the Western World and Riders to the Sea*, 52.

19  Johann Wolfgang von Goethe wrote the following lines of verse:

> Vom Vater hab' ich die Statur,
> Des Lebens ernstes Führen.
>
> [My father gave me his build,
> His earnest conduct of life.]

See Nicholas Boyle, *Goethe: The Poet and the Age, Vol I* (Oxford: Oxford University Press, 1991), 60.

20  Synge, *The Playboy of the Western World and Riders to the Sea*, 6.

21  ibid., 20.

22  ibid., 33.

23  Tomás Ó Máille, *An Ghaoth Aniar* (Dublin: Comhlucht Oideachais na hÉireann, 1920), 93–8.

24    Synge, *The Playboy of the Western World and Riders to the Sea*, 50.
25    Synge, *The Aran Islands*, 133.
26    ibid., 88.
27    Synge, *The Playboy of the Western World and Riders to the Sea*, 28.
28    ibid., 46.
29    ibid., 57.
30    In his essay 'Some Platitudes Concerning Drama', John Galsworthy stated that 'a drama must be shaped so as to have a spire of meaning.' John Galsworthy, 'Some Platitudes Concerning Drama', *The Inn of Tranquillity: Studies and Essays* (New York: Charles Scribner's Sons, 1912), 189.
31    This is a translation, by Bayard Taylor, of the closing lines of *Faust, Part II*:
             Das Unbeschreibliche,
             Hier ist es gethan;
             Das Ewig-Weibliche
             Zieht uns hinan.
32    In his *Poetics* (*c.*335), Aristotle defined tragedy as the imitation of noble actions, and comedy as the imitation of ignoble ones.
33    Synge, *The Playboy of the Western World and Riders to the Sea*, 57.
34    Francis Thompson (1859–1907) was an English poet and drug addict.
35    William Shakespeare, *King John* (1595), act iv, sc. ii.
36    T.S. Eliot, *Essays on Elizabethan Drama* (New York: Harcourt, Brace & Co., 1956), 52.
37    Jean Racine (1639–99) was a French dramatist, whose plays are marked by the prevailing passion of his characters and the speed and fury of his verse.
38    Anon., 'Mala an tSleíbhe Ruaidh', in Douglas Hyde (ed.), *Abhráin Grádh Chúige Connacht or Love Songs of Connacht* (Dublin: Gill & Son; London: T. Fisher Unwin [1893]; 1909), 20.
39    Synge, *The Playboy of the Western World and Riders to the Sea*, 37.
40    Anon., 'Úna Bhán', in Hyde (ed.), *The Love Songs of Connacht*, 60.
41    'The Pearl of the White Breast', in David Cooper (ed.), *The Petrie Collection of the Ancient Music of Ireland* (Cork: Cork University Press, 2002), 49–50.
42    Synge, *The Playboy of the Western World and Riders to the Sea*, 7.
43    Louis Charles Alfred de Musset (1810–57) was a French dramatist, poet and novelist.

*The Colonial Branch of Anglo-Irish Literature*

  1    Daniel Corkery, 'The Colonial Branch of Anglo-Irish Literature', *The Irish Press* (21 April 1937) [Courtesy of The National Library of Ireland]. In 1937, *The Irish Press* published a series of articles on 'the future of literature in Ireland'. The seven contributors to the series debated issues such as the extent and desirability of 'foreign' influences on Irish culture, and the relationship between the artist and the nation. M.J. MacManus, the literary editor of *The Irish Press*, opened the debate on 2 March 1937 by suggesting, in an article which makes a number of favourable references to Corkery's *Synge and Anglo-Irish Literature*, that Ireland was 'swamped culturally'. Corkery, Francis MacManus, T.C. Murray and Aodh de Blácam, in their contributions to the series, also expressed anxieties about 'foreign' influences. Frank O'Connor and Seán O'Faoláin took the opposing position, arguing that the influence of European culture was essential to the creation of a vibrant Irish national culture. The articles written by Frank O'Connor and Seán O'Faoláin for this series

('Ireland Reads – Trash!'; 'Let Ireland Pride – In What She Has') can be found in Part Four of this collection. It should be noted that while *The Irish Press* did employ a number of women writers at this point in time, including Dorothy Macardle and Máire Comerford, all of the invited participants in the debate were men.

2  In his poem 'Popularity', Robert Browning distinguishes between the 'true' poet and his less-talented followers and imitators ('Hobbs and Nobbs, and Nokes and Stokes'). Robert Browning, 'Popularity', in John Woodford *et al.* (eds), *The Poems of Robert Browning, Vol III* (Harlow: Pearson, 2007), 384–5.

3  Seán O'Faoláin, 'Let Ireland Pride – In What She Has', *The Irish Press* (2 April 1937). (See p. 233.)

4  Frank O'Connor, 'Ireland Reads – Trash!', *The Irish Press* (9 March 1937). (See p. 214.)

5  Corkery is referring here to Aodhagán Ó Rathaille's best-known poem, the *aisling* 'Gile na Gile' [Brightness most Bright].

Criostal an chriostail a goirmroisc rinn-uaine.

Crystal of crystal her eye, blue touched with green.

6  O'Faoláin, 'Let Ireland Pride – In What She Has'. (See p. 233.)

7  ibid. (See p. 234.)

8  Francis McManus, 'Faith – The Greatest Literary Force', *The Irish Press* (7 April 1937).

9  Daniel Corkery, *Synge and Anglo-Irish Literature* (Cork: Cork University Press, 1931), 26. (See p. 130.)

10  Ernest (Earnán) O'Malley (1897–1957) was a writer and republican, who, during the Civil War, became commander of the anti-Treaty IRA. When O'Malley's book *On Another Man's Wound* was published in London in 1936, the passages detailing his ill-treatment while under arrest in Dublin Castle were omitted. An unabridged version was published in America a year later under the title *Army without Banners*.

11  *Knocknagow* was first published (partially) in 1870 in serial form in the New York weekly *The Emerald*, and later in *The Shamrock*, Dublin. The novel was first printed in book form by A.M. Sullivan of Castletownbeare in 1873. It was published in Middle Abbey Street, Dublin. The novel's success began with its second edition, produced in Dublin by the Catholic publisher James Duffy in 1879.

12  O'Faoláin, 'Let Ireland Pride – In What She Has'. (See p. 234.)

13  Justin McCarthy, *Irish Recollections* (London: Hodder & Stoughton [1911]; 1912), 7.

14  James Agate (1877–1947) was one of England's most influential theatre critics. *Paul Twyning* (1922) was a three-act kitchen comedy written by George Shiels (1886–1949). The play, which features an itinerant labourer, was Shiels's first real success as a playwright.

15  T.C. Murray, 'Where the Modern Irish Novelist is at Fault', *The Irish Press* (13 April 1937).

16  The 'Mrs. Mulligan' referred to here is possibly the title character from 'Biddy Mulligan, the Pride of the Coombe', a song written by Seamus Kavanagh in the 1930s and made famous by the Dublin comedian Jimmy O'Dea. While the setting of the song is urban as opposed to rural, what connects this song to Lady Gregory's 'Kiltartanese' publications is that the metre of 'Biddy Mulligan, the Pride of the Coombe' suggests a strong accent in the singing. Furthermore, since the song,

especially when performed by Jimmy O'Dea, was part of a long music-hall tradition
in which ethnic minorities and the poor were treated as objects of fun, Corkery, by
referring to this song in conjunction with Lady Gregory, is perhaps suggesting that
her treatment of the rural poor of Kiltartan, Co. Galway is patronising.

## Jack B. Yeats Once More

1   Daniel Corkery, 'Jack B. Yeats Once More', *The Irish Monthly* (Sept 1945), 363–7.
2   In 1945, an all-Ireland committee organised a national loan exhibition of nearly 200
     Jack B. Yeats paintings. The exhibition was formally opened by Pádraig de Brún in
     the galleries of the National College of Art. During the three weeks that it lasted,
     thousands visited it from all over Ireland.
3   Walt Whitman, *Memoranda During the War* (Bedford: Applewood Press [1875];
     1990), 28.
4   Pádraig de Brún (1889–1960) was a priest, mathematician, translator and Irish-
     language poet. He is primarily remembered for his translations from the classics into
     the Irish language.
5   Seán Keating (1889–1977) was an Irish romantic-realist artist, who painted several
     iconic images of the War of Independence and the subsequent Civil War.

## PART THREE. THE NATION AND THE STATE

### Their First Fault

1   Daniel Corkery, 'Their First Fault', *Poblacht na h-Éireann* (31 Jan 1922). In this
     article, which was published shortly after the Dáil ratified the Treaty, Corkery
     compares the Free Staters to the foolish voyagers in Robert Browning's poem,
     *Paracelsus* (1835), whose 'first fault' is that they settle with their precious cargo on
     barren rocks while the land they seek lies just over the horizon.
2   Robert Browning, 'Paracelsus', *The Poetical Works of Robert Browning, 1833–1858,
     Vol II* (London: Hutchinson & Co., 1906), 116.
3   ibid.
4   ibid., 117.
5   ibid.
6   ibid.
7   ibid.
8   ibid.
9   ibid, 118.
10  ibid.
11  ibid.
12  ibid.

### A Landscape in the West

1   Daniel Corkery, 'A Landscape in the West', *The Irish Tribune* (18 June 1926). In
     June, July and August 1926, Corkery engaged in a bitter exchange in print with his
     former protégés Frank O'Connor and Seán O'Faoláin in the columns of *The Irish
     Tribune*. The dispute began on 18 June, when *The Irish Tribune* published an article
     by Corkery, 'A Landscape in the West', and an article by Sean Hendrick, 'The Heart

has Reasons'. The correspondence page of the next issue of *The Irish Tribune* carried a letter by O'Connor critiquing aspects of both Corkery's and Hendrick's articles. Corkery's dismissive response to this letter appeared in the paper the following week. O'Faoláin then entered the debate, writing a letter in defence of O'Connor's position. For further information on this exchange, see Paul Delaney, "'Fierce Passions for Middle-Aged Men": Frank O'Connor and Daniel Corkery', in Hilary Lennon (ed.), *Frank O'Connor: Critical Essays* (Dublin: Four Courts Press, 2007), 53–66.

2    The Harry Richmond referred to here can be found in George Meredith's romantic comedy *The Adventures of Harry Richmond* (1871). The novel also features Harry's dashing father, Richmond Roy, whose fantastical schemes provide much of the novel's entertainment.

## *The Book I am Writing Now*

1    Daniel Corkery, 'The Book I am Writing Now', UC/DC 400, The Papers of Daniel Corkery, University College Cork. This is an extract from a radio broadcast that Corkery gave in 1946 about a book he was working on at the time but never completed. The Corkery collection at University College Cork also contains notes for the work-in-progress, giving an outline of the book's contents, and discussing some of its main points under chapter headings (UC/DC 163). The manuscript of the broadcast is handwritten and quite difficult to read. While I have tried to ensure that my transcript is faithful to the original, in some instances I have had to surmise the intended word.

2    Edmund Spenser (1552–99) was born in London and went to Ireland in approximately 1580, where he was awarded lands that had been confiscated in the Munster Plantation. Spenser is best known for *The Faerie Queene* (1590–6), an epic poem and fantastical allegory celebrating the Tudor dynasty and Elizabeth I, and *A View of the Present State of Ireland* (1633), in which he argued that Ireland would never be 'pacified' until its language and customs had been destroyed.

3    Robert Stewart, Viscount Castlereagh (1769–1822), was elected to the Irish parliament in 1790 and became Chief Secretary in 1798. Following the Rising of that year, Castlereagh used every possible means, including bribery, to secure a majority in favour of union with Britain in the Irish parliament.

4    Edward Henry Carson (1854–1935) was a lawyer and politician, who became leader of the Irish Unionists in 1910 and played a key role in the establishment of the Ulster Volunteers.

5    Sir Henry Wilson (1864–1922) was a field-marshal in the British army who urged a policy of coercion in Ireland and was active behind the scenes in support of the Ulster Unionists in their opposition to Home Rule.

6    Thomas Edward (T.E.) Lawrence (1888–1935) was a British army officer renowned for his exploits as British military liaison to the Arab Revolt during the First World War. In 1914, his father, Thomas Chapman, inherited the title of seventh Baronet of Westmeath.

7    Gilbert Keith Chesterton (1874–1936) was an English journalist, novelist and essayist, who opposed the Boer War and advocated a patriotic anti-imperialism. Corkery is probably referring here to Part II of Chesterton's 1910 collection of essays, *What's Wrong with the World*, which is titled 'Imperialism, or, The Mistake of Man'.

8    After the Second World War, Germany was divided into four zones of occupation: the American zone, the British zone, the French zone and the Soviet zone.

9   Hilda Oakeley, *Should Nations Survive?* (London: George Allen & Unwin, 1942), 77.
10  Anthony Trollope (1815–82) was an English novelist of the Victorian era, who worked for the Postal Service in England for some years and, in 1841, moved to Ireland to take up the position of postal surveyor's clerk.

## The Struggle between Native and Colonist

1   Daniel Corkery, 'The Struggle between Native and Colonist', *The Sunday Press* (30 Aug 1953).
2   R.B. McDowell, *Public Opinion and Government Policy in Ireland, 1801–1846* (London: Faber, 1952).
3   Patrick Walsh (*c*.1885–1927) was a priest, Irish Irelander and collector of Irish-language songs.
4   An Irish-speaking region of Ireland.
5   Edmund Curtis (1881–1943) was a renowned Irish historian who was born in Lancashire and was professor of history in Trinity College Dublin, for twenty-nine years. Amongst his writings are *A History of Medieval Ireland* (1923) and *A History of Ireland* (1936). Curtis's Irish histories are characterised by an appreciation of both Gaelic and Anglo-Norman cultures.

## A Story of Two Indians

1   Daniel Corkery, 'A Story of Two Indians', *The Irish Press* (27 Sept 1953).
2   Margaret O'Leary was a playwright and novelist. Her writings include the plays *The Woman* (1929) and *The Coloured Balloon* (1944), both performed at the Abbey, and the novels, *The House I made* (1935) and *Lightning Flash* (1939).
3   Corkery refers again to this episode in 'What is a Nation' (1953), indicating that the book in question was a collection of essays by Thomas Babington Macaulay. There is a certain irony, perhaps not lost on Corkery, in this Indian student using a passage taken from the writings of Macaulay, whose very name is synonymous in India with colonial cultural alienation, to demonstrate his perfect pronunciation of the English language.

## What is a Nation?

1   Daniel Corkery, 'What is a Nation?', *The Sunday Press* (16 Oct 1953).
2   Daniel Corkery, 'A Story of Two Indians', *The Irish Press* (27 Sept 1953). (See p. 171.)
3   Thomas Babington Macaulay, *Reviews and Essays from 'The Edinburgh'* (London: Ward, Lock & Tyler, 188?).
4   The 1913 Nobel Prize in Literature was awarded to Rabindranath Tagore, making him the first Asian Nobel Laureate. In 1915, Tagore was knighted by the British Crown. He returned his knighthood following the massacre of unarmed Indians in 1919 at Jallianwala Bagh, a public garden in Amritsar in the Punjab province of India.
5   Rabindranath Tagore, *Nationalism* (London: Macmillan & Co., 1917), 9.
6   See Pádraic Pearse, 'The Spiritual Nation', *The Murder Machine and Other Essays* (Dublin: Mercier Press, 1976), 62–67. *The Spiritual Nation* was originally published as a pamphlet in February 1916.
7   Tagore, *Nationalism*, 110.

8    ibid.
9    ibid., 88.
10   ibid., 105.
11   ibid., 107.

## PART FOUR. CONTEMPORARY RECEPTION

### *A New Chapter of History:* The Hidden Ireland

1   P. de B., 'A New Chapter of History: *The Hidden Ireland*', *Irish Independent* (12 Jan
    1925). The author of this review is likely to have been the Irish-language scholar
    and translator Pádraig de Brún, with whom Corkery engaged in a celebrated debate
    in the pages of the short-lived journal *Humanitas* in the early 1930s about the
    translation of the classics into the Irish language. See Liam Prút (ed.), *Athbheochan
    an Léinn nó Dúchas na Gaeilge?: Iomarbhá idir Pádraig de Brún agus Domhnall Ó
    Corcora, Humanitas, 1930–31* (Coiscéim, 2005).
2   See Daniel Corkery, *The Hidden Ireland* (Dublin: Gill & Son [1924]; 1941), 188.

### *Gaelic Poets of Munster*

1   E.C., 'Gaelic Poets of Munster', *The Irish Times* (13 Feb 1925). This review is likely
    to have been written by the renowned historian Edmund Curtis.
2   The Irish Texts Society was founded in 1898 to promote the study of Irish-language
    literature through the publication of Irish-language texts.
3   Corkery discusses this poem by Donagh MacNamara (Donnchadh Ruadh
    MacConmara) in Chapter 10 of *The Hidden Ireland.*

### *A Book of the Moment: Gaelic Poetry under the Penal Laws*

1   Stephen Gwynn, 'A Book of the Moment: Gaelic Poetry under the Penal Laws', *The
    Spectator* (12 Sept 1925).
2   The mind moves the matter.
3   *The Hounds of Banba* (1920) contains nine stories, six of which are set just before the
    War of Independence and describe the experiences of a young Volunteer officer on
    the run from police for his involvement in the Rising, and three of which take place
    during the War of Independence.
4   William F.T. Butler, *Confiscation in Irish History* (Dublin: Talbot Press, 1917), 44.
5   The Irish-language poet Andrew Magrath worked, for a considerable time, as a
    pedlar, or traveling merchant, an occupation that gave him the nickname *Mangaire
    Sugach* or Jolly Pedlar.
6   Daniel Corkery, *The Hidden Ireland* (Dublin: Gill & Son [1924]; 1941), 134.
7   See ibid., 9. (See p. 28.)

### *The Other Hidden Ireland*

1   Aodh de Blácam, 'The Other Hidden Ireland', *Studies*, 23.91 (Sept 1934). This article,
    in which 'Gaeldom' is viewed as a composite of different races and creeds, is a critical
    rejoinder to *The Hidden Ireland*. It should be noted, however, that eight years prior to
    its publication de Blácam briefly intervened in the *Irish Tribune* debate between

Corkery, O'Connor and O'Faoláin in defence of that same book. See Aodh de Blácam, Correspondence: 'Have We a Literature?', *The Irish Tribune* (30 July 1926).

2 Lorcán Ua Muireadhaigh, 'Introduction', *Amhráin Sheumais Mhic Chuarta* (Dundalk: Preas Dhún Dealgan, 1925), 25.

3 Mícheál Coimín (Michael Comyn) (1688–1760) was an Irish-language poet and prose writer from Co. Clare. Piaras MacGearailt (Pierce Fitzgerald) (1700–91) was leader or 'high-sheriff' of a Court of Poetry that convened near Youghal. Corkery provides an overview of the life and poetry of these two poets in Chapter 10 of *The Hidden Ireland*.

4 William Bedell (1571–1642), under whose supervision the Bible was translated into the Irish language, was appointed Bishop of Kilmore and Ardagh in 1629.

5 William Daniel (Uilliam Ó Domhnaill) (1570–1628) completed a translation of the New Testament in 1602.

6 Richard Stanihurst (1547–1618) was a politician and historian who, in 1577, wrote one of the earliest histories of Ireland.

7 John Tillotson (1630–94) was an English preacher who became Archbishop of Canterbury in 1691.

8 John Wesley (1703–91), the founder of Methodism, visited Ireland over twenty times.

9 For further details on William Neilson (1774–1821), see Roger Blaney, *Presbyterians and the Irish Language* (Belfast: Ulster Historical Foundation, 1996), 56–63.

10 Michael Logue (1840–1924) served as Catholic Archbishop of Armagh and Primate of All Ireland (1887–1924).

11 See Blaney, *Presbyterians and the Irish Language*, 72.

12 Douglas Hyde, *A Literary History of Ireland* (London: T. Fisher Unwin, 1899).

13 Thomas MacDonagh, 'The Irish Mode', *Literature in Ireland: Studies Irish and Anglo-Irish* (Dublin: Talbot Press [1916]; 1919), 64–82.

14 W.E.H. Lecky, *A History of Ireland in the Eighteenth Century, Vol I* (Cambridge: Cambridge University Press [1892]; 2010), 246.

15 James Ussher (1581–1656) was the Church of Ireland Archbishop of Armagh from 1625 to 1656. One of the strategies employed by Ussher to prevent the use of the Irish language in the Church of Ireland was the obstruction of William Bedell's Irish-language translation of the Bible.

16 Whitley Stokes (1830–1909) was a lawyer and Celtic scholar.

17 E. Knott (ed.), *The Bardic Poems of Tadhg Dall Ó hUiginn (1550–91)*, 2 vols (London: Irish Texts Society, 1922, 1926).

18 Aodh de Blácam, *Gaelic Literature Surveyed* (Dublin: Talbot Press, 1929). The first issue of *Bolg an Tsolair* was circulated by the offices of the United Irishman newspaper *The Northern Star* in 1795. Thomas Russell (1767–1803), a librarian and United Irishman, was hanged following the uprising of 1803.

19 James Craig (1871–1940), 1st Viscount Craigavon, was a unionist politician and the first prime minister of Northern Ireland.

*An Irish Provincial*

1 Anon., 'An Irish Provincial', *The Irish Times* (12 June 1931).

2 Daniel Corkery, *Synge and Anglo-Irish Literature* (Cork: Cork University Press [1955]; 1931), 243.

3   *Cathleen Ní Houlihan* is a one-act play written by W.B. Yeats in collaboration with Lady Gregory in 1902. The play attracted a daily audience of approximately three hundred on its first production, with many contemporary critics, including Stephen Gwynn, commenting on the almost hypnotic effect that it seemed to exercise on its audience.

4   Corkery, *Synge and Anglo-Irish Literature*, 6. (See p. 116.)

5   The Censorship of Publications Act (1929) established a board of five members to advise the Minister of Justice on the proscription of 'corrupt' literature.

6   Corkery, *Synge and Anglo-Irish Literature*, 242.

### *Synge and Irish Life*

1   Anon., 'Synge and Irish Life', *The Times Literary Supplement* (23 July 1931).

2   Daniel Corkery, *Synge and Anglo-Irish Literature* (Cork: Cork University Press [1955]; 1931), 27. (See p. 131.)

3   ibid., 85.

4   ibid.

5   ibid., 104.

6   Cited in ibid.

7   ibid., 80.

8   ibid.

9   ibid., 109. The first sentence of this quote reads as follows in the original: 'Greatly moved on one occasion, he achieved the shedding of these prejudices, and wrote his masterpiece: *Riders to the Sea*.

10  Figure of fun.

11  Corkery, *Synge and Anglo-Irish Literature*, 152. The first part of this quote reads as follows in the original: '[N]o one reared in an Irish Catholic household would dream of creating a similar figure, unless of course he were, like Liam O'Flaherty, a mere sensationalist.'

12  Brinsley McNamara was the pen name of the novelist and playwright John Weldon (1890–1963). Weldon became a focus of national controversy with the publication of his first novel, *The Valley of the Squinting Window* (1918), which painted a somewhat grim picture of Irish rural life.

13  Eimar O'Duffy (1893–1935) was a member of the Irish Volunteers who, for practical reasons, opposed the Easter Rising and was sent by Eoin MacNeill to Belfast to call off the mobilisation there. His literary reputation rests on a trilogy of satirical fantasies – *King Goshawk and the Birds* (1926), *The Spacious Adventures of the Man in the Street* (1928) and *Asses in Clover* (1933) – in which he pilloried all aspects of the Irish Free State, including its economics and its acquiescence in clerical domination.

14  Peadar O'Donnell (1893–1986) was a writer and socialist, who fought on the anti-Treaty side during the Civil War. His novels *The Knife* (1930) and *On the Edge of the Stream* (1934) are concerned with small-town Irish life, while *Ardrigoole* (1929) is based on a true incident in which a mother and child died of starvation in a pro-Treaty area while her Republican husband was imprisoned.

15  Corkery, *Synge and Anglo-Irish Literature*, 5. (See p. 115.)

*Corkery's Synge*

1 'Chanel', 'Corkery's Synge', *The Leader* (8 Aug 1931). 'Chanel' was a pen name used by the Irish-Irelander Arthur Clery in his contributions to D.P. Moran's *The Leader*. *Synge and Anglo-Irish Literature* is often viewed as an attack on Synge. Clery's review indicates that the book was interpreted by some contemporary commentators as a defence of Synge against their harsher criticism. For an example of this harsher criticism, see Seán Tóibín's 'An "Playboy": Fear ón Oileán agus Synge', in which it is argued that *The Playboy of the Western World* has much in common with Charles Lever's *Harry Lorrequer*. Tóibín, 'An "Playboy": Fear ón Oileán agus Synge', *Misneach* (30 April 1921).

2 Hilaire Belloc (1870–1953) was an Anglo-French author, poet and historian, whose Catholic faith had a strong impact on his writings. *The Path to Rome* (1902) was an account of a walking pilgrimage that he made from central France to Rome.

3 O. Henry was the pseudonym of the prolific American short-story writer William Sydney Porter (1862–1910). His stories are famous for their witty narration and surprise endings.

4 J.M.W. Turner (1775–1851) was an English Romantic landscape painter whose work is regarded as a precursor to Impressionism.

*Synge and Ireland*

1 Austin Clarke, 'Synge and Ireland', *New Statesman and Nation* (29 Aug 1931).

2 George Moore's three-volume *Hail and Farewell* (1911–14) was a frank account of his ten years in Dublin.

3 Daniel Corkery, *Synge and Anglo-Irish Literature* (Cork: Cork University Press [1955]; 1931), 181.

4 Corkery, *Synge and Anglo-Irish Literature*, 20. (See p. 125.)

5 See ibid., 82.

6 ibid., 109.

7 ibid., 233–4.

8 ibid., 20. (See p. 126.)

*Daniel Corkery on Synge*

1 Dorothy Macardle, 'Daniel Corkery on Synge', *The Irish Press* (13 October 1931). Macardle (1889–1958) was amongst the first writers recruited by *The Irish Press* when it was established in September 1931.

2 Letter to Lady Beaumont, 21 May 1807. Cited in Stephen Gill (ed.), *The Cambridge Companion to Wordsworth* (Cambridge: Cambridge University Press, 2003), xvi.

3 Daniel Corkery, *Synge and Anglo-Irish Literature* (Cork: Cork University Press [1955]; 1931), 166.

4 ibid., 181, 132.

5 ibid., 105.

6 ibid., 1, 109.

7 See ibid., 138–9 for references to *Riders to the Sea* as evidence of Synge's 'gift of impassioned contemplation'.

8 ibid., 160.

9 ibid., 234.

*Synge and Irish Literature*

1   P.S. O'Hegarty, 'Synge and Irish Literature', *The Dublin Magazine*, 7.1 (Jan–Mar 1932).
2   Daniel Corkery, *Synge and Anglo-Irish Literature* (Cork: Cork University Press [1955]; 1931), 142.
3   ibid., 163.
4   ibid., 227.
5   ibid., 122.
6   ibid., 62.
7   William George (Willie) Fay (1872–1947) was an actor, theatre producer and one of the co-founders of the Abbey Theatre. Fay, who was particularly associated with comic roles, developed an acting style characterised by economy of gesture and movement.
8   Fred O'Donovan was an Abbey Theatre actor and director.
9   Francis John (Frank J.) Fay (1870–1931), brother of William George Fay, was an actor and co-founder of the Abbey Theatre.
10  William George Fay's recollections of the early years of the Abbey Theatre were published in 1935. W.G. Fay and Catherine Carswell, *The Fays of the Abbey Theatre* (New York: Harcourt, Brace & Co., 1935).
11  Corkery, *Synge and Anglo-Irish Literature*, 109.
12  ibid., 19. (See p. 125.)
13  Joseph Sheridan LeFanu (1814–73), author of *The House by the Graveyard* (1863), *Uncle Silas* (1864) and *In a Glass Darkly* (1872), is remembered primarily as a master of the mysterious and uncanny.
14  Corkery, *Synge and Anglo-Irish Literature*, 109.
15  See ibid., 236.
16  This saying is attributed to Charles Stewart Parnell. Cited in Robert Henry Murray, *Revolutionary Ireland and its Settlement* (London: Macmillan & Co., 1911), 416.
17  *The Racing Lug* (1902) was one of a number of plays that James Cousins wrote for the Abbey Theatre. The play was often compared to Synge's *Riders to the Sea* as the subject matter is quite similar.
18  Edward Martyn (1859–1923) was a playwright and co-founder of the Abbey Theatre. A number of his plays, including *The Heather Field* (1899) and *Maeve* (1899), were a study in Ibsen's symbolism with an Irish setting.
19  Henry David Thoreau's famous aphorism, 'the mass of men lead lives of quiet desperation', serves as an epigraph and part-title for Corkery's *The Threshold of Quiet* (1917).
20  *Clayhanger* is a 1910 novel by Arnold Bennett. *The Man of Property* is a 1906 novel by John Galsworthy.
21  William Allingham (1824–89), a Customs Officer and the editor of *Fraser's Magazine*, published several volumes of poetry and one play.
22  Samuel Ferguson (1810–86) was a poet and scholar who wrote both humorous verse and long narrative poems based on Gaelic legends.
23  William Molyneux (1656–98) was a philosopher and Irish patriot.
24  The English dramatist William Congreve (1670–1729) was a schoolboy in Kilkenny and an undergraduate at Trinity College Dublin, where he was a contemporary and friend of Jonathan Swift.

25   Laurence Sterne (1713–68), author of *Tristram Shandy*, was the son of an impover-
     ished army ensign and spent his early years in Irish garrison towns.

26   Johannes Scotus Eriugena (*c.*815–77), generally regarded as Europe's greatest
     philosopher of the early middle ages, was born in Ireland and spent some time at the
     court of Charles the Bald, grandson of Charlemagne.

27   George Berkeley (1685–1753) was a metaphysical philosopher who was born in Co.
     Kilkenny and, in 1734, appointed Bishop of Cloyne.

28   *John Sherman*, a short novel written by W.B. Yeats in 1888 and published in 1891,
     outlines Yeats's struggle, at a crucial point in his early years, in choosing a path in
     life.

29   *Under the Greenwood Tree* (1872) is an immensely popular novel by Thomas Hardy.

30   *The Words on the Window Pane*, first staged in 1930, features Jonathan Swift's ghost
     and is W.B. Yeats's most powerful exploration of the occult.

31   *Héloïse and Abélard* (1921) is set in France and is a retelling of a twelfth-century love
     story. *Aphrodite in Aulius* (1930), Moore's last novel, is set in ancient Greece.

32   *The Shaving of Shagpat* (1855) is an oriental tale by George Meredith.

33   *Under Western Eyes* is a 1911 novel by Joseph Conrad that is set in Russia and
     Switzerland.

34   *The Ring and the Book* (1868–9) is a long narrative poem by Robert Browning that
     is set in seventeenth-century Italy.

35   Corkery, *Synge and Anglo-Irish Literature*, 80.

36   The first performance of George Bernard Shaw's *The Apple Cart* (1928) was in
     Polish at Warsaw in June 1929.

37   Corkery, *Synge and Anglo-Irish Literature*, 229.

38   In 1927, Corkery addressed a mass meeting called to demand a ban on immoral
     publications. This may be the occasion to which O'Hegarty is referring.

## Correspondence: The Heart has Reasons

1   Frank O'Connor, Correspondence: 'The Heart has Reasons', *The Irish Tribune* (25
     June 1926). This letter is a response to two articles published in *The Irish Tribune* on
     18 June: Daniel Corkery, 'A Landscape in the West'; Sean Hendrick, 'The Heart has
     Reasons'.

2   Blaise Pascal (1623–62) was a French mathematician and physicist who wrote in
     defence of the scientific method.

3   Sean Hendrick, 'The Heart has Reasons', *The Irish Tribune* (18 June 1926).

4   ibid.

5   ibid.

6   The phrase, 'what a piece of work is a man!', comes from William Shakespeare's
     *Hamlet* (*c.*1599), act ii, sc ii.

7   William Stockley (1859–1943) was an academic and Sinn Féin politician. He
     occupied the Chair of English in University College Cork from 1905 until Corkery
     was appointed to it in 1931.

8   Daniel Corkery, 'A Landscape in the West', *The Irish Tribune* (18 June 1926).

## Correspondence: Have We a Literature?

1   Frank O'Connor, Correspondence: 'Have We a Literature?', *The Irish Tribune*
     (13 Aug 1926). This letter was written in defence of a series of articles by Seán
     O'Faoláin on the future of the Irish language.

2 Aodh de Blácam, 'Have We a Literature?', *The Irish Tribune* (30 July 1926). De Blácam's letter was primarily a response to the second of O'Faoláin's articles on the future of the Irish language.

3 Pádraic Óg Ó Conaire, *Solus an Ghrádha* (Dublin: Muinntir Dollard, 1923).

4 Julien Viaud ('Pierre Loti') (1850–1923) was a French novelist and an officer in the French navy.

5 Aodh de Blácam, 'Have We a Literature?'

6 ibid.

7 This is a reference to Aeschylus's Greek tragedy.

8 O'Connor is referring here to a ninth-century poem that Kuno Meyer popularised in a 1902 publication. Kuno Meyer, *Liadain and Curithir: An Irish Love-Story of the Ninth Century* (London: David Nutt, 1902).

## *Ireland Reads – Trash!*

1 Frank O'Connor, 'Ireland Reads – Trash!', *The Irish Press* (9 March 1937) [Courtesy of The National Library of Ireland]. This is O'Connor's contribution to the 1937 *Irish Press* debate on the 'future of literature in Ireland'.

2 Daniel Corkery, *Synge and Anglo-Irish Literature* (Cork: Cork University Press [1955]; 1931), 241. Cited in M.J. MacManus, 'Is Ireland Swamped Culturally?', *The Irish Press* (2 March 1937). MacManus's article was the first of the seven articles published in *The Irish Press* on the 'future of literature in Ireland'.

3 An Gúm was a government publishing agency which was established in 1926 to produce textbooks and literature in the Irish language. As indicated by O'Connor, much of its work has involved producing Irish-language translations of popular works written in English and other languages, but it has also published the work of some of the finest writers in the Irish language, such as Máirtín Ó Cadhain and Seosamh MacGrianna.

4 MacManus, 'Is Ireland Swamped Culturally?'

5 ibid.

6 Seán O'Faoláin's *Bird Alone* (1936), which features a hero-narrator who rebels against the political and religious establishments, was banned shortly after publication.

7 Corkery, *Synge and Anglo-Irish Literature*, 23. Cited in MacManus, 'Is Ireland Swamped Culturally?'

8 MacManus, 'Is Ireland Swamped Culturally?'

## *Synge*

1 Frank O'Connor, 'Synge', in Lennox Robinson (ed.), *The Irish Theatre* (London: Macmillan & Co., 1939).

2 Daniel Corkery, *Synge and Anglo-Irish Literature* (Cork: Cork University Press [1955]; 1931), 19. (See p. 125.)

3 ibid., 19, 212.

4 ibid., 24. (See p. 129.)

5 Patrick Augustine Sheehan (1852–1913) was a Catholic priest, novelist and poet. Amongst his publications are *My New Curate* (1900), *Luke Delmege* (1901) and *Mariam Lucas* (1912).

6 The theatre referred to here is the Abbey Theatre. This O'Connor piece was originally delivered as a lecture during the 1938 Abbey Theatre Festival.

7   A cloth stretched tight in an arc around the back of a stage set, often used to depict the sky.

8   *A Passage to India* (1924) is a novel by E.M. Forster set against the backdrop of the British Raj and the Indian independence movement. The central Indian character of the novel, Dr Aziz, is a young Muslim physician.

9   In later years, Lady Gregory is said to have often quoted from Aristotle: 'To think like a wise man, but to express oneself like the common people.' See Norman Jeffares and A.S. Knowland, *A Commentary on the Collected Plays of W.B. Yeats* (Stanford: Stanford University Press, 1975), 109.

10  Cited in W.B. Yeats, *Essays and Introductions* (London: Macmillan & Co., 1961), 523.

11  W.B. Yeats, *The King's Threshold: and On Baile's Strand* (London: A.H. Bullen, 1904), 23. The original reads:

> In ruin, poetry calls out in joy,
> Being the scattering hand, the bursting pod,
> The victim's joy among the holy flame.

12  For an account of this interchange between Yeats and Gregory, see Norman Jeffares, *W.B. Yeats: Man and Poet* (London: Routledge [1949]; 1962), 273. The poem from which this line is taken is 'Vacillation', which was first published, in its present form, in *The Winding Stair* (1933).

13  J.M. Synge, *The Aran Islands* (New York: Cosimo [1906]; 2005), 33.

14  See Corkery, *Synge and Anglo-Irish Literature*, 81.

*Irish – An Empty Barrel*

1   Seán O'Faoláin, 'Irish – An Empty Barrel', *The Irish Tribune* (16 July 1926). This is the second of a series of four O'Faoláin articles on the Irish language that were published in *The Irish Tribune* in the summer of 1926.

2   John Milton, 'Of Education', *The Prose Works of John Milton, Vol. I* (Philadelphia: Herman Hooker, 1845), 159.

3   A middle Indo-Aryan language of north Indian origin.

4   Alphonse de Lamartine (1790–1869) was a French writer, poet and politician, who was one of the key figures in the Romantic Movement in French literature.

5   'The Tyger', which was published as part of William Blake's collection *Songs of Experience* (1794), was the most popular classic poem taught in British primary schools in the twentieth century.

6   O'Faoláin is probably referring here to the 1842 Robert Browning poem concerning the Pied Piper legend.

7   The book in question is Pádraic Óg Ó Conaire's *Solus an Ghrádha* (Dublin: Muinntir Dollard, 1923).

8   Julius Pokorny (1887–1970) was an Austrian linguist and scholar of Celtic languages who had a particular interest in the Irish language.

*Correspondence: The Spirit of the Nation*

1   Seán O'Faoláin, Correspondence: 'The Spirit of the Nation', *The Irish Tribune* (23 July 1926). This is part of a bitter exchange in print that took place in the summer of 1926 between Corkery, O'Connor and O'Faoláin. Following Corkery's dismissive response to a letter by O'Connor critiquing articles by Corkery and Sean Hendrick, O'Faoláin writes this letter in defence of O'Connor's position.

2 Frank O'Connor, Correspondence: 'The Heart has Reasons', *The Irish Tribune* (25 June 1926). (See pp. 210–11.)

3 Daniel Corkery, 'A Landscape in the West', *The Irish Tribune* (18 June 1926). (See pp. 162–4.)

4 O'Faoláin is referring here to the building of the Ardnacrusha hydro-electric power station. The power station officially opened in 1929.

5 This is a reference to *The Irish Tribune* itself, a short-lived newspaper that was established in March 1926 as a nationalist alternative to *The Irish Statesman*.

## The Emancipation of Irish Writers

1 Seán O'Faoláin, 'The Emancipation of Irish Writers', *The Yale Review*, 23.3 (March 1934).

2 George Russell ('Æ') was a theosophist.

3 Daniel Corkery, *Synge and Anglo-Irish Literature* (Cork: Cork University Press [1955]; 1931), viii.

4 ibid., 26. (See p. 130.)

5 Katherine Tynan (1861–1931) was a poet, novelist, and journalist. Tynan was extremely prolific, publishing 161 books, as well as innumerable articles, essays, and stories. Her writings include the poetry collections *Louise de la Vallière and Other Poems* (1885) and *Irish Love Songs* (1892).

6 Kate O'Brien (1897–1974) was a journalist, playwright, travel-writer and novelist. Amongst her writing are *Without my Cloak* (1931), *The Ante-Room* (1934) and *The Land of Spices* (1941).

7 Henry Louis (H.L.) Mencken (1880–1956) was an American journalist, essayist, satirist and acerbic critic of American life and culture.

8 Falstaff is a fat, sensual and witty character who appears in three plays by William Shakespeare, including *Henry IV, Part 2* (*c*.1596).

9 Joxer is a comic character from Sean O'Casey's *Juno and the Paycock* (1924).

10 Alexander Pope (1688–1744) was an eighteenth-century English poet who is best known for his satirical verse.

11 Daniel Defoe (1660–1731) was an English writer, whose controversial pamphlets and political activities resulted in his arrest and placement in a pillory.

12 John Dryden (1631–1700) was an English poet, literary critic, translator and playwright, who is primarily remembered for his satiric verse.

13 *Wuthering Heights* (1847) is Emily Brontë's only novel. Now considered a classic of English literature, the novel was met with mixed reviews upon publication.

14 James Joyce, *Ulysses* (Oxford: Oxford University Press [1922]; 1993), 53–4.

## Daniel Corkery

1 Seán O'Faoláin, 'Daniel Corkery', *The Dublin Magazine*, 11.2 (April–June 1936).

2 Daniel Corkery, *Synge and Anglo-Irish Literature* (Cork: Cork University Press [1955]; 1931), 26. (See p. 130.)

3 ibid., 11, 26. (See pp. 120, 130.)

4 ibid., 12–13. (See pp. 120–1.)

5 Emil Cohn ('Emil Ludwig') (1881–1948) was a German biographer, journalist, playwright and poet, whose books were banned by the Nazi Party.

6 Lion Feuchtwanger (1884–1958) was a German-Jewish novelist and playwright whose strong criticism of the Nazi Party before it assumed power ensured that he

became the target of government-sponsored persecution after Adolf Hitler's appointment as chancellor of Germany in 1933. This persecution included the banning of his books and the inclusion of his name on a list of those whose German citizenship was to be revoked because of 'disloyalty to the German Reich and the German people'.

7   Ernst Toller (1893–1939) was a left-wing German-Jewish dramatist, poet and political activist. Following the Nazi Party's rise to power, Toller's citizenship was revoked, his books were banned and he was exiled from Germany.

8   *The Old Wives' Tale* is a 1908 novel by Arnold Bennett.

9   *The Country House* is a 1907 novel by John Galsworthy.

10   *The New Machiavelli* is a 1911 novel by H.G. Wells.

11   Corkery, *Synge and Anglo-Irish Literature*, 26. (See p. 130.)

12   ibid., 18. (See p. 124.)

13   ibid., 26. (See p. 130.)

## Let Ireland Pride – In What She Has

1   Seán O'Faoláin, 'Let Ireland Pride – In What She Has', *The Irish Press* (2 April 1937) [Courtesy of The National Library of Ireland]. This is O'Faoláin's contribution to the 1937 *Irish Press* debate on the 'future of literature in Ireland'.

2   This is a reference to M.J. MacManus's article 'Is Ireland Swamped Culturally?', *The Irish Press* (2 March 1937).

3   Frederick Robert Higgins (1896–1941) was a poet and a close friend of W.B. Yeats and Austin Clarke. Higgins's poetry, particularly his earlier work, incorporated elements of Gaelic poetry and was influenced by life in the west of Ireland.

4   Aodh de Blácam, 'Irish Letters: As Safe as the Irish Nation', *The Irish Press* (25 March 1937).

5   Daniel Corkery, 'Review of T.C. Murray, *Spring Horizon*', *Ireland To-day*, 2.3 (March 1937), 89.

6   Thomas Mann (1875–1955) was a German novelist, short-story writer, essayist, social critic and 1929 Nobel Prize laureate. In 1936, the Nazi government revoked Mann's German citizenship.

7   John O'Leary (1830–1907) was a poet, journalist, and member of the Fenian Brotherhood. He was sentenced to twenty years' penal servitude in 1865, but was released in 1874 on condition that he did not return to Ireland for fifteen years. Upon his return, he met W.B. Yeats with whom he became close friends.

8   After reading William J. Maloney's *The Forged Casement Diaries* (1936), W.B. Yeats wrote a protest poem titled 'The Ghost of Roger Casement' (1936).

9   *The Colleen Bawn* (1860) by Dion Boucicault was one of the most popular nineteenth-century melodramas. When staged in London in 1860, the play had a record run of 278 performances.

10   *The Way of the World* is a 1700 play by William Congreve. It was a failure with audiences when first performed but it has since come to be regarded as one of the greatest comedies in the English language.

11   Voice of the people.

12   Richard Alfred Milliken (1767–1815) wrote poetry, songs, plays and a novel. Many of his songs, including 'The Groves of Blarney', were extremely popular.

13  Thomas Parnell (1679–1718) was a Church of Ireland clergyman and a poet. Parnell was a friend of Jonathan Swift and helped Alexander Pope with his translation of Homer's *Iliad*.

14  Richard Alfred Milliken, *The River-side, A Poem in Three Books* (Cork: J. Connor, 1807).

15  *Lalla Rookh* is an 1817 Oriental romance by Thomas Moore.

*King of the Beggars*

1  Seán O'Faoláin, *King of the Beggars* (London: Thomas Nelson & Sons, 1938). In this biography of Daniel O'Connell, O'Faoláin challenges some of the key tenets of the Irish-Ireland movement. His praise for O'Connell was perhaps also an implicit critique of Eamon de Valera's leadership.

2  Art MacCooey (Art MacCumhaigh) (1738–73) was an Irish-language poet whose most famous work is 'Úirchill an Chreagáin', a poem about Greggan churchyard.

3  Tomás Ruadh Ó Súilleabháin (1785–1848) was an Irish-language poet and musician from Co. Kerry.

4  Cited in W.E.H. Lecky, *A History of Ireland in the Eighteenth Century, Vol I* (Cambridge: Cambridge University Press [1892]; 2010), 285.

5  The term 'Anti-Christ', as cited by Lecky, comes from George Sigerson, *The Last Independent Parliament of Ireland, with Account of the Survival of the Nation and its Lifework* (Dublin: Gill & Son [1918]; 1919), xxi.

6  Cited in Daniel Corkery, *The Hidden Ireland* (Dublin: Gill & Son [1924]; 1941), 157.

7  Asenath Nicholson, *Ireland's Welcome to the Stranger, or An Excursion through Ireland in 1844 & 1845* (New York: Baker & Scribner, 1847), 411.

8  See Daniel Corkery, *The Hidden Ireland*, 40–2.

9  ibid., 77.